CONCRETE *in*
SWITZERLAND

CONCRETE in SWITZERLAND

HISTORIES from the RECENT PAST

Edited by **SALVATORE APREA,
NICOLA NAVONE, LAURENT STALDER**
with a visual essay by **SARAH NICHOLS**

EPFL PRESS

This publication is released on the occasion of the exhibition *Beton* at the S AM Swiss Architecture Museum (November 20, 2021 – April 24, 2022) realised in coproduction with the Archives de la construction moderne, Archivio del Moderno, and gta Archiv of ETH Zurich.

Participating Institutions

The Archives de la construction moderne (Acm) is based at the École polytechnique fédérale Lausanne. Founded in 1989, it is currently directed by Salvatore Aprea.

The Archivio del Moderno (AdM) is based at the Università della Svizzera italiana. Founded in 1996, it is currently directed by Letizia Tedeschi (Director) and Nicola Navone (Deputy Director).

The gta Archiv is based at the Eidgenössische Technische Hochschule Zürich. Founded in 1975, it is currently directed by Bruno Maurer (Director) and Daniel Weiss (Deputy Director).

The S AM Swiss Architecture Museum is based in Basel. Founded in 1984, it is currently directed by Andreas Ruby.

Exhibition Impressum

Scientific Direction
Sarah Nichols, Rice University

S AM Curatorial Team
Andreas Kofler
Yuma Shinohara

Research Assistance
Ziu Bruckmann, Eidgenössische Technische Hochschule Zürich

Advisory Board
Salvatore Aprea, École polytechnique fédérale Lausanne
Nicola Navone, Università della Svizzera italiana
Laurent Stalder, Eidgenössische Technische Hochschule Zürich

Scenography
Graber & Steiger Architekten, Lucerne: Farhana Nizam Chowdhury, Beatrice Evangelisti, Pablo Filit, Niklaus Graber, Christoph Steiger

Production
Sandra Bachmann

Archival Follow-up
Barbara Galimberti and Joëlle Neuenschwander Feihl, Acm, École polytechnique fédérale Lausanne
Micaela Caletti, Renzo Iacobucci, and Matteo Iannello, AdM, Università della Svizzera italiana
Ziu Bruckmann and Daniel Weiss, gta Archiv, Eidgenössische Technische Hochschule Zürich

Texts
Sarah Nichols, Yuma Shinohara

Translations
Laura Haussmann, Yuma Shinohara

Copy Editing and Proofreading
Doris Tranter

Lending and Rights Coordination
Yuma Shinohara

Installation
Linus Baumeler, Christoph Bolli, David Häring, Marcel Jeker

Education
Olivia Jenni

Sponsoring and Fundraising
Anne Schmidt-Pollitz, Michèle Thüring

Marketing and Communication
Elena Fuchs, Anne Schmidt-Pollitz

Administration
Valérie Zuber

Accompanying Programme
Andreas Kofler, Andreas Ruby, Anne Schmidt-Pollitz, Yuma Shinohara

Graphic Design
Claudiabasel

Book Impressum

Edited by
Salvatore Aprea, École polytechnique fédérale Lausanne
Nicola Navone, Università della Svizzera italiana
Laurent Stalder, Eidgenössische Technische Hochschule Zürich

Editorial Coordination
Joëlle Neuenschwander Feihl, École polytechnique fédérale Lausanne

Translations
Jill Denton (essays by G. Marino; A. Muttoni)
Natalie Donat-Cattin (essays by S. Groaz, R. Gargiani)
Natalie Donat-Cattin and Maureen Young (essay by I. Giannetti)
Thomas Skelton-Robinson (essays by L. Stalder, M. Bächtiger, S. Berger Ziauddin, L. Stieger, M. Tschanz)
Maureen Young (essays by S. Aprea, N. Navone)

English Proofreading
Jo Nicoud-Garden

Graphic Design and Layout
Kim Nanette

Special thanks
to the following institutions and people for their invaluable help in researching and reproducing many of the archive documents published in this volume, as well as for having allowed the publication of them

Archives architectures Genève (Hervé Genton, Catherine Maudet); Archivio Storico Ufficio federale delle strade (USTRA), Bellinzona; Association Alain Tanner; Atelier 5 (Claudia Eugster); Bernhard Chiquet, Riehen; Commune d'Hérémence (Kilian Dayer); Espazium; ETH Bibliothek (Martin Bosshard, Meda Diana Hotea); Hochschularchiv ETH (Claudia Briellmann, Johannes Wahl); Leo Fabrizio; Filmverleih Stamm Film AG; Rudolf Guyer; gta Archiv ETH (Almut Grunewald, Sabine Sträuli); Herzog & de Meuron; Implenia (Philippe Gübelin); Made-in, Genève; Max Matter; Claudio Merlini; Mobimo Lausanne (Roman Loser); Musée de l'Élysée Lausanne; Musée historique de Lausanne (Sarah Liman Moeri); Radio Télévision Suisse; Cyril Schäublin and Silvan Hillmann; Schweizerisches Sozialarchiv Zürich; Staatsarchiv Basel (Patricia Eckert, Alexandra Tschakert); Stadtarchiv Bern (Ildikó Kovács, Brigitte Scheuner); Stadtarchiv Zug; Christian Schocher; Stadtarchiv Zürich (Anna Pia Maissen, Caroline Senn); Werk Bauen & Wohnen; ZHdK Plakatsammlung, Museum für Gestaltung Zürich (Patrizia Baldi, Alessia Contin, Bettina Richter).

Cover photograph: Jura-Simplon Railways, Simplon Canal, 1898 (Musée Historique, Lausanne)

EPFL PRESS is an imprint owned by the Presses polytechniques et universitaires romandes, a Swiss academic publishing company whose main purpose is to publish the teaching and research works of the Ecole polytechnique fédérale de Lausanne (EPFL).

PPUR, EPFL – Rolex Learning Center, CP 119, CH-1015 Lausanne / info@epflpress.org, tél.: +41 21 693 21 30, fax: +41 21 693 40 27.

www.epflpress.org

© 2021, First edition, EPFL Press
ISBN 978-2-88915-353-4

Printed in Switzerland

All rights reserved, including those of translation into other languages. No part of this book may be reproduced in any form – by photoprint, microfilm, or any other means – nor transmitted or translated into a machine language without written permission from the publisher.

Summary

7 Curatorial Statement

9 Message from the Director of the S AM

ESSAYS

13 Switzerland, A Technological Pastoral
    Laurent Stalder

25 Beton is a State of Mind: On the Representation
    of Concrete in Swiss Cinema
    Marcel Bächtiger

39 Nature, Science, and Enterprise: The Origins of the Success
    of Reinforced Concrete in Switzerland. The Introduction,
    Diffusion, and Supersedence of the Hennebique System
    Salvatore Aprea

53 Between Constraint and Freedom to Innovate:
    Swiss Standards to Innovate
    Aurelio Muttoni

63 The N2 Chiasso–Saint Gotthard Motorway:
    Design and Construction of One Hundred and Forty-Three
    Kilometres of Reinforced Concrete
    Ilaria Giannetti

77 Reinforced Country Below Ground
    Silvia Berger Ziauddin

89 Terraced Hillside Housing Architectures.
    When Vineyards Gave Way to Swiss Families
    Lorenzo Stieger

105 The Swiss Principle of *Béton Brut*: 'Betonkonstruktion'.
    A Debate between Theory and Practice, 1940s–1960s
    Silvia Groaz

115 *Gesamtschweizerische Plattenbau* – Large-Panel Construction
    in Switzerland. The IGECO Heavy Prefabrication System in Göhner
    Housing Estates: Serial Production and Variations (1965–1977)
    Giulia Marino

127 The Pluralities of the Possible
    Martin Tschanz

143 'In our country, it is practically impossible not to build in concrete'. Brief Notes on Exposed Reinforced Concrete in the Architecture of Ticino
Nicola Navone

159 Concrete in the Early Works of Herzog and de Meuron
Roberto Gargiani

173 Southern Fragments of Swiss Asbestos-Cement, 1940 to 2040
Hannah le Roux

CONCRETE STORIES
Sarah Nichols

189 Introduction

193 Concrete is Rock
205 Concrete is Underground
215 Concrete is Energy
223 Concrete is Second Nature
235 Concrete is Monolithic
243 Concrete is Composite
253 Concrete is Immaterial
261 Concrete is Praxis
271 Concrete is Fluid

279 Image Credits
285 Author biographies

Curatorial Statement

Although the initial and decisive steps in the development of reinforced concrete took place mainly in the United Kingdom, France, and Germany during the nineteenth century, Switzerland boasts a not inconsiderable record for the speed and breadth with which it adopted this new and composite material in the twentieth century, as well as for the capillarity with which concrete infiltrated all aspects of the material and cultural processes that enliven civil engineering and architecture, and move the construction sector, with considerable repercussions on the transformation and characterisation of the territory. Hence, what seems particularly striking for Switzerland is the close relationship between nation building, the institutionalisation of technical and scientific research, and the rapid industrialisation and growing welfare of the twentieth century, linked as it is to the wide availability of local cement.

As a matter of fact, concrete has probably done more than any other material to transform the Swiss territory. Not so much in the realm of formal innovation, however, since such transformation is always first and foremost an outcome of different types of expertise (statics, material science, geology, etc.), of new players (engineers, entrepreneurs, scholars), of new processes (construction and manufacture), and of new needs (circulation, energy, logistics, security), all of which have a profound and enduring impact on the Swiss territory. Accordingly, it has many repercussions both for the construction of a modern infrastructure with its civil engineering and subterranean structures and for the simultaneous reorganisation of knowledge in the parallel fields of geology, engineering, and architecture. It concerns technological issues as much as it does social, economic, and aesthetic considerations.

Over the course of the twentieth century, various structures built independently of one another (dams, bridges, bunkers, highways, and railways, as well as storage depots, factories, and housing) came to constitute an interdependent infrastructure network covering the Swiss territory in its entirety and encompassing everything in its path, from artificial networks (energy, transport) to natural ones (waterways) and from the built environment to topography. Not to mention the immaterial network of knowledge and expertise developed and disseminated through an efficient research and education system.

Hence, local Swiss insight about concrete and the manifold aspects of its production and use can act as a litmus test for understanding broader matters about the transformation of the built environment and its global consequences. And right now, in this very moment of historical importance, when concrete has become the climate's bitter enemy for the more than 4 billion tonnes of carbon dioxide deriving from its production annually and a symbol for environmental destruction, the three main architecture archives in Switzerland – the gta Archiv and the Archives de la construction moderne from the Swiss Federal Institutes of Technology in Zurich and Lausanne as well as the Archivio del Moderno of the Università della Svizzera italiana in Balerna – together with the S AM Swiss Architecture Museum based in Basel, thought that the time had come to make a historical assessment of the material. In 2019 a first symposium, financed by the Swiss National Science Foundation, was held in Zurich, bringing together national and international scholars, to both present and test the hypothesis of this work. The results of the research that preceded and followed the symposium are presented in an exhibition and in the present, collective book. The exhibition is being showcased at S AM from November 2021 to April 2022. It has been developed under the scientific direction of Sarah Nichols, in cooperation with a curatorial team from the S AM, and has been produced under the direction of Andreas Ruby.

The book, in turn, examines a series of moments in the history of reinforced concrete in Switzerland, from the early stages of its introduction (research, prototypes, tests, standards, etc.) to its production (in cement works and on construction sites) and use in civil engineering and architecture, right through to its reception and representation in different media (literature, cinema, photography, etc.). It consists of two parts. The first collects thirteen essays written by national and international scholars from the fields of history, history of architecture, engineering, and technology, while the second, using the register of the visual essay, presents nine stories illustrating the visual power of the material, from its extraction to its destruction. The essay is the result of Nichols's long archival research on concrete, and it formed the basis for the exhibition at the S AM.

As stated by its subtitle, the book approaches the subject from different perspectives. It is not intended to be exhaustive but more to enable the development of a future history of reinforced concrete in Switzerland, which is still to be written.

Message from the Director of the S AM

With the *Beton* exhibition, the S AM Swiss Architecture Museum opens a new chapter in its history, proposing a model of collaboration between the S AM itself and Switzerland's three major architectural archives: the gta Archiv and the Archives de la construction moderne (Acm), based at the two Federal Institutes of Technology in Zurich and Lausanne, and the Archivio del Moderno (AdM) at the Università della Svizzera italiana in Balerna.

When the S AM was founded in 1984, the public mission of conserving architectural drawings, plans, photographs, models, and other types of documents had been assumed in Switzerland by the gta Archiv. The Acm and AdM later joined the gta Archiv in this mission. What was still missing, however, was a platform to produce architectural exhibitions for a broader cultural audience at a federal level. And this was exactly what the founders of S AM intended the museum to do: showcase the importance of architecture within Switzerland's overall cultural landscape. Since then, the Museum has explored the past and present of architecture in Switzerland and abroad in almost 180 exhibitions and innumerable lectures, debates, guided tours, workshops, and symposia. It has worked closely on several occasions with some of the above-named institutions, for instance, in the exhibitions on Fritz Haller (2014) and André Studer (2016).

In 2017 the Museum initiated a collaboration agreement with the three archives, allowing them to make the best of their complementary assets. The archives develop their potential in the creation of architectural exhibitions thanks to the spaces, expertise, and audience of S AM, while the latter strengthens its mission through the archival holdings and academic knowledge in the history and theory of architecture offered by the archives. The four partners vowed to develop joint exhibitions and projects that would bring the richness of the archives into the limelight of architectural discourse in Switzerland by virtue of thematic exhibitions featuring crucial topics of building culture in Switzerland. The *Beton* exhibition is the first result issuing from this collaboration. It is an exhibition that not one of the four partners could have done alone. Many exhibits are being displayed to the public for the first time. By joining forces, the archives and the museum have created a model of architectural presentation that makes the content of the existing architectural archives from three different language regions available to the entire country and abroad. And it proposes a new model of how an architecture museum can work – a model which prioritizes use over ownership in order to create a whole that is larger than the sum of its parts and which in many ways corresponds to the logic of a federal state.

ESSAYS

Switzerland, A Technological Pastoral

Laurent Stalder

Bruno Taut's *Alpine Architecture* still continues to represent, at least from an architectural perspective, the most all-encompassing proposal for an artificial reshaping of the topography of Switzerland. Although the project extends far beyond the country to include the entire Alpine massif, as well as islands, continents, and the stars of the universe, it centres on the Swiss mountains – from the Wetterhorn above Grindelwald, whose mountainsides are adorned with iron thorns and whose summit is elevated by a glass sphere; to the Monte San Salvatore above Lugano, stepped into terraces for 'flight landing places' and as a 'spectator area' for performances of various sorts; to the Vorderglärnisch in the Alpine foothills, whose slopes have been smoothed and studded with crystals; or the Monte Rosa chain and the Matterhorn with their geometricised silhouettes. A further drawing shows the Roseg Valley in the Engadine close to Pontresina (fig. 1). It distinguishes itself from the other depictions: less due to its crystalline architecture than to the material deployed, because it is here, and only here, in the whole of *Alpine Architecture* that concrete is to be encountered, albeit it simply in the form of a reference to the 'concrete frames' of what are lancet-leave-shaped walls.[1]

As a rule, and rightly so, the significance of *Alpine Architecture* – composed by Bruno Taut in a garden city close to Cologne in the final years of the war from 1917 to 1918 – is judged to lie in its essence as an expressionist manifesto. This is evident in the culturally critical stance that saturates the work, the fantastical dimensions of Taut's architectural vision, or, expressed more prosaically, in the functionlessness of the buildings, the illustrious role ascribed to the architect as a leader, hero, and builder of worlds, or indeed in the late-Romantic idea of the world as a whole in which Architecture and Nature merge into a religiously or at least mystically heightened unity. This interpretation of *Alpine Architecture* as a utopian alternative to war and its destructive force was bolstered by Taut himself. As he recorded in an unpublished preface, the intention was to 'channel' all the 'achievements of nerves and energy' that Europe had proven itself to possess in the war 'into a more beautiful trajectory' in order to make the Earth a 'good dwelling place.'[2]

Nevertheless, all these interpretations that limit the facets of *Alpine Architecture* to the unrealisable, the reverie, the mystical, or the socially utopian[3] ultimately also reduce its significance to a critique of modernism, failing to realise that by the same token it can be read as an expression of modernism. By this, one has, however, to consider less the forms or even the materials that are characteristic for the Taut brothers' realised projects – such as the Glass Pavilion in Cologne with its spiral-shaped concrete venation, or the Wissinger family tomb, which translates the glass and crystal formations of *Alpine Architecture* into concrete[4] – rather far more the very specific technological and scientific milieu, with all its corresponding paraphernalia, that permitted these visions in the first place: the postcards or pictures in travel guides that served as a template for *Alpine Architecture*, the photographic cameras with which these scenes were captured, but also, and above all, the railway lines (such as the Gornergrat Railway from Zermatt, that of the Monte Generoso close to Lugano or of Muottas Muragl in the Engadine) that accessed these viewpoints and determined the perspectives. Add to this the rails and roads with their bridges and tunnels, avalanche barriers and galleries, that opened up the Alpine heights to increasing tourism; then, moreover, the dams and turbine halls that fed these railways with electricity; and which, together, rapidly transformed the Alps into a complex interconnected network of geographical and geological data and infrastructures through which nature also became systematised, combining to enable the dizzying sequence of Alpine panoramas that unfolds from sheet to sheet in *Alpine Architecture* to be popularly experienced as a sightseeing tour through Switzerland.

As sparsely as concrete is represented in *Alpine Architecture*, so rare was its initial presence in transforming the Engadine landscape. In the Bernina Railway, which runs from St. Moritz along the Roseg Valley to Italy and was opened in 1910, due to high acquisition and transport costs concrete was solely utilised – including for bridges and tunnels – 'in extremely exceptional cases.'[5] It was only in the 1920s that avalanche-protection galleries were erected in concrete, allowing the railway to operate in winter. The dam walls of the Lago Bianco reservoir, which supplies the railway with electricity, were likewise built in concrete but clad with stone arches.[6] However, both the hydraulic pressure pipes – an object of eternal fascination for the avant-garde architects of the ABC Group – and the generating plant buildings were made (save for the bearings for the turbines) of either steel or quarry stone. One notable exception is to be found further down the valley on the way to Austria, in Zuoz above the River Inn, namely the three-hinged bridge by Robert Maillart from 1901, which even if the abutments were built of untreated stone was executed entirely in concrete.[7] In buildings, on the other hand, concrete was rare, and if applied – such as in the viewing terrace at the Alp Grüm railway station – was limited to lone building elements and as a rule was dressed.[8]

Indeed, up until the first years of the twentieth century some of the major infrastructural works in Switzerland, including even the most imaginative projects, could dispense with concrete altogether. As such it is no coincidence that historians of the avant-garde, such as Sigfried Giedion (to remain with Switzerland), took France, not Switzerland, as their example when first delineating the significance of ferro-concrete, whilst simultaneously endeavouring to situate the country's predominance in the field in a specifically French tradition of construction stretching back to the Gothic.[9] Measured fifty years later, the

Swiss perspective had changed profoundly. The very thought of a built environment without concrete had become nigh on inconceivable. In his sweeping criticism of the building industry anno 1973, Rolf Keller in *Bauen als Umweltzerstörung* (fig. 2) pillories concrete – prefabricated or poured, as panels or entire building systems, prestressed or not, for housing, infrastructure, work or consumption facilities – as the main material behind the perceived malaise. Yet Keller only seldomly refers to concrete as the main reason for the comprehensive 'destructions' in Switzerland and beyond, instead locating it more broadly in the progress-driven ideology of modern society as a whole and the corresponding technocratic management of the environment. Without doubt the economic and technical performance of the material indeed perfectly fitted the goals of a growth-driven society. If current rates of growth were to continue, Keller notes in the last pages of the book, in 100 to 150 years Switzerland would be completely built over.[10] But in this equation concrete was the materialised expression, not its cause.

The opening reference to the Engadine has particularly useful connotations in that it serves as a model for other parts of the country: as an expression of the idiosyncratic connection or parallelism between 'political-institutional innovations and a period of economic growth and technical-scientific upswing' in the early phases of the Swiss Confederation, following the founding of the federal state in 1848.[11] This congruity would prove decisive for the transformation of the country into what can be called, borrowing from the literary scholar Leo Marx, a 'Technological Pastoral' – a place that is associated with 'rural peace and simplicity' but at the same time highly dependent on modern technology.[12] Several elements can be distinguished in this respect: Firstly, the map of the nation, the Dufour Map, a project undertaken between 1832 and 1865 based on a standardised surveying technique that generated a new 'space of truth', subjecting the previous individual representations and personal perceptions of the landscape of individual topographers and geodesists to a uniform technical-scientific method[13] and thus forming the basis for a sweeping reorganisation, transformation, and design of the Swiss territory.[14] Then, the telegraph network, which standardised the flow of information within the country and with other

1. Bruno Taut, Vorderglärnisch/Roseg-Tal, 1919. From Bruno Taut *Alpine Architektur* (Hagen i.W: Folkwang, 1919).

2. Rolf Keller, Biberbrugg/Neuenhof, 1973. From Rolf Keller, *Bauen als Umweltzerstörung* (Zürich: Verlag für Architektur Artemis, 1973).

countries. And, thirdly, the railway network, which from 1902 became almost entirely nationalised and which fundamentally transformed the spatial horizons of the country by means of levelling and its temporal horizons by means of acceleration. One could further mention the 'scientific systematisation of Nature', with which the Swiss waterscape was conceptualised as 'an interwoven system of rivers and lakes', coupled with the corresponding recognition of the potential of hydroelectric power.[15] Further, the systematic surveying of the geology and tectonics of Switzerland, constituting the basis for the monumental Alpine railway tunnels in the last quarter of the nineteenth century, the power stations from the Second World War onwards, and the motorways of the second half of the twentieth century. And finally, the foundation of the Swiss Federal Institute of Technology (ETH) in 1855, which would act as a scientific-administrative anchor for these endeavours and as a guarantor for the nationally acquired knowledge base, as well as serving as a training institution for the engineers that were so urgently needed. The political dimension of the ETH's founding cannot be underestimated: guided by the omens of science and technology it would also facilitate a tacit homogenisation of the differences in culture, belief, and language that were stumbling blocks to the unity of the country.[16]

Exemplary in this context was the research undertaken at the newly founded Department of Construction Engineering, which at the turn of the twentieth century would crucially contribute to the legitimisation of ferro-concrete building techniques by placing the various different processes propagated by individual companies on a 'scientific footing'. Or equally the founding at the ETH in 1880 of the Swiss Federal Laboratories for Materials Science and Technology (EMPA)[17] which would play a key role in standardisations in the cement and concrete industries. As early as 1903 provisional specifications were issued for the calculation of ferro-concrete constructions,[18] supplied with – and here the significance of norms for national particularities is especially evident – a key exemption clause for the Swiss engineering branch which stipulated that: 'In consideration of the newness of this building technique, deviations from the above-mentioned norms are permissible when substantiated by extensive tests and the judgements of proficient personages.'[19] Tellingly, Maillart's bridge in Zuoz had been approved a few years earlier after applying just this procedure in the form of an expert's assessment delivered by Wilhelm Ritter.[20]

Although Maillart's oeuvre allows us to trace the spread of concrete construction – in buildings as well as for infrastructures – to the furthest corners of Switzerland during the course of the inter-war years, and thus simultaneously revealing the importance of bridge building for railways and roads, nevertheless these interventions and the perceptions of them were still limited to individual objects. Max Bill's portfolio *Moderne Schweizer Architektur 1925–1945* (Modern Swiss Architecture 1925–1945)[21] gives an excellent overview of this tendency, not merely because it continued to illustrate particular and isolated constructions (rather than a network), but also because alongside a series of infrastructure buildings, such as dams, bridges, or stadiums, it also shows a series of residential, office, or community projects, all likewise executed in concrete (figs. 3–4).

Thus it is that we find Maillart's bridges (over the River Arve close to Geneva, in Schwarzenburg, or over the Salginatobel) together with Alexandre Sarrasin's arched bridges (in the Gorges du Trient or over the Laxgraben) or that by Charles Chopard (close to St. Gallen) quite naturally placed side-by-side with Karl Moser's St. Anthony's Church in Basel, Carlo and Rino Tami's library in Lugano, Marc Piccard's Plage Bellerive in Ouchy, or Otto Rudolf Salvisberg's Hoffmann-La Roche plant in Basel – all of them buildings that alternate between monolithic, flared-column-head and beam-and-column construction forms, thereby demonstrating the profound reciprocations between engineers and architects in Swiss modernism. This is even more evident in regard to building technology, for instance in how rapid, as has been convincingly shown by Sarah Nichols, the transfer of *Gussbeton* (cast concrete) was after the First World War from the power stations to such iconic representatives of architectural modernism as the St. Anthony's Church by Moser ten years later.[22]

Taken together, the factors outlined above formed some of the major scientific-technical bases for the subsequent boost in the concrete industry that first set in during the Second World War with the building of the fortification complexes and the so-called 'Reduit' on the Gotthard, turning upside down, both literally and metaphorically, Bruno Taut's vision of an alpine architecture as an alternative to the war efforts. After the war, the concrete industry experienced

3. Max Bill, *Modern Swiss Architecture* (Part II, Building for Traffic), 1949 (Alexandre Sarrasin, Pont sur les Gorges du Trient à Gueuroz, 1931–34). From Max Bill, *Moderne Schweizer Architektur = Architecture moderne suisse = Modern Swiss Architecture: 1925– 1945* (Basel: Verlag Karl Werner, 1949).

4. Max Bill, *Modern Swiss Architecture* (Part I, Building for Work), 1949 (Otto Rudolf Salvisberg, Betriebsgebäude Hoffmann-La Roche, Basel, 1938). From Max Bill, *Moderne Schweizer Architektur = Architecture moderne suisse = Modern Swiss Architecture: 1925– 1945* (Basel: Verlag Karl Werner, 1949).

Switzerland, A Technological Pastoral

an unparalleled boom, initially with the erection of central electric-power plants (which took up 8 to 9 per cent of all cement supplies in the post-war years), followed in the 1960s by the housing production industry[23] and the development of the national motorway network. In the process, cement consumption per inhabitant repeatedly topped international records.[24]

These facts and figures, and the central role that the concrete and cement industry played in Swiss politics, would by themselves be enough to attribute a special status to Switzerland. This particularity can be further highlighted by reference to three large-scale project types. The first is the construction of the large power stations in the Alps, such as Grande Dixence (1951–61), Oberhasli (construction and enlargement 1939–79), Maggia (1950–55) or Hinterrhein (1956–63)[25] – promoted first by energy suppliers during the Second World War and then by the national government after the war – as an urgent response to the economic upswing and the rapid increase in electricity demand during the 1950s and 1960s. What specifically characterises this expansion is the planning of supra-regional large-scale facilities as a combination of different reservoirs into an interlinked infrastructure network.[26] Over and above their territorial dimension, the resulting hallmark of these projects is a growing synchronisation between a natural and a man-made system, between a waterscape and an energy-scape, in which outflow is no longer determined by the rhythm of the seasons but by pure energy demand. In the process, rivers and streams, catchment basins, reservoirs, pressure tunnels, pressure pipes and turbine halls, but likewise mountains and valleys, became interconnected into a widespread network spanning cantonal, and in places even national, boundaries. Above ground the reservoir dams symbolically demonstrate the sheer scope of this operation, whilst the control centres were increasingly built underground in order to optimise their 'economic, functional, and operational conditions.'[27] This state of affairs embodies the 'scandalous contemporary actuality', to borrow from Paul Virilio,[28] of these constructions, being as they are an expression of the greatest possible 'functionality' and 'economy', and as such more faithfully mirroring present-day conditions than any other form of building. By their physical constraints and the immediacy of their answer to them, these tunnels, reservoirs, and energy control centres suggest implicitly the triviality of all other architecture.[29]

The second example is the federal motorways law, which came into force in 1960 and within a few decades enabled the construction of what would become the densest motorway network in the world. Although in terms of volume of construction it did not represent a particularly important sector for the cement industry,[30] it is nonetheless unique – at least in its symbolic impact – in that no other project so comprehensively mirrors the idea, enshrined since its inception, of the unity of the country. Its end effect is the closely meshed uniformity of the Swiss territory, at the same time introducing a new topography shaped by the speed of the motorised vehicle. Architect Rino Tami in the canton of Ticino, in response to the lack of overall planning on the Autostrada del Sole,[31] engineer Jean-Paul Piguet on the shores of Lake Geneva (fig. 5), and architects Flora Ruchat-Roncati and Renato Salvi in the canton of Jura – all of them interpreted 'the machine technique' (as Ruchat-Roncati called it) both as an object in the landscape and, seen from the perspective of the motorist, as a sequential series of signs, and correspondingly designed their objects to become an architecture of the territory, linked together with bridges, portals, and retaining walls in concrete.[32] And even where an overall design of this new infrastructural landscape was deemed unnecessary, as, for instance, in the case of the N1 motorway through the Mittelland, the new image of the territory afforded by the speeding car provided ample scope for the envisioning of iconic infrastructural buildings, such as the petrol station in Deitingen with its double-shell structure (recalling the logo of the client, BP) or the Kilcher company headquarters alongside the same road, both by engineer Heinz Isler (fig. 6).

Thirdly and finally, yet far less successful, are the attempts by architects and planners to formulate a national regional-planning strategy, which although already called for in 1933 by the architect Armin Meili only first came into effect as national law in 1980, and even then, still in a strongly federal form. Fragments of the conception of Switzerland as the 'decentralised metropolis of Central Europe' sketched out by Meili in 1933[33] can be seen, for instance, in the study for St. Moritz headed by Hans Schmidt and Werner Max Moser that transforms the topography of the Alpine location into a succession of flat roofs and terraces, entirely in keeping with the language of Neues Bauen[34] – a typology that would find its highly popular successor, architecturally trimmed to suit Swiss topography, in the innumerable anonymous stepped hillside houses of the post-war era. Probably the most prominent and architecturally refined example is the Siedlung Halen outside Bern by Atelier 5. It was built on the model of Le Corbusier's Roq et Rob project, striving to concentrate the settlement spatially while opening the individual step-down housing units to the un-built landscape. But perhaps more importantly, what distinguishes it from its French precursor, besides its almost complete realisation in concrete (from the foundation to the walls and ceilings), is the importance given to the car. The new housing

5. Jean Paul Piguet, Roland Hofer, and Maurice Tappy, Chillon viaduct, 1966–69. Photograph Franz Bock, September 1988.

6. Heinz Isler, gas station, Deitingen, 1967–68. Comet Photo AG. June 1986.

settlement was built within a set radius of 35 kilometres outside the city of Bern (linked as it is to the city by a major concrete bridge from 1913, the 'largest-span concrete bridge' of its time[35]) and features a large underground parking facility. As such it represents an architectural answer to the growing demand for housing outside the city, made possible precisely through these new infrastructures.[36]

Yet with the exception of the parking garage, in Halen, as elsewhere, infrastructure and architecture were conceived in isolation from each other. While as other built examples prove, ten years later almost nothing had changed in practice, in the architectural discourse their innate interdependency came to be increasingly recognised and thought about. A good example is the 1973 issues of the architectural and art journal *Das Werk*, the official organ of the Swiss Federation of Architects, covering such diverse topics as airports, holiday villages, urban utopias, housing, parking facilities, and shopping malls side by side, thus illustrating – if proof were needed – the deep interrelation between architecture and engineering in the transformation of the post-war environment. Through its pages, such large-scale infrastructural projects as the parking du Mont-Blanc built under Lake Geneva or Zurich Airport were, even if not designed by, at least brought to the attention of architects. Yet the issues published in the year of the oil crisis read also like a swansong for the proposals envisioned by such architects and planners as Team 2000, Justus Dahinden, Walter Förderer, Robert Frei, or Christian and Jakob Hunziker since the mid-1960s. These 'Urban Structures for the Future', to use the title of Dahinden's influential study on megastructures,[37] were pervaded by an infrastructural logic that until then was restricted to the movement of cars or railways. The projects, which relied on large-span structures used in bridge and underground engineering, were given telling titles such as Haldenstadt (Hill-slope City),[38] Hügeltektur (Hill-tecture) (fig. 7),[39] Stadtlandschaften (Urban Landscapes),[40] or, as an underground counterpart, Terra-Tekturen (Terra-tectures) (fig. 8).[41] The former, the Hill-slope City, for instance, envisioned new platforms giving open views across the – ideally otherwise un-built – landscape, while the Terra-tectures were conceived as an answer to the threat of atomic warfare and the primal need for protection. Like the hills and mountains conquered throughout the late nineteenth and twentieth centuries, they were equipped with so-called Höhenwege (Ridgeways), accessed

7. Justus Dahinden, Radio City, 1968–70. From Justus Dahinden, *Stadtstrukturen für morgen: Analysen – Thesen – Modelle* (Stuttgart: Verlag Gerd Hatje, 1971).

8. Pierre Zoelly, Heizkraftwerk, Aubrugg, 1974–78.

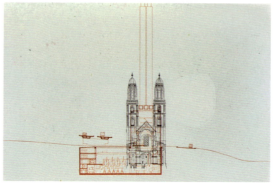

Concrete in Switzerland

by elevators and in some cases, in an almost too quintessentially Swiss way, via underground funiculars, or linked together by bridges or tunnels and adits. Enhancing, replacing, or digging deeply into the existing topography, they literally gave rise to the projection of a second, completely artificial, nature.

Indeed, what commonly characterises these different projects of the 1960s, even those that were subterranean, is a continued rigid counter-distinction between the existing topography and human interventions. Yet during the same period of time the shift from a construction on a landscape to the construction of a landscape (including its surfaces) is already visible in motorway designs, beginning with Tami and then later in those by Ruchat-Roncati and Salvi, where the repetition of typified construction forms aims at underscoring the folds of the hills and mountains.[42] From the late 1990s onwards, this design approach would become almost conventional – at least for architects – and can be found in a series of projects,[43] two of which (even if not realised) serve well to illustrate the fact. The first is Aurelio Galfetti and Jachen Könz's proposal for the northern dam of the Lago Bianco (1995) (fig. 9), situated along the aforementioned Bernina railway line. In addition to performing their primary function of turning an Alpine valley into a reservoir, the retaining wall and the mountain slopes are also formally linked together by a continuous geometrised curve that finds its origin in the shape of the valley as revealed by the precise positioning of the dam. This dimension is similarly evident in the proposal by the architects Made-in for the Porta Alpina (the evacuation shaft for the newly built railway through the Gotthard) in Sedrun (2010) (fig. 10), where the vertical infrastructure is transformed into an acoustic pipe. Produced by the passing trains, the sound is reverberated by the funnel shape of the mountains, unifying landscape, technology, and society through air. This last project is eloquent testimony to the fact that, by this point at the latest, the scope of design had shifted from the individual object to the whole environment, transforming a formerly inaccessible Alpine topography into a 'technological pastoral'.

Exploring a history of the built and designed environment in Switzerland decisively involves not only dealing with material artefacts but, perhaps even

9. Aurelio Galfetti and Jachen Könz, Lago Bianco Dam, Bernina, 1995.

10. Made-in, Galleria Alpina, Sedrun, competition 2010.

more importantly, with issues of their representation. It therefore requires treating both the physical transformation of the country and its status as a cultural construction in symmetry with each other. To understand how these two are intertwined, it might be useful to cast again an eye on *Alpine Architecture*, and from there maybe to allow the gaze to wander even further back to a series of sketches by John Ruskin from the middle of the nineteenth century. What unfolds when one compares Taut's aquarelles with Ruskin's sketches of Turnerian topography near Faido (where Tami's motorway was diverted into a tunnel a hundred years later) and then to recent photographs by Margherita Spiluttini (of dams covered with moss and rocks perforated by the ventilation shaft of a bunker) or those by Nicolas Faure (of highways dissecting the landscape or framing it) is first and perhaps foremost the long journey undertaken since the nineteenth century: from Turner's (and Ruskin's) recording and sublime remodelling of Swiss topography, to its architectural reworking in Taut's drawings, progressing to the later sweeping transformation of this territory in all its environmental dimensions (from water to air) throughout the twentieth century. What is equally striking is the shifting perspective on Swiss topography in these scenes: the perspective view from a mountain road, to that from a viewing platform, and finally to that of a seemingly all-accessible topography. But what is perhaps even more important are the changing conceptions of this territory represented in these images: from the territory as a sublime landscape to the territory as a *hyperville* (conceived in term of networks, and no longer of surfaces),[44] and finally to the territory as a technological pastoral, where the boundaries between a technologised nature and a naturalised technology become blurred.

Notes

[1] Bruno Taut, *Alpine Architektur in 5 Teilen und 30 Zeichnungen* (Hagen i.W: Folkwang, 1919), n. p.

[2] Bruno Taut, '[unpubliziertes] Vorwort des Herausgebers', in Matthias Schirren, *Bruno Taut: Alpine Architektur – A Utopia/Eine Utopie* (München: Prestel, 2004), 118.

[3] André Corboz, 'Schlussfolgerungen aus der Geologie – Von Viollet-le-Duc zu Bruno Taut' (1983), in *Die Kunst, Stadt und Land zum Sprechen zu bringen* (Basel: Birkhäuser, 2001), 201–18, here 209.

[4] Christophe Fischer, *Frühlicht in Beton: Das Erbbegräbnis Wissinger von Max Taut und Otto Freundlich in Stahnsdorf – Geschichte und Hintergründe der Entstehung, Dokumentation der Restaurierung 1987/88* (Berlin: Mann, 1989), 17.

[5] E. Bosshard, 'Die Berninabahn', *Schweizerische Bauzeitung* 59, no. 11 (1912), 145.

[6] Luzi Dosch, 'Eine Bergbahn als Gesmatkunstwerk: Geschichte und Architektur der Berninabahn', *Werk, Bauen + Wohnen* 80, no. 1/2 (1993), 6–13, here 13.

[7] Max Bill, *Robert Maillart* (Erlenbach-Zürich: Verlag für Architektur, 1949), 32–3. In this context one might also mention a further project attributed to Maillart from 1900 for a bridge near Thusis. See Jürg Conzett, 'Die Rheinbrücke der Albulabahn', *Bündner Monatsblatt: Zeitschrift für Bündner Geschichte, Landeskunde und Baukultur*, no. 4 (1989), 268–72.

[8] Kristiana Hartmann, *Baumeister in Graubünden: Drei Generationen Nicolaus Hartmann, 1850–1950* (Chur: Desertina, 2015), 100.

[9] Sigfried Giedion, *Bauen in Frankreich: Eisen, Eisenbeton* (Leipzig: Klinkhardt & Biermann, 1928), 68.

[10] Rolf Keller, *Bauen als Umweltzerstörung: Alarmbilder einer Un-Architektur der Gegenwart* (Zürich: Verlag für Architektur Artemis, 1973), 188.

[11] 'Politisch-institutionellen Innovationen, wirtschaftlicher Wachstumsphase und technischwissenschaftlichem Aufschwung' (David Gugerli, 'Die wissenschaftlich-technische Landschaft des jungen Bundesstaates', in Alexander Ruch, ed., *1848/1998: 150 Jahre schweizerischer Bundesstaat*, Zürich: Institut für Geschichte der ETH Zürich, 1998, 21–40, here 24).

[12] Leo Marx, *The Machine in the Garden: Technology and the Pastoral Ideal in America* (New York: Oxford University Press, 1964), here especially 19–24.

[13] Gugerli, 'Die wissenschaftlich-technische Landschaft' (see note 11), 24.

[14] See Sonja Hildebrand, 'Urbane Schweiz: Urbanistische Konzepte für die Schweiz von 1930 bis heute', in Karsten Borgmann et al. (eds.), *Das Ende der Urbanisierung? Wandelnde Perspektiven auf die Stadt, ihre Geschichte und Erforschung* (*Historisches Forum*, vol. 8) (Berlin, 2006), 69–83, edoc.hu-berlin.de/histfor/archiv.php.

[15] Gugerli, 'Die wissenschaftlich-technische Landschaft' (see note 11), 35.

[16] Wilhelm Oechsli, *Geschichte der Gründung des Eidg. Polytechnikums mit einer Übersicht seiner Entwicklung, 1855-1905* (Festschrift zur Feier des fünfzigjährigen Bestehens des Eidg. Polytechnikums, Part I) (Frauenfeld: Huber, 1905), 35–121.

[17] See Sarah Nichols, 'Opération Béton: Constructing Concrete in Switzerland', Diss., ETH Zürich, 2020, 29–57.

[18] Bruno Thürlimann, *Zur Geschichte der Konstruktion und Theorie im Betonbau* (*Bericht/Institut für Baustatik und Konstruktion ETH Zürich*, vol. 112) (Basel: Birkhäuser, 1981), 62.

[19] 'Mit Rücksicht auf die Neuheit dieser Bauart sind Abweichungen von vorstehenden Normen zulässig, wenn sie durch eingehende Versuche und Urteile kompetenter Persönlichkeiten begründet sind' (Art. 19 cit. in Thürlimann, *Zur Geschichte der Konstruktion und Theorie im Betonbau*, see note 18, 63). See the essay by Aurelio Muttoni in this book.

[20] David P. Billington, 'Wilhelm Ritter: Teacher of Maillart and Ammann', *Ingénieurs et architectes suisses* 113, no. 7 (1981), p. 98.

[21] Max Bill, *Moderne Schweizer Architektur = Architecture moderne suisse = Modern Swiss architecture 1925–1945* (Basel: Verlag Karl Werner, 1949).

[22] Nichols, 'Opération Béton' (see note 17), 312.

[23] Georges Spicher, Hugo Marfurt, and Nicolas Stoll, *Sans ciment rien ne marche: Histoire de l'industrie suisse du ciment* (Zürich: Éditions Neue Zürcher Zeitung, 2013), 196–97.

[24] Ibid., 199.

[25] Jürg Mutzner, 'Die Stromversorgung der Schweiz: Entwicklung und Struktur', *Bulletin des Schweizerischen Elektrotechnischen Vereins, des Verbandes Schweizerischer Elektrizitätsunternehmen* 86, no. 12 (1995), 58.

[26] Conradin Clavuot and Jürg Ragettli, *Die Kraftwerkbauten im Kanton Graubünden* (Chur: Bündner Monatsblatt, 1991), 108.

[27] Jürg Ragettli, 'Verborgene Reiche der Technik: die unterirdischen Anlagen der Wasserkraftwerke in der Schweiz', *Werk, Bauen + Wohnen* 91, no. 4 (2004), 12–20, here 20.

[28] Paul Virilio, *Bunker Archaeology* (New York: Princeton Architectural Press, 1994), 13.

[29] Ragettli, 'Verborgene Reiche' (see note 27).

[30] Mathias Eidenbenz, 'Asphalt, Beton, Kies und Schotter', in Martin Heller and Andreas Volk (eds.), *Die Schweizer Autobahn* (Zürich: Museum für Gestaltung, 1999), 300.

[31] On Tami, see the essay by Ilaria Giannetti in this book.

[32] Flora Ruchat-Roncati and Renato Salvi, 'Portails de tunnel pour la Transjurane', *Ingénieurs et architectes Suisse* 117, no. 24 (1991), 454.

[33] Armin Meili, 'Allgemeines über Landesplanung', *Die Autostrasse* 2 (1933), 17–21, here 17.

[34] Elena Chestnova, 'Die Planungs des Ausblicks: St Moritz Planungsprojekt 1942–44', elected subject in architectural theory, ETH Zürich, 2012, 14.

[35] 'Die weitest gespannte Betonbrücke' (*Inventar historischer Verkehrswege der Schweiz*, BE 1913.0.1, status 2002, 2).

[36] On Terrassenhäuser, see the essay by Lorenzo Stieger in this book.

[37] Justus Dahinden, *Stadtstrukturen für morgen: Analysen, Thesen, Modelle* (Teufen: A. Niggli, 1971).

[38] See Team 2000 / Famos + Scherer + Schenkel, 'Terrassensiedlung Burghalde in Klingnau', *Das Werk* 51, no. 10 (1964), 370.

[39] Dahinden, *Stadtstrukturen für morgen* (see note 37), 166.

[40] Walter Förderer [based on a conversation with notes by Lucius Burckhard], 'Stadtumbau auch ohne Bodenreform', *Das Werk* 53, no. 6 (1966), 241.

[41] Pierre Zoelly, *Terratektur: Einstieg in die unterirdische Architektur* (Basel: Birkhäuser, 1989).

[42] Flora Ruchat-Roncati, 'Eine Autobahn ist auch Architektur: Ein Gespräch mit Flora Ruchat-Roncati und Renato Salvi', in Heller and Volk, *Die Schweizer Autobahn* (see note 30), 264–83, here 274.

[43] For instance: baths in Bellinzona (Flora Ruchat-Roncati, Ivo Trümpy, Aurelio Galfetti, 1967–1970); housing development in Cellerina (Luigi Snozzi, 1973); chapel in Bonaduz (Rudolf Fontana, Christian Kerez, 1993); extension of the Freudenberg School (Joseph Schwartz, Christian Kerez, 2002).

[44] André Corboz, 'Die Schweiz als Hyperstadt / La Suisse comme Hyperville', *Anthos: Zeitschrift für Landschaftsarchitektur / Une revue pour le paysage* 42, no. 2 (2003), 4–9, here 8. The text is based on a conference paper given in 1997 before the Société française des architectes.

Beton is a State of Mind

On the Representation of Concrete in Swiss Cinema

Marcel Bächtiger

The titles and subjects of what are presumed to have been the first three films made on Swiss soil recount bucolic peasant idylls; we see Alpine scenery with wooden cabins, a rock face, and a waterfall (*Cascade*), village celebrations (*Fête au village*), and a festive procession descending from summer pastures (*Rentrée à l'étable*) (fig. 1). These three short film sequences were recorded in the summer of 1896 with the help of the *cinématographe*, the epoch-making invention of the Lumière brothers, which half a year earlier, on 28 December 1895, had made its first public appearance in Paris – a date generally deemed to mark the birth of cinema.[1] The distinctiveness and also the astounding success of the *cinématographe* lies in the fact that this small transportable device not only acted as a camera but with a few manual moves could also be transformed into a film projector. Strangely the Lumière brothers themselves lacked belief in the long-term success of 'living photographs', prompting them to concentrate on a rapid and concerted exploitation of their discovery. This involved the hiring of twenty so-called *opérateurs*, who travelled the globe in the following months presenting the spectacle of moving pictures to an awe-struck humanity for a fee, and who shot new films on the spot, which could then be shown to a picture-craving public back home.[2] For this reason, alongside the locomotive in the Lumière film *L'Arrivée d'un train en gare de la Ciotat* (1896), which went on to become one of cinema's iconic films, or the crowds of workers streaming out of the factory in *La Sortie de l'usine Lumière à Lyon* (1895), an extensive *Catalogue Lumière* exists – far less well-known but for that reason all the more fascinating – comprising 1,428 short documentary films shot between 1895 and 1905 at some of the most famous and obscure locations around the world.[3] The most productive *opérateur* in the service of the Lumière brothers in this respect proved to be a certain Alexandre Promio, whose inventory alone encompasses 348 films that he shot in the Sahara, Chicago, Jerusalem, the Antilles, or, indeed, Switzerland.

Moving Images of Artificial

Nevertheless, little is as it would seem in the realm of cinema, and indeed the closer and more precisely one studies, for example, the Lumière film *Rentrée à l'étable* shot by Promio, the more the Alpine pastoral begins to fracture; one is perplexed not only by the unending flow of people squeezing themselves through the tiny village, but one begins to wonder about the metropolitan elegance of the

1. Film still from *Cascade*, dir. Lumière brothers (Switzerland, 1896).

2. Film still from *An heiligen Wassern*, dir. Alfred Weidenmann (Switzerland/West Germany, 1960).

clothes that some of the participants in the processional descent from the pastures are flaunting. In reality, as the *Catalogue Lumière* records, the picturesque scenery was not filmed in the Alps at all, rather in Geneva, or to be precise at the Swiss National Exhibition of 1896. Amongst the undisputed main attractions of the exhibition was the *Village suisse*, the replica of an imaginary traditional Swiss hamlet on a scale of 1:1, transposed to nestle in an artificial landscape with mountains and a automatically operated waterfall – the ingredients of an image of Switzerland that circulated around the globe, not least thanks to the three Lumière films referred to above.[4]

However, the spectacular highlight of the *Village suisse* was hidden inside the artificial mountain, where the visitors were led through dark, cavernous tunnels before emerging again in the midst of an illusionistic Alpine panorama.[5] From the fundamental apparatus of a darkened audience space and a brightly illuminated pictorial space to the aesthetic ideal of the 're-creation of the world according to its own image',[6] panoramas were closely related and direct predecessors of cinema as it would evolve in the first years of the twentieth century. Set against this background it seems obvious to assume that Promio – an enthusiastic Lumière *opérateur*, who amongst other things was responsible for the invention of the tracking shot – selected the *Village suisse* not as a conveniently accessible ersatz for 'real' mountains but rather, and quite the opposite, because it was the illusionism and the requisite technical contraptions behind the scenes that excited his interest.[7]

In terms of the history of the cinematic representation of concrete, it would naturally be a happy coincidence had the artificial landscape and the chalet props of the *Village suisse* already been constructed using the newly discovered building material – parallel in that sense to François Hennebique's buildings erected for the Paris Exposition universelle de 1900, which four years later gave ferroconcrete its first worldwide platform. However, truth be told, the Alpine idyll of the Geneva Swiss National Exhibition was executed in conventional materials; the cliffs and chalets were props made of wood and plaster. Nonetheless, the three Lumière films from the Swiss National Exhibition already signal the sceptical-emphatic interest in the Swiss territory that would appear to be particular to cinema and filmmakers working in and on this country – an interest that applies far less to the landscape itself and far more to the image of the landscape, combined with an interest in the ambiguity of cinematic images that distort and manipulate reality, which itself in turn has often already been distorted and manipulated. As what follows sets out to demonstrate, when the cinematic gaze focuses on Switzerland, its attention is always drawn to the peculiar interplay of nature and technology, the uncanny intermeshing of landscape and infrastructure that would come to characterise the face of the Alpine republic in the twentieth century.

Harmless Collisions in a Well-ordered Country

If we begin, however, by turning our attention to early professional Swiss film production, all traces of this permeation, this overlapping of traditional landscapes and cultural spaces with the infrastructure networks of modernity that caused a gradual decomposing of past spatial hierarchies, are marked by their noticeable absence. On the contrary, it would appear that the early feature films that were shot in Switzerland insisted on this traditional dualism of the urban and the rural, as is eminently evident, for instance, in the first sound film in Swiss dialect, filmed in 1935 and appropriately titled with the vernacular phrase *Jä-soo!* (lit. now I get it!).[8] Directed by Leopold Lindtberg, the film tells the story of an aging married couple from a small country village who one day take the train to Zurich, where their daughter is earning her living in slightly dubious circumstances. Upon arriving in the city, the couple have to endure various adventures, including crossing the Limmatquai bustling with cars and trams – a humorous and at the same time morally laden, yet ultimately harmless collision between tradition and modernity that would be re-enacted on subsequent occasions with different variations. After Lindtberg it was the popular directors Kurt Früh and Franz Schnyder who almost single-handedly dominated mid-century Swiss cinema. Both figures reinforced the dichotomy of the city and the countryside through the respective focuses of their works: while Schnyder cultivated a form of rustic national cinema by mainly enacting adaptations of Jeremias Gotthelf, such as *Uli der Knecht* (1954),[9] Früh gained widespread popularity as the director of sentimental comedies and dramas set in Zurich's contemporary urban milieu. As the homely titles such as *Polizischt Wäckerli* (1955), *Bäckerei Zürrer* (1956), or *Oberstadtgass* (1957) suggest, the Zurich of Früh's films still remained a cosy little town that showed few similarities with the sheer dimensions and extremes of a modern metropolis.[10] Even though Schnyder and Früh worked on opposite settings, they actually communicated the same ideal: the image of a well-ordered Switzerland that would appear to be made up solely of picturesque landscapes and small towns, its appearance largely untouched by the radical ruptures of more recent times.

It was inevitable that the œuvre of Früh and Schnyder would therefore become the embodiment of what the filmmakers of the next generation would label 'Old Swiss Cinema', in that they regarded these films not only as hypocritical and reactionary but also, at a formal level, as hopelessly outdated.[11] In retrospect this criticism seems understandable but not necessarily justified; and it would later be relativised, not least by the representatives of the 'New Swiss Cinema' themselves, probably with most nuance in Christoph Kühn's astonishing personal rapprochement with the then 75-year-old Franz Schnyder in his 1984 documentary film *FRS: Das Kino der Nation* (FRS: The Nation's Cinema).[12]

Moreover, much of what progressive film theory and film practice somewhat too hastily and disdainfully pigeonholed under the description 'Heimatfilm'[13] in fact proves to be surprisingly revealing in terms of a cultural-historical reading. A film that deserves particular interest in our thematic context is *An heiligen Wassern* from 1960: a film that can clearly be classified as belonging to the Heimatfilm genre, but one that tells a story of modernisation, albeit from a fully affirmative standpoint.[14] Its topic is water supply in the mountains of Valais and the struggle to ameliorate the centuries-old system of timber-built conduits that steer glacial water over steep rock faces down to cisterns in the isolated mountain villages. Avalanches periodically destroy the open channels on the cliffs, whereupon a lone villager is selected by drawing lots to undertake the repairs – a fatally hazardous mission, as dramatically visualised in the first act of the film. The tragic plummet into the precipice is inescapable, but the accident is simultaneously the triggering moment for a long overdue march into the future. The victim's son, returning home from his years as an apprentice under the supervision of a British engineer in India, assumes the critical role in the film and provides the liberating idea; with a pneumatic drill and dynamite he blasts small tunnels in the rock, replacing the rickety wooden channels and safely controlling the flow of water down to the valley. From the surveying of the mountains and the drawing up of technical plans to the successful breaching of the cliff face, the feature film thus conveys a decisive moment in the transformation of the Swiss landscape: the transition from cultivated nature to operated infrastructure (fig. 2).

Imaginary Visions Become Real

Nevertheless, similarly in this case the illusionistic machinery of cinema is not entirely dependable. The mountainous canton of Valais in 1960 was by no means a region abandoned by technological civilisation, as the film suggests. On the contrary, it was the setting for a breathtakingly modern endeavour, far more ambitious and far larger than the diminutive water tunnels made by the heroes of our film. By this time construction had been continuing apace for over nine years on the Grande-Dixence Dam in the south of Valais, at the time the highest dam in the world. The gargantuan dimensions of the edifice guaranteed constant public interest in the project. Amongst the observers was a young Jean-Luc Godard, employed at the time as a telephone operator on the building site, who was inspired by his first-hand experience of the 'thousands of workers, at 2,500 metres above sea level […], erecting a concrete wall as high as the Eiffel Tower' to dedicate his first film to it: a short documentary worth mentioning in our context for its title alone

– *Opération Béton*.[15] The short film gained its own recognition over the years, but interestingly Godard was not the only young filmmaker to be captivated by the giant concrete wall high up in the world of the Swiss mountains. In 1960 Claude Goretta – who together with Alain Tanner, Michel Soutter, and others would later form the Groupe 5, a Geneva version of Nouvelle Vague – also shot a documentary film about the Grande-Dixence. Created for the Télévision Suisse Romande, *Grande-Dixence* proved to be a film of extraordinary visual beauty, staging the conveyer belts and cableways, the concrete buckets, silos, and mixing works as if they were imaginary visions become real (fig. 3).[16] The stance that both films assume vis-à-vis the edifice remains conspicuously affirmative. While Jean-Luc Godard revels in the recital of imposing facts and figures, Claude Goretta's interest in the faces and hands of the manual labourers culminates in a cinematic celebration of concrete and modernity. What at first glance might seem surprising (only a few years later emerging environmental protection movements would raise their voices in protest against similar projects) becomes comprehensible when set against the background of 'Old Swiss Cinema'; not only could the Grande-Dixence Dam be interpreted as an architectural portent of a new era, but above all the construction site provided the film cameras with entirely novel and exciting images – a world removed from the nostalgic settings of the Heimatfilm that still dominated the country's cinema screens. While Godard's and Goretta's films simultaneously echo with early cinema's pointed interest in trains, automobiles, and other machines in the silent-film era, this facet was also to be understood as a return to the modernity originally invested in film as a medium and to its intention to comprehend, enshrined in the Greek fantasy word 'cinematography' – the recording (*graph*) of movement (*kinema*).[17]

This fascination for such an unprecedented construction as the Grande-Dixence went hand in hand with an interest in spaces that previously had been overlooked or consciously ignored. In Alain Tanner's pioneering early films – *Charles mort ou vif?* (1969) and *La Salamandre* (1971) are particularly worth naming in this respect – the viewers are confronted with a peculiar mixture of settings. By foot, by bicycle or by car, Tanner's protagonists explore a space in which seemingly irreconcilable features lie un-jarringly adjacent to each other: stretches of pristine landscape, fragments of cities, historic alleyways and new housing estates, factories and single-family homes, farmyards and grain silos, modern streets, bridges, and railways lines.[18] What reveals itself in these films is a reality that had never been seen before on the cinema screen: the Swiss territory as it displayed itself at the end of the economic boom years in its whole ambiguous heterogeneity. While the construction of motorways, railway lines, and power stations had also brought about the emergence of a network that fanned out across and interconnected the country, by the same token this network also exhibited numerous gaps. This gave Tanner the opportunity to counter the by-now-proverbial *Diskurs in der Enge* (lit. discourse of narrowness)[19] with the freedom of the cinematic gaze. Loosened from the straitjacket of the rigid genre limitations of Heimatfilm, Tanner's cautious camera feels its way through all the niches that were similarly available to the outsiders and rebels who people his films.

3. Film still from *Grande-Dixence*, dir. Claude Goretta (Switzerland, 1960).

4. Film still from *Messidor*, dir. Alain Tanner (France/Switzerland, 1979).

Concrete Signs of an Inescapable Prison

By the end of the 1970s, almost as if these niches had subsequently gradually disappeared, very little remained of the quiet hope that had imbued Tanner's earlier films. In *Messidor* (1979), perhaps his most famous film, and which inter alia served as the template for Ridley Scott's *Thelma & Louise* (1991), the search for freedom and self-determination founders once again on the political and social realities of Switzerland during the Cold War.[20] The two young women, allowing themselves the liberty of travelling frivolously across Switzerland, inevitably first draw suspicion on themselves and are then found to be guilty of that suspicion. Their getaway from the police drives them, so to say, into the undergrowth of the Swiss Central Lowlands, where they end up between the massive struts of a newly built motorway viaduct (fig. 4). The iconic scene clearly demonstrates the shift in connotations: huge concrete infrastructures are no longer a source for the celebration of progress and modernity; instead they loom up like the gigantic feet of an omnipresent state apparatus – the pillars of an inescapable prison. Contextually this also provides an explanation for the strange melancholy that is woven into the images in *Messidor* and the pervading attitude that one would be more inclined to associate with 'Old' and not 'New Swiss Cinema'. With long aerial camera shots that glide over the land, juxtaposing meadows, woods, and mountains with the images of sweeping motorway intersections and viaducts, the opening sequence presents the evidence, seeped in nostalgia, that the Swiss landscape, as it existed over centuries, is in the process of disappearing, usurped by the autocratic concrete infrastructures that smother the landscape like a carpet.

However, criticism of the construction of ever more motorways, tunnels, dams, power stations, and oversized housing estates was by no means a new phenomenon. In 1971, a television documentary by the young filmmaker Kurt Gloor had sparked a vigorous nationwide debate. *Die grünen Kinder* was a sharply formulated indictment of the new housing estates that had sprung up everywhere across the Swiss Mittelland during the boom years.[21] The film portrays the Sunnebüel housing estate in Volketswil, built out of prefabricated concrete elements by the Swiss prefab pioneer Ernst Göhner, as a particularly bad, indeed barbaric example.[22] As a result of Gloor's social study, and fuelled shortly afterwards by the appearance of the book *Göhnerswil: Wohnungsbau im Kapitalismus*,[23] Göhner's housing estates soon became the symbols of a new alienation: habitats devoid of all homeliness.

Wanderings through a Foreign Country

An ingenious variation on this topic was represented, just under a decade later, in the opening scene of the legendary feature film *Reisender Krieger* by Christian Schocher: a car leaves the underground car park of a Göhner-designed estate, driven by a washed-up door-to-door cosmetics salesman called Krieger, whose journey across motorways and main country roads, through hairdressing salons, pubs, and hotels, forms the loose content of the semi-documentary film.[24] Schocher's model is nothing less than Homer's *Odyssey*, a provenance already signified in the film title, respectively the name of the salesman (Krieger, i.e., warrior).[25] It may be a simple coincidence that the towering concrete Göhner-ian pile in which Krieger has his apartment is aptly named 'Wohninsel Webermühle', but the background sounds of breaking waves and the cry of a muezzin accompanying the opening scene are obviously deliberate. In fact the irritating dissociative auditory departures from this everyday Helvetian scenery lead us directly to the film's core metaphor: Krieger's aimless wanderings through a now-foreign Switzerland in the same way that Odysseus strayed across the oceans – in search of a lost home that he can simply no longer reach (fig. 5).

One of the fascinations of *Reisender Krieger*, which was made in 1979, is that it almost prophetically pre-empts the youth riots that broke out in Switzerland a year later, as if from nowhere, and that sent lasting shockwaves through the rigid existing social order.[26] The forces that led to the violent upheavals in Switzerland's cities in 1980 are already tangible in the latent tensions and repressed aggressions captured in the documentary scenes of the film. In a similar manner, *Reisender Krieger* likewise anticipates the remarkable prominence that concrete as a building material would assume in the linguistic-symbolic context of the youth riots. Whereas Schocher's film still allows a more nuanced interpretation, for the youth movement of the 1980s the building material advanced to become one of the definitive metaphors in its already metaphor-laden language: concrete now stood for everything that deserved to be fought against, for the deplorable mentality of mainstream society and for the hostility of a country ruled by who else but '*Betonköpfe*' (i.e., blockheads, hardliners).[27] It is no coincidence that the first image in the 1980 film *Züri brännt* (lit. Zurich is burning) is a long tracking shot along the Rosengartenstrasse in Zurich to the newly opened Hardbrücke – the quintessence of an inhuman concrete structure that in the name of transportation and modernity devours its way uninvited through the fabric of the city (and which also made an identical appearance in *Reisender Krieger*).[28] The accompanying off-commentary is revealing, painting in a theatrical voice an apocalyptic picture of Zurich and its inhabitants: 'It didn't take long before Zurich went up in flames', says the voiceover, 'and as it finally began to burn there was nothing to feed the fire. Because the concrete sounds hollow and refuses to burn. An ugly hyper-security prison block may not be a pyre, but at least it is one thing: modern.'[29]

This cycle of films that were critical of modernity (and by substitute, of concrete) is complemented by Fredi M. Murer's *Grauzone* from 1979, a science-fiction film set in the here-and-now about a mysterious epidemic that spreads among the Swiss population, and whose cause is suspected to lie not least in the proverbial coldness of the concrete that the inhabitants of modern Switzerland are exposed to.[30] *Grauzone* mainly takes place in the Grünau housing development in Zurich-Alstetten, erected in 1976 in exposed concrete. For Murer, the high-rise tower, the repetitive facades, and the gaping distances within the estate serve as architectural symbols of alienation: human interactions are replaced by the detached gaze from windows and superseded by microphones, cameras, and binoculars.

Under the Spell of Concrete Aesthetics

However, this critical stance was not as explicit as it purported to be, partly evident in the fact that for the visually schooled eye the Grünau's meandering concrete buildings offer a certain undeniable charm. Murer, as a graduate of the photography department of the Zurich School of Applied Arts, naturally did not fail to notice this, especially when we consider that as a young man he had planned to make a documentary film about Le Corbusier, which despite the unexpected death of his main character nevertheless ended up as a modest spin-off in the form of his 1967 experimental film about the Centre Le Corbusier in Zurich.[31] Thus the socially motivated criticism in *Grauzone* is accompanied by an openly displayed architectural inquisitiveness, indicating that Murer felt innately drawn to expressing himself in aesthetic visual imagery, selective geometrical framings, and ingenious tracking shots. This does not exactly directly contradict the film's indictment of the anonymity of the modern living environment, but it does make it distinctly ambivalent. At a more general level, this phenomenon can also be seen in other films of the era. Ultimately, and in common, they were as interested in the cinematic representation of the object as in the object itself. In an act of reciprocal aesthetic permeation, the objects of criticism thereby became objects of cinematic desire, and the impression remains that the filmmakers were not only unable to resist the pull of the unique fascination of the Helvetic concrete landscape, but indeed willingly craved it. Significantly, of the films discussed here, *Züri brännt* is simultaneously the most political and formally the most extravagant; with its blurred images, captured in black and white on VHS film, its over-emotionally recited text, and raucous punk music, the film achieves an aesthetic coherence that undoubtedly distinguishes it as a work of art, but that by the same token tends to diametrically contradict the intended political message.

Similarly, the mythically underscored realism in *Reisender Krieger* is primarily a cinematic event. The concrete-made space of the Swiss territory experienced and driven through on the trail of the cosmetics salesman again plays a significant if not central role in this respect. The German-language newspaper *Die Zeit* referred to an 'insidious fascination'; to begin with one asks oneself where the journey is meant to end, but 'quickly one is beguiled and one's visual appetite for the very richness of these images becomes insatiable.'[32] Sure enough, what unfolds before the viewer is a unique panorama of 1970s Switzerland, the ingredients for which Schocher had feverishly studied and photographically documented in a prior journey right across the country. This must-see list of highlights naturally includes the construction site of the Gotthard motorway (fig. 6), just as it does the Glatt Shopping Centre, the concrete cube of the new multi-storey car park in Davos, and the dark chalice of the BIZ Tower in Basel. Likewise unmissable are the high street in Ebikon, celebrated as Switzerland's very own version of the American strip, and the newly opened Shop-Ville underneath the Zurich main station, which in the Helvetian reading of the *Odyssey* becomes its contemporary Hades. Although this 'image of a beton-ised Switzerland' continually striven for in the context of the film undoubtedly matches the overriding impression that the *Reisender Krieger*'s audiences come away with, this one-sidedness does not actually do the work full justice.[33] Alongside the mentioned landmarks of post-war Swiss modernism, both the film and the preparatory photo research also show settings that can be classed under completely different categories: for example, the Einsiedeln Abbey, the medieval alleys of the Zurich Niederdorf, or a mountain village in Grisons. Bygones are therefore still present and visible, and the only surprising aspect is how seamlessly they allow themselves to be assimilated within the visual stream of modern impressions that the film accumulates along the route of Krieger's travels. Thus behind the 'image of a beton-ised Switzerland' a far more multi-faceted country emerges, which can still hardly be called idyllic, but whose transfigured physiognomy is undoubtedly not only interesting but singular in its intertwining of characteristic landscape and infrastructure elements.

5. Film still from *Reisender Krieger*, Christian Schocher (Switzerland, 1981).

6. Film still from *Reisender Krieger*, Christian Schocher (Switzerland, 1981).

7. Film still from *Reisender Krieger*, Christian Schocher (Switzerland, 1981).

8. Film still from *Dene wos guet geit*, dir. Cyril Schäublin (Switzerland, 2017).

From Moving Images to a Motionless Camera

There are also moments of unexpected beauty in this ambiguous film. One scene unfolds on a sunny winter's morning with Krieger asleep at the steering wheel. The car is somewhere in snow-covered mountains at the start of a high narrow bridge, identifiable to aficionados as the Salginatobel Bridge by Robert Maillart (fig. 7). The scene itself can also be read with Homer's *Odyssey* in mind: the young farmer's daughter who speaks to Krieger corresponds to the mythical figure of Nausicaa, who encounters the shipwrecked Odysseus on the beach and who leads him to her parents' peaceful kingdom – in the film a simple mountain farmyard on the other side of the valley. Krieger drives over the graceful concrete edifice of 1930 remarkably cautiously, and whoever is inclined to do so can also interpret the bridge, which historically stands at the very beginning of the 'bet-on-isation' of Switzerland, as the approach to paradise.

This theme is re-adopted many years later in *Dene wos guet geit* (lit. those who are fine, 2017), the debut work of young filmmakers Cyril Schäublin and Silvan Hillmann.[34] The almost inescapable impression conveyed in this film is that in the meantime the built transformation of Switzerland has reached a conclusion. The carpet of visible and invisible infrastructures has now become densely knit; the last voids have been closed. With soft irony the film paints a portrait of society in the digital era: the aimless dialogues, which mainly revolve around WIFI and PIN codes, bank account numbers, health insurance, and roaming charges, correspond to the generic character of the built spatial environment shown to the viewer in mere fragments. The 'virtualized and mobilized gaze' of modernity – which commenced with the visual experience of panoramas and reached its classic form in cinema[35] – comes in this case to a sudden halt: the unceasing motion over the concrete roadways of Switzerland, as presented in Christian Schocher's *Reisender Krieger*, is replaced in *Dene wos guet geit* by the laconic gaze of a motionless camera. As a result, the images in this film lack all depth, instead exhausting themselves in the representation of surfaces shown from different perspectives: the surfaces of streets, walls, and squares. The people are pressed to the edges of the images, but as a result, what is visible of the locations is as stereotypical as it is interchangeable (fig. 8). In these irritatingly immaculate images, there is no indication whatsoever as to our possible location. Nonetheless, the flawless beauty of the concrete surfaces provides a reliable pointer to the fact that it must be somewhere in Switzerland.

Notes

[1] See Thomas Elsaesser, *Filmgeschichte und frühes Kino: Archäologie eines Medienwandels* (München: edition text+kritik, 2002), 37.

[2] Jean-Jacques Meusy, *Paris-Palaces ou le temps des cinémas (1894-1918)* (Paris: CNRS Éditions, 1995), 30.

[3] Michelle Aubert and Jean-Claude Seguin (eds.), *La production cinématographique des Frères Lumière* (Paris: Éditions Mémoires de cinéma, 1996). The catalogue has also become recently available online: https://catalogue-lumiere.com/, accessed 29 November 2019.

[4] Jacques Gubler, *Nationalisme et internationalisme dans l'architecture moderne de la Suisse* (Lausanne: L'Âge d'Homme, 1976), 29–32.

[5] Adolphe Ribaux, 'Le village suisse à l'exposition de Genève', *Journal officiel illustré de l'Exposition nationale suisse*, no. 39, 16 October 1896, 467.

[6] 'Wiedererschaffung der Welt nach ihrem eigenen Bild.' The formulation comes from André Bazin, who wrote in this context: 'True primal cinema, as existed in the fantasy of a mere dozen people in the nineteenth century, strove to completely imitate nature'. ('Les véritables primitifs du cinéma, ceux qui n'ont encore existé que dans l'imagination de quelques dizaines d'hommes du XIXe siècle, sont à l'imitation intégrale de la nature.' André Bazin, *Qu'est-ce que le Cinéma?*, vol. 1, Paris: Éditions du Cerf, 1958, 25).

[7] Alexandre Promio, 'Carnet de route', cited in Guillaume-Michel Coissac, *Histoire du cinématographe* (Paris: Cinéopse/Gauthier-Villars, 1925), 197.

[8] *Jä-soo!* dir. Leopold Lindtberg (Switzerland, 1935).

[9] *Uli der Knecht*, dir. Franz Schnyder (Switzerland, 1954); *Uli der Pächter*, dir. Franz Schnyder (Switzerland,1955); *Die Käserei in der Vehfreude*, dir. Franz Schnyder (Switzerland, 1958); *Anne-Bäbi Jowäger*, parts 1 and 2, dir. Franz Schnyder (Switzerland, 1960/1961).

[10] *Polizischt Wäckerli*, dir. Kurt Früh (Switzerland, 1955); *Bäckerei Zürrer*, dir. Kurt Früh (Switzerland, 1956); *Oberstadtgass*, dir. Kurt Früh (Switzerland, 1957).

[11] See, for example, *Alter und neuer Schweizer Film*, Cinema 22/1 (Zürich: CINEMA, 1976).

[12] *FRS: Das Kino der Nation,* dir. Christoph Kühn (Switzerland, 1984).

[13] Films redolent with the themes and values of nation, home, and hearth (TN).

[14] *An heiligen Wassern*, dir. Alfred Weidenmann (Switzerland/West Germany, 1960).

[15] 'À 2500 m d'altitude […], un millier d'hommes dresse un mur de béton aussi haut que la Tour Eiffel' (*Opération Béton*, dir. Jean-Luc Godard, Switzerland, 1955). The quote originates from the first text panel in Godard's film.

[16] *Grande-Dixence*, dir. Claude Goretta (Switzerland, 1960).

[17] On film and modernity see, for example, the collection of texts in Helma Schleif et al. (eds.), *Stationen der Moderne im Film*, vol. II: *Texte, Manifeste, Pamphlete* (Berlin: Freunde der Deutschen Kinemathek, 1990).

[18] *Charles mort ou vif?* dir. Alain Tanner (Switzerland, 1969); *La Salamandre*, dir. Alain Tanner (Switzerland, 1971). See Marcel Bächtiger, 'Odysseus im Mittelland: Urbane Landschaften im Schweizer Film', in Hubertus Adam and Evelyn Steiner (eds.), *Filmbau: Schweizer Architektur im bewegten Bild* (Basel: Christoph Merian Verlag, 2015), 102–10.

[19] See Paul Nizon, *Diskurs in der Enge: Aufsätze zur Schweizer Kunst* (Bern: Kandelaber Verlag, 1970).

[20] *Messidor*, dir. Alain Tanner (France/Switzerland, 1979); *Thelma & Louise*, dir. Ridley Scott (United States, 1991).

[21] *Die grünen Kinder*, dir. Kurt Gloor (Switzerland, 1971). See Werner Jehle, 'Die grünen Kinder: Zu einem Dokumentarfilm von Kurt Gloor', *Werk* 59, no. 4 (1972), 229–30.

[22] Patrick Schoeck-Ritschard and Fabian Furter, *Göhner Wohnen: Wachstumseuphorie und Plattenbau* (Zürich: Hier und Jetzt, 2013).

[23] Heini Bachmann et al., *Göhnerswil. Wohnungsbau im Kapitalismus* (Zürich: Verlagenossenschaft Zürich, 1972).

[24] *Reisender Krieger*, dir. Christian Schocher (Switzerland, 1981), director's cut, 2008.

[25] Christian Schocher in conversation with the author, September 2014. See also *Christian Schocher: Filmemacher*, dir. Marcel Bächtiger and Andreas Müller (Switzerland, 2015).

[26] See Felix Aeppli, 'Vom unerreichbaren Ort des unerreichbaren Glücks: Die 80er Bewegung im Spiegel des Schweizer Spielfilms', in Heinz Nigg (ed.), *Wir wollen alles und zwar subito: Die achtziger Jugendunruhen in der Schweiz und ihre Folgen* (Zürich: Limmat Verlag, 2001), 408–17. Here Aeppli argues that 'all the crucial themes, metaphors, strategies and behavioural conventions of the "movement"

('alle wichtigen Themen, Metaphern, Strategien und Umgangsformen der "Bewegung"') can already be found in the Swiss feature films of the second half of the 1970s.

[27] See Nigg, *Wir wollen alles* (see note 26).

[28] *Züri brännt*, dir. Videoladen (Switzerland, 1980).

[29] 'Es dauerte lange, bis Zürich brannte', 'und als es endlich Feuer gefangen hatte, fand dieses keine Nahrung mehr. Denn der Beton tönt hohl und will nicht brennen. Ein Supersicherheits-Klotz-Gefängnis ist kein Scheiterhaufen, aber: modern.' (*Züri brännt*, see note 28, 01:34 – 01:53).

[30] *Grauzone,* dir. Fredi M. Murer (Switzerland, 1979).

[31] Fredi M. Murer in conversation with the author, October 2015; *Centre Le Corbusier: Das letzte Bauwerk von Le Corbusier*, dir. Fredi M. Murer and Jürg Gasser (Switzerland, 1967).

[32] 'Schleichenden Faszination', 'bald schon ist man verführt und kann sich am Reichtum dieser Bilder nicht sattsehen' ('Verschlagen sein in der Verzweiflung: Christian Schochers "Reisender Krieger"', *Die Zeit*, 23 July 1982).

[33] In the context of a Christian Schocher retrospective, Pascal Blum wrote: 'It remains a film where what everybody says about it is right: there is no better image of beton-ised Switzerland' ('Es bleibt ein Film, bei dem stimmt, was alle sagen: es gibt kein besseres Bild der betonierten Schweiz.' Pascal Blum, 'Einer, der bleibt', *Tages-Anzeiger*, 21 August 2015).

[34] *Dene wos guet geit*, dir. Cyril Schäublin (Switzerland, 2017).

[35] For the concept of the 'virtualized and mobilized gaze' see Anne Friedberg, *Window Shopping: Cinema and the Postmodern* (Berkeley: University of California Press, 1994). On 'in-motion' architectural perceptions about new visual medias, see Mitchell Schwartzer, *Zoomscape: Architecture in Motion and Media* (Princeton: Princeton Architectural Press, 2002).

Nature, Science, and Enterprise: The Origins of the Success of Reinforced Concrete in Switzerland

The Introduction, Diffusion, and Supersedence of the Hennebique System

Salvatore Aprea

After the splendours of ancient Roman construction, the knowledge and technical skills for making concrete were passed down only locally until, in various regions of Europe over the course of the eighteenth century, a number of scholars and builders began studying the properties of limes, mortars, and cements. Their interest was sparked by ongoing archaeological studies of Roman hydraulic engineering works and by a general passion for geography and natural history, as well as by a growing demand for materials that could be used to build major works at the service of trade development and military defence.[1] Research by chemists made it possible to uncover the origin of the ability of certain types of lime to harden when exposed to water, a property called hydraulicity. Between the end of the eighteenth century and beginning of the nineteenth century, this property was attributed to the presence of clay minerals in the limestone. The discovery paved the way to the invention of modern cement, which became famous with the commercial name of Portland cement.[2]

The vast presence of calcareous, marly, and clayey deposits in the Alpine and Jura mountains meant that Switzerland had an abundant supply of the raw materials necessary for manufacturing lime. Local populations had been making use of ordinary lime since the time of the Roman presence in the Cisalpine territories,[3] though it seems they had only a very limited understanding of hydraulic property.[4] Nonetheless, the lime produced from the limestone of Saint-Gingolph and Chamonix was known for its ability to harden in water. This was reported by the Genevan naturalist Horace-Bénédict de Saussure, who studied the geology of the Alps and the composition of the rocks there in the second half of the eighteenth century.[5] Based on studies by the chemists Louis-Bernard Guyton de Morveau and Torbern Olof Bergman, Saussure was able to precisely attribute the origin of the hydraulic properties of Saint-Gingolph lime to the clay minerals contained in the local limestone.[6] Argillaceous limestone deposits for the production of medium hydraulic lime were later discovered in the Jura Mountains near

Basel when, in 1825, the Huningue canal lock was built by the French engineer Louis Alexis Beaudemoulin. In one of his memoirs, he would affirm that the local inhabitants were not aware of this type of lime and its properties.[7] The production of hydraulic limes was developed in Switzerland mainly from the mid-nineteenth century onward, by which time the marly deposits of Bodensee were also known,[8] and it remained predominant until the early twentieth century, when the demand for Portland cement began to prevail. The latter was first produced in Switzerland in 1871 by the Vigier Cement company in Luterbach (Solothurn). This launched the development of a flourishing industrial sector characterised by numerous small, locally owned limestone quarries in the Jura mountains.

The Combination of Iron and Concrete: Construction Principles

Alongside studies aimed at discovering the origin of the hydraulic property of certain binders, experiments were taking place that focused on the development of cement mortars and concrete, together with systems for combining these mixtures with iron bars. A few insightful initial hunches[9] were followed by a series of experiments over the course of the nineteenth century. Some concerned the invention of floor structures, while others aimed to define general methods for manufacturing various building elements and artefacts.[10] By the mid-1800s, these two lines of research revealed two fundamental ways of conceiving reinforcement within concrete: one involved concentrating the metal according to the tensile and shear stresses, while the other called for the use of wire mesh, uniformly distributed within the concrete mass. The first approach characterises the system that was patented in the United Kingdom by William Boutland Wilkinson in 1854. Wilkinson invented concrete floor structures 'reinforced with wire rope and small iron bars embedded below the central axis of the concrete',[11] obtaining surprisingly modern results for the time.[12] Joseph-Louis Lambot and Joseph Monier instead proposed the use of wire mesh reinforcement to produce various objects and minor construction works. The mesh was distributed uniformly in the concrete mass, generally positioned midway through the thickness of the slab. They deposited their patents in France in 1855 and in 1867. The application of these systems required the reinforcement to be modelled according to the shape of the object to be made, almost as if its main function were to ensure the desired shape of a material, concrete, which by its very nature is shapeless until the moment it sets. Hence, the plastic potential of concrete and a desire to create forms seemed to predominate over material strength considerations. Nonetheless, by 1885, it was precisely one of these systems, Monier's, that the German engineer Matthias Koenen would revisit and modify in the wake of that constructive rationality that Wilkinson had only intuited. After a careful analysis of construction techniques for walls and slabs in concrete reinforced with wire mesh, Koenen suggested moving the mesh from the midway line of the slab towards the area that is subjected to tensile stress. He also developed two rudimentary equilibrium equations for calculating the dimensions of a reinforced concrete slab.[13]

These experiments and studies led to the invention of numerous construction systems in the second half of the 1800s.[14] Of these, one would be widely adopted in Switzerland. It was based on a patent by François Hennebique, a French manufacturer based in Brussels and founder of a company of the same name.[15] Hennebique's first rudimentary concepts were aimed at reducing the amount of metal in floors built with concrete slabs and iron beams. He subtracted the webs from the beams, and he introduced a series of stirrups, the purpose of which was to maintain the remaining longitudinal elements in their intended position. Between 1886 and 1897, this initial idea was reworked several times, in various patents, up to the development of continuous beam systems on columns. The iron reinforcing was bent in response to the tensile and shear stresses, and to ensure an integral connection between the beams and columns.[16] Hennebique thus expanded on the constructive principles that had informed both Wilkinson's system and Koenen's revisitation of the Monier method.

The Hennebique System in Lausanne and Its Diffusion

It was the engineer Samuel de Mollins who first introduced the Hennebique system to Switzerland. Born in Paris but with origins in the canton of Vaud, Mollins completed his engineering studies at the École spéciale de Lausanne, the forerunner of the present École polytechnique fédérale, and he launched his professional career in Croix, France, in the region of Nord-Pas-de-Calais, where his parents had settled.[17] This was where he met Hennebique. He went into business with him in 1892, opening, in Lausanne, the first Swiss agency to represent the new construction system. For the realisation of future projects, Mollins worked with the entrepreneur Alexandre Ferrari, who became a licensee of the system, also in Lausanne.[18] For promotional purposes, the two performed a load test on a beam in September 1893.[19] Cleverly advertised with eye-catching photographs, the experiment garnered considerable attention, thus propelling the future commercial success of the system in Lausanne and in numerous other Swiss cities, where local entrepreneurs operated as licensees.[20] Many of the works made with the system were limited in scope, in particular floor structures, while others took on a certain importance in the history of construction and became prominent features in urban settings or, in a few cases, the landscape. These larger works consisted mainly of infrastructure and commercial, industrial, and residential buildings.

Shortly after they had performed their load test in Lausanne, Mollins and Ferrari were commissioned with building a storehouse for the Lausanne-Ouchy Railway Company in the valley of the Flon River, which was to become the city's industrial zone. The architects, Georges Corbaz and Jules Centurier, had planned on floor structures with double-T beams supported by iron columns, with concrete vaults between the beams. Mollins proposed the alternative of a structural frame (columns, beams, and floors) entirely in reinforced concrete. The perimeter bearing walls would be in masonry, while the lintels over the door and window openings would also be in reinforced concrete. The client analysed the two projects and chose the Hennebique system based on cost savings of over 10%.[21]

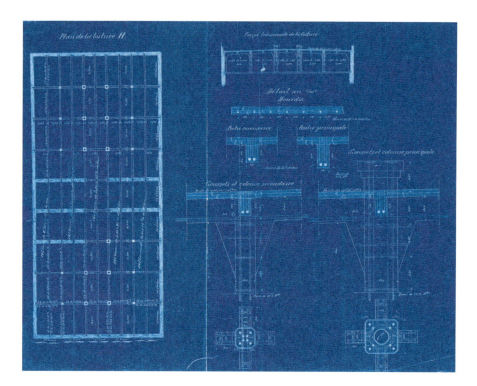

1. S. de Mollins, storehouse for the Lausanne-Ouchy Railway Company, Lausanne, 1895. Plan, section, and section details of the column and beam connection, May 1894.

After this building was completed, in October 1895, the same railway company launched the procedures for the construction of a second, similar storehouse just a few steps from the first.[22] At that time the two buildings were among the most representative of the Hennebique system in its most complete expression (much like the image that accompanied the Tourcoing textile mills project in France in 1893, which would later become the icon of the system itself).[23] In fact, with the exception of the perimeter walls, the storehouses in Lausanne each present a complete framework, the integral connections of the pillars and beams by means of reinforcing bars, and corbels (figs. 1–2).

The entire expansion zone of Lausanne, located between the medieval centre, the central train station, and the Flon Valley, soon became an enormous experimental construction site for the Hennebique system. It was used, on various scales, to build the Bonnard Frères department store and residential building (1900, architects Jacques Regamey and Henri Meyer); the Hôtel des Postes (1900, architect Eugène Jost); the Maison Mercier commercial and residential building, the Bel-Air freight station, and the Banque cantonale vaudoise (completed respectively in 1900, 1902, and 1903, all by the architect Francis Isoz); as well as the Galerie St-François shopping centre (1909, architect Georges Épitaux). The lintels over the openings facing the street on the ground floor of the Bonnard department store were surprisingly slender for their time.[24] Fearing they were insufficient to support the expected loads, the Director of Public Works for the City of Lausanne required a load test, which was conducted successfully in May 1898 (fig. 3). In the same years it became necessary to protect the Flon Valley from flooding by diverting the course of the river. This required the construction of three small bridges, which were designed by Mollins and Ferrari.[25]

Outside Lausanne as well, the Hennebique system was used to construct the floors, lintels, and entire concrete frames of numerous industrial, commercial, and residential buildings. In Geneva, where the entrepreneur Pierre Poujoulat was the licensee, Mollins managed to obtain the commission for the floors of the pump room of the Chèvres hydroelectric plant (completed in 1896 under the supervision of engineer Théodore Turrettini). In 1898, the plant was severely damaged by a fire that destroyed all the metal and timber structures, while the reinforced concrete floors resisted. This made it easy for Mollins to claim the superiority of the system he represented, and he was thus commissioned with both the reconstruction of the roofs and the expansion of the building.[26] In the meantime, for the 1896 Swiss National Exhibition in Geneva, the system was used to build the floors of various plant rooms at the service of the luminous fountains, as well as a monumental staircase, which was awarded a gold medal.[27] Other impressive achievements included the floors for an electrical cable factory in Cortaillod (Neuchâtel), built in 1898, and the floors of the Basel electric power station, completed in 1899.[28] Rudolf Linder, the licensee in Basel, used the system to build several residential buildings in that city, as well as the Sodeck commercial building (1898, architect Adolf Visscher van Gaasbeek), the structure of which consisted entirely of a reinforced concrete frame.[29] Hennebique also managed to open a breach in the nascent architecture of the great Swiss hotels. His system was used for the floors of the Grand Hôtel de l'Observatoire in Saint-Cergues sur Nyon (1899, architects Frédéric and Henri de Morsier and Charles Weibel); the entire structural frame of the Palace-Hôtel in Lucerne (1906, architect Heinrich Meili-Wapf); and the floors and supporting frame of the large dining room of the Beau-Rivage Palace in Lausanne (1908, architects Louis Bezencenet, Eugène Jost, and Maurice Schnell) (fig. 4).[30] Projects for new theatres also offered opportunities to develop original structural frameworks that were considered quite daring at the time. This was the case of the auditorium at the Casino in Morges (1900, architect Jacques Regamey), whose galleries were cantilevered on beams embedded in the masonry, and the Bern Theatre (1903, architect René von Wurstenberger), with its interior structure consisting of a reinforced concrete frame, including the roof of the large auditorium and the cantilevered balcony.[31]

2. S. de Mollins, storehouse for the Lausanne-Ouchy Railway Company, Lausanne, 1895. Interior view of one of the rooms of the storehouse during construction. Photograph Henri Gros, Fréderic Mayor, September 1895.

3. J. Regamey and H. Meyer, Bonnard Frères department store, Lausanne, 1900. Load testing of a lintel, from *Le béton armé*, 1898.

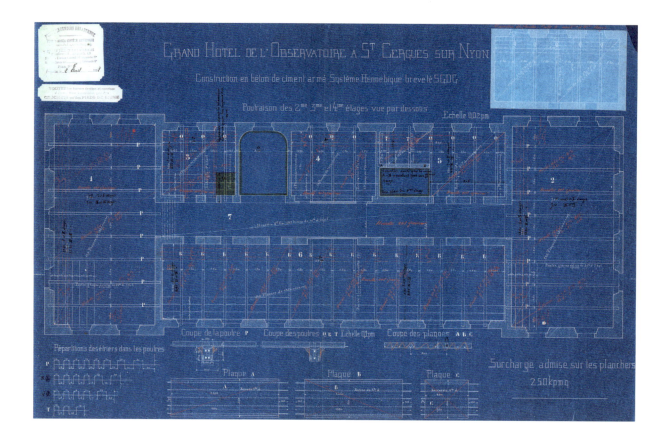

4. F. and H. de Morsier, Charles Weibel, Grand Hôtel de l'Observatoire, Saint-Cergues sur Nyon, 1899. Bétons armés système Hennebique, reflected ceiling plan of the second, third, and fourth floors, April 1898.

Buildings aside, however, perhaps it was railway infrastructures, more than any other type of construction, that most facilitated the diffusion of the Hennebique system in Switzerland. By their very nature, railways are networks, the construction of which requires experts who travel throughout the country, bringing their technical knowledge with them. In addition, the process of nationalisation of the various local railway networks had begun in 1902, and thus local information and knowledge were converging into the newly created federal offices, facilitating their diffusion throughout Switzerland. Very early on, the Jura-Simplon Railway Company began experimenting with the Hennebique system for the construction of reduced-span bridges, prompted by the engineers Édouard Elskes and François Schüle. Elskes was responsible for bridge construction for the railway company, while Schüle was responsible for construction supervision for the Federal Postal Services and Railways Department.[32] Four bridges were thus built between 1894 and 1898, one in Wiggen (Lucerne), one in Saint-Maurice (Valais), and two more in Rolle and Yverdon (Vaud).[33] And that was not all. Due to its incombustibility, reinforced concrete was identified as an excellent material for building the roofs and chimneys of locomotive sheds, in place of timber construction. Thus, the Hennebique system was used to build the locomotive sheds in Renens (1899, Vaud), St-Maurice (1902, Valais), and Sargans (1903, St. Gallen).[34] But the most extraordinary work stemming from the development of railway infrastructure was the Simplon Canal, which was used to transport water from the Rhône River to provide power for the construction of the railway

tunnel between Switzerland and Italy. It consists of a channel with a rectangular section, measuring over four kilometres long, three of which in Hennebique-reinforced concrete. Due to the difficult terrain, the canal is supported on trestles for much of its length.[35] The usual timber construction was in this case also replaced with concrete, as wood is not only inflammable but degrades in contact with water. The speed of execution created a further argument in favour of concrete. In fact, the canal was built in less than three months, from April to July 1898. It bears mentioning that, for this type of construction, Hennebique could already boast success in Switzerland: the canal for transporting water from the Suze River, at Frinvilliers, to the Évilard power station, in the canton of Bern (1897).[36] These reinforced concrete engineering works were the beginning of what would become, over the decades, a distinctive feature of the Swiss landscape (figs. 5–6).

Faced with the proliferation of the Hennebique system throughout the country, it was no surprise that Karl-Wilhelm Ritter, then the major authority in Switzerland in the field of structural calculations, would take an interest in it, analyse it, and then propose his own calculation techniques.[37]

However, the history of the Hennebique system in Switzerland was also marked by at least two disastrous events and some unsuccessful submissions for design contests. In 1901, the Hôtel Zum Bären in Basel collapsed while it was still under construction. In 1905, the set shop spaces of the Bern Theatre collapsed. These episodes were widely covered in the press, although it was later clarified, also as a result of analyses conducted by Ritter, that the causes were not attributable to the Hennebique system in itself.[38] Between 1894 and 1902, Hennebique's project submissions to competitions launched for the construction of three important bridges – Pont de la Coulouvrenière (1896) and Pont du Mont-Blanc (1903) in Geneva, and Pont Chauderon (1905) in Lausanne – were rejected, as his experience in the construction of this type of work was deemed insufficient. The Pont de la Coulouvrenière would be built with hinged concrete arches, unreinforced because the expected tensile stresses were considered negligible, while Pont du Mont-Blanc would be built with steel beams to a project

5. Jura-Simplon Railways, Simplon Canal, 1898. A section of the canal on trestles.

6. Frinvilliers Canal, Évilard (Bern), 1898. Partial bird's-eye view of the canal in the landscape, from *Le béton armé*, 1898.

7. E. Monod and A. Laverrière, Pont Chauderon, Lausanne, 1905. Construction of one of the vaults.

8. L. F. De Vallière, A. Simon, Pont des Planches, Ormont-Dessous (Vaud), 1913. Post card.

submitted by the engineer Georges Autran.[39] In making its decisions, the City of Geneva consulted with Elskes, Ritter, and Alphonse Vautier, an engineer from Lausanne with particular expertise in railway construction. Ritter's unfavourable opinions held sway in this context because he was carefully studying the Hennebique system and he would express doubts regarding its adequacy for the construction of bridges.[40]

The Pont Chauderon in Lausanne was built using the Melan system to a project by the architects Eugène Monod and Alphonse Laverrière.[41] Patented in 1891 in Brno by the Austrian engineer Joseph Melan, this system involved the use of a series of arched steel profiles with an I-section or double T-section, encased in concrete (fig. 7). The engineers Louis-François de Vallière and Albert Simon were the licensees for this system in Switzerland. They used the system again in 1913 to build the Pont des Planches – with a span of over 60 metres – in the territory of Ormont-Dessous (Vaud) (fig. 8).[42]

However, the competition was also encroaching on the field of floor construction. In fact, the system patented by the engineer François Brazzola in 1905, based on ribbed slabs and a reusable hollow metal formwork, enjoyed a certain amount of success.[43] The agents of Brazolla's system were the engineers Adrien Paris and Louis Berthod of Lausanne. They used it to build the floors of the headquarters of the Banque de l'État de Fribourg (1907, architect Léon Hertling), the Grands Magasins de l'Innovation (1907, architect Georges Épitaux), and the Hôtel Royal in Lausanne (1909, architects Charles Mauerhofer, Adrian Van Dorsser, and Charles Bonjour); a large terrace within the Montreux railway station (1909); and the floors of the Lumen Theatre (1911, architect Édmond Quillet) and the Maison Manuel Frères (1914, architects Georges Chessex and Charles-François Chamorel-Garnier) in Lausanne.[44] Solutions considered particularly daring for the time include the structural frame of the Royal Hôtel, with its floors suspended from the roof structure, the cantilevered floors of the Lumen Theatre and, in the same building, an avant-garde concrete column, 45 cm in diameter by 13.40 metres in height, reinforced with steel hooping.

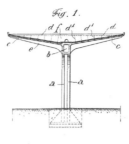
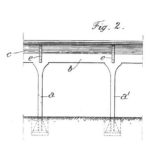

The Brazzola system also garnered some success in Ticino, where the licensee was Agenzia Tecnica e Direzione Generale dei Lavori, headed by the engineer Secondo Antognini. He had met both Brazzola and Paris at the construction site of the Simplon railway tunnel, a confirmation of the important role of the development of railway infrastructure in fostering relationships between professionals and the exchange of technical knowledge.[45]

And it was probably in response to the Brazzola patent that Mollins registered a system for reusable metal moulds for ribbed floor structures in 1907. He used it for various construction works, including the above-mentioned Palace-Hôtel in Lucerne, as well as the impressive vault of the meeting room of the Young Men's Christian Association in the Beau-Site building in La Chaux-de-Fonds (1907, architect Robert Convert) (fig. 9).[46] Mollins had, in fact, already made it clear that he was unwilling to limit himself to the role of sales agent. During the development of the project for the bridge at Coulouvrenière, he launched a harsh dispute by letter with Hennebique, mainly due to a disagreement about calculation methods.[47] It is not surprising that by the year 1900 Mollins had already begun depositing various patents for reinforced concrete applications. Of these, an umbrella-shaped canopy roof perhaps deserves mention, because, on a conceptual level, it appears that he was anticipating future developments, also and above all because he was already suggesting aligning structural elements in series (fig. 10).[48]

Epilogue

From the end of the nineteenth century to the beginning of the twentieth century, Switzerland made a significant contribution to the development of modern construction techniques in reinforced concrete, and it did so in particular through the numerous construction sites that employed the Hennebique system. Although skilfully orchestrated, the system's strong commercial protection, like that of many of its competitors, gradually lost its effectiveness with the success of reinforced concrete construction as a technique in the broader

9. Robert Convert, Beau-Site Building, La Chaux-de-Fonds, 1907. The meeting room of the Young Men's Christian Association under construction, from *Le béton armé*, 1907.

10. S. de Mollins, 'Abri léger, du type dit: parapluie ou auvent', patent no. 27898, Swiss Confederation, Federal Intellectual Property Agency, 10 January 1903.

sense, free of patent rights. The multiplication of national and imported patents, the dissemination of the calculation techniques developed by Ritter and the development of standards by the Swiss Society of Engineers and Architects would contribute, also in Switzerland, to the general process of transforming the numerous distinct systems into a technique in the public domain.[49]

At the same time, in terms of architecture, Hennebique's buildings, with their period facades concealing innovative structural systems, were soon superseded, not just by advances in civil engineering, but also by the innovative projects that had begun to spring from the minds and hands of the masters of the Modern Movement. The presence of reinforced concrete in the academic tradition probably facilitated its acceptance by urban, bourgeois architectural patrons, but it became an obstacle to overcome when a radical cultural change began to impose itself.

Robert Maillart, a student of Ritter, invented his own method of designing and building in reinforced concrete. He created both a bridge system (based on hinged, hollow box girders, which Hennebique erroneously predicted, or perhaps hoped, would not be viable[50]) and a structural frame system that reduced the usual forest of intersecting pillars and beams to just a few elegant mushroom columns supporting thin, flat-plate slabs. Maillart worked outside the confines of the above systems, and he developed his own interpretation of the nature and potential of reinforced concrete. In his opinion, the material had the advantages of stone but without the drawbacks, neither in terms of weight, because the sections of the various construction elements were considerably reduced, nor in terms of joints, because concrete is a material to be formed in moulds, like cast iron.[51] This approach allowed him to free reinforced concrete from the conceptual constraints that had been forcing it to mimic building elements borrowed from the past.[52]

The French architect Auguste Perret also refused to adhere to any pre-established system. Instead, he openly and generically declared himself to be a 'competitor'.[53] This afforded him the freedom to invent a new architectural language based on reinforced concrete. Between 1908 and 1909, at his studio in Paris, he trained an aspiring young Swiss architect, Charles-Édouard Jeanneret. The latter was certainly already familiar with the Hennebique system because it had been used to build the floors of the homes of Jules Jaquemet and Albert Stotzer.[54] Then, when Jeanneret went to see the terracotta, lime, and cement exhibition in Germany on behalf of the École d'Art in La Chaux-de-Fonds, he had the foresight to recognise the constructive and architectural potential of concrete, announce it in a pamphlet he published in 1912, investigate it in his design of Maison Dom-Ino, and use it for the construction of Villa Schwob – all before moving to Paris and becoming known as Le Corbusier.[55]

At this point, a new season had opened, and this book aims to represent some of its many and complex facets.

Notes

[1] See Roberto Gargiani, *Concrete, from Archeology to Invention 1700–1769* (Lausanne: EPFL Press, 2013) and Id., 'Les cônes de la rade de Cherbourg, ou du béton enseveli 1781-1788', in *matières*, no. 10, 2012, 80–9.

[2] Louis-Bernard Guyton de Morveau, Johann Wolfgang Döbereiner, Claude-Louis Berthollet, Tobern Olof Bergman, and Johann Friedrich John were among the most important chemists involved in this research.

[3] Lucienne Hubler, 'Chaux et ciments', in *Dictionnaire historique de la Suisse (DHS)*, version dating from 12.05.2015. Online: https://hls-dhs-dss.ch/fr/articles/014020/2015-05-12/, consulted on 24.08.2021.

[4] Ibid.

[5] Horace-Bénédict de Saussure, *Voyages dans les Alpes précédés d'un Essai sur l'histoire naturelle des environs de Genève* (Neuchâtel: Samuel Fauche, vols I–IV, 1779–1796). On the impressive number of explorations conducted by Saussure, see, in particular, vol. I, XIII.

[6] Ibid. (vol. II, 140–3). Saussure's theses were also later reported in the book by Jean-Henri Hassenfratz, *Traité théorique et pratique de l'art de calciner la pierre calcaire, et de fabriquer toutes sortes de mortiers, cimens, bétons, etc., soit à bras d'hommes, soit à l'aide de machines* (Paris: Carilian-Goeury, 1825), 166–7. On these reflections, see also, Cyrille Simonnet, *Le béton. Histoire d'un matériau* (Marseille: Éditions Parenthèse, 2005), 11–5.

[7] Louis Alexis Beaudemoulin, *Recherches théoriques et pratiques sur la fondation par immersion des ouvrages hydrauliques, et particulièrement des écluses* (Paris: Carilian-Goeury, 1829), 8.

[8] Max Joseph von Pettenkofer, 'Bemerkungen zu Hopfgartner's Analyse eines englischen und eines deutschen hydraulischen Kalkes', *Polytechnisches Journal* 113, no. 17 (1849), 371.

[9] In 1774, the French inventor Antoine-Joseph Loriot suggested using a compound – which he himself developed and defined as 'cement' – for the production of various building and decorative elements, such as balustrades, stairs, flat arches, and parastas, and increasing its strength by means of an iron core. See Antoine-Joseph Loriot, *Mémoire sur une découverte dans l'art de bâtir* (Paris: A. Lemoine, 1774), 28.

[10] On the various systems for the fabrication of floor structures, see Thomas Potter, *Concrete: Its Use in Building and the Construction of Concrete Walls, Floors, etc.* (London: E. & F. N. Spon, 1877); for the systems for building minor construction works and other artefacts, see further in this same paper.

[11] William Boutland Wilkinson, U.K. Patent 2293, 1854, cit. in Gustav Haegermann, *Vom Cæmentum zum Zement* (Wiesbaden, Berlin: Bauverlag, 1964), 26.*

[12] This was the case of the first floor of a small house built by Wilkinson in Newcastle-upon-Tyne in 1865. Demolished in 1954, the structure of this house was documented by William Fisher Cassie, see W. F. Cassie, 'Early Reinforced Concrete in Newcastle upon Tyne', *Magazine of Concrete Research* 7, no. 19 (1955), 25–30.

[13] Matthias Koenen, 'Für die Berechnung der Starke der Monierschen Cementplatten', *Centralblatt der Bauverwaltung* 6, no. 47 (1886), 462.

[14] See Paul Christophe, *Le béton armé et ses applications* (Paris: Librairie polytechnique Ch. Béranger, 1899, 1902).

[15] According to Karl-Wilhelm Ritter, an authoritative professor of statics at the Swiss Federal Institute of Technology of Zurich, while the Monier method spread throughout Germany and Austria, the Hennebique system prevailed in Switzerland. See K. W. Ritter, 'Die Bauweise Hennebique', *Schweizerische Bauzeitung* 33, no. 5 (1899), 41.

[16] Jacques Gubler, 'Les beautés du béton armé', in Gwenaël Delhumeau et al., *Le béton en représentation. La mémoire photographique de l'entreprise Hennebique 1890–1930* (Paris: Hazan, 1993), 17; Gwenaël Delhumeau, *L'invention du béton armé. Hennebique 1890–1914* (Paris: Norma, 1999).

[17] Gubler, 'Les beautés du béton armé' (see note 16), 18–9.

[18] The business structure of the Hennebique company consisted of the parent company, a network of agents in various countries who maintained contact with the parent company, and numerous licensees, that is, the local builders who worked with the agents.

[19] See Samuel de Mollins, 'Le béton de ciment armé. Procédé Hennebique', *Bulletin de la Société vaudoise des ingénieurs et des architectes* 19, no. 6/7 (1893), 105–7, Alphonse Vautier, 'Le béton de ciment armé. Procédé Hennebique', ibid. 20, no. 8 (1894), 177–8. Also see the essay by Aurelio Muttoni in this book.

[20] Among the main cities: Geneva, Neuchâtel, Fribourg, Bern, Solothurn, Basel, Zurich, and St. Gallen. See the lists of agents and licensees published in the Hennebique company's promotional magazine, *Le béton armé*.

[21] Joëlle Neuenschwander Feihl, 'Magasins L-O No 1 et No 2. Lausanne, Rue de Genève No 19 and No 21', historical report commissioned by the Mobimo company (Épalinges: 2016), 10.

[22] Ibid., 24–35.

[23] See fig. on page 258 of this book.

[24] 'Une intéressante épreuve', *Le béton armé* 1, no. 2 (1898), 1–2.

[25] 'Correction du Flon', *Le béton armé* 1, no. 3 (1898), 1–2.

[26] 'L'incendie de l'usine de Chèvres', *Le béton armé* 1, no. 4 (1898), 1; 'Troisième congrès du béton de ciment armé', ibid. 1, no. 9 (1899), 4–5.

[27] 'Escalier monumental de 11m de portée', *Le béton armé* 1, no. 7 (1898), 3–4.

[28] 'Fabrique de la société d'exploitation des Câbles électriques à Cortaillod', *Le béton armé* 1, no. 9 (1899) 16–7; 'Elektrizitätswerk der Stadt-Basel', ibid. 2, no. 21 (1900), 7.

[29] 'La transformation de la Freienstrasse, à Bâle', *Le béton armé* 6, no. 66 (1903), 88–9. See also the lists of the 'Travaux du mois', ibid. 2, no. 13 (1899), 8 and ibid. 2, no. 16 (1899), 18.

[30] See Archives de la construction moderne EPFL Lausanne, fonds Morsier et Weibel, dossier 0164.04.0072; Samuel de Mollins, 'Le Palace-Hôtel de Lucerne', *Le béton armé* 10, no. 103 (1907), 65–6; Id., 'L'Hôtel Beau-Rivage à Lausanne', ibid. 12, no. 136 (1909), 129–130.

[31] 'Théâtre de Berne', *Le béton armé* 5, no. 57 (1903), 157–8 ; 'Le nouveau théâtre de Berne', ibid. 6, no. 67 (1903), 105.

[32] Schüle would later become a professor at the École d'ingénieurs at the University of Lausanne (1899–1901) and at the Swiss Federal Institute of Technology of Zurich (1901–1924), as well as the director of the Swiss Federal Laboratories for Materials Testing and Research (Eidgenössische Materialprüfungs- und Forschungsanstalt, EMPA). See also the essay by A. Muttoni in this book.

[33] 'Les ponts des chemins de fer', *Le béton armé* 1, no. 1 (1898), 2–6; Édouard Elskes, 'Trente ans de béton armé', *Bulletin technique de la Suisse romande* 50, no. 23 (1924), 285–90.

[34] Elskes, 'Trente ans de béton armé' (see note 33), 289.

[35] Samuel de Mollins, 'Tunnel du Simplon. Dérivation du Rhône actionnant les installations de la tête nord', *Bulletin de la Société vaudoise des ingénieurs et des architectes* 25, no. 5 (1899), 171; 'Troisième Congrès du béton de ciment armé', *Le béton armé* 1, no. 9 (1899), 3–4; 'Le canal d'amenée du Simplon', ibid. 1, no. 11 (1899), 13; 'Achèvement du canal du Simplon', ibid. 2, no. 18 (1899), 12–3; Salomon Pestalozzi, 'Die Bauarbeiten am Simplontunnel', *Schweizerische Bauzeitung* 38, no. 18 (1901), 191–4, no. 19 (1901), 205–9, no. 20 (1901), 215–7, no. 22 (1901), 241–4; Elskes, 'Trente ans de béton armé' (see note 33), 285.

[36] 'Canalisation de Frinvilliers en béton armé système Hennebique', *La construction Lyonnaise* 20, no. 5 (1898), 54–5, later reprinted in *Le béton armé* 1, no. 1 (1898), 8.

[37] Ritter, 'Die Bauweise Hennebique' (see note 15), 41–3; ibid., no. 6 (1899), 49–52, and ibid., no. 7 (1899), 59–61.

[38] The incident in Basel was one of the events that led to the development of Swiss standards for reinforced concrete construction. Also see the essay by A. Muttoni in this book.

[39] G. M., 'Referat über den Vortrag von Professor W. Ritter: "Ueber den Neubau der Coulouvrenière-Brücke in Genf"', *Schweizerische Bauzeitung* 27, no. 14 (1896), 100–1; 'Reconstruction du pont du Mont-Blanc, à Genève', *Bulletin technique de la Suisse romande* 28, no. 22, (1902), 294–9.

[40] Ritter, 'Die Bauweise Hennebique', (see note 15), 42. Nonetheless, Hennebique built over 1300 bridges throughout the world between 1892 and 1909; see Jacques Gubler, 'Prolégomènes à Hennebique', *Études de Lettres: revue de la Faculté des lettres de l'Université de Lausanne*, no. 4 (1985), 64.

[41] Alphonse Vautier, 'Concours pour l'exécution du pont Chauderon-Montbenon', *Bulletin technique de la Suisse romande* 28, no. 2 (1902), 13–4.

[42] Albert Hahling, 'Dans la vallée des Ormonts, un intéressant monument d'histoire technique : le pont des Planches, près du Sépey', *Revue historique vaudoise* 98 (1990), 85–100; Archives de la construction moderne EPFL Lausanne, fonds Hahling, 0189.01.0004, 0189.01.0005.

[43] François Brazzola, 'Poutre en béton armé', patent no. 33308, Swiss Confederation, Federal Intellectual Property Agency, 18 March 1905; Id., 'Appareil pour la fabrication, en béton armé, de poutres évidées, de planchers évidés, etc.', patent no. 34202, Swiss Confederation, Federal Intellectual Property Agency, 4 July 1905.

[44] Léon Hertling, 'Hôtel de la Banque de l'État de Fribourg', *Schweizerische Bauzeitung* 52, no. 3 (1908), 31–4; Roland Zehnder-Spoerry, 'Die elektrische Zahnradbahn Montreux-Glion', ibid. 54, no. 2 (1909), 22–3; 'Le Royal Hôtel, à Lausanne', *Bulletin technique de la Suisse romande* 36, no. 1 (1910), 5–6; Adrien Paris, 'Planchers suspendus en béton armé, au Grand Hôtel Royal, à Lausanne', ibid. 34, no. 21 (1908), 245–9; Id., 'Le théâtre Lumen, Lausanne', ibid. 40, no. 9 (1914), 97–103; Id., 'Construction en béton armé des grands magasins de l'Innovation, Lausanne', ibid. 39, no. 3 (1913), 27–9; 'Une maison lausannoise', ibid. 40, no. 21 (1914), 243–5.

[45] Nicola Navone examined the arrival of the Brazzola system in Ticino at the conference 'Concrete in Canton Ticino: An Overview' in the workshop 'Béton Fédérateur', Swiss Federal Institute of Technology, Zurich, 26 January 2019.

[46] Samuel de Mollins, 'Moule métallique renforcé pour hourdis', patent no. 39409, Swiss Confederation, Federal Intellectual Property Agency, 28 March 1907 ; Id., 'Les planchers creux en béton armé. Système Hennebique sur moule d'acier breveté', *Le béton armé* 10, no. 105 (1907), 17–24.

[47] See Delhumeau, *L'invention du béton armé* (see note 16), 127–31.

[48] Samuel de Mollins, 'Abris léger, du type dit: parapluie ou auvent', patent no. 27898 Swiss Confederation, Federal Intellectual Property Agency, 10 January 1903.

[49] On the development of the standards for reinforced concrete and on the general validity of the calculation methods developed by Ritter, see the essay by A. Muttoni in this book.

[50] Gubler, 'Prolégomènes à Hennebique' (see note 40), 72.

[51] Robert Maillart, 'Aktuelle Fragen des Eisenbetonbaues', *Schweizerische Bauzeitung* 111, no. 1 (1938), 1; David P. Billington, *Robert Maillart: Builder, Designer, and Artist* (Cambridge: University Press, 1997), 18.

[52] Maillart, 'Aktuelle Fragen des Eisenbetonbaues' (see note 51), 1.

[53] Delhumeau, L'invention du béton armé (see note 16), 300.

[54] Jacques Gubler, 'À l'heure des horlogers jurassiens', *Revue neuchâteloise* 23, no. 90 (1980), 28.

[55] Charles-Édouard Jeanneret, *Étude sur le mouvement d'art décoratif an Allemagne* (La Chaux-de-Fonds: École d'art, 1912).

Between Constraint and Freedom to Innovate: Swiss Standards to Innovate

Aurelio Muttoni

A Swiss engineer who designs a load-bearing structure has the right to derogate from the standards in force, if in possession of the requisite theoretical or empirical expertise. This is explicitly stated in the article that is commonly known among engineers as the 'exemption clause' – a piece of legislation that has undoubtedly been essential for the evolution of structural engineering and the development of innovative solutions. This essay addresses the origins of the clause in Switzerland in the late 1800s and early 1900s, as well as the various approaches taken to structures of steel, reinforced concrete, or timber, and the consequences for the development of Swiss engineering.

A Brief History of Swiss Standards for Steel Structures

The industrialisation of Switzerland and the concomitant growth of a transport network rapidly spawned railway bridges, platform canopies, industrial buildings, and other steel structures throughout the country. A first standard for elements to be taken into account when designing bridges, or roof and floor structures, was drawn up by the Swiss Railway Inspectorate on the occasion of the first Swiss National Exhibition, which was held in Zurich in 1883;[1] it was immediately published by the Swiss Society of Engineers and Architects (SIA).[2]

In the early 1890s, at the instigation of Professor Ludwig von Tetmajer, this standard was replaced by a regulation.[3] More restrictive than the standard, the regulation concerned not only the forces acting on load-bearing structures, but also certain rules on the design of steel structures, such as those for compression members, to prevent buckling. Tetmajer, as of 1880 founding director of the Building Materials Testing Institute (later EMPA),[4] also co-authored a theory on the buckling of timber and steel compression members taking into account the negative effect of material imperfections and non-linear behaviours.[5] These research findings proved to be crucial for metallic structures, because they demonstrated that in the case of long and slender compression members, the Euler formula in use at the time to predict the critical buckling load led to the design of undersized steel structures. The need for regulation became patently clear when a passing train provoked the collapse of the Birs bridge in Münchenstein in the canton of Basel on 14 June 1891, a disaster which killed seventy-three people.[6] Expert consultants Professors Wilhelm Ritter[7] and Ludwig von Tetmajer were able to show that the steel truss bridge, designed and built in 1874 by the Ateliers Eiffel, collapsed after certain compression members insufficient both in size and steel grade buckled under the weight of the train.[8] Soon after the disaster, a series of measures was taken to improve the safety of all railway bridges on the Swiss network, including the assessment of their static resistance, in line with a new directive issued by an expert commission under the aegis of the Federal Department of Post and Railways.[9] It was on the basis of this directive that the Federal Council introduced a new regulation on 19 August 1892 – one that could now be legally enforced. Highly prescriptive, it regulated not only the actions to be considered, but also material properties, the allowable stresses, and the buckling resistance of all compression members.[10] In addition to the design of new structures, it defines load tests and the inspection procedures for existing structures; indeed, the latter was one of its primary aims.[11] Given its title, the regulation would appear to refer solely to Swiss railway bridges and structures, yet it covered road bridges, too. A revised version was issued by the Swiss Federal Railways four years later, in the form of new regulations.[12] Doubtless because the systematic inspection of all Swiss rail network bridges, as decreed in the wake of the Münchenstein disaster, had meanwhile been completed, the focus was then on the calculation and construction of new structures. A further version of the regulation was issued in 1913, again by the Federal Council,[13] and as in the original version and that of 1892, this one, too, covered building structures and road bridges, which suggests that these texts served as a basis for designing all kinds of load-bearing structures, not only steel ones. This was the case up until 1935, the year the SIA published new standards for the design, construction, and maintenance of structures built of steel and reinforced concrete.[14]

The Case of Reinforced Concrete Structures: A Standard for a New Construction Method

The origins of the standards for the design and construction of reinforced concrete structures are similar to those for steel structures in certain respects, yet differ considerably in others. By the turn of the twentieth century, reinforced concrete was progressing in leaps and bounds.[15] In 1900, more than twenty systems were known in Switzerland,[16] the most widespread of which was based on a patent filed by François Hennebique in 1892,[17] and meanwhile represented in Switzerland by an agent in Lausanne, the engineer Samuel de Mollins.[18] The systems differed with regard not only to the reinforcement itself – the where and how of its incorporation – but also to the composition of the linear elements (beams, slabs columns) and planar elements (slabs, walls, and shells) in what was generally a monolithic structure.[19] The Hennebique system was soon franchised to several Swiss companies and it quickly spread throughout the country.[20] To demonstrate its reliability, a first load test was carried out under Mollins's direction in 1893, in Lausanne, by the Ferrari company[21] (fig. 1). The same reinforced concrete floor slab was load tested to breaking point several months later,[22] under the supervision of François Schüle,[23] inspection engineer for bridge construction at the Federal Department of Post and Railways. Construction methods and theoretical

1. The first load test of a reinforced concrete beam in Switzerland, conducted in 1893 in Lausanne, under the supervision of S. de Mollins and F. Schüle.

knowledge developed rapidly between 1890 and 1910. In 1899, Wilhelm Ritter published his famous article 'Die Bauweise Hennebique' (Hennebique System), in which, in addition to presenting the system, he described the design methods for the bending moment, shear force, and stability of slender compression members.[24] In fact, despite the title of the article, the design methods he described were universally valid: they applied to many of the concrete structural systems in vogue at the time and to this day have lost none of their topicality. The need to have standards in place for the design and construction of concrete structures was recognised first by the Swiss Hydraulic Lime and Cement Association (Société des fabricants suisses de chaux hydrauliques et ciments, now cemsuisse), and as early as 1901, it invited the SIA to cooperate to that end.[25] This was made terribly clear by the collapse in August that same year of a Hennebique-system building under construction in Basel.[26] In their report, the Zurich city architect and SIA President Alfred Geiser and Professors Ritter and Schüle attributed the collapse to the insufficient resistance of the ground-floor concrete columns (itself a result of low-quality aggregates and inadequate compaction), the failure to monitor the strength of the concrete, the incorrect assessment of the internal forces in these elements, and the inappropriate removal of shoring during work on a critical column. In addition, the experts continued, the fact that the design of the structure had been carried out by Hennebique's technical office in Paris had led to problems of coordination that were exacerbated in turn by the lack of technical competence among the staff in charge of the project in situ.[27] In concluding their report, the experts, while emphasising that a scientifically based dimensioning method was not available, nonetheless proposed some general rules for the planning of future buildings.[28]

So, once again, it took a major accident to bring about rapid action on standards. However, unlike in the case of steel structures, the SIA's approach here was characteristically federalist: on 25 May 1902 its assembly of delegates called on the cantonal sections to comment on Geiser, Ritter, and Schüle's proposals and to make some of their own regarding the content of the future standard.[29] The consultation produced varied results, from very general proposals to more detailed provisions.[30] Nonetheless, the three experts' position on the Basel accident carried sufficient weight, and the arguments for less prescriptive standards held sway. Several cantonal sections felt that the new standard should on no account hinder the system of construction but, rather, allow it to further develop.[31] The Zurich section even proposed a clause that would permit derogation from it: 'In view of the novelty of this type of construction, derogation from the aforementioned standards is permitted, if justified by scientific testing and appraisal by competent experts'.[32]

In August 1903, the new provisional standard was finally published by the SIA, along with a commentary by François Schüle.[33] Extremely succinct – six pages of standard and ten of commentary – it contained no precise rules in relation to design methods, while the derogation clause proposed by the Zurich section was reproduced in full, with one minor modification, 'scientific tests' being replaced by 'detailed tests'. It was one of the first regulations of this sort to attain international scope: its French counterpart followed in 1904 and the Austrian in 1907.[34] Certain German cities had had one in force for some time.[35] In line with the Geneva section's request, it applied to buildings as well as to bridges – 'because there is no difference between the behaviour of reinforced concrete in buildings and in bridges'.[36] It was surely this last feature, typical of a standard written by engineers for engineers, which fostered fruitful interdisciplinary exchange in the following years, so enhancing creativity and quality in the structural design of bridges and buildings.

The Importance of Being Able to Derogate from Standards, in the Early Twentieth Century and to This Day

The clause permitting derogation from the requirements of the 1903 provisional standard for reinforced concrete structures was entirely justifiable, given that construction methods were still evolving at the time and design methods were still rudimentary. Nonetheless, the clause was adopted in slightly modified form in all subsequent versions of the standard for reinforced concrete structures (1909, 1935, 1956, 1968, 1989, 2003, and 2013). That since 1989 this option is always the first clause in the standard is a sign of its great importance to engineers. A similar clause has been part of the standards for steel structures since 1935[37] and for timber structures since 1936.[38] The novelty of the materials in question, which was used to justify the derogation clause in the first standard of 1903 for reinforced concrete structures, appeared to be less relevant in the case of standards for steel or timber structures. Nevertheless, the derogation clause in the standard for steel structures explicitly mentions the evolution of construction methods (1935) or new knowledge of materials and calculation methods (1990). In the case of timber structures, the standard refers not only to test-based empirical methodologies, but also to methods based on experience (1953).

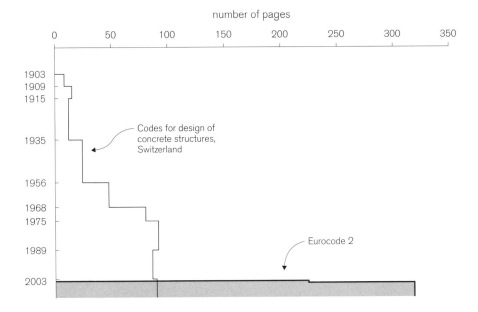

2. Growth in the number of pages devoted to building regulations.

The fact that structures evolve, or that engineers should not be prevented from introducing innovations, has thus been deliberately taken into account in all Swiss structural standards for several generations. Engineers are aware of this, all the more so since the price to pay is a greater liability.

It should be noted also that since 1903, the standards have become increasingly detailed and prescriptive (fig. 2). It is interesting to see that Robert Maillart protested this development as early as 1938: 'Unfortunately, official regulations, especially when used as teaching material or applied to the letter by inspectors, tempt or force the engineer to apply them in a strict and mechanical fashion. Slightly relaxing the regulations in order to put more responsibility on the structural engineer would go a long way towards improving the quality of our buildings. Above all, the student should not be taught the regulations, as to do so can only narrow the scope of his vision. A very simple calculation method is therefore the sole possible and adequate option. In any case, the prudent assessment of its results will produce a more uniformly secure construction than the strict but thoughtless application of any calculation method riddled with finer points.'[39]

This position is hardly surprising, considering that Maillart was probably behind the first proposal for a derogation clause in 1903. Indeed, the young engineer was very active in discussions of this topic by the Zurich section of the SIA[40] and is listed as the first of the five members of the working group that drafted the proposal.[41] Besides, had the Swiss standards not granted such freedom, Maillart would have found it more difficult to innovate throughout his career, both in structural design and methods of calculation.[42] The examples in Figure 3 finely illustrate the outcome of such freedom. In the case of the Tavanasa bridge (fig. 3a), the overall form is optimised on the basis of experience with masonry bridges, while the amount of material is minimised by removing all unnecessary concrete parts and choosing the appropriate sections (T-section for the arch to better carry asymmetrical loads and assure the required stability).

3 a. Robert Maillart, bridge over the Rhine in Tavanasa (Grisons), 1905–06. Photograph Carl Anton Lang.

b. Robert Maillart, concrete decks and columns in the Federal Granary, Altdorf (Uri), 1912. Photograph H. Wolf-Bender.

c. Robert Maillart, bridge over the Arve, Vessy (Geneva), 1936. Photograph Fred Boissonnas.

Flat slabs follow the same logic (fig. 3b): the Hennebique system beams are no longer necessary, as a slab simply resting on columns can easily resist uniformly distributed loads – on condition, however, that the columns have capitals, to prevent the risk of punching.[43] In this case, intuition was corroborated by innovative calculation methods and confirmed by a series of tests.[44] This enabled Maillart not only to optimise the use of the materials, but also to determine, through analysis, the capitals' ideal form. There was, moreover, no dichotomy for Maillart between calculation and design, the former serving not only to ensure a sufficient level of safety, but also, and above all, to determine the ideal form of the structure and optimise the amount of material used. The Vessy bridge is the very epitome of this idea (fig. 3c): the form of the arch no longer responds either to experience or to aesthetic considerations, which have nothing to do with neo-Gothic reminiscence, but is the result solely of calculation.[45] The same goes for the X-shaped piers which, as the original calculation note clearly shows, are given this form so as to minimise the effect of the deformation necessarily deriving from the different behaviours of the deck and the arch respectively. It should be noted that the validation of Maillart's designs often depended on detailed

Concrete in Switzerland

measurements made by his friend and colleague Mirko Roš.[46] The process from intuition to test-based validation (itself a source of future intuition and optimisation) via modelling, calculation, optimisation of form and dimensioning, and design and construction was accordingly able to unfold in Maillart's work, without hindrance by overly restrictive standards.

The present author's personal experience as a structural designer suggests that the situation today is not so very different. When it comes to constructing a 93-metre-long and 52-metre-wide ellipsoidal reinforced concrete shell with a thickness varying between 100 and 120 mm (fig. 4), the standards currently in force are not only of little use, but even a hindrance – especially those pertaining to the reinforcement cover and the minimum dimensions of elements with shear reinforcement – so much so, that the clause permitting derogation from them is of paramount importance.[47] Of course, more extensive specific analyses and laboratory tests on parts of the structure are indispensable, too. The same considerations can be given to the evolution of materials and methods of construction. Even though more than a century separates us from the pioneers of reinforced concrete, this material is still evolving. Today, lightweight, durable, and sustainable reinforced concrete structures are feasible, thanks to ultra-high-performance fibre-reinforced concretes or textile concretes.[48] In the case of the new roof for the Olympic Museum in Lausanne, for example (fig. 5), it was possible to design large-span beams merely a few centimetres thick, using the standard in force but adapting its provisions to the characteristics of the new material, which is six times more resistant than ordinary concrete.[49] Here, too, it was the derogation clause and specific tests which made it possible.

Returning now to the fact that standards are becoming increasingly detailed (fig. 2), and to Maillart's remark in 1938 that 'a very simple calculation method' and, hence, concise standards are to be preferred, the following considerations are essential. In the design of ordinary structures, simple methods should still be given preference today. Increasingly, they are proving necessary also as a means to quickly check 'by hand' the complex calculations made with the latest advanced computer tools. Yet, since simple calculation methods tend to be overly conservative, sophisticated methods remain vital, if the goal is to build more cost-effectively. This is particularly the case now when assessing existing structures, so as to avoid expensive and unnecessary retrofittings. The debate between advocates of simple and concise standards or comprehensive and detailed standards is therefore no longer relevant, as the two solutions each meet different requirements.

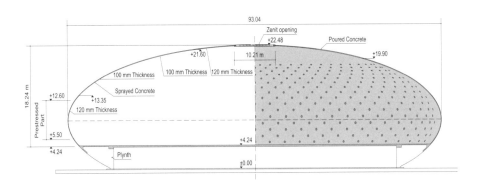

4. Aurelio Muttoni, Franco Lurati, and Miguel Fernández Ruiz, engineers, and Elio Ostinelli, architect, Centro Ovale, Chiasso, 2010. Longitudinal section drawing of the reinforced concrete shell.

Today, the optimal solution should allow for several levels of approximation. Given that a calculation is always a simplified approximation of reality, engineers in the design of simple structures should be able to use simple methods (first level), and then, as the requirements increase, improve the level of approximation while still using those same methods. Accordingly, for a more accurate calculation, they must apply themselves to a more time-consuming analysis. In order to simplify engineers' tasks, standards today should be detailed yet at the same time allow for simple calculations, whenever these suffice.[50] Furthermore, both simple and more detailed calculations should be based on one and the same theory, so as to afford a consistent transition between different levels of approximation.

Conclusions

The first Swiss standards for steel structures and those for concrete structures have some points in common, but also some substantial differences. In both cases, their development was the consequence of major accidents that impressed public opinion at the time, but because concrete structures were still in a pioneering phase (both in terms of construction methods and calculation methods), it was decided to keep the standard as non-prescriptive as possible and to allow for derogations if the engineer had the necessary knowledge. This openness facilitated the evolution of construction methods and allowed engineers a more creative approach to design. This possibility is still relevant today, because developments are still possible, and because the standards have become very detailed and prescriptive. As in the early twentieth century, creativity in structural design should not be hampered by overly prescriptive documents.

5. Muttoni & Fernández Ingénieurs Conseils SA and Brauen Wälchli Architectes, new roof of the Olympic Museum, Lausanne, 2012–13. Photograph by author.

Notes

1. 'Verordnung betreffend Berechnung und Prüfung der eisernen Brücken- und Dachconstructionen auf den schweizerischen Eisenbahnen (von 19. August 1892)', *Schweizerische Bauzeitung* (now *SBZ*) 20, no. 13 (1892), 86, note**.
2. *Belastungsverhältnisse der Brücken- und Dachstuhlconstructionen*, bearbeitet vom technischen Inspectorat schweiz. Eisenbahnen. See *SBZ* 1, no. 25 (1883), 158.
3. *SBZ* 20, no. 13 (see note 1).
4. Bruno Meyer, 'Tetmajer Przerwa, Ludwig von', in *Dictionnaire historique de la Suisse* (now *DHS*), version dating from 29.10.2013. Online: https://hls-dhs-dss.ch/de/articles/031686/2013-10-29/, last accessed 15 April 2021.
5. L. Tetmajer, 'Die Knickungsfestigkeit der Bauhölzer', *SBZ* 2, no. 22 (1883), 141–3; L. Tetmajer, 'Zur Theorie der Knickungsfestigkeit', *SBZ* 10, no. 16 (1887), 93–6; L. Tetmajer, 'Das basische Convertereisen als Baumaterial: ein Beitrag zur Frage der Dimensionsberechnung von Eisenconstructionen', *SBZ* 16, no. 18 (1890), 111–4.
6. *SBZ* 18, no. 2 (1891), 10.
7. Rudolf Mumenthaler, 'Ritter, Karl Wilhelm', in *DHS*, version dating from 10.11.2010. Online: https://hls-dhs-dss.ch/fr/articles/031637/2010-11-10/, last accessed 15 April 2021.
8. W. Ritter, L. Tetmajer, 'Bericht über die Mönchensteiner Brücken-Katastrophe', supplement to *SBZ* 18, no. 26 (1891).
9. *SBZ* 18, no. 2 (1891), 11.
10. *SBZ* 20, no. 13 (see note 1), 86–9.
11. Ibid.
12. *Allgemeine Bedingungen und technische Vorschriften für die Berechnung und Ausführung von eisernen Brücken- und Dachkonstruktionen* (Bern: Schweizerische Eisenbahnen, 1896).
13. 'Verordnung betreffend Berechnung und Untersuchung der eisernen Brücken und Hochbauten der, der Aufsicht des Bundes unterstellten Transportanstalten (Vom 7. Juni 1913)', in *Sammlung der auf das schweizerische Eisenbahnwesen bezüglichen amtlichen Aktenstücke* 29, (1913), 63–92.
14. *SIA 112. Normen für die Berechnung, die Ausführung und den Unterhalt der Bauten aus Stahl, Beton und Eisenbeton* (Zürich: SIA, 1935).
15. Gwenaël Delhumeau, *L'invention du béton armé. Hennebique 1890–1914* (Paris: Norma, 1999); Tullia Iori, *Il cemento armato in Italia dalle origini alla seconda guerra mondiale* (Roma: Edilstampa, 2001), 266.
16. Josef Rosshänder, 'Anwendung und Theorie der Betoneisen-Konstruktionen', *SBZ* 36, nos. 10, 11, 12, 14 (1900), 93–5, 101–2, 109–10, 129–33.
17. Delhumeau, *L'invention du béton armé* (see note 15).
18. Joëlle Neuenschwander Feihl, 'Mollins, Samuel de', in *DHS*, version dating from 26.11.2008. Online: https://hls-dhs-dss.ch/fr/articles/031531/2008-11-26/, accessed 15 April 2021.
19. See, for example, below, Maillart's remarks in 1938 on the subject.
20. See, for example, advertisements in the *SBZ* 35, no. 5 (1900), III or *SBZ* 37, no. 8 (1901), VIII.
21. S. de Mollins, 'Le béton en ciment armé, procédé Hennebique', *Bulletin de la Société vaudoise des ingénieurs et architectes* (now *BSVIA*) 19, no. 6/7 (1893), 105–7.
22. Alphonse Vautier, 'Le béton de ciment armé, système Hennebique', *BSVIA* 20, no. 8 (1894), 177–9.
23. Peter Müller-Grieshaber, 'Schüle, François', in *DHS*, version dating from 23.08.2011. Online: https://hls-dhs-dss.ch/fr/articles/031665/2011-08-23/, last accessed 15 April 2021.
24. W. Ritter, 'Die Bauweise Hennebique', *SBZ* 33, nos. 5–7 (1899), 41–3, 49–52, 59–61.
25. *Bulletin technique de la Suisse romande* (now *BTSR*) 28, no. 10 (1902), 136.
26. 'Gebäude-Einsturz in der Aeschenvorstadt Basel am 28. August 1901' *SBZ* 39, no. 19 (1902), 211; 'Expertenbericht betreffend den Gebäudeeinsturz in der Aeschenvorstadt Basel am 28. August 1901', *SBZ* 39, nos. 20–21 (1902), 213–20, 226–30.
27. 'Expertenbericht betreffend den Gebäudeeinsturz' (see note 26), 213.
28. 'Expertenbericht betreffend den Gebäudeeinsturz' (see note 26), 226–30.
29. *SBZ* 40, no. 11 (1902), 122.
30. 'Zürcher Ingenieur- und Architekten-Verein. Entwurf für eine provisorische Norm zur Berechnung und Ausführung von Beton-Eisenkonstruktionen', *SBZ* 41, no. 14 (1903), 159–160. For proposals of the Vaud and Fribourg cantonal sections, see *BTSR* 28, no. 23 (1902), 314–16 and *BTSR* 29, no. 3 (1903), 45–8.
31. *BTSR* 28, no. 23 (see note 30); 'Zürcher Ingenieur- und Architekten-Verein. Entwurf für eine provisorische Norm' (see note 30).
32. 'Mit Rücksicht auf die Neuheit der Konstruktion sind Abweichungen von den vorstehenden

32. Normen zulässig, wenn sie durch wissenschaftliche Versuche und Urteile kompetenter Persönlichkeiten begründet sind' ('Zürcher Ingenieur- und Architekten-Verein. Entwurf für eine provisorische Norm', see note 30, 160, III. Ausnahmen. Art. 14).

33. *Provisorische Normen für Projektierung, Ausführung und Kontrolle von Bauten in armiertem Beton*, aufgestellt vom Schweizer Ingenieur- und Architektenverein, nebst einem erläuternden Berichte von Prof. Schüle (Zürich: SIA, August 1903).

34. E. Mörsch, *Der Eisenbetonbau, seine Theorie und Anwendung* (Stuttgart: Konrad Wittwer Verlag, 1912).

35. 'Règlements de la police des constructions pour l'exécution de travaux en béton armé. (Système Hennebique, etc.)', *BTSR* 28, no. 23 (1902), 308–13.

36. 'Ein prinzipieller Unterschied in dem Verhalten des armierten Beton bei Brücken und Hochbauten besteht ja nicht' (*Provisorische Normen für Projektierung*, see note 33, 10).

37. SIA 112 (see note 14).

38. SIA 111. *Provisorische Normen für die Berechnung, die Ausführung und den Unterhalt von Hölzernen Tragwerken* (Zürich: SIA, 1936).

39. 'Leider verführen oder zwingen die amtlichen Vorschriften, besonders wenn sie als Lehrstoff benützt und von den Kontrollbeamten buchstäblich angewendet werden, den Ingenieur zu deren strikter mechanischer Anwendung. Eine allgemeine Lockerung der Vorschriften im Sinne der Zuweisung einer grössern Verantwortung an den konstruierenden Ingenieur würde sehr zur qualitativen Verbesserung unserer Bauwerke beitragen. Vor allem dürften die Vorschriften nicht schon dem Studierenden angelernt werden, da dies der Freiheit seines Blickfeldes nur abträglich sein kann.
Eine ganz einfache Berechnungsweise ist also einzig möglich und genügend. Die vernünftige Beurteilung ihrer Resultate ergibt jedenfalls eine Konstruktion von gleichmässigerer Sicherheit als die strikte, aber gedankenlose Anwendung einer mit allen Feinheiten ausgestatteten Rechnungsmethode.' (Robert Maillart, 'Aktuelle Fragen des Eisenbetonbaues' *SBZ* 111, no. 11, 1938, 2).

40. *SBZ* 41, no. 7 (1903), 84.

41. 'Zürcher Ingenieur- und Architekten-Verein. Entwurf für eine provisorische Norm' (see note 30).

42. Markus Hottinger, 'Gemeisterte Materie (Robert Maillart: 1872 bis 1940)', *Das Werk* 27, no. 11 (1940), 324–9; Max Bill, *Robert Maillart* (Erlenbach-Zürich: Verlag für Architektur, 1949).

43. R. Maillart, 'Zur Entwicklung der unterzugslosen Decke in der Schweiz und in Amerika', *SBZ* 87, no. 21 (1926), 263–5; Armand Fürst and Peter Marti, 'Robert Maillart's Design Approach for Flat Slabs', *Journal of Structural Engineering* 123, no. 8 (1997), 1102–10; Andreas Thuy and Mario Rinke, 'The Mushroom Column. Origins, Concepts and Differences', in Ine Wouters et al. (eds.), *Building Knowledge, Construction Histories,* Proceedings of the 6th International Congress on Construction History Brussels 2018, vol. 2 (Boca Raton: CRC Press, 2018), 1271–8.

44. Bill, *Robert Maillart* (see note 42); Fürst and Marti, 'Robert Maillart's Design Approach for Flat Slabs' (see note 43).

45. R. Maillart, 'Évolution de la construction des ponts en béton armé', *BTSR* 65, no. 7 (1939), 85–93.

46. Mirko Roš, *Versuche und Erfahrungen an ausgeführten Eisenbeton-Bauwerken in der Schweiz* (Zürich: EMPA, 1937).

47. Aurelio Muttoni, Franco Lurati, and Miguel Fernández Ruiz, 'Concrete Shells – Towards Efficient Structures: Construction of an Ellipsoidal Concrete Shell in Switzerland', *Structural Concrete* 14, no. 1 (2013), 43–50.

48. Aurelio Muttoni et al., 'Textile Reinforced Concrete for Sustainable Structures: Future Perspectives and Application to a Prototype Pavilion', *Structural Concrete* 21, no. 6 (2020), 2251–67.

49. Aurelio Muttoni et al., *A New Roof for the Olympic Museum at Lausanne, Switzerland*, International Symposium on Ultra-High-Performance Fibre-Reinforced Concrete, Marseille, 2013.

50. Aurelio Muttoni and Miguel Fernández Ruiz, 'Levels-of-Approximation Approach in Codes of Practice', *Structural Engineering* 22, no. 2 (2012), 190.

The N2 Chiasso–Saint Gotthard Motorway: Design and Construction of One Hundred and Forty-Three Kilometres of Reinforced Concrete

Ilaria Giannetti

With its 143 kilometres of reinforced concrete, the N2 Chiasso–Saint Gotthard is recognised by architectural historians as one of the most accomplished works of the architect Rino Tami, the 'aesthetic consultant for the motorway'.[1] It remains an important symbol of the modernisation of Ticino in the second half of the twentieth century. The focus of this article is a reconstruction and analysis of the history of the realisation of the N2 motorway, based on studies already dedicated to Tami's work and on previously unexplored archives, including reports by the engineer Renato Colombi[2] (head of the National Roads Office) and the documentary and iconographic heritage of the Federal Roads Office's historical archive (Ufficio federale delle strade or USTRA).[3] Cross-referencing the above resources with the technical literature of the time and the documentation preserved in the Rino Tami holding at the Archivio del Moderno[4] has permitted us to establish a factual chronicle of the motorway's lengthy construction process (necessary for fully understanding its characteristics) and to analyse the construction history of some of the most significant structural solutions realised along the route. This verification of events has also provided a basis for further reflection, within the context of the history of the canton of Ticino in the second half of the twentieth century, on the processes and concepts behind the design of this singular infrastructure.

In the Beginning: The National Roads Section

The project had its start in 1954 when the Swiss Federal Council set up a Commission for the development of the motorway network. At that time, motorway development was also at the heart of infrastructure planning in Italy, Germany, and France.[5] The Commission issued its first report in 1958. For Ticino, a primarily two-lane road was proposed, while tunnelling under the Gotthard Pass was not even contemplated. On 5 April 1959, the politician Franco Zorzi was elected head of the canton's Department of Construction. As a strong believer in the fundamental role of infrastructure[6] in the modernisation of Ticino (and for ending the isolation of the canton from the rest of Switzerland), he adamantly opposed the modest federal programme. In its place he proposed the vision of a full four-lane motorway in Ticino, to be completed by a tunnel under the Gotthard Pass. With this in mind, Zorzi met with the civil engineer Renato Colombi (1922–2015) on 5 May.[7] Colombi, a graduate of the Swiss Federal Institute of Technology (ETH), was employed in the hydroelectric sector for the company Blenio SA and was particularly experienced in large reinforced concrete works. Zorzi informed Colombi of his decision to form a new section within the Department – a team of engineers who, under his leadership, would be committed exclusively to the motorway project. This section was established on 7 July of the same year, under the name of the National Roads Section. It would later be renamed the National Roads Office.[8]

As chief engineer, Colombi began recruiting a team specialised in large reinforced concrete works. This was a necessary step to enable Ticino to build its own new infrastructure, given the economy of the canton[9] and its complex topography, which at the time was traversed only by a few state roads. Thus, on 6 August, he paid a visit to Zorzi, accompanied by the engineer Francesco Balli (1925–2015), a fellow graduate of the Swiss Federal Institute of Technology and employee of Blenio SA, who would soon be named head of the Design section of the National Roads Office.[10]

The Office, as it became known, began working unofficially on 1 October 1959.[11] On 7 October, competitive examinations were launched to select draftsmen and a total of eight civil engineers. The latter, required to be graduates of the Swiss Federal Institute of Technology, were hired for a one-year probationary period at salaries comparable to those paid by private industry.[12] During the recruitment process, between 14 and 18 October, Colombi travelled to Italy with Balli and a small delegation of engineers to study the Autostrada del Sole (A1 motorway), which had become a fundamental point of reference in the field of reinforced concrete motorway construction.[13] The official start date of the Office's activities was 1 January 1960. The team was made up of eight engineers, assisted by six draftsmen and a secretary in charge of expropriation procedures. Despite its limited staff, the Office was already divided into three departments: Design, directed by Balli; Geotechnical Laboratory and Materials Testing, directed by the engineer Marco von Krannichfeldt; and Administrative Services, directed by Renzo Sailer. In April of that year, the Project Management section was added. Directed by the engineer Glauco Nolli, it would be deployed in several locations along the future construction sites.

The team's first task was to re-examine the proposed route at the scale of 1:25,000.[14] From the south end they began with the design of the section from Chiasso to Lamone, and from the north end with the 'semi-motorway' section, which, while waiting for the completion of the tunnel, led from Airolo to the Gotthard Pass, thus replacing the old Val Tremola road. In the meantime, the first construction sites for Lots 7a and 7b were opened in Bissone, the birthplace of Francesco Borromini. A strip was cleared between the railway and the village to make way for the N2 motorway, which, at thirty-metres wide, would constitute an astonishing innovation in the local landscape.[15]

The Ticino Motorway (1961–1968)

Twenty-five per cent of the motorway was built between 1961 and 1968. While the construction works were focused on the Chiasso–Lamone section, inaugurated in December 1968, and on the 'new Tremola' section, opened to traffic in 1967, the Office was developing its own particular methodology.

The Design section prepared the 1:1,000 scale plan based on the 1:25,000 schematic plan, while invitational design competitions were held for the most challenging structures. The first such competition, for the Melide viaduct, was announced on 4 January 1961. It would establish the procedure used from then on for procuring the designs of the structural elements along the entire route. Five Swiss engineering firms (most of which were from Ticino) were invited to take part in the competition. The jury included the architect Rino Tami,[16] who had been a member of the Swiss Association for Urban Planning (Associazione svizzera per la pianificazione del territorio, ASPAN) since 1963. Tami was officially designated 'consultant in aesthetic matters for motorway works', a role he would hold until 1983. Based on the schematic drawings (plans and sections) produced by the Design section, the competitors were required to submit their final project for the viaduct, complete with cost estimates. The task of the jury was to evaluate the proposals based on both the traditional criteria for road construction and the more unusual category of 'aesthetics'.

The A2 had a promising start. In 1963, 'the motorway works were inserted in the construction plan',[17] with the section between Chiasso and Grancia declared entirely under construction. In 1964, twenty-five contractors were present at the construction sites, with a peak of 2,200 workers hired. In 1968, the Office's staff reached 168 people, while the number of consulting engineering firms reached thirty-eight, having risen from three in 1961.[18] In 1964, however, budget cuts due to the first counter-cyclical measures[19] were already threatening to compromise future planning. Zorzi went to Bern on 11 August to discuss the issue with the federal authorities.[20] This was to be the final contribution to the N2 motorway on the part of the man who invented it. Zorzi lost his life on 4 September in an accident on the Basodino glacier[21] and was succeeded by Argante Righetti[22] as head of the Department of Construction. The effects of the economic situation on the construction of the N2 were not felt until the autumn of 1967,[23] when a new federal programme was issued that delayed the works on the central section, near Monte Ceneri, by almost ten years. The federal scheme overturned the cantonal approach of 'rational and systematic succession of major road sections',[24] thus concluding the first phase of development.

'Keep the Construction Sites Alive' (1969–1980)

Between 1969 and 1980, the Office adapted its work methodologies in accordance with the new federal programme, and the second quarter of the motorway was – laboriously – built, including the 9.6 kilometres of the Gotthard Tunnel.[25] The work focused on sections that were 'stitched' into the motorway: the

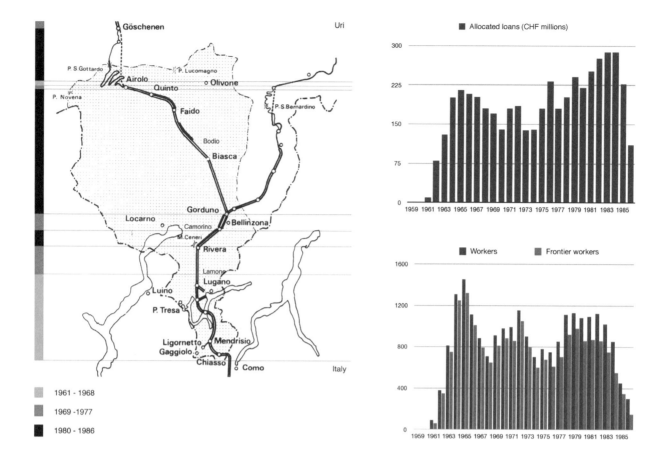

1. Plan of the N2 motorway with indication of the construction period.

Allocated loans 1961–85 (carried over to 1984) and annual averages of workers on the building sites (1961–85).

Bellinzona bypass, the four kilometres between Airolo and Varenzo, the eight kilometres of the semi-motorway between Airolo and Foppa Grande, and the eleven kilometres between Lamone and Rivera. In 1980, the stretch from Gorduno to Varenzo, which represented fifty per cent of the N2 and was the most technically difficult section, had not yet been built.[26]

In 1969, the federal budget (700 million Swiss francs per year) turned out to be insufficient, drastically influencing the planning; while the Hürlimann Commission was reviewing national financing, construction did not begin on any new road sections in Ticino. Furthermore, the design of the entire path to the Gotthard Tunnel – locally called the 'ramp' – also became a subject of debate between municipal, cantonal, and federal authorities, particularly heated regarding the section of road in the Faido area. Then, in 1971, ten years after the start of the works and with only thirty per cent of the motorway complete, the federal authorities set out a new programme that would further lengthen construction times: no opening was planned before 1977 and the opening of the 'ramp' to traffic would have to wait until 1982 – five years after the planned opening of the tunnel.[27]

These federal decisions were quickly followed by cantonal memorandums, site inspections by authorities, and subsequent drafts of long-term programmes.[28] In 1974, the Office's motto was to 'keep the open construction sites alive',[29] particularly because, after the Rivera–Lamone section was inaugurated in 1973, thanks to early completion on the part of the contractors, three hundred workers were

Concrete in Switzerland

transferred or dismissed, cutting more than a quarter of the total workforce.[30] Thus, in October 1975, when the competitions were announced for the viaducts in the Biasca area, the most challenging structures of the entire motorway path,[31] they seemed only an act of faith in the uncertain future of the motorway.

In the spring of 1976, however, something changed: on 26 May, the federal authorities launched an optimistic, long-term programme that provided for renewed financing throughout the decade to follow. In that year, the canton of Ticino was granted the extraordinary sum of 176 million Swiss francs, which meant that the contractors could be paid and, in 1977, the two Airolo sections could be completed. In August, once the long-awaited decision on the Faido section was pronounced by the Council of State, the 'ramp' could finally be built[32] (fig. 1).

Towards the Gotthard (1980–1986)

On 5 September 1980, in the motorway's twentieth year of construction, the Gotthard Tunnel was opened to traffic. The effects were immediately visible: more than eight thousand vehicles passed through the tunnel every day, with a fifty per cent overall increase in traffic on the motorway. In 1981, the construction of the 'ramp' had become a national problem. 'Finally!' was Colombi's comment.[33] On 23 June, the Federal Government was present *in corpore* on the construction sites. On 23 October 1982, the definitive projects for the last sections of the motorway were approved. The extraordinary concession of 278 million Swiss francs[34] and, in 1983, the approval of the new constitutional article on the allocation of fuel taxes for motorway works made it possible to begin and rapidly conclude the construction of fifty per cent of the motorway, which until then had existed only on paper. At Piottino, the construction of four tunnels and four large viaducts proceeded briskly, while construction sites were opened for the Biaschina Tunnel and the six challenging bridges that would provide access to it from the north[35] and the south,[36] while maintaining the road at an altitude high above the valley floor. Construction had also begun of the structures for bridging the difficult descent from Monte Ceneri to Bellinzona, along the 'stitched in' section between Robasacco and Camorino.[37] In 1984, the Office celebrated its twenty-fifth year of activity with a series of early openings and, the following year, for the first time, they closed the year with a surplus.[38] The motorway was opened on 23 October 1986.[39]

Fragmentation vs Unification

In 1986, 'the massive and definitive transformation of the Ticinese territory' could be considered complete.[40] Entirely passable from Chiasso to Airolo, the N2 motorway – first conceived in 1959 and constructed in fragments over an arc of twenty-five years – now presented itself as an extraordinarily unified work, characterised by clear rigour and aesthetic coordination between its various structures.[41]

In 1961, Bruno Zevi, in reference to the Autostrada del Sole,[42] attributed the cause of its inorganic and inharmonious appearance to the 'fragmentation of the works', citing the eighteen contractors and twenty-seven engineers involved in the construction of the original eighty-four-kilometre tract across the Apennines.[43] That same year in Ticino, twenty-five engineering firms and twenty-five general contractors (along with various associations, committees, communities, consultants, and consortiums) were involved in the realisation of the first 20.6 kilometres of the Chiasso–Grancia motorway. Furthermore, considering only the viaducts of the substructure over the entire route of the N2, seventy-eight structures were built between 1961 and 1968, while 115 structures were built between 1980 and 1986, the latter incorporating twenty years of technological developments.

It is clear, therefore, that the organic design of the N2 is not the result of the centralised approach advocated by Zevi (and as impossible to implement in Ticino as it had been in Italy[44]), but of a strategy of 'coordination', which, as personified by Tami,[45] the 'aesthetics consultant', has been amply confirmed by numerous episodes of the history of the construction of the motorway.

The Office and the Consultant

Most importantly, the reconstruction of the chronicle of the motorway's construction, made possible by studying the diaries of the Office Director, Renato Colombi, articulates (and amplifies) the effect that Tami's coordination work has had across time and on a multiplicity of actors.[46] This history testifies to the development of an ongoing dialogue between the 'aesthetic consultant' and the numerous engineers and contractors involved in the definitive project phase, based on the effective working practices developed by the National Roads Office between 1961 and 1968 and replicated until 1986.

The Design section, assisted by the engineers involved by means of the design competitions, simultaneously carried out three tasks: preparing, section by section, the definitive projects for the motorway, including, as mentioned above, adapting the drawings from 1:25,000 to 1:1,000 scale; preparing the projects for the motorway elements to be entrusted to competitions (both for the definitive projects and for their construction); and preparing and verifying the construction details of the contracted works under construction.

An essential tool used by the Design section, both for preparing projects in-house and for examining proposals submitted to the competitions, was the technique of photomontage, which made it possible to insert new structures into images of the landscape and in relation to the adjoining structures.[47] Tami, who maintained contact with the Office on a daily basis,[48] had the extraordinary opportunity to intervene in the design of each section of the motorway and of every structure (portrayed by means of photomontages). Later, during production of the working drawings, he would 'correct' the details.[49] Though the economic, technical, and aesthetic choice of reinforced concrete as the only material used in the motorway did not in itself ensure visual unity, it played a crucial role in favour of the aesthetic coordination provided by Tami, as it made it possible to 'redesign' the details of structures in the definitive project phase or even during construction (figs. 2–3).

2. National Roads Office, competition for the Melide viaduct. Photomontage of proposal 60 60 40, 1961.

National Roads Office, competition for the Fornaci viaduct. Photomontage of proposal 15 27 33, 1962.

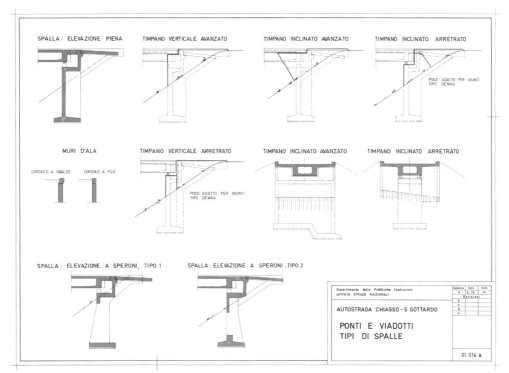

3. National Roads Office, schematic plans for bridges and viaducts: Types of abutments, April 1974.

The Structural Theme

In addition to the Office's work methodology (and again thanks to the use of reinforced concrete), the effectiveness of Tami's aesthetic coordination was due to the decision – accurately confirmed by the documents conserved in the Roads Office archives – to use a single structural type, which, with only a few variations, was suitable for the construction of (almost) all the substructure's viaducts. In line with the most common type of viaducts of Swiss motorways in the 1960s, the N2 viaducts are, with very few exceptions, characterised by slender piers and continuous prestressed box girders.[50]

In the jury-led design competitions of the 1960s, the elements of this structural type – judged both in terms of 'aesthetics' (a criterion introduced by Tami) and the more usual 'structural and constructive concept'[51] – were gradually renamed: the abutments were called 'headers' or 'ground connections', the spaces between the piers were referred to as the 'rhythm of the load-bearing elements', the width of the traditional double overhang of the section of the caisson deck

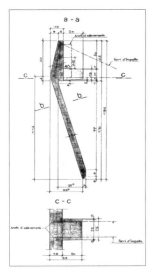
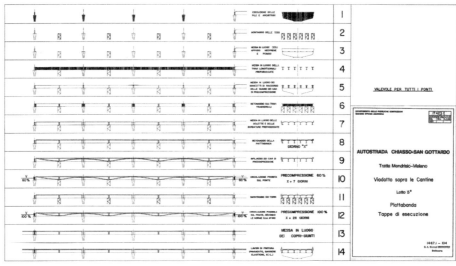

4. SA Conrad Zschokke, viaduct above Le Cantine, deck. Construction stage, 3 September 1965.

SA Conrad Zschokke, prefabricated 'edge contours', 25 November 1965.

was called 'profile' (or 'shadow strip'), while 'sleekness' was the term used for the ratio between the height and length of the deck.[52]

Tami's new names for the structural elements and forms encouraged the exploration of new design themes, which, within the confines of the chosen structural type and thanks to the plasticity of reinforced concrete, helped ensure rigorous formal coordination between the structures and between the structures and the surrounding context.[53] While the piers, spaced at forty-metre spans, were unified by either 'slim rectangular' or 'cylindrical' cross-sections, the abutments of the viaducts presented new additional elements – inclined vertical 'tympanums', advanced or retracted – that were to be employed taking strictly into account the contours of the terrain, the types of joints, and the geometry of the adjoining structures.[54] Thus, having devised a way to create, through adherence to a standard type, the unified image of a 'sleek' viaduct, on 'orderly supports', and profiled by an elegant 'shadow strip', it was necessary to rigorously respect this standard along the entire motorway, even at the cost of relinquishing structural clarity by implementing certain construction artifices during the execution phase.

An exemplary case, in this sense, is the Cantine (or Capolago) viaduct. Tami explicitly claims credit for the design of its forms and for the solution devised for the 'ground connections'.[55] To understand the true anatomy of the deck of the viaduct (now replaced),[56] one must imagine a transverse section: the superstructure is composed of six prefabricated double-T beams (in prestressed reinforced concrete), framed laterally by specially contoured elements.[57] These 'edge contours', designed when the viaduct was already contracted out, were composed of 495 prefabricated, one-metre-long elements per side, differing in form between the valley and mountain sides, with the aim of 'contouring' and lightening 'the appearance [of the viaduct], both from the road below and from the motorway itself'.[58]

Only the intermediate supports of the typical N2 viaduct, between the piers and the deck, remained 'anonymous', entrusted to the experimentation of the engineers. Indeed, in the shadow of the overhanging deck, the systems they devised

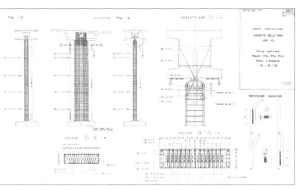

5. Bernardi-Gerosa engineering office, Bisio viaduct, 1964.

Luigi Pini, Tana viaduct, 1964. Pier reinforcement and details of the pendular supports in reinforced concrete, 5 February 1964.

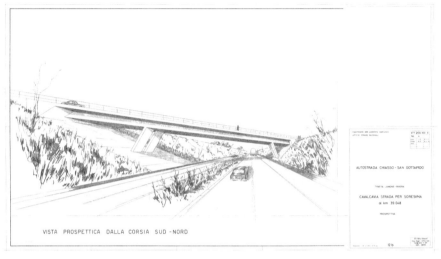

6. Ervino Kessel, Soresina overpass. Perspective drawing, 25 May 1970.

present a great variety of structural types that 'personalised' them on a technological level. Between 1962 and 1964, to cite only a few cases, Bernardi-Gerosa and Pini, respectively for the Bisio and Tana viaducts, designed elegant pendular supports in reinforced concrete with crossbar hinges, while both Hartennach & Wenger and Frey preferred to use prefabricated steel devices for the Campaccio[59] and Lenaccio[60] viaducts (figs. 4–6).

Thanks to the use of reinforced concrete, the elements that had been codified for the viaducts of the motorway substructure were also used for the overpasses, in this way contaminating the usual structural type used for overpasses, 'inclined piers'. Also in this case, 'inclined tympanums' were combined with the 'shadow strips' formed by the deck overhangs, and even the characteristic finish of the roadbed contributed to the composition of the forms of each element.[61] Similarly to the viaducts, the creation of the aesthetic image of the typical N2 overpass was supported by certain construction 'stratagems', such as inserting a second pillar into the slope of the roadbed to maintain the 'sleekness' of the deck, and the use of polystyrene fill to reduce the load of the heavy 'headers'.[62]

In the meantime, above the level of the road, a series of new 'objects' were defined as necessary to assure formal homogeneity between the structural elements belonging to the different families: between the viaducts and tunnels, and between the road surfacing and the roadbed, various 'grafts' and 'wounds' appeared[63] that needed to be compensated by means of special 'contoured joints', 'portals', and 'scarps and counterscarps'. These episodes, central to the creation of the unified visual experience of traveling on the N2, remained the exclusive domain of Tami.[64] He was in constant dialogue with the engineers, who alternated between implementing his solutions with their own.[65]

The 'Motorway Dialect'

While 'portals', 'counterscarps', 'inclined tympanums', and 'headers' were, in the early 1960s, neologisms in the design of infrastructure, over the years they became part of a common vocabulary among the drawing boards of the Office. Was this the genesis of a new Ticinese *koiné*, well-suited to describing the contamination of the forms of the most common structural elements of motorways?

The development of this shared idiom was certainly also supported by the fact that the thousands of border workers hired on the construction site developed their own language around the process of cast-in-place concrete, which permitted them to implement the design strategies aimed at unifying the N2. At the same time, it constituted a defence, until the 1970s, against competition from the more mechanised foreign contractors. In fact, already in the 1960s, the cast-in-place concrete of the motorway concealed numerous construction stratagems that had been executed with the aim of realising the unified image, coordinated during the design phase, of the structural elements. The subordination of construction technologies to the image of the 'sleek' and 'contoured' viaduct, already codified in the 1960s, was made more evident in the 1980s by the conspicuous mechanisation of the construction site.

Between 1980 and 1986, for the realisation of the bridges in the gorges of Piottino and Biaschina and in the descent from Ceneri, the use of 'traditional' scaffolding (by then strictly in steel) was alternated with innovative gantry cranes, lateral cantilevers on special trolleys, and free cantilevers. Nonetheless, despite their having demonstrated the real economic advantages of mechanisation (even at the cost of 'infiltration' by foreign contractors),[66] no recognisable constructive changes were made to the aesthetic forms of the N2 viaduct, which had already been defined in the 1960s.

Only in the case of the Biaschina bridge – the most demanding work of the entire section – does the free cantilever construction system remain clearly legible in the structural design of the element. Though on the one hand the technical achievements of the prestressed concrete bridge, still under construction, earned it the cover of the 1982 book *Prestressed Concrete of Switzerland*, on the other hand they made it difficult to visually link the bridge to the adjacent structures (also because they defeated the stratagem of inserting the 'inclined tympanums').[67]

The Office engineers chose the Biaschina viaduct as the background for the group photograph taken on the day the motorway was inaugurated.[68] We like to imagine them standing in the shadows of its tall, slender piers, talking amongst

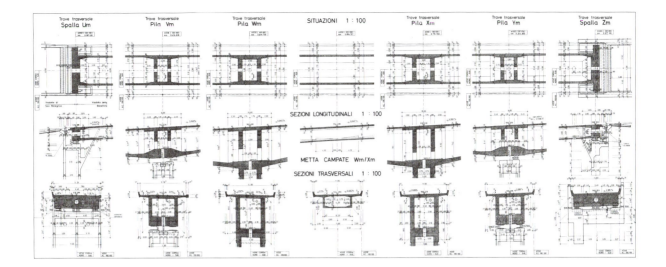

themselves about the success of their shared endeavour, using, however, that 'motorway dialect'[69] that had continued to expand and become more refined over the twenty-five years of the road's construction.

Indeed, while the images of the N2's structural elements effectively illustrate Tami's best-known writings, *Problemi estetici dell'autostrada*[70] and later, *L'autostrada come opera d'arte*,[71] the construction history of the motorway limited the potential 'professional audience' of these publications to the small community of engineers who participated, under the guidance of their 'aesthetic consultant', in the continuous cultural training that accompanied its construction. Thus, over time, a unique technical culture emerged within Ticino's community of engineers that – for its ability to adapt static and constructive functions to precise 'aesthetic directives' (even to the most authoritative architectural solutions of infrastructure built in the years that followed, such as the Transjurane motorway[72]) – has enriched, 'with proud modesty', the history of structural engineering (fig. 7).

7. Guzzi SA engineering office, Biaschina viaduct, transversal beams. Schematic plans, 1982.

Biaschina viaduct under construction.

The N2 Chiasso–Saint Gotthard Motorway…

Notes

[1] 'Consulente in materia estetica dell'autostrada'. For the contribution of Tami to the design of the N2, see Serena Maffioletti, 'L'"orgogliosa modestia" della N2', in Kenneth Frampton and Riccardo Bergossi, *Rino Tami. Opera completa* (Mendrisio: Mendrisio Academy Press, 2008), 137–75; Nicola Navone, 'Rino Tami, architecte-conseil de l'autoroute Chiasso–Saint-Gothard', *fabricA* 11 (2017), 12–43.

[2] Rendiconti annuali, 1959, Archivio del Moderno Balerna, Fondo Renato Colombi (now AdM, Colombi).

[3] The historical archive of the Ufficio federale delle strade (now USTRA), Bellinzona branch. With thanks to engineer Marco Fioroni and archivist Davide Campana for their help with research. The iconographic documentation is conserved at the Archivio di Stato del Cantone Ticino, Fondo della Sezione Strade Nazionali, Photo Library (now ASTi, USN, Photo Library).

[4] Archivio del Moderno Balerna, Fondo Rino Tami (now AdM, Tami).

[5] Cf. German Bundesminister für Verkehr (ed.), *Ausbauplan für die Bundesfernstraßen (Bundesstraßen und Autobahnen)* (Bonn, February 1957); Italian law 21 May 1955: Measures for the construction of highways and roads and modifications to motor vehicle taxes; On 18 April 1955, French law 55-435 was adopted 'relating to the status of motorways'.

[6] News bulletin on Swiss-Italian radio, 25 September 1954; 'L'eredità di Franco Zorzi, a 50 anni dalla scomparsa', online archives of the Radiotelevisione Svizzera italiana RSI, 4 September 2014, audio, 50.27, https://www.rsi.ch/rete-uno/programmi/intrattenimento/millevoci/Leredità-di-Franco-Zorzi-a-50-anni-dalla-scomparsa-2071208.html.

[7] Ilaria Giannetti, Matteo Iannello, and Nicola Navone (eds.), 'Dalle dighe all'autostrada: Renato Colombi. Un'intervista a Luigi Colombi' (Balerna: Archivio del Moderno, 6 June 2018), www.ticino4580.ch/interviste/luigi-colombi/.

[8] *Ufficio strade nazionali. 1959–1984, 25 anni di attività* (Bellinzona: Ufficio delle strade nazionali, 1984). On page 4 of the volume, see the Council of States' resolution of 7 July 1959. See page 6 for the name change to 'Ufficio strade nazionali' to bring it in line with federal nomenclature.

[9] Silvano Toppi, 'La crescita economica (1945–1975): la scommessa industriale', in Raffaello Ceschi (ed.), *Storia del Cantone Ticino. L'Ottocento e il Novecento* (Bellinzona: Edizioni Casagrande, 1998), 600–8.

[10] Office from now on in this text.

[11] Orio Grassi, '19 ottobre 1959', in *Bollettino Ufficio strade nazionali*, printed brochure conserved in the private archive of Luigi Colombi, 1979. The Office was installed in a small villa on Via Ghiringhelli in Bellinzona. A memory from one of the first days of work at the Office: the first of the engineers to arrive was Mr Krannichfeldt, followed by Zinniker and Pedrini.

[12] Rendiconti annuali, 1959 (AdM, Colombi).

[13] Tullia Iori and Sergio Poretti (eds.), 'Fotoromanzo SIXXI. 5. L'Autostrada del Sole', in *SIXXI 3 – Storia dell'ingegneria strutturale in Italia* (Roma: Gangemi, 2015), 108–55.

[14] Federal Law on National Roads, 8 March 1960.

[15] ASTi, USN, Photo Library, lot 7a, lot 7b.

[16] Viadotto di Melide, 1961 (AdM, Tami, RT S107/2).

[17] 'Le opere autostradali entrano nel piano dell'attività realizzativa' (Rendiconti annuali, 1963, AdM, Colombi).

[18] Rendiconti annuali, 1960–1968 (AdM, Colombi).

[19] Toppi, 'La crescita economica (1945–1975)' (see note 9).

[20] Rendiconti annuali, 1964 (AdM, Colombi).

[21] 'La tragedia del Basodino', *Notiziario della Svizzera Italiana*, 25 September 1964.

[22] Righetti was director until 1979. His successor was Ugo Sadis, in office until 1983, followed by Claudio Generali.

[23] In 1965, the fifth service of the Office was put in place, the Maintenance section, directed by engineer Guelfo Piazzini.

[24] 'Della razionale e sistematica successione delle grandi tratte' (Rendiconti annuali, 1968, AdM, Colombi).

[25] Only 6.6 kilometres of the tunnel are in the Ticino territory.

[26] Rendiconti annuali, 1968–1979 (AdM, Colombi).

[27] Rendiconti annuali, 1971 (AdM, Colombi).

[28] II federale programma 1972, III programma federale 1973, IV programma federale 1974 (Rendiconti annuali, 1972–1974, AdM, Colombi).

[29] 'Mantenere in vita i cantieri già aperti.'

[30] Rendiconti annuali, 1973–1974 (AdM, Colombi).

[31] Concorso Biaschina, 1972 (AdM, Tami, RT S107/2). *N2 Concorso viadotto S. Pellegrino-Biaschina* (Bellinzona: Ufficio delle strade nazionali, 1977).

[32] Rendiconti annuali, 1976–1977 (AdM, Colombi).

[33] Rendiconti annuali, 1981 (AdM, Colombi).

[34] Rendiconti annuali, 1982 (AdM, Colombi). The credit came to twenty-six per cent of the national total.

[35] Viaducts of Chiggiona, Nivo, and Ruina.

[36] Viaducts of Biaschina, San Pellegrino, and Altirolo.

[37] Viaducts of Ronchi, Costa Revoira, and San Leonardo.

[38] Rendiconti annuali, 1985 (AdM, Colombi).

[39] Rendiconti annuali, 1987 (AdM, Colombi). This was the Office's last report. It was still active in 1987 before being absorbed into the Department of Construction in 1988.

[40] 'L'immane e definitiva trasformazione del territorio Ticinese' (Paul Guidicelli, 'Una conquista di Civiltà', *Corriere del Ticino*, 24 October 1986, 33).

[41] 'Autostrada del Ticino', *L'architettura. Cronache e storia* 27, no. 2 (1981), 82–3.

[42] Bruno Zevi, 'Dittatori dell'asfalto. Le superstrade della disunione nazionale', *L'Espresso*, 19 February 1961.

[43] Tullia Iori, 'La strada dell'unità nazionale. L'Autosole nella storia costruttiva italiana', in Carmen Andriani (ed.), *Le forma del cemento. Dinamicità* (Roma: Gangemi, 2011), 8–21. Tullia Iori, 'L'Autostrada del Sole', in Alfredo Buccaro, Giulio Fabricatore, and Lia Maria Papa, *Storia dell'Ingegneria*, vol. 2 (Napoli: Cuzzolin, 2006), 1111–20.

[44] Toppi, 'La crescita economica (1945–1975)' (see note 9).

[45] Maffioletti, 'L'"orgogliosa modestia" della N2' (see note 1); Navone, 'Rino Tami, architecte-conseil de l'autoroute Chiasso–Saint-Gothard' (see note 1).

[46] Ibid.

[47] ASTi, USN, Photo Library.

[48] Correspondence between Rino Tami and the Ufficio strade nazionali, 1961–1980 (AdM, Tami).

[49] Rino Tami, 'L'autostrada come opera d'arte', in Tita Carloni (ed.), *Rino Tami, 50 anni di architettura* (Lugano: Fondazione Arturo e Margherita Lang, 1984), 122–44.

[50] Christian Menn, 'Comparison of Casts and Material Quantities for Some New Highway Bridges in Switzerland', in *Prestressed Concrete of Switzerland*. Proceedings of the 9th International Federation for Structural Concrete Congress in Stockholm (Wildegg: Technischen Forschungs- und Beratungstelle der Schweizerischen Zementindustrie, 1982).

[51] 'Concezione strutturale e costruttiva' (Verbali giurie di concorso, 1961–1977, AdM, Tami, RT S107/2).

[52] Concorso viadotto di Melide, Relazione della giuria, 1962; Concorso per il viadotto di Bisio, Relazione della giuria, 1962 (AdM, Tami, RT S107/2).

[53] Schema testata tipo, drawing 879 60, 10 July 1967 (AdM, Tami, RT S107/2).

[54] 'Piani tipo', Ponti e viadotti: tipi di spalle, drawing 01.014a, April 1974 (USTRA).

[55] Rino Tami, 'Problemi estetici dell'autostrada', *Rivista tecnica della Svizzera italiana* 60, no. 24 (31 December 1969), 1607–20.

[56] The viaduct deck and the tops of the piers were replaced in 2004 in the structural restoration project by the firm Muttoni-Grignoli. 'Viadotto delle Cantine', Tratto Mendrisio–Lugano, Progetto esecutivo, impalcato, 2 February 2004 (USTRA). Franco Lurati and Francesco Caggia, 'Progetto Generoso: Viadotto delle Cantine', *Archi*, no. 2 (2006), 57–9; René Hornung, 'Flick, Abbruch oder Neubau?', *Hochparterre* 17, no. 3 (2004), 24–6.

[57] SA Conrad Zschokke, Viadotto sopra Le Cantine Elemento prefabbricato di 'bordatura', tipo 2 (a valle), drawing 12281 E, 25 November 1964 (USTRA).

[58] 'L'aspetto [del viadotto], sia dalla strada sottostante che dall'autostrada medesima' (Rino Tami, 'Problemi estetici dell'autostrada', see note 55, 1612).

[59] Hartennach & Wenger, Viadotto Campaccio, appoggi tipo 'corroweld', drawing 12875 E, 9 April 1964 (USTRA).

[60] H. R. Frey, Viadotto di Lenaccio, appoggi prodotti dalla Mageba, drawing 13012 E, 6 July 1964 (USTRA).

[61] Rivestimento scarpate sotto i manufatti, piani tipo, drawing 01.010, October 1980 (USTRA).

[62] Ilaria Giannetti, 'Cavalcavia della strada per Soresina', in *Architettura nel cantone*

Ticino, 1945–1980, online guide, n.d., www.ticino4580.ch/mappe.

[63] Portale Sud Galleria Melide Grancia. Considerazioni sul progetto, 3 December 1963, typescript (AdM, Tami, RT S107/2).

[64] Maffioletti, 'L'"orgogliosa modestia" della N2' (see note 1); Navone, 'Rino Tami, architecte-conseil de l'autoroute Chiasso–Saint-Gothard' (see note 1).

[65] Consulting of the USTRA technical documentation: in general, the 'standard plans' do not show details of the profiles of the counter-walls and the elements of the portals. The structures are detailed, in numerous drafts, by the various engineers in charge of their respective projects.

[66] Menn, 'Comparison of Casts and Material Quantities for Some New Highway Bridges in Switzerland' (see note 50). The 'consortium of the Biaschina viaduct' was managed by the Italian company LGV, already active in Ticino for the construction of hydroelectric plants. The Ruina and San Pellegrino viaducts were built using construction site systems from Austrian companies.

[67] Guzzi SA, Viadotto della Biaschina, Travi trasversali, piano sinottico, drawing 1006, 1982 (USTRA).

[68] Christian Balli Private Archive, group photograph of the office staff at the bottom of the Biaschina viaduct, 23 October 1986.

[69] The expression is borrowed from the Ticino idiom 'dialect of the railway', a simplified version of the Lombard dialect, which makes the speakers of the different areas of the region more intelligible to each other, from Chiasso to Airolo. See Repubblica e Cantone del Ticino (ed.), *Vocabolario dei dialetti della Svizzera italiana* (Lugano: Mazzuconi, 1952–).

[70] Tami, 'Problemi estetici dell'autostrada' (see note 55).

[71] Tami, 'L'autostrada come opera d'arte' (see note 49).

[72] Silvana Maffioletti, 'Composizioni infrastrutturali. I sogni a occhi aperti di Flora Ruchat-Roncati', in Silvana Maffioletti, Nicola Navone, and Carlo Toson, *Un dialogo ininterrotto* (Padua: Il Poligrafo, 2018), 159–85.

Reinforced Country Below Ground

Silvia Berger Ziauddin

This essay deals with a type of shell made of reinforced concrete in Switzerland that reaches huge dimensions and whose prevalence in the domestic sphere is unparalleled worldwide. Despite their literal mightiness, their location under the ground and their profane architectural form mean that they are barely noticeable. The category referred to is that of the civil defence shelter built throughout the duration of the Cold War. Based on the *Schutzbaugesetz* (Civil Defence Construction Law) passed in 1963 and the civil defence concept that was formulated shortly afterwards, the Swiss authorities accelerated the construction of highly standardised defence shelters in order to provide each and every inhabitant with a 'modern' protective space that would not only shield them from the devastating effects of an atomic-bomb attack but from chemical and biological weapons as well. With an expenditure of approximately 12 billion Swiss francs, Switzerland nowadays boasts 360,000 such atomic shelters. Strung out in sequence, these subterranean cells made of reinforced concrete – built in the cellars of single-family houses, but also under school complexes, municipal town halls or parking garages – would give a traversable route of 1,200 kilometres, equivalent to the distance between Zurich and Algiers.[1]

Even if the figures are unparalleled by any other country in the world, these Swiss survival catacombs should not be reduced simply to their undoubtedly impressive material and monetary dimensions. The reinforced concrete cells, which are to be found in almost every apartment building, are closely interlinked with specific rationalities and expertise in Switzerland during the Cold War, with its politico-cultural self-images and identity discourses. In this respect the built civil defence environment should also be understood as political plastic, as the ideological and material armour of Switzerland in the Atomic Age. Conceived and implemented in the 1960s and 1970s, at the latest by the 1980s, this cemented Switzerland under the ground has begun to erode.

I will initially examine the formation of civil defence spaces as a realm of technical knowledge as generated by engineers, specified in technical guidelines and, finally, as materialised in concrete during the course of the 1960s.[2] In the second part I outline the hegemonial imaginational arsenal and the identity discourses that engineers and officials spun around these concrete shells, before finally concluding in the third part with a civil-societal critique of concrete and the armour-plated Switzerland of the Cold War.

Calculating and Materialising the Apocalypse

Before and during the Second World War, in order to protect the civilian population against aerial attacks, civil defence organisations, authorities, and the military encouraged the voluntary construction of makeshift air-raid shelters. Due to the fact that the additional costs had to be largely borne by house owners and tenants, and because existing construction regulations varied greatly from canton to canton, the population initially showed very little self-initiative during the war in building such air-raid shelters, so that by the end of 1945 provisional defence shelters existed for only 15 per cent of the population.[3] In the immediate post-war years, and as a result of the general peace euphoria, the Swiss Federal Council initially focused on terminating all air-raid protection measures. However, only a short time later differences in the positions of the United States and the Soviet Union on how the world should be re-ordered emerged, leading to the division of Europe into two enemy power blocs, whereupon the conviction also began to spread in Switzerland that civilian defence measures were a necessity. Faced with the recurring crises that threatened from one day to the next to drive the world to the precipice of a nuclear catastrophe, the characteristic atmosphere of this newly dawning Atomic Era was one of fear. In 1951, during the course of the Korean War, the Federal Council decided that air-raid cellars should be included in all new buildings and remodelling projects. The guidelines published at the time by the Air-raid Defence Section (Abteilung für Luftschutz) of the Military Department (Militärdepartement) clearly demonstrate that such protective structures were largely intended to withstand conventional warfare scenarios, for instance involving high explosive and incendiary bombardments.[4] The main focus lay in securing the entrances against bomb shrapnel and debris (which was achieved by simply reinforcing the rooms with timber bracings and sand sacks), the provision of fire-fighting equipment, and the installation of escape routes and emergency exits. Reinforced concrete was first-and-foremost viewed as a means by which to reinforce the ceilings.

Over the course of the 1950s, as thermonuclear war scenarios terrified the world and the threat of atomic radiation grew to be a prime concern, it became apparent that the perceived threats and defence measures to date no longer matched the new nuclear reality and that know-how about modern nuclear-shelter construction was lacking. As a response the newly founded Federal Civil Defence Office (Bundesamt für Zivilschutz, BZS) created a special task force for civil defence construction, and at the beginning of the 1960s the Research Institute for Military Construction Technology (Forschungsinstitut für militärische Bautechnik) at the Swiss Federal Institute of Technology in Zurich constituted a parallel institution dedicated to the development of construction guidelines for the Atomic Age. In order to rapidly acquire the available knowledge in the field of the effects of nuclear weapons and the corresponding means of defence construction, a small circle of civil engineers (many of them with research and professional experience in the United States), architects, physicists, and chemists concentrated on setting up an international and above all US network of experts and on the transfer of data and studies on the effects of nuclear weapons. As of the mid-1950s the United States partly declassified technical reports in this field, with the aim of giving other countries the opportunity to develop their own protective measures via this controlled access to the data.[5]

Two premises were crucial for Swiss attempts to achieve a balanced dimensioning in the question of atomic-defence shelters: first they should be economical, and second they should be effective against all the consequences of a nuclear attack. In terms of the desired uniform protection, those responsible judged reinforced concrete to be an ideal construction material.[6] Due to its mass and its ductility, when used for underground structures it was able to withstand both dynamic and static pressure, in addition providing a shield against heat radiation and primary nuclear radiation, as shown in US nuclear test trials in the Nevada Desert and in evaluations of the A-bomb attacks on Hiroshima and Nagasaki.[7] This preference for concrete as a construction material was undoubtedly helped by the fact that at an early stage the Swiss cement industry promoted the material-technical advantages of reinforced concrete for air-raid defence and cultivated close ties with the officials responsible for built civil defence engineering.[8] As opposed to the guidelines issued around 1950, by the mid-1960s the BZS stipulated that in the future, civil defence shelters should be built solely in reinforced concrete. In addition, it became obligatory that all such structures be equipped with mechanical ventilation using ABC (atomic, biological, and chemical) gas filters.

In order to achieve the premised economic rationale the experts drew on cost-benefit analyses, and by applying complex mathematical and quantitative methodologies derived from the field of operations research arrived at an 'optimal' constructional scope that promised to save the most lives per franc invested in built protective measures. The upshot of these optimisation studies was the prediction that with an expenditure outlay of 1,000 Swiss francs per person and a constructional protective scope of 1 atmosphere (a pressure resistance of 10 tonnes per square metre) the number of lives lost in Switzerland as a result of any potential attack could be reduced to one-tenth.[9] These study findings and calculations, driven in turn by a belief in technical feasibility and a faith in progress, were then broken down into detailed standardisations for the planning and building of shelters in new buildings, as codified in the 1966 *Technische Weisungen für den privaten Schutzraumbau* (Technical Directives for the Construction of Private Shelters, *TWP 1966*).[10] The reinforced concrete shelters were to be installed as deeply as possible in the terrain and, as a rule, to consist of a rectangular floor plan and cross section. As well as planning principles and detailed specifications for the concrete thickness of the roof (35 centimetres), floor (20 centimetres), and the perimeter walls facing the cellar (freestanding 80 centimetres, fully submerged 25 centimetres, partially submerged 50 centimetres), *TWP 1966* also contained information about the space requirements per shelter placement, secure surface and sealing elements, ventilation installations, and, for instance, the arrangement of the entrances and exits. In terms of material technology *TWP 1966* discussed the compressive cube strength and adhesive strength of the concrete to be used and stipulated that plastering or insulation was not to be applied on the inner sides of the shelter walls and ceilings. The guidelines likewise supplied civil engineers with rules for the dimensioning and the construction of standard small defence shelters, accompanied by a reinforcement scheme and material specifications for the concrete (fig. 1).

TWP 1966 boosted shelter construction in Switzerland, helped at the same time by a swell in public finances, which defrayed 70 per cent of the additional costs for shelter construction, as well as by the simultaneous beginning of the housing construction boom. Between 1970 and 1973 residential building enjoyed growth rates of 10 per cent per annum,[11] entailing a corresponding burgeoning in civil defence construction. It is therefore hardly surprising that the consumption of cement exploded, rising from 4.3 million tonnes in 1966 to 6 million in 1972, representing an increase of over 40 per cent.[12] It is impossible to calculate what proportion of this was accounted for by the newly emerging concrete survival infrastructure, but that individual civil defence projects indeed used up enormous amounts of cement is clear, for instance, in the example of the Urania Parking Garage in Zurich. In the 'Peace Version' the seven-storey underground car park in the centre of the city afforded space for 610 cars (fig. 2). In the 'War Version' it served as a defence shelter that could contain 10,000 people and was to be sealed using a gigantic reinforced concrete door (fig. 3). One thousand rail carriages of cement and 460 rail carriages of reinforcing material were carted to the building site in order to construct the mass public shelter. Nevertheless, as one of the few large-scale collective shelters it was also dimensioned to provide a considerably higher protection standard, designed to withstand 6 atmospheres (a pressure resistance of 60 tonnes per square metre). The costs totalled 22 million Swiss francs, 12 million francs of this alone for the construction and installation of the civil defence shelter, including drinking-water storage tanks, two emergency power generators, thirty-four gas filters, and a command system.[13]

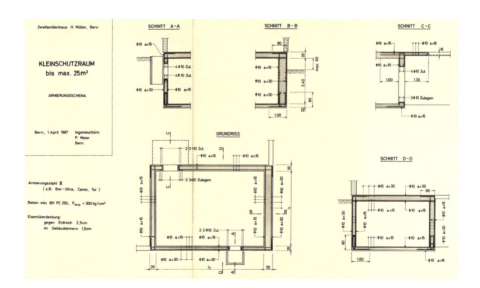

1. Model for the construction of a small standardised defence shelter.

 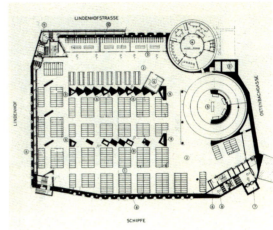

High-Tech Capsules of the Nation and the Family

These protective shelters, considered to be the actual 'backbone' of the country's civil defence, were omnipresent in civil defence brochures and official public information films of the 1960s and 1970s. Using a technicistic imagery, the films and the photos familiarised viewers with the technical aspects of the constructional and material design of these subterranean survival realms, promising 'almost total protection'.[14] They are enacted as scientifically optimised, technologically elaborated, brightly lit, and mostly automated defence capsules. Tracking camera shots, positioned at eye level and moving at a walking speed, guide the viewers through clinically immaculate catacombs devoid of people, along endless corridors with plentifully stocked storage rooms and fully equipped operation theatres, and past lounge chairs with carefully folded woollen blankets, chrome-covered kitchens, and gleaming technical installations. The passage from the world above to the world below is mostly staged as a movement from darkness into light, or indeed overexposed light for that matter.[15] This invests the grey concrete capsules with a sacred aura – an effect that is underscored in many of the films by the slow automatic opening of the steel-reinforced doors.[16]

What is also identifiable in parallel to this enthronement of defence shelters as modern, scientifically optimised, and overly high-tech capsules is an ideological cloaking of these shelters in official descriptive strategies. In this process engineers and civil defence authorities compounded the subterranean concrete cells with the traditional self-perceptions and politico-cultural arsenal of images propagated after the Second World War under the auspices of a revived *Geistige Landesverteidigung* (i.e., spiritual or intellectual national defence), targeted at consolidating a common spirit of defence and resistance against Communist totalitarianism.

In the 1950s the proponents of air-raid defences were already extolling the virtues of such constructions as the 'citizens' reduit', an image the population was judged to 'organically' identify with.[17] Alongside the symbolic force of the reduit mentality, which following the war advanced to become a national myth, engineers and officials resorted to one of the central Swiss self-images that had

2. 'Peace' modus: garage level in the Urania Parking Garage.

3. 'War' modus: shelter-space organisation of a level in the Urania Parking Garage.

been in circulation since the very beginning of the twentieth century: that of a peace-loving 'island' sealed off from the outer world. Thus one civil defence engineer described the subterranean concrete shell in 1968 as follows: 'The image of a defence shelter, that continues to live on in a sea of destruction after the breaking off of contacts to the world outside, can be vividly encapsulated in the term "island of survival".'[18] This idea of Switzerland as an island buffeted by enclosing seas and isolated from the outside world corresponds to a topos that had already been perpetuated in postcards and paintings during and shortly after the First World War.[19] As Peter von Matt demonstrates, this vision of 'Switzerland as a small pure homestead on an island in the stormy ocean' experienced a revival during the Second World War and helped to obscure the profound political and economic dependencies the country found itself in.[20] After the defeat of Nazi Germany civil defence planners transposed this island metaphor to the new underground reinforced concrete shells, now intended to serve as the locus of survival for Switzerland and everything Swiss.

That which was to be guaranteed a continued existence in such shelters was, first and foremost, Switzerland as a federal and nationally organised republic and as an exclusively male domain. This is ideally represented in civil defence training material showing the symbolic image of a territorial map with stalwart rows of male figures visually embedded in the unbroken rectangular outline of the shell of a shelter (fig. 4). However, the inherent substrate, and the ideological core of Switzerland during the Cold War, was situated in the bourgeois image of the family. The defence shelter was directly referred to as the 'survival island of the family' in which the 'democratic substance of Switzerland' could continue to exist.[21] In the symbolic images of the bunker as a protective shell the family mostly appears nuclear – consisting of a father, mother, and one or two children (and occasionally a dog) – endowed with the traditional middle-class patriarchical role allocations and attributes. The husband and father reads a newspaper, controls the technical equipment, and is responsible for listening to the radio. The wife and mother, dressed in a prim skirt, looks after the children and is responsible for feeding the family and preserving family bonds.[22] This image of the nuclear family in the shelter acts simultaneously to underline the preserving unity of national independence, thus aggregating the 'civic cell of national resistance'.[23] The resistance required to triumph in the total war with the enemy from the East is sustained not merely by a spirit of combat directed outwards but, more crucially, in an inward ideological fortification. This dualism of an externally combat-ready and internally integrated defensive collective community found its most striking expression in the symbolic image of the hedgehog, its spiky rear directed to the East and its body framing the rectangular shell of a shelter with an integrated territorial map of Switzerland (fig. 5). As an emblem of *Geistige Landesverteidigung* and the embodiment of 'Fortress Switzerland', the hedgehog was also manifested in the Swiss National Exhibition that took place in Lausanne in 1964, in the form of an army pavilion adorned with 141 spikes.[24] As opposed to the symbolic image of the hedgehog in the civil defence literature, in which the material of the rectangular shell of the shelter remains

4. Switzerland as a male-dominated, federal republic in a shelter, 1976.

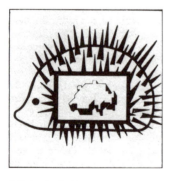

5. Swiss territorial map framed by a civil defence shelter within the hedgehog, 1976.

unarticulated, the spikes of the army pavilion made of heavy concrete pyramids directly amalgamated with the popular ideological self-image of Switzerland.

Cold and Dark Concrete Worlds

In the 1950s and 1960s, when civil defence was politically propagated and the constructional-technical guidelines were formulated, this future narrative of technical progress, economic growth, and social prosperity exercised a powerful integrational pull. However, during the course of the 1970s, and in particular by the beginning of the 1980s, the symptoms of a new understanding of the future began to make themselves felt. A general perception of economic and social crisis, triggered by the 1973 oil shock, became combined with fears about the depletion of natural resources and the destruction of the environment. Expectations about the future darkened further with the increasingly negative connotations associated with urbanisation and the sprawling over-development of the national landscape, made all the more acute by a background of heightened geo-political tensions. This last factor worsened with the NATO Double-Track Decision of December 1979, which justified the installation of new nuclear-warhead rockets and missiles in Western Europe, ushering in a renewed climax in the East-West Conflict.

In around 1980, as these various feelings of crisis intensified, civil defence infrastructure projects began to be greeted with ever more hostility. Defence shelters, and namely the concrete used to build them, became objects of radical dissent or indeed came to be demonised by a combination of peace activists, rioting youths, and socially critical writers, culminating in an outright rejection of the innate rationale of these concrete shells and their promises of protection. The youth protest movement of the early 1980s, which exploded in cities like Zurich ('Greenland'), Geneva ('Calvingrad'), and Lausanne (Lôzane bouge) against the perceived coldness and rigidity of society, dethroned concrete and adopted it instead as the intrinsic symbol of alienation and of a complete stasis in any vision of the future. Thus, for instance, the slogan 'No Future' appears in the activist film *Günz, Mündel, Riss und Würm* (lit. Günz, Legal Minor, Crack and Worm) as an accompaniment to a tracking shot along a sequence of underground concrete rooms reminiscent of a civil defence installation.[25] 'Concrete – grey like the future', 'Do you want total concrete?' or 'How much concrete does a person need?' were some of the graffiti sprayed by the youth-movement activists on Zurich's concrete walls in the early 1980s.[26] In 1984, after the struggle for autonomous spaces had shifted to the house-squatting scene, in an insolent act of defacement and refusal a group of young activists encased their *Zivildienstbüchlein* (the personal document recording civil defence service) in cement in a concrete cylinder. This was then dropped into the River Sihl, accompanied by a speech emphasising that as a contemporary monument the concrete block articulated how they felt about the institutions and an entire country that had become cold and unyielding. 'Civil defence', so ran their battle cry, 'means nothing but opposition for us from now on'.[27]

Peace activists, on the other hand, focused their criticisms in particular on the concrete of the civil defence shelters and on the official promises of survival and protection they were said to offer, which considering the studies about a so-called 'nuclear winter' and the devastating long-term effects of an atomic war seemed less and less believable. Instead of survival islands, they referred to them as 'concrete coffins', 'concrete dungeons', and 'concrete sardine tins' that would imprison the population in the 'torpid weapon-bristling hedgehog' and ultimately leave them to perish.[28] During a large Demonstration for Peace and Immediate Disarmament in December 1981, Switzerland was also described as a society with a 'worldwide common destiny', thus rejecting the image of the country as an island. One female speaker asked the 30,000 women, men, and children who had gathered on the Bundesplatz in front of the Swiss parliament what exactly they thought they were going to do 'crammed up' in these 'concrete holes' when faced with an 'atomic holocaust'.[29] Personal fear was invoked by her and other activists as the driving force and a new sanity against the 'cold' rationality of the experts that was based on mathematical calculations – an opposition that challenged the 'necrophilic' thinking of civil defence experts extolling atomic bunkers instead of nurturing 'liveable' lives.[30]

Writers likewise preoccupied themselves in their novels with the impossibility of survival following a Third World War, mercilessly depicting scenes of death in the concrete cells in all its wretchedness. An early and little-known example of this rising wave of German-language apocalypse literature is Gertrud Wilker's story 'Flaschenpost' (i.e., message in a bottle).[31] Her text, begun in 1969 but first published in 1977, describes the last weeks and days of a woman who, together with her two teenage children, has sought refugee in the collective public shelter of a Swiss municipality after the explosion of an atomic bomb. In order to stop going 'bunker stir-crazy' and to fight against forgetfulness the protagonist writes out 'radiation-resistant' words in her notebook – words intended to reinvigorate life again afterwards.[32] They are interspersed in the story with flashbacks to the time before the nuclear attack and with detailed scientific descriptions of the effects of nuclear weapons and measures to shield against the blast waves and the nuclear radiation. Thus, for instance, Wilker calculates that a protective layer of 12 centimetres of concrete is necessary to reduce the primary radiation by half, and 6 centimetres of concrete to reduce the secondary radiation.[33] As more and more people begin to die in the shelter and the life of the protagonist also begins to rapidly fade, a handful of youths, including her daughter and son, ram the concrete doors open. With no hope left and with her last remaining strength she records: 'Well, the bolt is gone. I think they're just pushing the concrete doorwings apart. They can see daylight (I can't). I don't want to think how intense the radiation dose must have been for them and what this means for them.'[34] With her last words she writes: 'I can't hear anything anymore either. It's becoming cold, always colder.'[35]

Perhaps the most negative visual monument to a cemented-over Switzerland was set by the book *Schutzraum Schweiz* (Shelter Switzerland), issued in 1988 by a group of historians, left-wing politicians, peace activists, and doctors.[36] The

6. Switzerland as a concrete slab, drawing by Bernhard Chiquet, 1988.

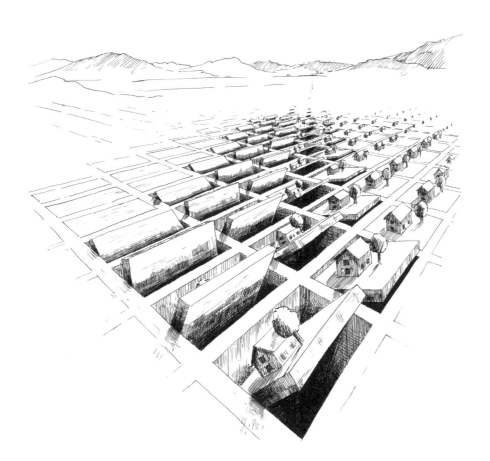

7. Swivelling concrete compartments, drawing by Bernhard Chiquet, 1988.

Reinforced Country Below Ground

85

cover of the book is adorned with the drawing of a concrete roof surface from which a steep ramp leads down into the dark concrete underground (fig. 6). In the book itself one of these ramps is populated by a faceless mass of people, pressing themselves into the massive concrete container as tank battalions are already beginning to rumble over up above. A further drawing shows Switzerland as a subdivided landscape of single-family houses. Each house stands on a concrete lid, with some of the concreted-over segments already tilting downwards, thus swivelling the individual houses down into the underground darkness (fig. 7). Switzerland as a whole degenerates into an endless concrete slab and a death zone.

Notes

1. Jost auf der Maur, *Die Schweiz unter Tag: Eine Entdeckungsreise* (Basel: Echtzeit, 2017), 114.
2. For the development of nuclear-shelter construction know-how, see Silvia Berger Ziauddin, 'Superpower Underground: Switzerland's Rise to Global Bunker Expertise in the Atomic Age', *Technology and Culture* 58, no. 4 (2017), 921–54.
3. See Beat Tscharner, 'Die Wiedereinführung der privaten Luftschutzkeller', *Protar* 18, no. 7/8 (1952), 78–81, here 79.
4. The 1949 guidelines for built air-raid protection focused on high-explosive, incendiary, rocket-propelled and winged bombs, as well as artillery and infantry shells, and only mentioned the effects of an atom bomb in passing. See Beat Tscharner, 'Die neuen Richtlinien für den baulichen Luftschutz I', *Protar* 15, no. 9/10 (1949), 105–14.
5. See Berger Ziauddin, 'Superpower Underground' (see note 2), 928.
6. See Walter Rimathé, 'Bauliche Massnahmen zum Schutz gegen Atombomben', *Cementbulletin* 26, no. 10 (1958), 1–8; Theo Ginsburg and Alex Haerter, 'Technische Grundlagen des Schutzraumbaus', *Neue Zürcher Zeitung*, 23 June 1965.
7. See Samuel Glasstone, *Die Wirkungen der Kernwaffen* (Köln: Heymanns, 1960), 633; Alex Haerter and Gottfried Schindler, *Handbuch der Waffenwirkungen für die Bemessung von Schutzbauten*, implemented by the Arbeitsgruppe für den baulichen Zivilschutz für das Bundesamt für Zivilschutz (Bern: Bundesamt für Zivilschutz, 1964), 320.
8. See 'Der Beton im Luftschutz', *Cementbulletin* 9, no. 7 (1941), 1–6; Rimathé, 'Bauliche Massnahmen' (see note 6).
9. See Berger Ziauddin, 'Superpower Underground' (see note 2), 937.
10. Eidgenössisches Justiz- und Polizeidepartement, Bundesamt für Zivilschutz, *TWP 1966: Technische Weisungen für den privaten Schutzraumbau* (Bern: Eidgenössische Drucksachen- und Materialzentrale, 1966).
11. P. G. Rogge and H. Bülow, 'Die Stellung der schweizerischen Bauwirtschaft in einer sich ändernden Umwelt', *Schweizerische Bauzeitung* 93, no. 4 (1975), 56–61, here 57.
12. Georges Spicher, Hugo Marfurt and Nicolas Stoll, *Ohne Zement geht nichts: Geschichte der schweizerischen Zementindustrie* (Zürich: Verlag Neue Zürcher Zeitung, 2013), 199.
13. 'Der Schutzraumdienst am Beispiel der Organisation im öffentlichen Schutzraum Urania', *Zivilschutz* 22, no. 11/12 (1975), 348–51; 'Grösstes Zürcher Parkhaus in der Innenstadt offen', *Tages-Anzeiger*, 30 November 1974; 'Doppelleben im Untergrund', *Neue Zürcher Zeitung*, 23 October 2012.
14. According to a diagram in the red Civil Defence Book, which in 1969 was sent to all Swiss households, defence shelters provided 90 per cent 'safety'. Eidgenössisches Justiz- und Polizeidepartement (ed.), *Zivilverteidigung* (Aarau: Miles-Verlag, 1969), 74.
15. This is impressively shown in the civil defence film *Blumen und tote Fische*. In one scene the camera moves slowly along a gloomy curved passageway before suddenly revealing the opened doors to the shelter. The light streaming from inside the installation makes the massive threshold and the doors themselves shine like an aureole. *Blumen und tote Fische*, dir. Roland Bertschinger, produced on behalf of the Bundesamt für Zivilschutz (1969), 6′41″–7′11″.
16. Ibid., 9′16″–9′26″.
17. 'Reduit der Bürger', *Protar* 18, no. 7/8 (1952), 91.
18. 'Das Bild eines Schutzraums, welcher nach Unterbrechung aller Kontakte mit der Aussenwelt in einem Meer von Zerstörung weiterexistiert, kann anschaulich mit dem Begriff "Überlebensinsel" beschrieben werden' (Werner Heierli, 'Der Schutzraum als Überlebensinsel', *Schutz+Wehr* 34, no. 9/10, 1968, 120–2, here 120).
19. See Philipp Sarasin, 'Die Insel der Seligen und die Kultur der Bedrohung', in Brigitta Gerber and Damir Skenderovic (eds.), *Wider die Ausgrenzung: Für eine offene Schweiz*, vol. 3: *Akteure* (Zürich: Chronos, 2011), 11–34; Beatrice Ziegler, 'Switzerland: An Island of Peace', in *1914–1918-Online: International Encyclopedia of the First World War*, issued by the Freie Universität Berlin 2018-04-11. DOI: 10.15463/ie1418.11239.
20. 'Das kleine saubere Schweizerhaus auf der umbrandeten Insel im Weltmeer' (Peter von Matt, 'Kritischer Patriotismus', in *Die tintenblauen Eidgenossen: Über die literarische und politische Schweiz*, München: Carl Hanser Verlag, 2001, 131–143, here 134).
21. 'Überlebensinsel der Familie' (Heierli, 'Der Schutzraum als Überlebensinsel', see note 18,

122); 'demokratische Substanz der Schweiz' (Bundesamt für Gesundheit, ed., *Zivilschutz-Konzeption 1971*, Bern: Eidgenössische Drucksachen- und Materialzentrale, 1971, 3).

[22] See, for instance, *Zivilverteidigung* (see note 14), 55.

[23] Werner Heierli, *Überleben im Ernstfall* (Solothurn: Vogt-Schild, 1982), 120.

[24] Gustav Däniker, 'Konzept und Entstehung der "wehrhaften Schweiz"', *Schweizer Soldat* 39, no. 17 (1963/1964), 385.

[25] *Günz, Riss, Mündel und Würm*, prod. Geschichtsladen Zürich, Lehrlingstreff Zürich, Videoladen Zürich (1986), 3'33" (Schweizerisches Sozialarchiv Zurich, F_Videos Stadt in Bewegung/Vid V 033).

[26] 'Wollt ihr den totalen Beton?' 'Beton Grau wie die Zukunft' 'Wieviel Beton braucht der Mensch?' (Schweizerisches Sozialarchiv Zurich, Fotoarchiv Gertrud Vogel, F 5107, Na-10-107-032; Na-10-116-007; Na-10-115-026)

[27] 'Heisst für uns fürderhin nichts als Widerstand' (Schweizer Fernsehen DRS, 'Zivilschutz-Verweigerer', *DRS Aktuell*, 9 November 1984; *Günz, Riss, Mündel und Würm*, see note 25, 40'30").

[28] 'Nuklearen Winter', 'Betonsärge', 'Betonverliesse', 'Sardinenbüchsen aus Eisenbeton', 'waffenstarren Igel'. Konradin Kreuzer, 'Der schweizerische Zivilschutz: Ein Beitrag zum Krieg', in Hans A. Pestalozzi, *Rettet die Schweiz: Schafft die Armee ab* (Bern: Zytglogge, 1982), 129–39, here 135; Konradin Kreuzer, 'Die Bunkerschweiz', *Arch+* 16, no. 71 (1983), 26–8, here 26; 'Rede von Christine Perren anlässlich der Friedensdemonstration vom 4.12.1981 in Bern', in Komitee für Frieden und Abrüstung (ed.), *Friedensdebatte in der Schweiz* (Bern: A.G. Friedensdebatte KFA, 1982), 16; Flugblatt Schutzraum – Schutzraum (Schweizerisches Sozialarchiv Zurich, QS 45.3C*25, 1960–1984).

[29] 'Weltweite Schicksalsgemeinschaft', 'eingepfercht', 'Betonlöchern', 'atomaren Holocaust' ('Rede von Christine Perren', see note 28).

[30] See Kathrin Huber, 'Angst, Bedrohung, Verteidigung aus weiblicher Sicht: Referat in der Arbeitsgruppe "Leben ist bedroht – Sicherheit ist gefragt – Was für eine Sicherheit"', in Frauen für den Frieden Region Basel (ed.), *Aufbruch der Frauen: Dokumentation Frauen-Symposium, 25–26 April 1987 in Basel* (Basel: Frauen für den Frieden Region Basel, 1987), 66–70, here 70.

[31] Gertrud Wilker, 'Flaschenpost', in *Winterdorf: Erzählungen* (Frauenfeld: Huber, 1977), 47–90.

[32] Ibid., 60, 70.

[33] Ibid., 53.

[34] 'Also ist der Riegel weg. Sie schieben, glaube ich, eben die Betonflügel auseinander. Sie können Tageslicht sehen (Ich nicht). Ich will nicht daran denken, wie stark die Strahlungsdosis für sie gewesen sein muss und was das für sie bedeutet. […] Auch höre ich nichts mehr. Es wird kalt, immer kälter' (ibid., 86).

[35] 'Auch höre ich nichts mehr. Es wird kalt, immer kälter' (ibid., 89).

[36] Peter Albrecht et al. (eds.), *Schutzraum Schweiz: Mit dem Zivilschutz in die Notstandsgesellschaft* (Bern: Zytglogge, 1988).

Terraced Hillside Housing Architectures

When Vineyards Gave Way to Swiss Families

Lorenzo Stieger

'The architects are saying to themselves one should make a virtue of a necessity, and it appears that Switzerland will become a country of terraced hillside housing estates.'[1]

The hectic pace of building activity after the Second World War led, within a few years, to widespread urban sprawl in the Swiss Mittelland. From the 1950s onwards the sun-kissed, undeveloped southern slopes of the Jura region were thought to represent an attractive alternative. The advantages of the steep topography had been recognised by planners since the turn of the century, but it was only by resorting to a legal loophole that it first became possible to also exploit the region for housing. Since the introduction of the modern Civil Code in 1912, Switzerland's citizens had been legally prohibited from acquiring flats in most parts of the country. Concerned about the legal-structural problems that inheritance laws had caused in the past with the part-division of houses, individual housing ownership had been conditional upon simultaneous land ownership. This legal stipulation made it obligatory that house ownership had to demonstrate a physical connection to the land as property. On the one hand this guaranteed the ownership of single-family homes, and on the other it prevented the sale of individual flats in multiple-family dwellings to interested buyers. In essence, hillside terraced housing owes its early success in Switzerland to this legal obstacle. In 1957 the ingenious architects Fritz Stucky and Rudolf Meuli spotted steep hillside slopes as an opportunity to overcome this legal hurdle.[2] By virtue of a diagonal stacking of the apartments parallel to the slope each unit stood on a minimal plot of land. With this sleight of hand, the subdivision of the building land into narrow strips allowed each apartment to be assigned the status of a single-family house in the land registry, each with their separate entrances (fig. 1).

A further legal manoeuvre involved contractually regulated building authorisations between the individual house owners that constituted the legal basis for the overlapping of the residential units of terraced housing projects. This meant that the first housing estate by the Stucky Meuli architectural office on the symbolically christened *Terrassenweg* (i.e., terrace lane) in the city of Zug was not only erected on relatively cheap land, which until then had been considered

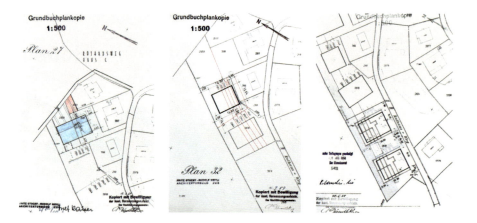

1. Fritz Stucky and Rudolf Meuli, Terrassenweg project, Zug, 1957–60. Sub-division of the escarpment, plan and drawing.

almost undevelopable, but also that potential buyers could be wooed with the argument that their future hillside home required a land purchase that was merely a third of the size of the actual living space. Once tried and tested in Zug, this model of property sub-allocation quickly advanced to become a common practice amongst architects, aimed at obtaining official permission for this hitherto largely unfamiliar building design (fig. 2). At the same time the various building authorities lacked uniform guidelines to evaluate the terraced housing developments, which due to their elongated architectural dimensions along the dip of the slopes obliged the granting of exemption permits.

The approval procedure for a stepped multi-family house by the architect Claude Paillard in Witikon, in Zurich, clearly shows that in 1959 there was still a lack of clarity about the criteria by which such a building type set on sloping land should be measured. According to the cantonal building laws, the number of floors facing downhill was to be counted from the juncture where the first residential storey emerged above the building plot, whereas the municipal building regulations considered the street level facing uphill to be decisive. These opposing interpretations resulted in the new development requiring the issuing of two special permits that could hardly have been more contradictory. On the one hand an exception was granted to construct a high-rise block with seven storeys, and on the other to erect a two-storey house with four additional basement levels (fig. 3). However, this combination of a deficit in professional experience amongst the building authorities and the absence of a vocabulary for terraced construction approaches in the building laws also opened up considerable freedoms in design scope, as is strikingly evinced in the projects by architectural offices such as Team 2000 and Atelier 5. This tandem of topography and multi-occupancy dwellings was seized as an opportunity to test out new forms of housing projects focused on inner-scheme community living. The vagueness of prevailing building laws coupled with the unfamiliar building design constituted an energy field that provided dedicated architects with a chance to realise just such approaches using a new plastically shaped physical presence. In this sense the steep slope became a locus of planning uncertainty and a source of architectural innovation in equal measure.

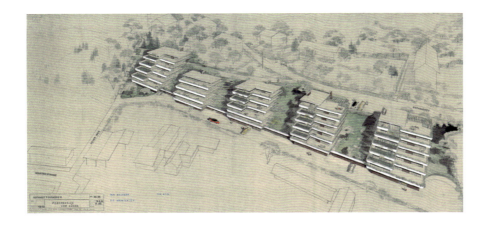

2. Fritz Stucky and Rudolf Meuli, Terrassenweg project, Zug, 1957–60. Sub-division of the escarpment, perspective drawing.

Keeping the Flatlands Free: Hillside Terraced Housing as a Spatial Planning Instrument

> 'How delightfully the three co-joining little houses are staggered on the steep escarpment, each a little higher than the next, perfectly aligned to the slope [...] three houses and yet nonetheless only one!'[3]

In the issue 'Junge Form' of the cultural magazine *DU* in 1963, the author Silvia Kugler highlighted the special status given to urban development in numerous projects by a new generation of Swiss architects.[4] Featured as a prominent example was a double-rowed terraced housing project erected in the canton of Aargau in front of the fortified walls of the small town of Klingnau, between the vines on an until then largely pristine site.

The Burghalde (lit. castle escarpment) housing estate was the initial realisation of what the young architect Hans Ulrich Scherer would later describe as the built fragment of a real *Haldenstadt* (lit. escarpment town). The idea of a modern city on a hillside was based on his urbanistic vision to build a continuous linear city in the form of terraced hillside housing along the entire length of the Jura Mountains, stretching all the way from Geneva to Brugg.[5] Scherer was first able to concretise this leitmotiv in the regional model Brugg 2000 in 1958, demonstrating that in Scherer's thinking the idea of terraced hillside housing encompassed both architectural-constructional and spatial planning aspects. Team 2000 – Scherer's team together with befriended architects, construction engineers and sculptors – presented their radical planning proposal to residents and municipal representatives from the building authority in an exhibition in Brugg, specifically put together for this purpose (fig. 4). By the symbolically laden year 2000, the historical core of the town was to be expanded by a modern commercial district and eleven flanking residential towers. The up-and-coming municipality was to be equipped with an extensive industrial zone running along the railway lines, while families with children were to be provided with desirable housing in the form of a terraced *Teppichsiedlungen*[6] on the sun-drenched Bruggerberg adjacent to the countryside. Accompanying this highly densified urbanisation of the hillside

3. Claude Paillard, terraced housing in Eierbrecht, Zurich, 1960. Illustrative model contrasting a standard construction procedure conforming to the building regulations with a sloped terraced house as a permitted exemption. Photograph P. Grünert.

Terraced Hillside Housing Architectures

4. Visionary regional model Brugg 2000. The new style of living at the turn of the century in the Haldenstadt on the Bruggerberg.

areas, the authors formulated an urgent demand that the lowlands be protected against the forces of further sprawl and be preserved as a vital natural and agricultural space for the population – a landscape conservation agenda *avant la lettre*.

There were two key factors that encouraged these young architects in their aspiration to combine modern architectural practices with a root-and-branch urban and regional planning perspective. One aspect was that futurologists had predicted rapid economic and demographic growth rates for the region in the coming years. This would present small municipalities with new challenges, the meeting of which would require the coordinated collaboration of interdisciplinary teams. The first omens of these prognoses were already to be seen in the arrival of global-player industries, the imminent linkage to the national motorway network or the projected construction of a new-generation nuclear power plant.[7] The other aspect was that these young architects were swayed by the thinking of prominent personalities demanding a new planning approach for tackling pressing future settlement issues. In their pamphlet *Achtung: Die Schweiz*, authors Max Frisch, Lucius Burckhard, and Markus Kutter called for nothing less than the construction of a whole city from scratch. Built to accommodate 10,000 inhabitants, it was envisioned to provide an urban model whose features would exclusively conform to the most modern planning principles.[8] Although this idea was fundamentally anchored in the functional separation of living, working, industry, and recreation as propagated in Le Corbusier's *La Charte d'Athènes* (1943), in the meantime the theoretical discourse in modern urban planning had undergone a paradigm shift. The new objective was to respond to these growth projections with a housing strategy based on qualitative and social guiding principles. The discussions concerning a more humane 'habitat' were marked by a resumed search for a densified urban atmosphere and new collective forms of living. Traditional and vernacular settlement structures, such as the Arab kasbah or the historical Zähringen town layout, were adopted as paradigm archetypes for new planning impulses in the conception of contemporary settlements. A younger generation was considered to be under an obligation to harness architecture to serve the community again. In addition, by virtue of their 'social imagination'[9] architects were ideally positioned to deliberately shape a complex living environment that could once more act as a wellspring of identity and meaning for the modern individual.

Under these circumstances it was hardly surprising that the canton of Aargau's small medieval towns should possess a real model character for Scherer in terms of the spatial organisation and architectural articulation of terraced hillside housing. A transfer of ideas with conventional forms of urbanisation was not yet explicitly expressed in the radical regional model for Brugg, which excited both a favourable curiosity and deep antipathy amongst the visitors to the exhibition. The model presentations were too large-scale and the building plans too schematic to derive a spatial impression of what community existence on the Bruggerberg might look like. However, in the following years this discursive spirit fused with technical solutions that made large-scale terraced housing projects on steep slopes realisable. The Mühlehalde housing estate, built between 1964 and 1971 in three stages, would emerge as the most fully developed manifesto of the new hillside town. In addition to the shared facilities and varied layout configurations, its distinguishing characteristics were above all an ingenious network of paths and the world-first mechanically driven inclined lift system in a housing scheme. The differentiated prioritisation of the individual circulation and access forms resulted in a multi-faceted arrangement of narrow byways, widely configured stairways and expansive open spaces between the layered architectural volumes. This structured the housing project, distinguishing between private and public areas, which in turn served the residents either as individual havens or places to pause collectively. As the most prominent voice and early pioneer of the Swiss terraced hillside housing, Hans Ulrich Scherer happily referred to what he called 'a spider's web of new urban forms of living.'[10] However, the accolade of energising terraced hillside housing with a renewed impulse, and thereby demonstrating a ground-breaking spatial and programmatic virtuosity, lies with the architects of Atelier 5. In their unrealised Bühnenberg project they successfully coupled two principles: the resurrection of the idea of diagonal circulation, harking back to a traditional Italian hilltop town, and united with a rigid yet organic topographically embedded structure (fig. 5).

Buttressing the Slope and Shaping Living: Concrete between Statics and Structural Freedom

> 'We don't believe it right that a person has to conform to the apartment – a supposition dictated by official regulations, by the profit margins of real-estate developers or by the ideologies of architects. [...] The problem thereby concerns... both furnishing possibilities in a limited volume and the opportunities to expand or reduce in conformity with the cycle of human lifespans.'[11]

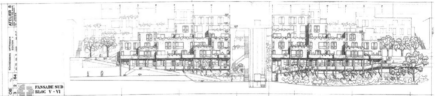

5. Atelier 5, Bühnenberg project, Oftringen, 1973 onwards, unrealised. A dynamic hillside housing development between traditional urban morphology and technical progress.

In the 1950s, at the same time as the first of these housing projects was being completed in Switzerland, the question of the appropriate construction material no longer revolved around whether terraced hillside housing should be built in concrete, but instead focused on which foundation techniques and construction methods could be most efficiently applied on sloping terrain. Land treatment and slope stabilisation were inevitably compelling cost factors, pushing architects and structural engineers to reduce excavation work to an absolute minimum and to test out new foundation methods wherever possible.[12] Moreover, the deployment of the technical advantages of the composite material was due to the fact that inclined stepped building entailed a swivelling – from the vertical to the horizontal – of the classic order of base structure, central structure and roof. While the rear part of the building was submerged beneath the ground, the terraces jutted out towards the sky, so that both the construction and the material were equally weathered by ground damp and the changing seasons. The architects of the first terraced hillside housing development in Zug tried to elegantly sidestep this problem by using an experimental method. Due to the fact that the overall concept was based on two different building approaches, in terms of construction engineering the apartments could be divorced from the bedrock. The foundations were built in the form of parallel set strings, which essentially simply rested on the inclined terrain, supported by a massive retaining wall at the base of the slope. In keeping with the spirit of industrial prefabrication, the apartments were conceived as autonomous spatial modules that – simply placed on the concrete steps – would settle diagonally one above the other. Theories aside, realities showed that local building contractors had yet to convert to industrial construction techniques. Instead of stacking one spatial cell above the next using cranes, and contrary to the architectural vision, each storey had to be successively built level by level while the walls were executed using traditional bricklaying.

Despite this setback the new technical capabilities in concrete construction and the advance of industrial assembly led to a closer collaboration between architects and civil engineers in developing new building approaches to frame construction and with prefabricated modular design systems. The ambitions went as far as to liberate terraced hillside housing from a rigid floor plan by deploying frame systems and pre-stressed tension cables, as in bridge engineering. Because the rear of the terraced building had to simultaneously perform a slope-supporting function and the inner walls had to bear the accumulated weight of the levels above, resulting in massive configurations, the apartment floor plans allowed no scope for structural alterations whatsoever. On the other hand, the advantages of frame construction in terms of statics lay in the point-focal load transfer in the form of a three-dimensional spatial grid, which from then on enabled both horizontal and vertical spatial configurations over multiple storeys. Thanks to the standardisation of the building elements and a flexible arrangement of the apartments, the architects believed that the inhabitants could be already included as participants in the design phase of the planning process. Moreover, the adaptability of the apartments could anticipate future use scenarios, which could be implemented internally, without interfering with the load-bearing structure, due to the lightweight construction method. The architect Erwin Mühlestein was one such protagonist who over a period of many years successively pursued the implementation of modular and adaptive module-based systems in his terraced housing designs (fig. 6).

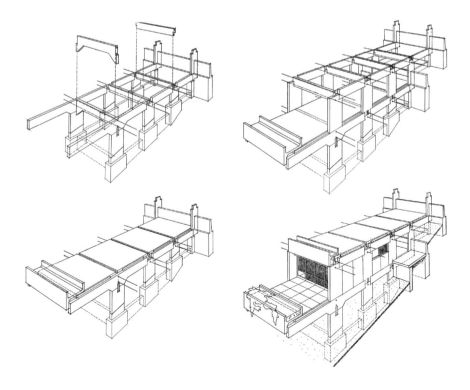

6. Erwin Mühlestein, the variable terraced hillside housing construction system imbued by the spirit of participation and adaptation.

Terraced Hillside Housing Architectures

Despite the strong desire of the engineers and architects involved to experiment with modular principles, the inherent inconveniences of hillside building plots – including, for instance, cumbersome access to the building site, structural project complexities, the high production costs of the building elements, and lengthy transport distances – meant that prefabricated-based construction processes never became an established practice. The on-site realisation of terraced housing developments additionally took advantage of a cheap labour pool of migrant workers, whose manual skills were limited to traditional building. The upshot was a large discrepancy between the theory, concerning what was technologically achievable with concrete in mass-housing developments at the time, and the practice, in terms of the extent to which such building methods were basically implementable on steep topographies in the first place.[13] One of the architectural leitmotifs propagated in the 1950s and 1960s was architectural and social renewal, but terraced housing developments offered little scope in realising these aims, not least because the living form was closely tied to the idea of being a surrogate for house ownership and thus remained reserved to a small segment of the general population who could afford to purchase property. Discussing a particular terraced housing development built based on a flexible 4D construction-element system (Kamm and Kündig), the architectural critic Benedikt Loderer came to the conclusion in the 1990s that: 'The idea of a democratisation of planning via residents' participation proved to be a democracy for those who could afford to pay for it. Therefore, flexible structures do not automatically lead to more fairness – they can merely assimilate it.'[14]

Expressive Sculptural Force and Fragmentation as Distinguishing Characteristics – a Verdict on the Quintessence of Swiss Architecture?

> 'The sensation of exiting the apartment and entering the sheltering cellar space across a single level undoubtedly satisfies the primal soul of the mountain dweller in the same way as a dovecote-like projecting or overhanging panoramic window does.'[15]

The fact that the majority of such buildings had to be realised in situ could be taken as proof that some of the architects involved focused above all on the aesthetic potential of concrete as a monolithic building material and less on its technical properties. Especially in the first terraced hillside housing projects, the choice of stylistic means and material appearance were more often than not closely interlinked with the personal biographies of their authors, their education, and the principles of the architectural discourse. The works of Frank Lloyd Wright and Alvar Aalto were held in considerable awe, both of them exercising a marked sway over Swiss architectural creativity after the Second World War. Thus the clear formal design of the terraced hillside housing in Eierbrecht and its material execution in red exposed brick can be explained by Claude Paillard's affinity for Aalto's architecture. Fritz Stucky, on the other hand, chose to train

7. Team 2000, Mühlehalde terraced hillside housing development, Umiken, 1966. Expressive plasticity and Mediterranean bulkiness in the aesthetic tradition of Le Corbusier's *béton brut*.

in Taliesin under Frank Lloyd Wright instead of learning architecture at the Swiss Federal Institute of Technology in Zurich, which can inevitably be read in his recital of various aesthetic design elements in his numerous hillside housing projects. Thus the particular emphasis given to the horizontal and the massiveness of concrete deployed again and again in Stucky's work refers to specific projects by the American master and his former mentor.[16] Nevertheless, the deliberate use of concrete to articulate a new plasticity in modern architecture was undoubtedly above all the hallmark of Le Corbusier's late works, which certainly attracted the most admirers amongst Swiss architects. The members of Atelier 5, the sculptor-architect and 'facade renegade'[17] Walter Maria Förderer, as well as Hans Ulrich Scherer were amongst the closest adherents of a *béton brut* architecture. In his Mühlehalde housing project the latter consciously relied on a material aesthetic, form design, and colour elements that were prominently found in Le Corbusier's buildings (fig. 7).

This architectural idiom, as defined by the plasticity of concrete, was discussed by architectural critics such as the Austrian Friedrich Achleitner or the British Reyner Banham either as a short style episode in Swiss architecture or as part of the wider aesthetic tradition of international Brutalism. Against the backdrop of these savants' speculations, the local population often perceived this sculptural concrete architecture woven into the landscape as positive, because, according to Christoph Allenspach, building in concrete in the Alpine region was often combined with an association of 'progress and prosperity' – both factors that were embodied in infrastructure edifices, for instance dams, which, 'as the work of fathers, brothers and sons', were 'the pride of the whole population'.[18]

However, it was the sociologist Lucius Burckhardt, as the editor-in-chief of the journal *Werk*, who proved to be particularly persuasive in increasingly equating dwelling in hillside terraced housing with a Swiss self-image, as associated with the ways of living of the country's mountain inhabitants. Such a perception was also coupled with a political dimension that represented the core features of terraced housing as a democratic architectural form. The dissolving of facades and proportions – Burckhardt juxtaposed the 'contemporary terraced hillside house' with the '"facade-front house" of the past'[19] – and the penchant for tranquil spatial divisions echoed supposedly typical Helvetic traits, at the same time underscoring the dismantlement of the totalitarian claims to power abusively embraced during the Second World War in the two official tendencies of Nazi Classicism and Stalinist Folklore.[20] In Switzerland a moderateness of spatial order was felt to correspond with the repeatedly stressed sovereignty of the people, with hillside complexes and the layout of their individual spatial units considered to be ideal expressions of this marriage, in particular in terms of an oft-cited human scale. The architectural critic Friedrich Achleitner considered this small-scale segmentation, produced by manipulations of 'stepping, stacking or swivelling', as 'a new widespread notion of the spatial' that had become a 'kind of common denominator' in Switzerland and was 'possibly an expression of an altered social situation, a democratic form of living'.[21] The prominence given to the individual within a larger community seemed to correspond to the socio-political structure of federalist Switzerland, and the revision of single-storey owner-occupancy rights in 1965 was similarly imbued with the 'basic democratic spirit'[22] that each and every citizen should possess their own home and thus financial security.[23]

In a special issue of the architectural journal *Werk* in 1966 dedicated to terraced hillside projects, the architect Hans Ulrich Scherer emphasised that Switzerland could by no means claim a monopoly on the building type, naming numerous examples of terraced projects in England.[24] Indeed, thanks to the promotional programmes of their respective national tourism ministries, numerous terraced holiday complexes had sprung up along the French and Italian Riviera since the 1950s.[25] Nevertheless, in terms of the history of the idea, the terraced hillside housing development as a typical Swiss architectural form remained, intimately tied to the argument of the country's distinct national topography and the dwindling space for settlement development. In comparison to its German-speaking neighbours Austria and Germany, where the first projects had been realised from 1965 and 1970 onwards, respectively, the rapid spread of the type had already begun relatively early along the foot of southern slopes of the Jura Mountains. Moreover, this Swiss-centric image was further fostered via a coordinated media campaign about national building endeavours in numerous foreign professional journals, propelled at the time by a small circle of enthusiastic architects. To take one prominent example, it was the efforts of Lucius Burckhard, Hans Ulrich Scherer, Erwin Mühlestein, Walter Maria Förderer, and others that led to the French architectural journal *Architecture d'Aujourd'hui* prominently featuring hillside terraced housing in a number of articles in 1965.[26] The title page of the special issue about current architectural activities in Switzerland was illustrated with two high-profile terraced hillside developments executed in exposed concrete, prominently embedded, as an unmistakable message of the neighbouring country's new identity, in the emblem of the Swiss cross.

8. Max Matter's work from the series Überbauung from 1969. Painting as an architectural and planning critique of hillside developments.

According to the announcements by developers and investors in the 1960s, the clientele most attracted by this individual hillside living style included young, open-minded people who did not lead traditional middle-class lives and who had intellectually challenging jobs.[27] And so it was: the general interest in apartment properties with their own private seating areas and pristine panoramas was great enough to slowly but surely inscribe terraced hillside housing into the image of Swiss housing. The resulting creeping but steadily encroaching transformation of the Swiss national landscape was registered not only by experts but also increasingly among the public at large.[28] Within the context of confronting the force of everyday phenomena, the artist Max Matter, for instance, unerringly sensed the extent to which this persistent urge to build more and more had now colonised the hillside slopes to its own ends under the disguise of a postulated modernism in architecture (fig. 8).[29]

9. Atelier 5, sketch showing a rigid structure for a Siedlung, as if a tenement block had been pushed against the hillside.

It did not take long before it became a common proverb that the majority of terraced housing complexes were little more than tenement blocks tilted onto the hillside (fig. 9).[30] Tax competition between municipalities, rising hillside property prices, speculative practices by construction companies and investors, newly issued hillside zoning plans, but also building regulations with rigid design parameters, collectively acted to ossify the form of terraced housing as a building typology. On the one hand this provided planning security, but on the other meant that the design parameters became successively suffocated in an ever-tighter corset. As an 'anthology' of advertising texts and prospectuses for terraced hillside apartments in *Werk* already showed in 1966, the outcome of these growing trends was often schematic developments with minimal architectural originality.[31] New zoning plans incorporating hillside slopes and yet reserving them for housing resulted in programmatic impoverishment and stymied planning proposals advocating a functional mix on slope sites.[32] Amongst both the population and architects, the opinion eventually prevailed that the construction of terraced hillside housing entailed a marring of the country's visual appearance.[33]

For Switzerland, the circumstances at the time, coupled with a curiosity on the part of the architects involved, could have perhaps acted as nothing less than a beacon for the formulation of a pioneering planning ideology, bridging the gap between control and laissez-faire. Instead, ultimately all we are left with are a few built examples and project sketches – fragments pointing to the fact that this unique interplay between the new, the unknown, and a healthy portion of insecurity inherent to terrace hillside housing architecture could have perhaps truly been a rich seam for the architecture of the country.

Notes

1. 'Man soll aus der Not eine Tugend machen, sagen sich die Architekten, und es sieht so aus, als werde die Schweiz das Land der Terrassensiedlungen' ('Terrassensiedlung – Bauform der Zukunft?', *Wohnen* 42, no. 4, 1967, 103–4, here 103).

2. Fritz Stucky pointed out in the journal *Werk* that as a type, steep building plots stimulated them as architects to examine new hillside housing forms that offered a suitable solution in terms of construction, laws, and economics. The architecture duo had already experimented with a legal hybrid form with their 1955 Bohlgutsch House, consisting of a single-family house and two attached rental apartments. The insights into ownership rights in hillside multi-apartment dwellings were applied from 1957 onwards in the design of their first terraced housing development. See Fritz Stucky, 'Terrassenhäuser in Zug: 1957/60, Architekten Frütz Stucky und Rudolf Meuli, Zug', *Werk* 48, no. 2 (1961), 58–60; Fritz Stucky, 'Haus mit 3 Wohnungen in Zug', *Bauen + Wohnen* 11, no. 1 (1957), 14–17.

3. 'Wie entzückend die drei aneinandergebauten Häuslein sich an der steilen Berghalde staffeln, jedes ein wenig höher als das andere, ganz dem Hang folgend [...] drei Häuser und doch nur eins' (Wolfgang Müller, 'Der Kindergarten "Munothalde" in Schaffhausen', *Der Schweizerische Kindergarten: Monatsschrift für Erziehung im Vorschulalter* XXVI, no. 1, 1936, 8–11, here 8, 9).

4. See Silvia Kugler, 'Städtebau ist wichtig!', *Du* 23, no. 11 (1963), 11–25.

5. See 'Terrassensiedlung Burghalde in Klingnau', *Werk* 51, no. 10 (1964), 370–3; Hans Ulrich Scherer, 'Terrassenbauten', *Werk* 53, no. 6 (1966), 201–7.

6. Hans Ulrich Scherer, 'In ein paar Jahrzehnten', *Brugger Neujahrsblätter* 69 (1959), 49–62, here 56. *Teppichsiedlungen*: lit. a carpet housing development, that is, an intricate varied housing pattern based on interlocking low-rise units and courtyards or gardens (TN).

7. The architect summarised the local development in the region in the *Brugger Neujahresblätter* of 1959, mentioning the 'prognosis of a statistician' ('Prognose eines Statistikers') who predicted that the canton's population would double to reach 600,000. By 2000 three-quarters of the newcomers were anticipated to settle in the areas around Baden and Brugg. Ibid., 49–50.

8. See Lucius Burckhardt, Max Frisch, and Markus Kutter, *Achtung: Die Schweiz. Ein Gespräch über unsere Lage und ein Vorschlag zur Tat.* Basler politische Schriften vol. 2 (Basel: Verlag Karl Werner, 1955).

9. 'Sozialen Imagination' (Sigfried Giedion, *Architektur und Gemeinschaft: Tagebuch einer Entwicklung*, Hamburg: Rowohlt, 1956, 96).

10. 'Spinnweb neuer urbaner Lebensform!' ('Terrassensiedlung Brüggliacher in Rohrdorf AG', *Werk* 51, no. 10, 1964, 375).

11. 'Wir halten es nicht für richtig, daß sich der Mensch der Wohnung anzupassen hat - einer Vorgegebenheit, die durch behördliche Bestimmungen, durch Renditegesichtspunkte von Baugesellschaften oder durch Ideologien von Architekten fixiert ist [...] Dabei geht es [...] sowohl um Einrichtungsmöglichkeiten in einem begrenzten Volumen - als auch um Expansions- und Reduzierungsmöglichkeiten, die dem Zyklus menschlichen Lebens entsprechen' (Harald Deilmann, 'Zu diesem Heft [Die Wohnung: Variabilität – Flexibilität]', *Bauen + Wohnen* 24, no. 3, 1970, 76).

12. Based on the premises of Neues Bauen, the minimisation of excavation costs by staggering the architectural volumes on inclined terrain had already been an important criterion in housing development prior to the Second World War. Thus, for example, the Neubühl housing estate (Haefeli, Moser, Steiger, Roth, Artaria) or the GWAD housing estate (Fischli) – both of them built during economic crises (the Great Depression and the Second World War, respectively) – were executed as stepped ribbon developments on hillsides with the aim of keeping excavation costs as low as possible.

13. Erwin Mühlestein's plans for a terraced housing development in Orselina based on standardised building elements were featured in the journal *Bauen + Wohnen* in 1964. The architect referred to the fact that 'the whole architectural complex can be constructed for significantly less than traditionally built houses' ('die ganze Baugruppe wesentlich billiger zu stehen kommen wird als Häuser in traditioneller Bauweise.' Erwin Mühlestein, 'Terrassensiedlung in Orselina ob Locarno', *Bauen + Wohnen* 18, no. 4, 1964, 155–8, here 158). Nevertheless, photographs of the building site in the journal *L'Architecture d'Aujourd'hui* from around

1965 document the construction work being executed in cast-in-situ concrete. André Bloc, 'Suisse', *L'Architecture d'Aujourd'hui* 35, no. 121 (June-July 1965), 20. As late as 1977 Mühlestein was obliged to admit in the journal *Werk-Archithese* that participatory and adaptable terraced developments did '(not) yet' exist, and concluded: 'They exist, at best, on paper, as theoretical entities … whose realisation today is stymied by factors other than technical capability' ('Sie existieren bestenfalls als papierene, theoretische Gebilde […], deren Verwirklichung heute andere als technische Hindernisse im Wege stehen.' Erwin Mühlestein, 'Partizipative Siedlungsstrukturen', *Werk-Archithese* 64, no. 11/12, 1977, 52–4, here 52).

[14] 'Die Idee der Demokratisierung der Planung durch Bewohnermitsprache erweist sich als Demokratie für diejenigen, die sie zahlen können. Flexible Strukturen schaffen also nicht automatisch mehr Gerechtigkeit, sie können sie nur aufnehmen' (Benedikt Loderer, 'Alte Wahrheiten in neuer Lage', *Hochparterre* 5, no. 10, 1992, 61–3, here 63).

[15] 'Die Sensation, von der Wohnung ebenerdig in einen bergenden Kellerraum zu gelangen, ist sicher eine ebensolche Befriedigung eines Urgefühls des Bergbewohners wie etwa ein vorspringendes oder überhängendes, taubenschlagähnliches Aussichtsfenster.' (Lucius Burckhardt and Urs Beutler, *Terrassenhäuser*. Werk-Buch vol. 3, Winterthur: Werk, 1968, 3).

[16] A horizontal alignment was germane to all of Wright's works but was expressed in its most spectacular form in Fallingwater. The concrete parapets in Stucky's terraced housing projects are inspired both aesthetically and materially by the rooftop terraces of the Suntop Homes.

[17] 'Fassadenrenegate' (Scherer, 'Terrassenbauten', see note 5, 205).

[18] 'Fortschritt und Wohlstand' 'als Werk von Väter, Brüder und Söhne der Stolz der gesamten Bevölkerung' (Christoph Allenspach, *Architektur in der Schweiz: Bauen im 19. und 20. Jahrhundert*, 2nd updated ed., Zürich: Pro Helvetia, 2002, 99).

[19] 'Terrassenhaus der Gegenwart' '"Fassadenhaus" der Vergangenheit' (Lucius Burckhardt, 'Das Terrassenhaus – Eine Hausform für die Schweiz?', in Burckhardt and Beutler, *Terrassenhäuser*, see note 15, 7).

[20] See Adolf Max Vogt, Ulrike Jehle-Schulte Strathaus, and Bruno Reichlin, *Architektur 1940–1980* (Frankfurt: Ullstein, 1980), 27–34.

[21] 'Stufung, Stapelung oder Drehung' 'eine weitverbreitete, neue Auffassung des Räumlichen' 'Art Gemeingut'; 'möglicherweise ein Ausdruck der veränderten gesellschaftlichen Situation ist, einer demokratisierten Lebensform…' (Friedrich Achleitner, 'Extreme, Moden, Tabus', in *Die Architekturabteilung der Eidgenössischen Technischen Hochschule Zürich, 1957–1968*, Zürich: ETH Architekturabteilung, 1970, 8–10, here 8).

[22] 'Demokratischen Grundgedanken' (Romano Diem, 'Stockwerkeigentum – pragmatisch, aber nicht immer frei von Problemen', *Wohnwirtschaft HEV Aargau*, no. 10, 2006, 10–11, here 10).

[23] The reintroduction of single-storey owner occupancies was prompted by rising land prices and shrinking investment opportunities in the real estate market, intended to also offer private individuals new perspectives in planning their pension arrangements.

[24] See Hans Ulrich Scherer, 'Beispiel England', *Werk* 53, no. 6 (1966), 210–11.

[25] Early examples are the terraced holiday housing complex Pineta di Arenzano (1958–1965) by Ignazio Gardella in Arenzano to the west of Genoa and the holiday home complex Torre del Mare (1957) by Mario Galvagni and his Swiss colleague Carlo Fellenberg in Bergeggi. Further residential developments appeared along the coast in places such as Spotorno or Varazze. The undoubtedly most famous French example of a free-standing terraced housing project are the pyramid-shaped buildings by architect Jean Balladur, erected from 1963 onwards (until 1984) in the tourist spot La Grande-Motte. See, for example, Martin Feiersinger and Werner Feiersinger, *Italo Modern: Architektur in Oberitalien 1946–1976* (Wien: Springer, 2012), 124; Benedikt Huber, 'Architektur des Zufalls', *Werk* 50, no. 7 (1963), 264–71, here 269.

[26] See Bloc, 'Suisse' (see note 13). The national Swiss report in the German journal *Neue Heimat* emphasised the dominance of this building typology, whereby geographical and topographical shortcomings were identified as the supposed driving forces behind this development. See Hansdietmar Klug, 'Schweizer Terrassenhäuser – Architekten auf neuen Wegen', *Neue Heimat: Monatszeitschrift für neuzeitlichen Wohnungsbau* 14, (1967), 28–41. At the beginning of the 1960s, numerous interested foreign parties (such as the Constance municipal council, student groups from

Stuttgart, Darmstadt and Delft, but also architects and sociologists such as Egon Eiermann or Ulrich Conrads) took part in so-called 'information tours' to visit the projects, including those by Fritz Stucky, Claude Paillard, or Hans Ulrich Scherer. The mediating role of promoting these Swiss artefacts abroad was assumed not only by the Federation of Swiss Architects (BSA/FAS), the Swiss Society of Engineers and Architects (SIA) or Pro Helvetia Foundation, but also the ETH Professor Werner Max Moser. See Werner Luz, 'Endgültiges Reiseprogramm der Besichtigungsreise des Konstanzer Gemeinderates', 9 June 1965; BSA/Bund Schweizer Architekten, 'Studentengruppe Prof. E. Neufert', 13 February 1962; Werner Max Moser, 'Besuch der Stuttgarter Studenten', 13 February 1962 (gta Archiv Zurich ETH, Nachlass Claude Paillard, Sig. 181-091.2/2).

[27] Asked in an interview in the journal *Modernes Bauen* what kind of people chose 'to live in terraced hillside housing', a Park Immobilien AG representative responded: 'They are people from intellectually challenging professions who are less rooted in "plain middle-class" traditions and who are open-minded about architectural innovations' ('Es sind Leute mit geistig anspruchsvollen Berufen, die wenig der "gutbürgerlichen" Tradition verwurzelt sind und Neuerungen in der Architektur aufgeschlossen gegenüberstehen.' 'Terrassensiedlung Brüggliacher in Oberrohrdorf', *Modernes Bauen* 14, no. 1, 1969, 7–10, here 7). Roman Brunner from the Historic Building Conservation Office Zug was similarly quoted in a property development magazine as follows: 'Back then the futuristic construction type was considered unusual. Terraced hillside housing targeted open-minded people who were searching for novel densified housing forms beyond the model of the single-family house' ('Damals galt die futuristisch wirkende Bauweise als ungewohnt. Die Terrassenhäuser hätten sich an aufgeschlossene Menschen gerichtet, die nach neuartigen verdichteten Wohnformen jenseits des Einfamilienhauses gesucht hätten.' David Strohm, 'Die Familienbühne', *Residence: Das Magazin für Wohnen und Immobilien*, 2015, 20). The sales brochures of the time deliberately advertised the attractiveness of terraced hillside housing by drawing attention to the tax reductions in the respective municipalities. See Uto Wohnbau AG, 'Uto baut Terrassenhäuser Chilacher II Uitikon a/Albis' (1969) (ETH Bibliothek, ORL-Archiv, Conv. 661); Park Immobilien AG, 'Terrassensiedlung Brüggliacher Oberrohrdorf/Baden' (1967) (gta Archiv Zurich ETH, Nachlass Hans Ulrich Scherer).

[28] In the early 1970s two books appeared that focused on the transformation of the Swiss landscape, albeit from completely different perspectives. In his children's book Jörg Müller presented the various stages of developments over a period of many years, subtly criticising the loss of identity that the country had been subjected to through the breakneck pace of building activity. Jörg Müller, *Alle Jahre wieder saust der Presslufthammer nieder, oder Die Veränderung der Landschaft* (Aarau: Sauerländer AG, 1973). Peter Keller explained the existing state of the landscape, encapsulated in numerous photographs of buildings and urban vignettes, as evidence of the environmental destruction caused by building. Rolf Keller, *Bauen als Umweltzerstörung: Alarmbilder einer Un-Architektur der Gegenwart* (Zürich: Artemis, 1973).

[29] Matter offered a 'special perspective on things' ('besondere Sicht auf die Dinge') in the architectural journals of his flatmate in which the artist confronted 'what is being newly developed in building' ('was im Bauen neu entwickelt wurde'. Stephan Kunz, ed., *Ziegelrain '67–'75*, Aarau: Aargauer Kunsthaus, 2006, 15). The works, which revealed his critical stance 'vis-à-vis contemporary architecture and urban sprawl' ('gegenüber zeitgenössischer Architektur und Zersiedelung'. Annelise Zwez, 'Max Matter', 1998/2017, in *SIKART Lexikon zur Kunst in der Schweiz* http://www.sikart.ch/KuenstlerInnen.aspx?id=4001293&lng=xx, accessed 19 May 2021), were exhibited in December 1969 in the ETH Zurich's Globus-Provisorium (a repurposed temporary department store building) under the title 'Malerei als Architekturkritik' – a criticism that was 'in Max Matter's case always a social critique' ('bei Max Matter immer auch Gesellschaftskritik'. Gruppe Agitation, 'Uitikon: Eine Oase der oberen Zehntausend', *Agitation: Aktions-Zeitschrift der fortschrittlichen Arbeiter, Schüler und Studenten – FASS* 2, no. 9, 1970, 4–7, here 7).

[30] Lucius Burckhard noted in the 1968 book *Terrassenhäuser*: 'But unfortunately reality shows that the majority of these objects

will simply be tenement blocks tilted onto the hillside, because the speculators have eagerly recognised their chance' ('Aber leider zeigt die Wirklichkeit, daß die Mehrzahl dieser Gebilde lediglich gegen den Hang gekippte Mietskasernen sein werden. Denn die Spekulation hat rasch ihre Chance begriffen') (Burckhardt and Beutler, *Terrassenhäuser*, see note 15, 7). This statement originated in an article about Swiss terraced hillside housing first published in French in 1965. See Lucius Burckhardt, 'Les habitations en terrasse', *L'Architecture d'Aujourd'hui* 35, no. 121 (June-July 1965), 14. The architectural office Atelier 5 revived Burckhardt's analogy in the context of readdressing this housing typology in the 1970s and 1980s. See Atelier 5, 'Oftringen und Dahlerau (D): Projekte für Hangbebauungen', *Werk* 60, no. 11 (1973), 1383–4; A[natole] d[u] F[resne] and R[alph] G[entner], 'Gruppenhokuspokus', *Werk, Bauen + Wohnen* 67, no. 7/8 (1980), 26–7.

[31] See Scherer, 'Terrassenbauten' (see note 5), 202. Three years later Erwin Mühlestein likewise complained that a lot of planning applications that 'failed' to match 'the model' were being rejected by building authorities and rarely received bank financing, making the building projects rich pickings for the speculative business practices of 'finance companies' whose main purpose was to develop the increasingly scarce hillside building land 'at a profit'. Erwin Mühlestein, 'Zur Entwicklung des terrassierten Bauens', *Modernes Bauen* 14, no. 1 (1969), 5–6, here 6.

[32] See Willi Strickler et al., 'Wohnbebauung in Hanglagen: Forschungsbericht im Auftrag des ORL-Institutes ETH Zürich' (1969); Heinrich Huber et al., 'Empfehlungen für die Beurteilung, Zonung und Überbauung von Hanglagen, Berichte zur Orts-, Regional- und Landesplanung no. 34' (Zürich: Institut für Orts-, Regional- und Landesplanung, 1976).

[33] Numerous newspaper reports commented on the 'bad reputation' ('schlechten Ruf') of hillside developments, which were considered to be 'ugly and unfavourable in terms of energy consumption' ('als hässlich und energetisch ungünstig'). Larger-scale building projects were thought to be 'massive intrusions into the vineyards' ('massiver Eingriff in den Rebberg'), whereby complaints were loud not only about stylistic 'gimmickries' ('Spielereien') but repeatedly about the 'stereotypical' ('stereotyp wirkende') appearance of the realisation, 'lacking any allure' ('ohne Ausstrahlung') and 'lacking any attention to detail' ('ohne grosses Engagement fürs Detail'). A 2017 initiative to legally ban terraced hillside housing in the municipality of Ennetbaden was welcomed, amongst others, by 'star architect' Mario Botta. See Benjamin Gygax, 'Ganz oben auf dem Sonnendeck', *Sonntagszeitung*, 23 February 2013, business section, 59; Ulrich Scheibler, 'Nicht immer glücklich am Hang gebaut', *Der Landbote: Tagblatt von Winterthur und Umgebung*, 20 January 2007; Pirmin Kramer, 'Stararchitekt Mario Botta befürwortet das Verbot für Terrassenhäuser', *Aargauer Zeitung*, 26 March 2017, local Ennetbaden section.

The Swiss Principle of *Béton Brut*: 'Betonkonstruktion'

A Debate between Theory and Practice, 1940s–1960s

Silvia Groaz

In the context of the affirmation of *béton brut*, discovered during the construction of the Unité d'habitation in Marseille, Switzerland's cultural position is emblematic. Whilst in international debates this technique is often characterized by theoretical and ideological accents (converging in the definition of New Brutalism and International Brutalist Style), in Switzerland, exposed concrete takes on a particular meaning, emancipated from the desire to investigate its intrinsic theoretical and artistic concepts, and devoid of any search for decorative textures. Instead, it is the engineering tradition that confers to concrete a technical and scientific vision which admits a certain degree of imperfection in its implementation, even if confined within the limits of material economy or construction site logic. Exposed concrete, informed by the principles of the engineering tradition, is marked in the Swiss culture of the 1950s by a 'rational' character and becomes the pretext to assert the refusal of any formal or intellectual designations other than that of the most radical construction.

Exposed Concrete, or the Myth of Perfection

The world conflicts of the twentieth century generated cultural isolation and important economic restrictions in Switzerland. The debates focusing on the sentimentalism of Heimatstil and the functionalism of Neues Bauen are contaminated by international research striving for an increasingly 'humanist' and 'plastic' architecture.[1] These different currents diverge and intertwine as much in debates as in built works, and it was only at the beginning of the 1960s that the affirmation of trends capable of undermining the technicality originating from the 1920s became visible.

Precisely because of its neutrality during the Second World War, Switzerland (in addition to Scandinavian nations) is one of the first countries to which critics and architects turn in search of examples of reconstruction and pragmatic solutions for a simple and economic architecture. The common question faced by Western architectural culture on the fate of the Modern Movement – its precepts and materials, and its typological and urban solutions – can only increase interest

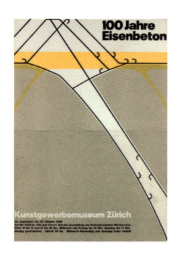

1. Poster by Richard Paul Lohse for the exhibition '100 Jahre Eisenbeton' at the Kunstgewerbemuseum in Zurich, 1950.

in this 'small democracy', seen as the pioneer of a certain trend within the Modern Movement.[2] It is not the rise of a new movement that shifts the attention towards Switzerland, but a particular alchemy of influences that demonstrates a hypothetical development and synthesis of European architectural culture. The characteristic features of 'minimum of means' and 'technical perfectionism' are coloured by different European influences ranging from Perret's 'concrete-classicism' to the 'Corbusier-direction' and to the impact of Italian rationalism.[3]

In the preface to the catalogue for the *Switzerland Planning and Building* exhibition, organized in 1946 in London and then staged in various European capitals, Hans Hofmann affirmed: 'Today we think of the Modern Movement as already belonging to the past.'[4] Hofmann was a professor at the Swiss Federal Institute of Technology and had been the curator of the Swiss National Exhibition that had taken place in Zurich in 1939. What Hofmann means by 'Modern Movement' is the particular Swiss connotation of 1930s and 1940s functionalism and the obsession with the canons of utility and function, which in the Neues Bauen had dictated an 'almost invariable choice of concrete or reinforced concrete as a building material.'[5] For Hofmann, 'functionalism', 'technical style', and 'concrete style' become synonyms. In the same way, the intrinsic alliance between an 'appropriate use of material', a certain 'style', and the search for a 'painstaking execution' turns into a crucial paradigm for the critical reception of exposed concrete in the second post-war period, remaining anchored to a vision of technical perfection, expressed by the material itself. 'Where the functional conception is projected into the external appearance, concrete is used in a manner suitable for the material', continues Hofmann, confirming the indissoluble influence of the functionalist culture that contaminates the vision of the material.[6]

However, other components – derived from a cultural dimension aimed at overcoming the simple technique – contribute to turn this trajectory of strong functionalist character into a more complex affair. Concrete takes on the appearance of a material shaped by the 'special feeling for precision, for economy, hygiene and democratic simplicity' that Max Bill attributes to Swiss architecture between the 1920s and 1940s.[7] In the malleability of reinforced concrete exemplified by Robert Maillart's structures, Bill identifies the apex of the search for a primarily cultural synthesis between an 'intensity of technical expression' and an aesthetic vision,[8] resulting in a 'beautiful fluidity' expressive of the material's nature and economy of construction, as declared by Maillart himself.[9]

The aspiration to the 'democratic simplicity' that innervates the vision of concrete finds confirmation in the particular geographical condition of a territory to be structured. It is the great tradition of infrastructural engineering that lays the foundations for a Swiss identity. Switzerland is perceived as a pioneer in its use of reinforced concrete, which appears in all its great power in the colossal dams in Wäggital and Valais, in bridges and roads, and factories and hangars, building up an imagery supported also by travelling exhibitions such as *Hundert Jahre Eisenbeton* (fig. 1), organized in 1950. These engineering works demonstrate a daring use of reinforced concrete and reveal its potential impact on form. This is at the expense of architecture, which expresses, according to the organisers, more conventional traits, of which only the works of Karl Moser constitute an exception in the Swiss territory.[10]

Despite the quest to overcome the abstraction of Neues Bauen, in the early 1950s, concrete is still made 'socially acceptable', as it is hidden by layers of plaster or other materials, according to what Alfred Roth regretfully calls an 'Angst vor der Fläche', or 'fear of the surface', intended as visible material.[11] However, in the slow process of a desired renunciation of cladding, it is not the artistic expression of the material that is sought, but a controlled and precise nature. 'Is there anything more powerful and more beautiful than the clearly precise, well-proportioned surface?' asks Roth, invoking not a compositional 'modulor' but a 'module' of construction science, or rather a scientific variable able to concretise what he defines as the 'beauty of rational construction' associated once again with Maillart's bridges, thus confirming them as an essential reference for architectural culture.[12]

The role of these 'pioneers' in the engineering use of concrete emerges as the decisive Swiss cultural trait in various international commentaries, to the point that even Louis Kahn recognizes how in Switzerland 'concrete is asserting itself as a material of beauty born of necessity and economy'.[13] The shapes of the avant-garde bridges of Maillart or the large parabolic vault of the Vevey market (1933–35) by Schobinger, Taverney, Gétaz, and the engineer Sarrasin return to the international scene in the 1950s to demonstrate how material economy and precise structural research can aspire to an architecture capable of reducing 'to rational terms that controversial structural material – reinforced concrete.'[14]

The vision informed by the 'rational' use of concrete translates into the search for a unity of material and structure, and based on a construction process that economises on framework construction, as George Everard Kidder Smith observes in his fresco on Swiss architecture, in which he notes how 'concrete is the most important structural medium.'[15] Exposed concrete, in buildings such as the institutes at the University of Bern by Otto Rudolf Salvisberg (1928–31) or the church in Zurich-Altstetten by Werner Max Moser (1939–41), demonstrate the achievement of a monolithic structure, which admits other materials only due to war-time restrictions, as observed in Dubois & Eschenmoser's Saurer factory in Arbon (1943–46): 'When the war broke out in 1939, and even this material became more and more scarce, the solid concrete building disappeared. It was replaced by the concrete frame with brick infill.'[16]

In September 1952, while the two large Swiss dams of Mauvoisin and Grande Dixence are being built, a committee of the Société suisse des ingénieurs et des architectes visits the major infrastructure works in the United States – the same that had inspired Le Corbusier to uncompromisingly embrace the *béton brut* technique.[17] The colossal concrete casting is admired for its bold aesthetic, monumental impact, and the care and precision of its surface – 'very meticulous and smooth, but without cladding'.[18] The use of exposed concrete for infrastructure turns the material into a synonym for Swiss engineering and technological progress. The dams appear as an example in this sense, and are among the rare works listed by Max Frisch to convincingly demonstrate the ability to redeem, through a quest for monumentality, a certain nostalgia and intimacy which otherwise would render Swiss architectural culture 'serious, so serious', confined within an obsession for an 'exclusively material perfection', stuck in an 'over-proliferation of detail' until it fades into 'monotony'.[19]

The emancipation from a restricted vision focused on details is for Frisch not achieved through the experimentation of new forms or materials, but through the territorial planning envisaged in the radical proposal of a satellite city that can accommodate up to 15,000 inhabitants – generated by rapid mobility and developed upwards thanks to prefabrication systems that he will describe in 1954 together with Lucius Burckhardt in the book *Achtung: Die Schweiz*, published in 1955.[20] The 'moderation', 'compromise', and 'cabinetmaking architecture' that Frisch attributes to the Swiss culture of the 1950s are the cultural legacies preventing the affirmation of a 'radical' vision.

The Swiss Reception of Le Corbusier's *Béton Brut*

A profound renovation of Swiss architecture takes place concurrently with Le Corbusier's most important works in the second post-war period, capable of raising decisive questions on the implications of concrete – its form, structural development, and finishing. The concerns raised by Swiss architects and critics are reported in the *Œuvre complète*, in which Le Corbusier accuses his fellow citizens being unable to grasp the pure and brutal manifestation of the material: 'How often visitors (particularly the Swiss, the Dutch and the Swedes) have said to me: "Your building is very beautiful, but how badly it has been executed".'[21]

Although the Unité is appreciated as a new model of 'habitat', in sociological and urban terms,[22] the acceptance of its materiality is hampered by the search for an obsessive perfection. As Hans Girsberger, the Swiss publisher of the *Œuvre complète*, consciously acknowledges: 'The Swiss love a meticulous, careful execution too much to overlook certain defects and to be able to measure the "beauté du béton brut" as Corbusier sees it.'[23]

Even when, at the end of the 1950s, *béton brut* finds acceptance as a successful technique (now considered Le Corbusier's 'signature'[24]), its conception still appears to be subjugated to the functionalist myth of the Neues Bauen. This can be observed in the case of the administrative building of the Mutuelle Vaudoise Accidents (1952–56) in Lausanne by Jean Tschumi, in which the perfectly controlled exposed concrete transmits a feeling of structural lightness.[25] The *noblesse* of the *béton brut* is expressed by Tschumi through the precise execution of the sharp edges and through the careful composition of the compound, with white cement and light Vaulion sand making it similar to limestone.[26]

It is not only the concrete finishing that raises concern, but also its plasticity of form, as in the case of the Ronchamp chapel. Here Roth identifies the genesis of a 'form-Anarchism' opposed to the certainty of the skeleton of Miesian absolutism, and the symptomatic outcome of a deviation from the founding principles crystallized in the 'five points'.[27] Beyond its material and crafted components, Ronchamp is read by the editorial staff of *Bauen + Wohnen* as the apex of the curve's formal potential, whose origin is once again traced into the purity of the surface of the thin concrete shells, derived from a profound reflection on material economy and structural efficiency.[28]

The tendency to see in *béton brut* the traits of 'unique' workmanship and the values of a 'noble' technique[29] – adapted in the name of perfection – evolves at the end of the 1950s into a different attitude, which leads to an excess of constructive and logical factors. The combination of concrete's 'rational' component – as described by Roth – and the Corbusian vision, generates a new form of *béton brut*, derived from the tension between construction site economy and perfection, capable of admitting a certain degree of controlled roughness.

Béton brut, subordinated to a pragmatic logic, is reflected in the proposals of Atelier 5 and in particular in Flamatt 1 and in the Siedlung Halen, presented for the first time on the occasion of the exhibition *Elf Architekten stellen aus* organised by the Bernese gallery Klipstein & Co in March 1956.[30] The works on display testify to the birth of a new sensibility that goes beyond perfectionism and measured, controlled detail.[31] This new attitude to imperfection is supported by some critics, who free the interpretation of *béton brut* from an obsession with technical and economic principles – consolidated in the general debate. Critical reception of concrete opens up to an artistic vision, as demonstrated by Silvia Kruger, who finds in the strong and primordial character of matter the nineteenth-century myth of Michelangelo's *non finito*.[32]

The admission of a certain degree of imperfection in the concrete finishing is, however, devoid of the conceptual declinations implicit in Le Corbusier's experiments on 'unexpected' and 'unintended' effects. Instead, *béton brut* becomes an instrument through which humanistic components can be investigated; the surface, marked by 'judicious' proportions and finally stripped of its 'expensive' cladding reveals the 'nobility' of the material. As Dolf Schnebli observes in regard to Le Corbusier's works in Chandigarh: 'As we contemplate Le Corbusier's constructions, we realize to what extent concrete loses its force of expression when covered in all kinds of costly cladding, as is the case for most construction in Switzerland.'[33] The 'rational' meaning of concrete thus evolves from the vision linked to Roth's abstract surface to an invitation to a new construction site economy. 'It would be as absurd', explains Schnebli, 'to criticize the imperfections in the concrete of these constructions as to be surprised by unevenness in the rough-stone surface of a masonry wall.'[34]

The concepts Le Corbusier associated with the ability of concrete to become a transcription of a sometimes unwieldy and crude gesture – sublimating the defects intrinsic to *béton brut*'s 'nobility' – are interpreted by Swiss culture in a technical process oriented to economic and expressive simplicity. Indeed, *béton brut* becomes the expression of an extreme form of construction, as in the case of George Brera's Villa Maier in Cologny, where the 'authentic' technique of *béton brut* is functional to the graphic transcription of the different structural behaviour of the load-bearing and infill walls.[35]

Construction and Form or Ethics and Aesthetics?

The theoretical issues present in international debates about the affirmation of exposed concrete remain marginal in Swiss publications. Only from 1958, when Franz Füeg becomes editor of the magazine *Bauen + Wohnen*, do various critical positions begin to take shape, which measure, on the one hand, the masters' legacy and the essence of 'modern architecture', and, on the other hand, the question of form and construction.

The desire of Swiss critics to not attribute – to the vision of concrete – values defined in the contemporary debate is reflected in a striking silence on the definition of New Brutalism, which is occasionally employed only to confirm the distance from an intellectual discourse and the total rejection of any labels. The definition of New Brutalism can only lead to an exclusively superficial and formal interpretation of architecture according to Füeg: 'Stock phrases and catch-words are insidious.'[36] Swiss critics agree in seeing the definition of New Brutalism as an obstacle for critical objectivity. 'Unfortunately, the word "brutalism" which designates a direction in architecture, is quite literary and produces emotions that complicate objective appreciation,' is *Bauen + Wohnen*'s comment on the issue on New Brutalism by the Italian review *Zodiac*, defined not without perplexity as 'an architecture magazine for which words are more important than images'.[37] When the critics – all coming from a pro-Germanic epicentre, such as Benedikt Huber – accept the category of New Brutalism, the latter is used to describe what is already consolidated in the international debate, and therefore confined to the British context and the works of Le Corbusier and Vittoriano Viganò. Indeed, the definition of New Brutalism is not extended to include some Swiss buildings with a similar appearance, also characterized by the use of the 'untreated, massive, unfinished' concrete.[38] The worn-out feeling of the style that Huber ascribes to the Swiss architectural culture of the 1960s explains the reason why the definition of New Brutalism is carefully avoided, even if, when discussing the works of Walter Förderer, Ernst Gisel, Lorenz Moser, Werner Gantenbein, and Wolfgang Behles, parallels are drawn with themes already ascribed to the definition of New Brutalism – such as *tachisme* and Action Painting, or the admission of the category of chance and the irregularity of form.[39]

The increasingly strong reference to Le Corbusier's work – identifiable in Jacques Schader's Kantonsschule in Zurich (1954–60) or in Fritz Haller's Schulhaus Wasgenring in Basel (1953–55), and in the Siedlung Halen of Atelier 5 (1955–61) – is recognised by the German critic Jürgen Joedicke in *Bauen + Wohnen* as a Swiss stance against the inevitability of technique and the predestination of form, demonstrated through structural accentuation and the building's inclusion in the urban tissue. Joedicke's willingness to not align Swiss examples to the international experiences of New Brutalism seems justified by a particular Swiss attitude: 'The Helvetic mentality is such that it only welcomes the unusual with caution.'[40]

When in 1963 editorial staff at *Bauen + Wohnen* decide to republish Le Corbusier's position against the definition of New Brutalism, their choice is symptomatic of the rejection of its intellectual elaborations: '"Brutaliste" is an Anglicism. Like "versatile", which in English means many-sided capacity, wealth. In French, however, "versatile"' (unreliable) has a highly pejorative meaning. I have employed rough concrete, "béton brut" (rough = brut). The outcome is a hundred-percent fidelity to the material, a perfect precision in casting, a building material that cannot lie [...] The rough concrete says: I am concrete!'[41]

Once again the review *Bauen + Wohnen*, despite an initial lack of interest in the issue of New Brutalism, becomes, thanks to Joedicke's contribution, a protagonist and vehicle for the affirmation of that definition at an international level. Indeed, in November 1964, the review publishes a monograph issue entitled *Brutalismus in der Architektur*[42] (fig. 2). This decisive change is consequent to the appointment to the editorial staff of Joedicke, who, since November 1962, has been in contact with Reyner Banham about the publication of the book *New Brutalism: Ethic or Aesthetic?*[43] The monograph on the theme of New Brutalism is conceived by Joedicke as an anticipation of Banham's book, which outlines a decisive balance on the origins and current developments of New Brutalism and its international manifestations in the United States, England, Germany, and the Netherlands (fig. 3). Surprisingly, no Swiss case is included in the examples described, although Joedicke had already compiled a list of buildings to illustrate Banham's book, including works by Atelier 5, Förderer, Otto, and Zwimpfer.

In Banham's book, the Swiss examples play a crucial role in documenting the international agenda and the extension of New Brutalism, demonstrating its complexity and aporia. Banham identifies in the 'Swiss school' one of the cores of the Brutalist style, which finds its epicentre in the works of Schnebli, Förderer, Otto, Zwimpfer, and Atelier 5. It is precisely in the Swiss school that Banham sees the reiteration of Corbusian figures that lead to the question of style, from which his major 'disappointments' derive: the academic declination of New Brutalism and the reduction of the phenomenon's complexity to 'just an affair of exposed concrete.'[44]

The Swiss school therefore ends up representing, according to Banham, the 'excesses' of the Brutalist style in the most exasperated forms, ranging from the 'mannerism' of the Haus in Rothrist and the factory in Thun (both by Atelier 5) to Schnebli's 'eclectic and historical approach' and an 'extremism' recognised in Förderer, Otto, and Zwimpfer's school in Aesch, guilty of reducing architecture to a play of sculptural forms.[45]

The culmination of the Brutalist-style phenomenon, defined by Banham as a 'high-period of concrete Brutalism', is materialized in the 'habitat' of the Siedlung Halen, which shows how an ethical impulse can come to life again in the 'brut' and 'heroic' aesthetics of exposed concrete. The photograph taken by Albert Winkler of the Siedlung Halen rising above the trees, is selected by Joedicke – according to Banham's critical reading – for the cover of the book *The New Brutalism: Ethic or Aesthetic?* (fig. 4) Although in the Siedlung Halen Joedicke identifies a possible synthesis between ethical impulses and aesthetic factors – aiming to solve the dilemma posed by Banham in the book subtitle – for Banham, instead, the cover 'does not seem to typify the content of the

2. Cover of *Bauen + Wohnen*'s monograph issue on Brutalism, November 1964.

3. Jürgen Joedicke, advertisement for the book *Brutalismus in der Architecktur* in *Das Werk*, September 1966.

4. Cover of Reyner Banham's book *Brutalismus in der Architektur*, 1966.

5. Cover of Walter Häberli's book, *Beton, Konstruktion und Form*, 1966.

book.'[46] Banham's perplexities show that his vision of New Brutalism diverges from the example of the Swiss school, in which he sees the end of a phenomenon consumed in a triumph of styles, redeemable only through a technological accentuation of the mechanisms of the project.

The response of Atelier 5 members is indicative of a typically Swiss attitude of resistance to any style category. Indeed, when the publishing house Krämer Verlag requested their photos of the Siedlung Halen, they replied: 'As for the New Brutalism book, we cannot decide to participate. Hence, I would like to ask you to take our buildings off the list. In our works, we hardly ever cared about the idea of Brutalism. Even if some buildings may suggest it, the reasons are elsewhere, e.g., in limited building costs that dictate the choice of material.'[47]

Following the forced inclusion in the historiographic construction of Brutalism, Atelier 5 outline their position in a typescript document entitled *Sichtbeton*, which demonstrates how exposed concrete, beyond any style, corresponds to a radicalism linked to pure construction, confirming once again the concept of rationalism permeating the matter: 'The terms beauty and clarity are related to one another. A condition for clarity in building is visibility of construction. To judge whether a house is good or bad, you want to know how it is made. Exposed concrete is therefore not the name for a special surface treatment, but is visible concrete construction.'[48] In the document, the reasoning of Atelier 5 on monolithism, on the value of traces of casting phases and the transformation of the surface over time, and on the liquid nature of the material, which can be moulded at will, converge into a vision constantly renewed within the limits of an strictly economic principle: 'The restrictions come from economy: with as little material and formwork as simple as possible.'[49]

Concurrently with the release of *The New Brutalism: Ethic or Aesthetic?* a manual is published in Zurich, which can be considered the Swiss antithesis to Banham's book. Written in 1966 by engineer Walter Häberli, *Beton, Konstruktion und Form* becomes the herald of a vision of concrete restored to its essential foundations of construction and form, with its techniques and components (fig. 5). Concrete is seen as a material derived from an engineering science attentive to its expressive potential and formal issues, in order to redeem the material from the conceptual and ideological structures pervading it.[50] *Beton, Konstruktion und Form* confirms a cultural vision of exposed concrete, devoid of any issues related to style, anchored instead in construction site practices. In the name of a 'Sichtbetonkult',[51] at the end of the 1960s, concrete is still there to demonstrate how – as summarized by Stanislaus von Moos and Jul Bachmann – 'the force of present Swiss architecture lies in its close combat with reality, rather than the theoretical field, in technical and construction experience rather than creative speculation and imaginative outlooks.'[52]

Notes

1. Alfred Roth, 'Zeitgemäße Architekturbetrachtungen. Mit Besonderer Berücksichtigung der Schweizerischen Situation', *Werk* 38, no. 3 (1951), 65–76.
2. Alfred Roth, *La Nouvelle Architecture: présentée en 20 exemples = Die Neue Architektur = The New Architecture* (Erlenbach-Zürich: Les Éditions d'Architecture, 1946), 8.
3. John Summerson, 'Swiss Architecture in London', *The Listener*, 26 September 1946, 412–3.
4. Hans Hofmann, 'Thoughts on Contemporary Architecture in Switzerland', *Switzerland Planning and Building Exhibition* (Zürich: Orell Füssli, Arts graphiques SA, 1946), 19–23. Repr. 'Wo Steht die Schweizerische Architektur Heute?', *Schweizerische Bauzeitung* 65, no. 13 (1947), 166–70.
5. Ibid., 20.
6. Ibid.
7. Max Bill, 'Introduction', in *Moderne Schweizer Architektur: 1925–1945 = Architecture moderne suisse = Modern Swiss Architecture* (Basel: Verlag Karl Werner, 1949).
8. Max Bill, *Robert Maillart* (Erlenbach-Zürich: Verlag für Architektur, 1949). See, in particular, the chapter 'Der Künstlerische Ausdruck der Konstruktion', 27–30.
9. Robert Maillart, 'Aktuelle Fragen des Eisenbetonbaues. Gestaltung des Eisenbetons', *Schweizerische Bauzeitung* 111, no. 1 (1938), 1–4; reproduced in Max Bill, *Robert Maillard* (see note 8), 15–6.
10. Berchtold von Grünigen, 'Vorwort', in *Hundert Jahre Eisenbeton,* exhib. cat. (Basel: Gewerbemuseum of Basel, 19 March–30 April 1950), 1–2.
11. Roth, 'Zeitgemäße Architekturbetrachtungen' (see note 1), 74.
12. 'Gibt es etwas Kraftgespannteres und Schöneres als die klar umrissene, wohl proportionierte Fläche?' (Ibid., 75).
13. See Louis Kahn, *Preliminary Report on Housing in Israel*, 7 June 1949, cited in Roberto Gargiani, *Louis I. Kahn: Exposed Concrete and Hollow Stones, 1949–1959* (Lausanne: EPFL Press, 2014), 24.
14. 'Swiss Architecture', *The Architect and Building News*, 20 September 1946, 170–72, here 172. See also 'Not to Miss', *The Architect's Journal*, 26 September 1946; Edward Passmore, 'Swiss Architecture', *The Builder*, 27 September 1946; 'Swiss Architecture Exhibition', *National Builder*, October 1946.
15. George Everard Kidder Smith, *Switzerland Builds: Its Native and Modern Architecture* (New York: Bonnier, 1950), 86.
16. Ibid.
17. Mardges Bacon, 'Le Corbusier and Postwar America: The TVA and Béton Brut', *Journal of the Society of Architectural Historians* 74, no. 1 (March 2015), 13–40.
18. 'Voyage d'étude de la S.I.A. aux États-Unis, du 20 août au 14 septembre 1952', *Bulletin d'information de la Société Suisse des Ingénieurs et des Architectes* 79, no. 3 (June 1953), 42–5 (supplément à *Bulletin technique de la Suisse romande* 79, no. 13, 1953).
19. Max Frisch, 'Cum Grano Salis: eine Kleine Glosse zur Schweizerischen Architektur', *Werk* 40, no. 10 (1953), 325–9.
20. Lucius Burckhardt, Max Frisch, and Markus Kutter, *Achtung: Die Schweiz. Ein Gespräch über unsere Lage und ein Vorschlag zur Tat*. Basler politische Schriften vol. 2 (Basel: Verlag Karl Werner, 1955).
21. Le Corbusier, *Le Corbusier. Œuvre complète 1946-1952, vol. 5* (Zürich: Éditions Girsberger, 1953), 191.
22. Alfred Roth, 'Der Wohnbau "Unité d'Habitation" in Marseille', *Werk* 41, no. 1 (1954), 20–4.
23. 'Der Schweizer liebt allzusehr eine gepflegte, sorgfaltige Ausführung, um über gewisse Mange! hinwegzusehen und die "beauté du béton brut", so wie Corbusier sie sieht, geniessen zu konnen.' (Hans Girsberger, 'Zum Erscheinen des 7. und Letzten Bandes des Gesamtwerkes von Le Corbusier', *Schweizerische Bauzeitung* 84, no. 35, 1966, 625–7, here 627).
24. 'Nef à trois Proues, triomphe du verre et du béton armé. Le Palais de l'Unesco affirme dans le site le plus classique de Paris l'audace des bâtisseurs modernes', *Habitation* 30, no. 1 (1958), 22–3.
25. 'Bâtiment administratif de la Mutuelle Vaudoise Accidents, Lausanne', *Werk* 44, no. 3 (1957), 82–7.
26. Ibid.
27. Alfred Roth, 'Die Wallfahrtskapelle in Ronchamp', *Werk* 42, no. 12 (1955), 375–85.
28. 'Am Rande. Machine und Architektur', *Bauen + Wohnen* 13, no. 9 (1959), 297.
29. Maurer Fritz, 'Das Dominikanerkloster "La Tourette"', *Werk* 47, no. 6 (1960), 190–5.
30. The participants in the exhibition, together with Atelier 5, are Alfred Gysin, Niklaus Morgenthaler, Werner Peterhans, Edwin Rausser, Rolf Siebold, and Rudolf Werder.

Elf Architekten stellen aus (Bern: Gutekunst & Klipstein, 1956); 'Ausstellungen', *Bauen + Wohnen* 10, no. 5 (1956), 121.

[31] Peter F. Althaus, 'Erinnerungen an die Anfangszeit des Ateliers 5 und das Projekt Halen', *Werk, Bauen + Wohnen* 67, no. 7/8 (August 1980), 16–7.

[32] Silvia Kugler, 'Le Corbusier, "non finito" Architekt?', *Kulturelle Monatsschrift* 19, no. 4 (1959), 55–6.

[33] 'En contemplant les constructions de Le Corbusier, on se rend compte à quel point le béton perd de sa vigueur d'expression quand on le recouvre de toutes espèces de revêtements coûteux, comme c'est le cas pour la plupart des constructions en Suisse' (Dolf Schnebli, *Bulletin du ciment* 28/29, no. 12, 1960, 1–10, here 8).

[34] 'Il serait aussi absurde de critiquer les imperfections du béton de ces constructions que de s'étonner des inégalités de la surface d'une maçonnerie en moellons bruts' (ibid., 7).

[35] George Brera, 'Villa à Cologny, Genève', *Werk* 46, no. 12 (1959), 429–34.

[36] Franz Füeg, 'Am Rande: Kristalline Architektur', *Bauen + Wohnen* 14, no. 12 (1960), 427.

[37] 'Leider ist das Wort "brutalism", das eine Richtung der Architektur bezeichnet, recht literarisch und erzeugt Affekte, die eine objektive Würdigung erschwert'; 'Zodiac ist eine Architekturzeitschrift, bei der das Wort wichtiger ist als das Bild!' ('Buchbesprechungen', *Bauen + Wohnen* 13, no. 10, 1959, 28.) The original article is by Alison and Peter Smithson, Jane Drew, and Maxwell Fry, 'Conversation on Brutalism', *Zodiac* 4 (1959), 73–81.

[38] Benedikt Huber, 'Epigonen', *Werk* 46, no. 12 (1959), 419–22, here 420.

[39] Benedikt Huber, 'Architektur des Zufalls', *Werk* 50, no. 7 (1963), 264–71.

[40] 'Die Mentalität des Schweizers verhält sich dem Außergewöhnlichen gegenüber abwartend.' (Jürgen Joedicke, '1930-1960', *Bauen + Wohnen* 15, no. 10, 1961, 360–73, here 362).

[41] '"Brutaliste" = anglicisme. Tout comme "versatile" en anglais, signifie multiplié, abondance, richesse. En français, "versatile" est un qualificatif très dépréciatif. J'ai employé du "béton brut" (en anglais: rough concrete). Résultat: une fidélité totale, une exactitude parfaite du moulage, un matériau qui ne triche pas. [...] Le béton brut dit: je suis du béton!' ('Am Rande: 5 Fragen an Le Corbusier', *Bauen + Wohnen* 17, no. 3, 1963, 95–6, here 96 ; English translation 96; original publication 'Cinq Questions à Le Corbusier', *Zodiac*, no. 7, 1960, 50).

[42] Jürgen Joedicke, 'New Brutalism: Brutalismus in der Architektur', *Bauen + Wohnen* 18, no. 11 (1964), 421–5.

[43] Banham's book is published at the same time in German by Krämer Verlag and in English by the Architectural Press. Reyner Banham, *Brutalismus in der Architektur* (Stuttgart: Krämer Verlag, 1966).

[44] Reyner Banham, letter to Jürgen Joedicke, 5 December 1966 (Archive Krämer Verlag, Stuttgart).

[45] Banham, *Brutalismus in der Architektur* (see note 43), 90.

[46] Raymond Philp, 'Jacket for book "The New Brutalism"', letter to Nora von Mühlendahl, 25 August 1966 (Archive Krämer Verlag, Stuttgart).

[47] 'Was das Buch "Neuer Brutalismus" anbetrifft, können wir uns leider nicht entschliessen mitzumachen. Ich möchte Sie desshalb bitten, unsere Bauten von der Liste zu streichen. In unseren Arbeiten haben wir kaum jemals den Gedanken des Brutalismus gepflegt. Wenn einzelne Bauten den Anschein erwecken, so liegen die Ursachen anderswo, z.B. in beschränkten Baukosten die die Materialwahl diktiert.' (Rolf Hesterberg, letter to Heinz Krehl, 18 December 1964, Archive Krämer Verlag, Stuttgart).

[48] 'Eine Bedingung für Klarheit im Bauen ist Sichtbarkeit der Konstruktion. Um zu beurteilen, ob ein Haus gut oder schlecht gemacht ist, möchte man wissen, wie es gemacht ist. Sichtbeton ist deshalb nicht der Name für eine besondere Oberflächenbehandlung, sondern heisst sichtbare Betonkonstruktion.' (Atelier 5, *Sichtbeton*, typewritten document, Archive Atelier 5, Bern, 19 November 1968, 1–2, here 1).

[49] 'Die Beschränkungen kommen von den Oekonomie: mit möglichst wenig Material und möglichst einfachen Schalung.' (Ibid., 2).

[50] Walter Häberli, *Beton, Konstruktion und Form* (Dietikon-Zürich: Verlag Stocker-Schmid, 1966).

[51] Friedrich Achleitner, 'Extreme, Moden, Tabus', in *Die Architekturabteilung der Eidgenössischen Technischen Hochschule Zürich, 1957–1968* (Zürich: ETH Architekturabteilung, 1970), 8–10.

[52] Jul Bachmann and Stanislaus von Moos, *New Directions in Swiss Architecture* (New York: Braziller, 1969), 14.

Gesamtschweizerische Plattenbau – Large-Panel Construction in Switzerland

The IGECO Heavy Prefabrication System in Göhner Housing Estates: Serial Production and Variations (1965–1977)

Giulia Marino

Ernst Göhner was a visionary entrepreneur. He also planned and produced numerous major housing estates in the 1960s and '70s. His goal was clear: to make an above-average quality of comfortable housing rapidly available to the middle class at affordable prices. The means to do so were equally explicit: industrialised construction based on proprietary systems of serial production. Systematic recourse to heavy prefabrication techniques thus became the pivotal feature or even veritable guarantee of the Göhner programme's commercial success. One strategic mainstay was the effective, long-term collaboration with IGECO, a manufacturer of heavy prefab systems that was based in the canton of Vaud but also active in German-speaking Switzerland – which was rare and remarkable. This 'marriage of convenience' enabled the Zurich-based property developer and general contractor to put an average of nine hundred housing units a year onto the market: no mean feat in 1960s Switzerland.

Ten years later, a new generation of architects proved to be vocal critics both of the production line of the Göhner-IGECO partnership and *grands ensembles* in general: large-scale housing estates comprised of regimented slabs and blocks, their facades lacklustre and drab owing to the repetitive deployment of mass-produced construction components – or so went the allegedly radical reappraisal. The questions raised were: How to reconcile deliberately devised strategic innovations in modern urban housing with the constraints of supplying industrialised construction sites? How to counter the impression of 'monotony' conjured by the relentless juxtaposition of large prefab panels of reinforced concrete in the *Plattenbau* type? How to enliven and lend more character to this sort of residential development? In other words, how to make these housing estates 'more human', while yet retaining the great economic and practical benefits of industrialised construction systems? Here, we examine in particular the last large-scale Göhner-IGECO undertaking, namely the Avanchet-Parc housing estate[1] in Geneva (1969–77), which was planned in response to these urgent questions. A showcase operation, firmly anchored in the culture of its day, the Geneva estate is emblematic of a period of transition. On the one hand, it demonstrated a novel approach to housing development, in which design research and technological experimentation were successfully combined at last. Yet on the other hand, this final Göhner project exposed the limitations of the heavy prefab systems in production since the 1950s, for while it is true that such systems easily satisfied the new criteria – both aesthetic and social – the requisite investment was considered far too costly, and barely justifiable once the oil crises had rocked the construction industry to its foundations.

Ernst Göhner, 'an Open-minded General Contractor'

Ernst Göhner (1900–1971) inherited his father's carpentry workshop in Altstetten between the First and Second World Wars. A shrewd businessman, he never ceased developing the small family concern, transforming it initially into a factory for standardised doors and windows and then, by acquiring other factories for secondary construction components, into an industrial group with international scope. Besides expanding this dynamic general contracting business and broadening its product range, Göhner assumed the role of property developer not only in Switzerland but also in Berlin, Munich, Ljubljana, and – a rare accomplishment for a European company at the time – in North America, too.[2]

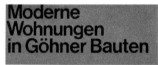

1. Advertisement for Ernst Göhner AG, 1966.

Following crucial trials with the Schindler–Göhner brand of the industrially manufactured housing unit, which was sold 'in kit form' in England from as early as 1946, Göhner massively increased investment in housing throughout the post-war period.[3] His goal was to make an above-average quality of comfortable housing rapidly available to the middle class at affordable prices. The method was simple: recourse to the most advanced industrialised construction systems would assure competitive production costs. It was a case, therefore, not only of drawing on the vast range of components produced and supplied by Göhner AG itself – from Bauwerk flooring to EGO windows – but also of deploying the proprietary heavy prefabrication system developed by IGECO (Industrie Générale pour la Construction SA), a construction company with which collaboration was to prove profitable and long-lasting. Among the joint undertakings of IGECO and (in its role either of developer or general contractor) Göhner AG number some of the most striking Swiss housing ensembles of the 1960s and '70s: the Benglen Garden City (H. Litz, 1970–74), the Siedlung at Langgrüt in Zurich (Steiger+Partner and W. M. Förderer, 1968–71), and those at Greifensee, Grafenwis, Müllerwis (H. Litz, 1967), Im Langhacher (J. Schilling, H. Litz, Schneider & Busenhardt, 1967–69) and Am Pfisterhölzli (Schneider & Busenhardt, 1969–75). Mention must be made also of the Siedlung Sonnhalde at Adlikon (Steiger+Partner and W. M. Förderer, 1966–74), which clearly presaged later experiments, and of the widely publicised Siedlung Sunnebüel at Hegnau-Volketswil (Gelpke & Düby, 1965-73). But as we will see, of all the projects realised by Göhner and IGECO, it was the Avanchet-Parc in

Geneva (P. Steiger, F. Amrhein, W. M. Förderer, 1969–77) which marked a crucial moment in the history not only of housing in Zurich but of Swiss housing construction overall, and in several respects (fig. 1).

Göhner AG and IGECO, a Long-standing Partnership

Collaboration between the Zurich-based developer and the first heavy prefabrication plant in French-speaking Switzerland, founded in 1957 by the engineer and architect César Tacchini,[4] began in the mid-1960s. By this time, IGECO had already gained an impressive portfolio: in only twelve years, the 'factory prodigy'[5] based in the small town of Étoy had built a considerable number of housing units, thereby compensating the fact that Switzerland overall was lagging behind in the prefab market.[6] The building that IGECO completed in the late 1950s for a cooperative society, Les Ailes, in the Cointrin district of Geneva (J. Duret, F. Maurice, J.-P. Dom, 1958–59) was a fêted prototype – 'one floor in a week, one unit in six minutes!' the press enthused.[7] It was followed by the En Champs-Mogins estate in Nyon (M. Lasserre, 1965–66) and the Ancien-Stand estate in Lausanne (AAA Atelier des Architectes Associés, 1961–67). The entire Ancien Stand development numbers among the most significant projects of the era, a true bench test, not least in light of the design opportunities afforded by the assembly of heavy prefab panels, either solid or fenestrated, in a regular grid, but also simply in terms of its scale and architectural qualities. This, the AAA's first experience with IGECO – the results of which were very favourably received by architects in French-speaking Switzerland, who recognised the potential in rationalised on-site production – was quickly followed by the second stage of the Cité Meyrin (A. and F. Gaillard, 1961–69) and the beautiful development at La Gradelle (J. Hentsch, J. Zbinden, 1961–67), with its striking horizontal and vertical alternation of prefab panels. As for the remarkable Pont des Sauges housing estate in Lausanne (B. Calame, J. Schlaeppi, D. Gilliard, 1965–70), which entailed the coordinated assembly of fifty-four types of prefab components 'according to the modular system'[8] developed by the engineer Jean-Marie Yokoyama, it proved to be a particularly accomplished feat of architecture, with stunningly sculpted and fluted concrete panels cleverly arranged as a recessed facade.

The commission for an apartment block in Alchenflüh, near Bern, with Göhner on board as developer, opened up the Swiss-German market to the Vaud-based company, where rapid growth soon prompted it to open IGECO branches in Lyssach in the canton of Bern[9] and Volketswil in the canton of Zurich. Of particular note is that the Volketswil operation directed by Ernst Ulmer was launched specifically in order to produce a system of room-sized insulated double panels for the Siedlung Sunnebüel. Under the watchful eye of engineers Walter Böhler and J. Schleutermann, this site, which turned out 'the concrete components for four apartments every day, that is, approximately […] one hundred and five components',[10] came to be a linchpin of Göhner's serial production of housing (fig. 2).

2. Advertisement for IGECO, 1969.

3. IGECO factory in the 1960s, Étoy.

IGECO, a Tried-and-tested Method for Heavy Prefab Systems

The IGECO system therefore gained an exceptional market foothold in the 1960s, benefiting also from the strong reputation of an operation which brought together 'a team of talented young professionals: the architect Georges van Bogaert, the engineer Georges Steinmann, of Zschokke Holding AG, and his colleague Jean-Marie Yokoyama, who had just left steel engineering firm Zwahlen & Mayr.'[11] These cutting-edge planners and programmers proved their worth particularly when it came to devising strategies for coordinating the dimensions of components, which is the very foundation of industrialised construction.

The production process was based on the Danish patent of Larsen & Nielsen, to which the company in Étoy held the exclusive rights for Switzerland. Everything was set up to enable construction to proceed quickly and without hindrance. To keep assembly operations to a minimum, the heavy large concrete panels (weighing in at four to ten tonnes) were manufactured to the specific width of each room. They constituted the structural system (that is, the traditional load-bearing infrastructural components generally cast on site) but were produced at the factory in 'vertical batteries composed of vibrating and heated formwork panels, which guaranteed excellent compaction of the concrete' as well as a rapid curing time and, hence, 'a faster production rate'[12] (fig. 3).

The means of assembling the components, in the upper part of each panel, was another major asset of the process. It 'consisted in the panels' rebated edges (cells would achieve the same effect)',[13] in combination with the metal plate couplings incorporated in the panels during casting. This method assured immediate stability, allowing assembly to proceed independently of grouting operations and regardless of the weather, which was clearly advantageous with regard to speed and site management. The vertical panels were further stabilised 'prior to grouting… by means of lugs that temporarily wedged them in place. The bearing surface of the lugs was lined with a compressible material which subsequently assured uniform transmission of the vertical loads'.[14] Of course the couplings, too, assured a perfect seal, which was essential for soundproofing apartment buildings. Progress on site was accelerated by this assembly system and, moreover, by the very nature of the concrete panels themselves, in which 'some of the finishing components were incorporated [as necessary] during production',[15] at times even the electrical wiring or the wallpaper (fig. 4).[16]

4. Installation of IGECO heavy prefab components. Comet Photo AG, September 1966.

Concrete in Switzerland

A Critical Review of the *Plattenbau* (Large-panel Construction) Type

Göhner's string of commissions for *grands ensembles* enabled IGECO to perfect its system. The basic principle was very similar in essence to the famous Camus panel components patented in France, which came to be a synonym for the *Plattenbau* heavy prefab system and were widely exported, internationally. The Francophone-Swiss company optimised implementation of the system, notably with regard to the couplings. But while the efficacy of the process was never in doubt, the aesthetics of the load-bearing shells made of (exposed or painted) concrete and accentuated by a regular grid that finished flush with the edges of the prefab components, proved for its part a far thornier question.

This crucial point was raised as early as November 1962, at the conference 'On the Current State of Prefabrication Technology in Switzerland' organised by the Swiss Federal Institute of Technology. While specifying that 'the share of this construction method in the total volume of construction is currently still low, but should likely increase in the years to come'[17], speakers confirmed the benefits of heavy prefabrication yet remarked that the challenges it posed called for a specific approach, namely 'far more consistent and accurate planning down to the last detail'.[18]

In parallel, some fears were voiced with regard to the mass housing sector as epitomised by the Siedlung Rietholz in Zollikerberg:[19] 'More than 2,000 apartments have already been built and as many more are under construction. In eastern Switzerland there are some new developments […], where efforts are being made above all to find a compromise between the trend towards standardisation and the pronounced individualism of the population of our country'.[20] This critique of the idea that the excessive standardisation of facades was an inevitable or 'natural' aspect of industrialised production was anything but subtle.

Despite statements by the advocates of heavy prefabrication, the look of concrete panels continued to be debated in trade journals, where opinion was divided between defence of the system's efficiency and criticism of its, at times, sheer tedium. Over the years, the remarks became more scathing and the 'boring' architectural forms of these 'contemporary rabbit hutches' or 'termite mounds' which had sprung up on city outskirts were regularly called into question. In Switzerland, as indeed everywhere in Europe, the experiments of the 1960s proved controversial.

Thus, scepticism prevailed once the euphoria over the first satellite cities had died down. The Göhner housing estate found themselves in the firing line and the neologism 'göhnerite' was coined to depict the phenomenon of 'large-housing disease', which in France had been named 'sarcellite' after the Sarcelles estate (J.-H. Labourdette, R. Boileau, 1955–76). *Plattenbau* facades, the hallmark of any Göhner housing estate, were decried by their detractors as an emblem of a production process which had absolutely no regard for the human scale; and critics likewise targeted the simple volumes of Göhner's linear blocks, which were limited in height to four or five floors in order to facilitate the assembly of the prefab panels. In 1972, Göhner found himself in the limelight, and it was none too flattering: the Siedlung Sunnebüel in Volketswil was put up for debate, first in a critical documentary showing the daily life of a child there, directed by Kurt Gloor,[21] and then in the pamphlet *Göhnerswil. Wohnungsbau im Kapitalismus*, in which researchers at Swiss Federal Institute of Technology gave vent to their harsh critique both of the Volketswil estate and a production process which was widely – yet mistakenly – believed to be the result of the most abject speculation.[22]

At the turn of the 1970s, therefore, while waiting for historical judgment to finally do justice 'to these facades of classic twentieth-century architecture',[23] large housing estates were thoroughly stigmatised. It was the fashionable position to take, at a key moment when society was seeking to move beyond the very idea of 'a satellite city', which had increasingly become synonymous with 'a dormitory city'. It was a transitional period in the history of architecture: the end of three decades of post-war growth and prosperity coincided with the demise of the *grands ensembles* programme, and throughout all of Europe. While waiting for the clustered habitat (or grouped co-habitat) to assert itself as a viable alternative to those giant 1950s and '60s housing estates created simply by juxtaposing high- and low-rise blocks within an elementary grid, experimentation became the order of the day. In this context, heavy prefabrication systems and, more broadly, the industrialisation of construction overall, were singled out as 'a kind of combinatorial enclave in which the architect's hands are tied by industrialisation, […] the notion of "process" suggesting that of a restriction of compositional logic'.[24] Inevitably, the term 'monotony' once again reared its head (fig. 5).

Put an End to Monotony! The Avanchet-Parc, a Showcase Venture

Avanchet-Parc in Geneva, the last and most important of Ernst Göhner's large-scale housing estates, was very much a child of its time, conceived precisely to dispel these prejudiced views of 'standardised' production. Architects Peter Steiger and Walter Maria Förderer, both very active in the Swiss Werkbund for the renewal and the enhancement of multi-family dwellings, joined the Geneva project in 1969, along with their colleague Franz Amrhein. Göhner was sceptical, initially, but then encouraged them to experiment with new forms. Accordingly, the new operation in French-speaking Switzerland was a bench test that built on experience recently gained at the Siedlung Sonnhalde near Zurich, where attempts had been made to overcome some of the constraints ensuing from industrialised construction methods.[25] Avanchet-Parc was patently a showcase venture and no one tried to deny it. On the contrary, contrasting the monotonous effect of the grid of prefab reinforced concrete components was pivotal to the design brief from the start – a veritable *crescendo* of all possible means was deployed to this end: the open, asymmetrical layout was articulated around a central infrastructure spine; volumes were modelled by means of intervals, angles and (sawtooth) recesses inspired by a clever combination of typologies; the colour scheme drew on optical principles so as to heighten the residents'

sense of identification with the site and help them find their way around it easily; and the grounds were landscaped or, one might say, the topography literally sculpted by the artist Jürg Altherr and the landscape architect Christian Stern so as to provide a myriad of very different spaces in which plant varieties, too, served as additional signage for better orientation. The architects sought inspiration and insights from the latest trailblazing projects. They visited the Märkisches Viertel in Berlin or the Grande Borne in Grigny – like Bernard Lassus, Émile Aillaud even took a trip to Geneva to defend the Avanchet-Parc approach then under fire from the cantonal architectural commission. A great array of devices was brought into play to 'make architecture more human', to cite the catchphrase of the day. Yet everything was so admirably arranged as to simultaneously permit the extreme rationalisation of industrialised construction or, in other words, keep costs and time frames under control, which for Göhner was a major consideration. It was a tour de force and IGECO engineers were kept busy adapting operations to the new constraints, one of which was now – and increasingly – reflection on the architectural qualities of industrialised production (fig. 6).

5. Ernst Göhner (property developer), Wendel Gelpke & Hans Düby (architects), Siedlung Sunnebüel, Hegnau-Volketswil. Comet Photo AG, August 1972.

6. Avanchet-Parc, aerial view. Swissair Photo AG, September 1984.

Heavy Prefabrication and High-rise Construction

At the Avanchet-Parc, the IGECO heavy prefabrication system was used to construct the entire shell of a building, from the ground-floor slab upwards. Hence the system had to be optimised, for only then would it be possible to attain giddy heights (of up to 50 meters) and rebut the frequent criticism of the Göhner projects' excessively uniform volumes. As the engineer Jean-Marie Yokoyama has noted, the statics remained relatively simple, in line with the regular heavy prefab system: 'The vertical loads of the floors are borne entirely by the ground-floor columns and the stairwell walls, which together provide bracing for the whole building'.[26]

On the other hand, 'the static independence of each building, which was due to the double walls at the expansion joints',[27] amounted, in combination with the panels' angled profile and the building height of up to thirteen floors, to a whole new ball game, especially given that heavy prefab systems had until then generally been used to turn out far smaller buildings. The engineers at Volketswil were thus obliged to adapt the standard process, namely by deploying at each building's core an ingenious system of partial prestressing that would restore and stabilise the building's monolithic behaviour. Up to the tenth-floor slab, therefore, the four corners of the stairwells were fitted with prestressing tendons – doubly fitted, even, on the lower floors – which novel device opened up new possibilities in volumetric construction design.

'An average of two apartments every day!'[28] noted the admiring press, in light of the rapid progress underway at Avanchet-Parc, despite the colossal size of the estate foreseen for seven thousand people. The 'total output following the positioning and assembly of components prefabricated on site'[29] was indeed exceptionally high. 'It takes around 150 hours of labour to turn out [the components for] a medium-sized, 90-square-metre apartment. Thanks to particularly effective lifting equipment, the normal assembly rate is thirty to thirty-five units per montage team per day'[30] – quite a feat (fig. 7).

Ventilated Facades at Avanchet-Parc: a Pioneering Choice

Besides the approximately five hundred types of basic components cast in reinforced concrete (from slabs to walls, stairways, or even elevator shafts, the latter a new IGECO 'product line' launched in the 1970s), balconies, in their multiple variations, were made by assembling a range of precast components made at the Étoy factory. This method was exemplary also in terms of energy management, a declared goal of the Avanchet-Parc. Balconies that were completely independent of the main load-bearing structure were stacked one above the other and this 'tower' then anchored to the front of each floor slab by a metal dowel cast in place during fabrication. Accordingly, there was none of the thermal bridging normally assured by the indoor/outdoor continuity of the lamellar (thin-plate) load-bearing structure.

This same principle came to bear on the design of the building envelopes and was, in engineering terms, undoubtedly one of Avanchet-Parc's most technologically advanced features. The entire estate has a ventilated facade, a continuous skin that was set in front of the prefab reinforced concrete supporting structure and thus prevented any thermal bridging. The construction technique used was the 'Ickler Norm 100 System', a sub-construction of aluminium T and angled profiles, fixed to the supporting structure by means of cast aluminium plates and stainless-steel screws. Following insulation, the facade was clad in Pelichrom panels, an Eternit flagship product first featured in its 1964 catalogue.[31] Use was made too, logically enough, of the blocks of standardised windows produced by the EGO company in Altstetten, a part of the group since the 1940s.[32] When it came to airtightness, these timber-framed 'box windows' were strikingly sophisticated: their composite double simple-glazing assured an excellent thermal and acoustic performance – which was vital given the proximity of the airport.

7. Avanchet-Parc under construction.

8. Avanchet-Parc today. Photograph Claudio Merlini.

While primarily a pragmatic choice, the ventilated envelope was also a pioneering feature, ahead of its time: on the one hand, in comparison to traditional painted or coated concrete formwork, this constructive method afforded great freedom of plastic expression, which the architects made the most of, with virtuosity. In construction terms, on the other hand, the design of this 'stable, adjustable and economical' facade relied almost entirely on the industrialised production of primary and secondary construction components, which was the veritable common thread in the Avanchet-Parc project as well as the spearhead of all the Göhner AG operations.

The choice of material for the envelopes at Avanchet-Parc was, moreover, a harbinger of the paradigm shift in construction materials that was soon to follow on the oil crises of 1973 and 1979, namely the increasingly widespread use of peripheral insulation. Cost-effective development and reduced maintenance costs were now presented as key assets, and for good reason. At the same time, the combination of prefab panels and ventilated facades cost considerably more to build – yet the developer and his architects not only assumed this additional expense in full but even openly defended it as strategic foresight.

The goal at Avanchet-Parc had been to break new ground, and the gamble paid off. There was, furthermore, another major asset to this choice of typology, also and not least in terms of the on-site management of teams who worked simultaneously at diverse trades to complete the structure and the envelopes. In other words, the IGECO system earned its stripes as a rationalised and cost-effective production process that was smart and flexible enough to accommodate the new issues at stake; and yet in terms of profitability, it had certain drawbacks. It was these which would propel the decline of heavy prefab systems, or even their proscription, over the following decades,[33] on a construction market increasingly attuned to the strategic installation of cellular elements that could be externally insulated at less expense. Moreover, while the financial planning of the developer and general contractor Göhner was more than viable in the case of a large-scale project like the 2,240 apartments in Geneva, such investment was disproportionate to the smaller-scale operations in demand in the 1980s once building *grands ensembles* had been dropped on grounds as much economic as political. The context was changing fast: Avanchet-Parc was an irrefutable success yet would remain a relatively isolated phenomenon (fig. 8).

Adapting the Industrialisation of Construction: a Manifesto

Peter Steiger, Walter Maria Förderer, and Franz Amrheins' housing estate was a conscious response to the practice of their day, at a time when this was being called into question. The architects sought to make a clean break. By means of an implacable project process, expertly led, incidentally, by the architect Christian Hunziker (who in the 1980s was to mastermind another key constructive experiment in the prefab field, namely the Schtroumpfs estate in Geneva), the Avanchet-Parc designers delivered a daring showpiece. Its curved or skewed lines, complex volumes, concave or convex facades, polychrome colour schemes, and material heterogeneity were an explosion of shapes and volumes, colours and textures. Just as the pioneers of the interwar period had radically rejected historicism and the sanctioned canon, so too, the 1970s new generation of architects aimed for nothing less than a *tabula rasa*, the overthrow of all established precepts; but this time it was the theories of 'the Modern movement' that came under fire. Now, it was a matter of adapting industrialised construction techniques, which yet retained their strengths and were finally perfectly mastered, to a new way of thinking about large housing estates from which all forms of 'monotony' would be banned. Punctuated by pioneering achievements – from Ralph Erskine to Lucien Kroll – it was a prolific period of extreme experimentation, also with regard to construction techniques. New and innovative configurations came about, with obvious and openly declared implications for society. There can be no doubt that the Avanchet-Parc in Geneva was the epitome of this new vision of building ambitious housing for the greatest possible number of people as well as a remarkably consistent example of a design rooted in state-of-the-art application of the theoretical and technical tools of industrialised construction. The excellent state of Avanchet-Parc to this day is proof of this – and owes much, besides, to the active involvement and commitment of the residents who appreciate living there[34] (figs. 9–10).

9. Avanchet-Parc today. Photograph Claudio Merlini.

10. Avanchet-Parc today. Photograph Claudio Merlini.

Notes

[1] 'Cité Avanchet-Parc', now Avanchet-Parc.

[2] The first of the Göhner *Wohnblöcke* (apartment blocks), those comprising the City Park housing estate, saw the light of day in Toronto in 1946.

[3] 'The Schindler-Göhner prefabricated house system', *Schweizerische Bauzeitung* 128, no. 4 (1946), 41–3. On Göhner, see also the excellent publication: Fabian Fürter and Patrick Schoeck-Ritschard, *Göhner Wohnen. Wachstumseuphorie und Plattenbau* (Baden: Hier+Jetzt, 2013).

[4] Franz Graf, 'Préfabrication "haute couture" (IGECO) versus "prêt-à-porter" (HA)', in Uta Hassler and Catherine Dumont d'Ayot (eds.), *Bauten der Boomjahre. Paradoxen der Erhaltung* (Gollion: Infolio, 2009), 120–33. See also Dominique Zanghi, 'Espoirs et aléas de la préfabrication en Suisse romande. Le cas de l'usine IGECO à Étoy', *matières*, no. 3 (1999), 86–95. The IGECO factory at Étoy was inaugurated in January 1959. With its substantial production capacity, estimated to lie between 1,000 and 1,200 cubic metres of concrete turned out by a production site of likewise never-before-seen dimensions (92,000 square metres!), IGECO was a pioneer in Switzerland. Ramelet and, later, Léonard Gabella took over management of the factory in 1962.

[5] 'Usine-prodige' ('Une "première" suisse à Étoy. Inauguration d'une usine de préfabrication', *Gazette de Lausanne*, 12 January 1959).

[6] [Pierre Jeanneret], 'La préfabrication à l'ordre du jour. À Étoy, s'installe une grande entreprise romande', *Journal de la construction de la Suisse romande* 34, no. 3 (1959), n. p. From the early 1960s on, the prefab market in French-speaking Switzerland was in the hands of four companies that had acquired patent licenses, in particular French ones: Induni & Cie in Geneva (from 1958 on, the Barets system), E. Cuénod SA in Geneva (the Estiot system), the Swiss branch of Constructions Balency in Vich (the Balency system), and IGECO SA which had acquired the Danish patent of Larsen & Nielsen.

[7] 'Un étage en une semaine, une pièce en six minutes!' ('Un immeuble locatif pour le personnel de l'aéroport', *Journal de Genève*, 19 December 1958).

[8] 'Coordonnés selon le système modulaire' ('Cité Pont des Sauges, Lausanne', *Das Werk* 57, no. 4, 1970, 237–9, here 237).

[9] And let's not forget the housing development comprising 219 apartments on Giacomettistrasse in Bern, realised with IGECO by the architects C. Naeur and K. Scheurer and the engineers J. Bächtold and J. D. Robert, in 1967.

[10] 'Sont fabriqués chaque jour les éléments en béton pour 4 appartements, soit […] 105 éléments environ' (Ernst Göhner A.G., 'Programme pour la visite des chantiers du 25 novembre 1970', Archives Communauté genevoise d'action syndicale, Geneva).

[11] 'Une équipe de jeunes professionnels de talent: l'architecte Georges van Bogaert et les ingénieurs Georges Steinmann de l'entreprise Zschokke ainsi que Jean-Marie Yokoyama qui vient de quitter l'entreprise Zwahlen & Mayr' (Graf, 'Préfabrication "haute couture"', see note 4, 124).

[12] 'Des batteries verticales formées de banches vibrantes et chauffantes assurant un excellent compactage du béton et une accélération du rythme de production' (IGECO SA, 'Vorfabrikation-Préfabrication, IGECO Étoy-Bern', factory catalogue, undated [ca. 1971], Archives de la construction moderne, EPFL, Lausanne, fonds IGECO).

[13] 'Assurée par des redans en bord de dalle (les alvéoles faisant le même office)' (Jacques Bovet, 'La préfabrication lourde à Genève', *Bulletin technique de la Suisse romande* 89, no. 10, 1963, 192–8, here 195).

[14] 'Est réalisé avant le bourrage des joints, par l'intermédiaire d'ergots permettant ainsi leur calage provisoire. La surface d'appui des ergots est garnie d'un matériau compressible assurant ultérieurement une transmission uniformément répartie des charges verticales' (IGECO SA, 'Vorfabrikation-Préfabrication, IGECO Étoy-Bern', factory catalogue, undated [ca. 1967], Archives de la construction moderne, EPFL, Lausanne, fonds IGECO).

[15] 'Est incorporée [le cas échéant] une partie du matériel du second œuvre' (ibid.).

[16] On this topic, see Giulia Marino, 'Variations on the Theme of *Plattenbau*. Heavy Prefabrication and Total Industrialisation in the Experience of the Göhner Housing Estates in Switzerland (1966–1979)', in S. D'Agostino and F. R. D'Ambrosio (eds.), *History of Engineering – Proceedings of the 3rd International Conference* (Napoli: Cuzzolin, 2020), 869–80.

17 'Der Anteil dieser Bauweise am gesamten Bauvolumen ist derzeit noch klein, dürfte aber in den kommenden Jahren grösser werden' ('Der Stand der Vorfabrikations-Technik in der Schweiz', *IABSE Congress Report* 7, 1964, 205–16, here 216).

18 'Viel konsequentere und bis in das Detail gehende Planung' (ibid.).

19 Architects: A. Hubacher-Constam, H. Hubacher, and P. Issler; engineers: Weder & Prim, 1959–61.

20 'Über 2000 Wohnungen sind dort bereits ausgeführt und noch einmal so viele im Bau begriffen. In der Ostschweiz sind einige Neuschöpfungen zu verzeichnen […] bei denen vor allem versucht wird, einen Kompromiss zwischen den Normierungs-Tendenzen und dem ausgeprägten Individualismus der Bewohner unseres Landes herzustellen' ('Der Stand der Vorfabrikations-Technik in der Schweiz', see note 17, 212).

21 *Die grünen Kinder*, dir. Kurt Gloor (Switzerland, 1971, 87 min). See also *Zur Wohnungsfrage*, dir. Hans and Nina Stürm (Switzerland, 1972, 30 min).

22 Heini Bachmann et al., *Göhnerswil. Wohnungsbau im Kapitalismus* (Zürich: Verlagenossenschaft Zürich, 1972). See also Furter and Schoek-Rischard, *Göhner Wohnen. Wachstumseuphorie und Plattenbau* (see note 3).

23 'À ces façades de l'architecture classique du XXᵉ siècle' ('Pont des Sauges. Habitations collectives préfabriquées', *Schweizer Baublatt*, no. 99, 10 December 1968, n.p.).

24 'Una sorta di *enclave* combinatoria cui l'industrializzazione costringerebbe l'architetto, […] timori riferiti all'idea di "procedimento" cui la chiusura in senso compositivo è strettamente connaturata' (Giuseppe Ciribini, 'Prefazione', in G. Mario Oliveri, *Prefabbricazione o metaprogetto edilizio*, Milano: Etas-Kompass, 1968, XI). Ciribini refers especially to the criticisms voiced by Pier Luigi Spadolini and Marco Zanuso.

25 Supported in the initial phase by a working group comprised of Swiss Werkbund affiliates, the Siedlung Sonnhalde directed on behalf of Göhner by Peter Steiger and Walter Maria Förderer was intended as a pioneering project capable of overturning certain practices of its day. Yet in spite of extensive research – into topics such as the layout and the architectural expression of the buildings – the end result was a compromise, because industrialised construction imposes a logic of its own. Peter Steiger and Hansruedi Meier, *Die Sonnhalde in Adlikon* (Buchs: Heimatkundliche Vereinigung Furttal, 2014).

26 'Les charges verticales des étages sont entièrement appliquées sur les piliers du rez-de-chaussée et les murs de la cage d'escaliers, qui assurent le contreventement de l'ensemble de l'immeuble' (Jean-Marie Yokoyama, 'Description générale du gros-œuvre du bâtiment', *Chantiers*, spec. Issue, June 1975, 28).

27 'L'indépendance statique de chaque immeuble, due aux doubles murs des joints de dilatation' (Jean Perrin, 'Préfabrication en grands panneaux', *Chantiers*, spec. Issue, June 1975, 33–6, here 33).

28 'Chaque jour, deux appartements en moyenne voient le jour!' (Michel Baettig, 'Avanchet-Parc à Genève: bientôt 7000 habitants!', *Gazette de Lausanne*, 21 June 1973).

29 'Rendements totaux réalisés lors de la pose et de l'assemblage des éléments préfabriqués au chantier' (Perrin, 'Préfabrication en grands panneaux', see note 27, 35).

30 Préfabrication lourde et construction industrialisée. Inauguration des premiers immeubles d'Avanchet-Parc, 19 juin 1973 (private archives of Claude Graber, Versoix).

31 These were asbestos cement panels, 7–8 mm thick, extremely compressed and hermetically sealed then given a colour coating that was fired and chemically treated so as to assure long-lasting performance as well as excellent fire-resistance. The colour palette has been extensively studied by Franziska Gehrig, a colourist trained at the famous Institute of the Psychology of Colours in Salzburg.

32 By this same logic of integrating standardised secondary construction components, the EBO company's prefab bathrooms, produced on site, inclusive of all fittings and finishes, were hailed as a major innovation.

33 Like Avanchet-Parc, La Bourdonnette housing estate at Lausanne (J.-P. Desarzens, 1966–73) is one of the last large-scale projects realised by IGECO. In difficulty since the 1970s, the company was bought out in 1984 by Prelco in Geneva and Piersa in Marin-Epargnier then shut down for good in 1986.

34 Franz Graf and Giulia Marino, *Avanchet-Parc: 'Cité de conception nouvelle et originale'* (Gollion: Infolio, 2020).

The Pluralities of the Possible

Martin Tschanz

Concrete as a Building Material in Swiss Architecture around 1970

Prior to the first oil crisis of 1973, in a period still drunk on the imminent arrival of the future, concrete was unparalleled as a building material in its impact on architectural culture. It is hardly surprising that on looking back voices talk critically of a concreting-over of the landscape,[1] or more even-handedly about the left-behind 'concrete monstrosities' as half-quaint, half-gruesome but in any case alien and interesting compositions, and hence worthy of saving.[2] From the motorways, those endless ribbons that made the faraway near, to the bunkers, erected to defy an impending nuclear strike, and on to the churches, intended as mighty fortresses for God and His congregation, this synthetic mineral material was flexible enough to satisfy widely differing needs. Its sheer unending malleability was a boon to the experimental passions of designers, yet at the same time its resilient hardness and solidity created a counterpoint to the extreme dynamism of the times, and its restrained tone constituted an appropriate background for the exploding colourfulness in current fashions and arts.

Exposed concrete had already proven its worth in the endeavour to reach an 'objective' architecture prior to the Second World War,[3] and later, Le Corbusier's Unité d'habitation in Marseille found its embodiment as an artistic means of expression. The free form-flexibility and the expressive materiality of *béton brut* matched the tendency of the era away from abstract volumes towards plastically moulded bodies. Because this then endured as one of the main currents in architectural progression up until the 1970s, later examples of sculptural concrete architecture were – for good reasons – identified as part of a Corbusian tradition even when they in fact had very little in common with the works of the master himself.[4]

However, in the joy of experimentation of the late 1960s, the potential of concrete was explored in not one but many ways. The three following examples, which are introduced in greater detail below, each used the building material in their own exemplary but directly contrary ways. As the discussion will show, upon examining them even such a commonly used term as 'exposed concrete' becomes dubious, and indeed the corresponding variety inevitably poses the question whether we can talk of a specific concrete architecture at all.

In around 1970, concrete had almost gone full circle back to the broad range of expressive possibilities that it had once previously possessed at the beginning of the twentieth century. This clearly demonstrates how narrow and tendentious the image of the material had been, as circumscribed in superficially serious publications such as the 1928 book *Beton als Gestalter*.[5] A more differentiated and in terms of content richer, but equally far less attractive publication, such as *The Ferro-Concrete Style* by Francis S. Onderdonk[6] had little chance of challenging this all-powerful imagery, and as a result concrete tended to remain uniformly grey. However, the period of renewed experimentation in the economic boom years proved to be similarly short: following the subsequent recession, when the building material experienced another renaissance, even dyeing was considered innovative.

St Nicholas's Church in Hérémence (1961–1971) by Walter Maria Förderer

Walter Maria Förderer was one of the most idiosyncratic and influential Swiss architects of his era.[7] Although it includes a handful of schools, his architectural catalogue predominantly consists of churches – building assignments that afforded his sculptural creativity great freedom. St Nicholas's Church in Hérémence belongs undoubtedly to his most impressive works[8] and can be understood, if one so will, as a sum of his architecture (fig. 1).[9] Its unusually long planning and construction period encompassed almost the whole span of his life as an architectural practitioner, which began in 1956 and had already come to an end by the mid-1970s, at which point he withdrew from building and dedicated himself entirely to his free artistic work and to teaching.

Nevertheless, even in his building activities Förderer, who began his career as a sculptor, viewed himself primarily as an artist. Architecture attracted him because it enabled him to work spatially at a large scale and to create works that could be traversed. It also allowed him to combine his interests in the concave and the convex, which in his earlier works he had pursued separately from one another.[10]

He originally obtained the requisite building know-how during an intensive traineeship in the studio of Hermann Baur from 1954 to 1956. As he later formulated it, he soon realized that the only way to put his 'sculptural intentions into practice was through architecture, and more particularly by the utilization of spatial elements whose meaningful formation depended less on a grasp of organizational and functional features than on the requirements of atmosphere.'[11] His perhaps unattainable aim was to create a 'structure of elevated – or essential – purposelessness' in which his individual artistic expression would acquire a relevance for the public at large. 'Its artistic power and sculptural aura' should radiate over the surroundings, for which the building as a piece of complete art could be a pivotal nucleus.[12]

The client that tolerated such ventures most frequently was the Catholic Church, which at the time had a large requirement for buildings and was open to reforms. Nevertheless, for Förderer the demands set out in the programme were little more than the starting point. Certainly, the site and functional requirements had to be initially met via a number of basic decisions, but the built composition was intended to ultimately be able to stand for itself, largely independently of its use.[13]

1. Walter Maria Förderer, St Nicholas's Church in Hérémence, 1961–71. Photograph by author.

The appropriate path to achieving this was outlined by Förderer as follows: 'Once I have assured myself by means of sketch plans and models that the imperatives of the environment and the programme have been observed and will be secure even in the event of the alterations that are to be expected, the most exciting part of the work begins. At this stage, I see nothing but the "sculptured building" with all its details, and for some time I have paid no attention to anything but the models of the interior and the exterior. Having previously worked out the methods of construction and the materials to be used, I am able to devote myself entirely to the spatial, three-dimensional realization of my concept as unrestrictedly as if it were pure sculpture. The results of this modelling are then transformed into plans and thus represent the spatially-visualized product of spatial, three dimensional experiments. This product must proclaim the special features of the place in which it is to be built, the purposes for which it is intended, the man who shaped it and through him the age out of which and for which it was created. The finished building must underscore the messages foretold by the model (fig. 2). And incidentally, all my buildings, irrespective of their purpose and of the materials in which they have been built, have a common factor: they speak my own architectural language. The messages may vary, but the language does not.'[14]

2. Walter Maria Förderer, St Nicholas's Church in Hérémence, Model.

It therefore comes as no surprise that Förderer's preferred building material was massive, monolithic concrete – in the case of St Nicholas's Church with walls that were generally 50 centimetres thick. This construction method enabled him to translate his large-scale wooden-cardboard models into built, or in fact cast forms in the straightest manner possible. In the last resort the building is nothing other than an enlarged casting of its model.

Although Förderer's architectural archive is not extant it is still possible in the case of the church in Hérémence to approximately trace how the project evolved.[15] To begin with, the planning for the project encountered a number of difficulties. A competition for the replacement of the existing church, damaged in the major earthquake of 1946, was announced in 1961. The brief also involved the planning of a school and municipal facilities on the steep and somewhat constricted plot. The result of the competition, which was followed by two rounds of revision with variation studies, was a splitting of the commission between the originally second- and third-place winners: the architects Morisod, Kyburz and Furrer planned the school and took over construction management while Walter Maria Förderer, on the other hand, designed the church.[16]

Förderer's[17] competition projects no longer exist,[18] but the state of the project in spring 1964, shortly before the division of labour between the architects was fixed, does. The difference in the essential disposition of this pre-project and what was built consists simply of very minor aspects. In Hermann Baur's studio, Förderer had not only learnt how concrete should be treated, but also how a modern church should be organised. The clam-shaped layout, typical for Förderer's churches, has one noticeable deviation: the liturgical space shifts more decisively into the centre of the congregation than had been proposed in Baur's designs. This appears to anticipate the results of the Second Vatican

The Pluralities of the Possible 129

Council, which had been convoked while St Nicholas's was in its project phase.[19] Amongst the interesting specifications are the additional uses: the tower houses a library and community rooms, accessed via an outer staircase. Later, in the course of the planning, this was supplemented by a village shop located on the lower entrance level.[20]

Both the floor plan and the elevation of the pre-project still appear largely abstract and somewhat clumsy, above all in regard to the openings, set either as grouped series or as isolated perforations in the surfaces (fig. 3). It would be safe to assume that at this stage the status of the project differed little from the revised competition entry, which the jury considered to be overly outlandish. Specifically they criticised the complexity of the details and the severity of the appearance; in general they wished a more elegant and supple character.[21] Following the second round of revisions they in particular found the ambulatory too theatrical and recommended giving the rear wall to the altar a calmer appearance and to heighten the architectural expression of the tower and the clerestory.[22] These comments indicate a desire for greater clarity, for a differentiation between the individual parts, and in general for greater simplicity. Were Förderer to have heeded these recommendations, what would have undoubtedly emerged would have been a church of the type that Hermann Baur was building in Ennetbaden and Moutier at the time.

However, the objective of the reworking was to pull things in the opposite direction. Thus, the first project state still exhibits rudimentary sheer walls, between which the light would have fallen as oblique streaks of radiance – an approach that Bauer had already taken in the past to solve the problem of the wall. Förderer, on the other hand, was striving to find a closed shell and subsequently eliminated anything that might be considered joints. He facilitated perforations through the shell by interpolating mediating threshold spaces: the light cavities in the roof and in the wall, but also the ambulatory criticised by the jury. Furthermore, he moulded the surfaces as a relief that was designed to be spatially active.[23]

A hand-drawn item in section C of May 1964 demonstrates the trajectory the revision was taking (fig. 4); while the disposition remained untouched, the overall sculptural design was enriched, always orientated towards the perception of the visitor. The relief accompanies the real and imagined movement of the beholder, traced simply by eye, thus becoming the guiding perceptional pointer. Forty-five-degree angles create a continuity between the partial surfaces, both in the size of the wall segments and in the detailing. The edges are generally bevelled so that the surfaces are framed by lines, simultaneously mediating between the two.

It was an important design principle that these lines should run continuously, and they were correspondingly set with the utmost care. Wherever a dead end was unavoidable the chamfer had to cease 15 centimetres beforehand, for instance, 15 centimetres above the ground in the case of a column. These points provide the eye, so to speak, with a head start.

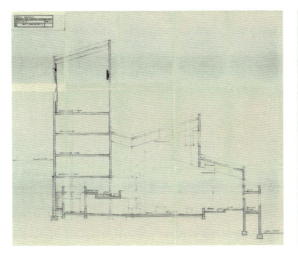
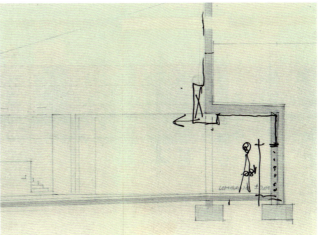

Förderer had a relatively long time for this 'most exciting part of the work' in the Hérémence project, during which he could work on the building 'as if it were pure sculpture'.[24] Construction work did not begin until three years later, in 1967, and the consecration ceremony was finally held on 31 October 1971. Although he was a consummate draughtsman with enormous powers of spatial imagination, his preferred working tools were models in white-coated wooden cardboard. In this case, besides a general model there was a model on a scale of 1:50, equipped not only with a removable roof but also an opening underneath through which a person could stick their head. This work model has unfortunately disappeared.[25] The only extant item is a fragment of the outer steps to the forecourt, which bears the marks of the design process: suggestions for alterations in the relief arrangement and the openings have been made in pencil, although none of them were carried out.

It is evident that model photos, sketched over to amend them, also played an important role in the phase of thinking through the sculptural design. This manifests Förderer's interest in pictorial, perspectival perception. As built, his spaces confirm that the design rests on preferred viewing points and lines of sight and is very precisely calibrated to the eye level of the standing or sitting visitor.[26]

Communications between the architecture office and the building site were carried out conventionally in the form of plans. That the model was employed on the building site, 'on which the workers could orientate themselves',[27] sounds plausible but is nevertheless denied by project architect Willy Jeiziner.[28] The plans had to be as complete, precise, and clear as humanly possible so that no additional decisions had to be made on-site, and where the treatment of the walls played a central role (fig. 5).

Strictly speaking these drawings were plans for the casting forms of the building; the shuttering plans of the engineers were little more than precisely dimensioned architectural plans. In detail the formwork pattern was mainly given by the horizontal board shuttering conventional at the time. The details, however, also demonstrate that those implementing them understood and adopted the

3. Walter Maria Förderer, St Nicholas's Church in Hérémence. Section A drawing, project status May 1964.

4. Walter Maria Förderer, St Nicholas's Church in Hérémence. Section C drawing (excerpt), project status May 1964.

The Pluralities of the Possible

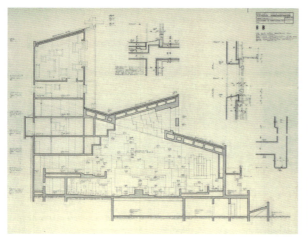 

5. Walter Maria Förderer, St Nicholas's Church in Hérémence. Section A drawing, project status March 1967.

6. Walter Maria Förderer, St Nicholas's Church in Hérémence. Interior space. Photograph by author.

explicit architectural goals, for example, in the ceiling underside on the outer stairway in the tower that reinforces the continuity between space and movement. Jeiziner's presence on the construction sight may well have played a crucial role in details like this.

Exposed Concrete?

St Nicholas's in Hérémence is a paradigm example of what concrete is able to accomplish as a monolithic building material (fig. 6). Förderer himself said that he envisioned a fallen boulder into which he had chiselled the church.[29] Despite this, the surface of the composition is by no means stone-like: instead the concrete prominently bears the imprinted texture of the wooden moulding forms. It is not the materiality that is paramount, rather the shape. In this sense, this type of exposed concrete is similar to bronze casting.

When unclad, and thus defining the appearance of the architecture, concrete is normally described as 'exposed concrete', even when its texture is determined by the formwork and very little of the material itself makes an appearance. In the church in Hérémence one can certainly see the grain of the roughly sawn shuttering planks, right down to the finest structures, but in terms of concrete as a material the only thing visible is the fine, homogenous skin of hydrated cement and sand powder. The essence of concrete as a conglomerate remains, by contrast, completely hidden.

Contrary to common usage, one should actually therefore only refer to exposed concrete when it has no casting crust, so that the components that make up the building material are openly evident. In this case, however, its properties are fundamentally different, and therefore it is slightly confusing that both types of concrete are not more clearly distinguished from one another.[30] The term 'artificial stone', which is sometimes used to differentiate from 'raw-shuttered concrete', is almost as indistinct in this respect as the term 'exposed concrete'. It stresses the stony materiality that is dominant in those types of concrete where the surface is not determined by the interplay of cement crust and casting form, but this classification similarly fails to discriminate: concrete is per se artificial stone.

Additional Buildings of the Teacher Training College in Kreuzlingen (1965–1972) by Rudolf + Esther Guyer

The materiality of concrete is a core theme in the buildings for the college in Kreuzlingen by Esther + Rudolf Guyer. The complex extends the baroque monastery, which was restored following a major fire and which dominates its surroundings with its mighty walls and high roofs. The new buildings form a contrast to this arrangement. Abundantly subdivided architectural volumes congregate around a central free space (fig. 7), and with their halls and differentiated threshold spaces create a spatial range that complements the long corridors of the historical substance.

Involving a systematic evaluation process, the architects searched for a material that would not clash with the abstract whiteness of the whitewashed surfaces of the old building and its sandstone jambs, but instead would harmoniously complement them. Light tones were disqualified 'because they would have distended the volumes of the new buildings and robbed the monastery of its dominant position.' Likewise rejected was tinted plaster and grey exposed concrete, which 'have a slightly volume-stifling effect in large successive surfaces, especially in our foggy grey climate.' The upshot was to concentrate on a material that had 'a warm, earth-coloured hue' and with its rich, raw texture had the ability to enliven the large wall expanses.[31] After further deliberations – during which amongst others 'corduroy' concrete, with its texture of grooves and broken ridges (also sometimes known as 'Paul Rudolph concrete'), was eliminated – the decision was taken to erect six large-scale samples, based on which the building commission was able to quickly and confidently make a choice.

7. Rudolf + Esther Guyer, Teacher Training College in Kreuzlingen, 1965–72. Photograph by author.

Two brick variations proved unusable due to the fact that the desired animated irregularity of English brick-built architecture was unachievable using local bricks and due to the Swiss 'precision-watchmaker mentality' of the bricklayers.[32] High hopes were set in the two types of grouted-aggregate concrete that had been experimented with as an analogy to Eero Saarinen's Morse and Ezra Stiles Colleges at Yale University. Because no precise technical data had been made available, an equivalent construction method had to be developed using their own experiments based on the sparse literature available. Layered quarry stone was cast into a conglomerate by grouting it with low-viscosity cement mortar, whereby the largest stone-fracture surfaces where aligned to face the shuttering and then freed from the cement overlay after removing the formwork. The result was satisfactory regarding its structure but less so regarding its colouring, due to the fact that the contrast between the stone available within a reasonable local radius and the cement was considered to be too great.[33]

In tests with raw-shuttered concrete dyed with ferric oxide stains appeared, and it was moreover feared that a lighter toning might produce a sugary effect. So it was that the choice was made to use a dyed concrete reworked with a double-chisel pick hammer before it completely hardened. This treatment removed the cement crust and splintered the gravel to give a relatively coarse but nonetheless uniform and quasi-soft texture. The model for this surface finish was the town hall in Asker in Norway by the architects Lund & Slaatto, which was known to the Swiss architects from an English publication.

The architectural formulation of the project evolved in accordance with the choice of material. With its ribbon windows, their horizontality reinforced by the use of brise-soleils, the initial competition design largely corresponded to the conventions of late-modern architecture (fig. 8). However, one particular perspective drawing already indicates that that overall composition of staggered cubes with closed wall surfaces was more important than the lighting rhetoric of the ribbon windows. This latter element was eliminated during the revision of the project by replacing the horizontal sunshade slats with deep vertical pillars that emerge seamlessly from the wall surfaces. Something akin to a colossal order, these elements connect multiple floors by virtue of their recessed setting within the parapet elements, their smooth concrete signifying them as a secondary infill. In this manner the horizontal arrangement of the competition project is replaced by a vertical one, which either finds an upright contact with the ground or cuts into the edge of the roof and dovetails with the sky like battlements. With this approach the architectural volumes take on a standing, even reposing character and the complex is able to completely forego the blustering modernist muscle-flexing of protruding or 'floating' elements. This also meant that it perfectly met the demands that the historic preservation officer Albert Knoepfli had formulated in his written opinion for the competition: 'Although, for various reasons, it is not possible for the new buildings to simply adopt the "load–support" construction principle of the historic buildings, nevertheless the new buildings should refrain from boastfully showcasing today's "stressed construction". The "stationary visual equilibrium" that contributes so greatly to the calm, supported

8. Rudolf + Esther Guyer, Teacher Training College in Kreuzlingen. Competition perspective drawing, 1965, and architectural project.

effect in the old buildings should be taken into account in terms of its ethos in the new ones. Vice versa, aggressive initiatives would lead here to disharmony.'[34]

With its compact, red-hued wall surfaces, the project as ultimately built is reminiscent of loam architecture, whereby the red paving of the courtyard and the intermediary spaces serve to additionally emphasise the close bond between earth and architecture. Prior to studying architecture Rudolf Guyer had lived in Morocco for eight months in order to sketch.[35] The influence of this experience is obvious, even though the architecture by no means lapses into the exotic, instead speaking a language of its own commensurate with the task set.

Concrete and Time

The concrete of the Kreuzlingen teacher training college evidently has a completely different character to that of the church in Hérémence. In Kreuzlingen the raw, stone-like surface that emerges from the conglomerate of gravel and cement, and in which a faint horizontal stratification appears, has echoes of the close and primary relationship between concrete and pisé construction techniques. Here the concrete manifests itself to the beholder as artificial stone, monolithic in its conglomeration. Its cast production only plays a part in so far as no joints are visible and the demeanour of the building is not that of a construction in the true sense of the word.

Taken together this means that this type of concrete interacts differently with the dimension of time than raw-shuttered concrete. The latter fossilises the moment of its hardening, causing it, as Adrian Forty has wonderfully described, to resemble a photograph.[36] Admittedly it may assume the traces of the weathering of time, but these are added accretions. As in other forms of casting, namely art-bronze casting, it is never entirely clear whether these traces should be understood as a valuable patina or as an undesirable impurity.

The Pluralities of the Possible

9. Rudolf + Esther Guyer, Business Training College for the Sales Personnel Department in Zurich, 1967–73. Photograph by author.

When, on the other hand, concrete is exfoliated and its stony materiality revealed, the moment of its hardening essentially plays no role in its appearance. As is true of all massive materials, concrete in this form can not only acquire a patina or become grubby but can also erode. When this occurs, its ageing may leave noticeable traces, but this nonetheless does not alter the essence of the material. In general, artificial stone ages not only as well but also in the same way as natural stone – or at least as long as constituents of the conglomerate that should remain hidden are not exposed, such as the reinforcing rods.

The aspect that such thoroughly different types of concrete have in common is their monolithic character. What emerges through the hardening of the mouldable mass is an entire whole, not an assembled composite, entirely independently of whether either the casting form or the inner essence of the solidified material determines its appearance. That this shapeability should be readily exploited in architecture is self-evident, especially because the manifold load-bearing capacity of reinforced concrete lends the sculptural structure great stability. Having said this, the monolithic quality can also be harnessed at different scales: the corresponding possibilities are not only exploited in buildings that appear as a whole like a formed stone or formed earth, but equally in buildings assembled out of elements plastically formed out of poured stone.

Business Training College for the Sales Personnel Department in Zurich (1967–1973) by Rudolf + Esther Guyer

In considering this second approach, there is hardly a comparable building that goes to such extremes as the Business Training College building in Zurich (fig. 9), developed by Rudolf and Esther Guyer parallel to the building complex in Kreuzlingen discussed above. In this project they were able to draw upon their experience with the Bremgarten Barracks (1959–68), for which they had developed a specialised construction system. This 'System "Kabre"' was adapted for the college so that already existing steel shuttering could be partly reused. However, this extra rationalisation was probably not the key reason for the choice of construction system. The architects were well aware that it would not result in any cost savings and that 'the commonly held perception of multipurpose concrete elements for differing functions' was 'unrealistic'.[37]

The college is composed of 26 element types, ranging from '01: facade columns' to '26: flower troughs' (fig. 10). Due to the fact that varying loads and connections required alterations in the detailing, for example in the reinforcement rods, of the total 2,458 assembled elements in the building, the architects still had to individually draw 1,056 of them. Despite this and the fact that their experience with the predecessor building in Bremgarten must have meant that they were perfectly acquainted with what it entailed, the architects willingly shouldered this enormous planning effort, concentrating instead on the calculated advantages of a short construction schedule, 'but above all regarding quality and the potential for a richer architectural design.'[38]

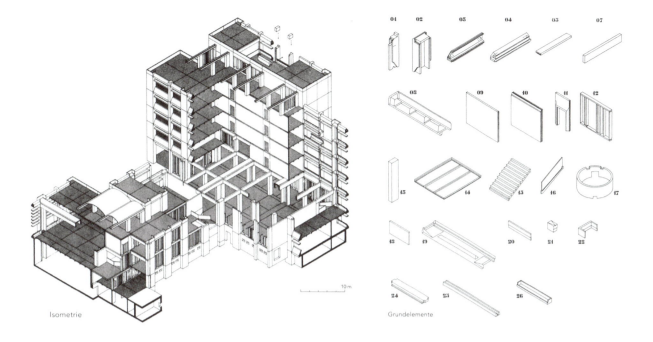

The spatial three-dimensionality of the elements was employed to integrate the service installations, for example in the U-shaped girders and facade supports or in the parapet elements, which housed the ventilation and heating. However, this plasticity is also an architectural means of expression, both at the level of the connections and joints, which give the space rhythm, and at the level of the individual elements. Thus, the entrance hall is divided into different zones using simple columns and U-supports, single and double binding joists and U-girders without interrupting the open spatial continuum (fig. 11). Similarly with the doors, where the wall elements swell out facing the corridor as if the rooms behind them were subject to an inner pressure. This also creates a connection between the openly displayed concrete carcass and the likewise poured fittings and fixtures made of polyester, in particular to the almost identically formed display cases. The shiny coloured plastic and the concrete complement each other as two related yet different synthetic materials. That this process entailed an interest in the materiality and colouring of the concrete, and that this was duly applied in a controlled manner, goes almost without saying.

The walls, supports and girders were generally ground so that the grain is hinted at in the smooth outer surfaces. Other parts were sandblasted or simply abraded, while the parapet elements were washed, and the stairs and the floors of the day rooms consist of terrazzo dyed, as are the parapets, with ferric oxide. But raw-shuttered surfaces also make an appearance, for instance in the ceiling slabs. They were described as 'moulding smooth', and indeed here, too, the materiality and the structure of the formwork only play a role in so far that they leave no visible traces behind in the perfect cement surfaces.

Casting as a process, on the other hand, remains unarticulated. Thus, for instance, the ceilings produce the effect of stone ceilings in the sense of an

10. Rudolf + Esther Guyer, Business Training College in Zurich. Construction system.

11. Rudolf + Esther Guyer, Business Training College in Zurich. Entrance hall with graphic artwork by Hansruedi Scheller. Photograph by author.

The Pluralities of the Possible   137

Antique strotere, the fine ribs of which structure the surface and intimate a direction, whereby occasional fields are eliminated to be re-assimilated by acoustic elements. The elements of the building appear as large plastically formed artificial stones with a configuration that combines aspects of classical tectonics with those of stereotomy.

Concrete Architecture?

The expectation must be that the architectural expression of a concrete architecture worthy of its name is characterised, or at least significantly co-determined, by the properties of concrete as a material, and, in the process, that concrete is applied according to its nature. This unquestionably applies to all three of the examples discussed above. Just like the monolithic nature of St Nicholas's Church, the configuration of the Business Training College in Zurich is 'true' to concrete, which in turn equally applies to the explicit casting accompanied by a suppression of its own materiality in Hérémence as it does to the staging of the materiality in Kreuzlingen.

Between the poles, on the one hand, of the monolithic and the assembled vis-à-vis structure and the poles, on the other, of the cast-stamped and the materially determined vis-à-vis appearance stretch two fields of possibilities that can easily be combined to give a matrix. Most of the concrete-made buildings in which the potential of the material can generally be combined and mixed can be pinpointed within this matrix. The overwhelming variety of the possibilities that emerge from this are rooted in the nature of concrete, which as an initially amorphous and supple mass only acquires its shape in the process of hardening. To pity concrete for this reason, and like Frank Lloyd Wright to believe that it is eternally searching for its innate essence,[39] would be mistaken.

Finally, in the interests of completeness, and indeed to make matters even more complicated, it is also worth recalling sprayed concrete as yet a further variety, which takes on its form not via shuttering but via its adhesion to a substrate. Applying sprayed concrete produces an individual monolithic type that yet again differs fundamentally from those described so far. Even though this technique is mostly used in civil engineering, corresponding examples do exist in the field of Swiss architecture in around 1970, for example, St Michael's Church by Donat Ruff, which was dynamited out of the cliff face in Raron from 1971 to 1973 and was lined with gunite vaulting.[40] In addition, from the mid-1970s onwards, Peter Vetsch began with his long series of Earth Houses. Their complex shell forms were produced very directly and simply using sculpturally shaped reinforcement nets and sprayed concrete, dispensing with the need for complex shuttering.[41] This archaic technology has now acquired a renewed significance in combination with automatically produced high-precision reinforcements, but that, as they say, is another story.[42]

Notes

1. See, for instance, 'Erwachende Sensibilität für die Landschaft', in Bundesamt für Umwelt (BAFU) and Eidg. Forschungsanstalt für Wald Schnee und Landschaft (WSL) (eds.), *Wandel der Landschaft: Erkenntnisse aus dem Monitoringprogramm Landschaftsbeobachtung Schweiz (LABES)* (Bern: Bundespublikationen, 2017), 19–20.
2. *SOS Brutalismus – Rettet die Betonmonster!* exhibition, Deutsches Architekturmuseum, Frankfurt am Main, 9 November 2017–2 April 2018.
3. As an aside it is worth mentioning that in Switzerland this tendency continued up until the 1970s, for example with the railway buildings of Max Vogt.
4. Thus, for instance, Jul Bachmann and Stanislaus von Moos, *New Directions in Swiss Architecture* (London: Studio Vista, 1969), 20: 'Le Corbusier's style often dries up into a more or less hectic but essentially dessicated [sic] formalism.'
5. Julius Vischer and Ludwig Hilberseimer, *Beton als Gestalter: Bauten in Eisenbeton und ihre architektonische Gestaltung* (Stuttgart: Julius Hoffmann Verlag, 1928). As is well known, the publication was an amalgamation of two book projects that were combined by the publisher Julius Hoffmann to suit market requirements by issuing it as the fifth volume in his series of books on building.
6. Francis S. Onderdonk, Jr., *The Ferro-Concrete Style: Reinforced Concrete in Modern Architecture* (New York: Architectural Book Publishing Co., 1928). The book, with a polychrome neo-Romanesque concrete capital on the jacket, was ill-suited to appeal to the tastes of European modernism.
7. His language of forms influenced numerous architects, particularly Otto Glaus. His ideas on church building were widely discussed both in architectural and church circles, and his views on the potential and limits of architecture fascinated and influenced such differing opinion leaders as Max Bächer and Lucius Burckhardt.
8. A wonderful appraisal of the building by Pierre Imhasly (text) and Oswald Ruppen and Jacques D. Rouiller (pictures) is to be found in *Hérémence Béton* (Lausanne: Grand Pont, 1974). For the author's own attempt at an emphatic description, see Martin Tschanz, 'Licht, Raum, Materie', in *Bauen in Beton / Construire en béton* (2014/15), 4–15.
9. This is certainly how Förderer himself saw it: This 'special case […] embodies much which had concerned me from one building to the next during that period. And […] it alludes to many of the spatial and three-dimensional possibilities [räumliche und plastische Möglichkeiten, AN] I had thought individually in other buildings but only brought to interaction in this one.' (Max Bächer, *Walter M. Förderer: Architecture – Sculpture / Architektur – Skulptur*, Neuchâtel: Éditions du Griffon, 1975, 38).
10. Ibid., 128.
11. Ibid.
12. Ibid., 117.
13. Förderer published two sketches in the periodical *Kunst und Kirche*: 'Hérémence "Kirche"' (lit. church of Hérémence) and 'Hérémence Touristenzentrum statt Kirche' (lit. Hérémence tourist centre instead of church), the latter being the same building rededicated with a small number of minor amendments. In the text Förderer specifies: '"Form" does not follow "function", although it can be a stimulus for many forms' ('"Form" folgt nicht "Funktion", aber diese kann Anstoss zu vielen Formen sein.' Walter M. Förderer, 'Kunst für kirchliches Bauen', *Kunst und Kirche* 35, no. 3, 1972, 109–24, here 110 text and 113 drawings).
14. Bächer, *Walter M. Föderer* (see note 9), 29. The English translation 'sculptured building' seems to the author to be somewhat unsatisfactory in comparison with the German expression 'Bau-Skulptur'.
15. The municipality of Hérémence possesses an unusually large collection of documents. During the building phase Willy Jeiziner, who drew almost all of the final plans for the church, founded his own architectural office in Visp, together with his fellow Förderer member of staff Xavier Furrer, in order to build his own, strongly Förderer-influenced church in Riddes and to simultaneously supervise the construction works in Hérémence. When the office of Furrer & Jeiziner dissolved, the plans and models of the St Nicholas's Church were donated to the municipality of Hérémence, which in turn generously gave me access to their archive. The only uncertainty is whether I was able to consult all of the holdings.
16. The competition is documented in detail in the bequest of Hermann Baur (gta Archives, ETH Zurich), who guided the jury, albeit not officially as its president.

17. The pre-project still bears the plan stamp 'Förderer + Otto + Zwimpfer'. The office partnership was only dissolved in 1964, but it was Förderer who had played the major part in the competition project.
18. Numerous models from the competition are stored in the municipal archive in Hérémence, but it was not possible to identify the winning project as being among them.
19. The Constitution on the Holy Liturgy was published on 4 December 1963. See Fabrizio Brentini, *Bauen für die Kirche: Katholischer Kirchenbau des 20. Jahrhunderts in der Schweiz* (Luzern: Edition SSL, 1994), 145–8.
20. The embedding of ecclesiastical functions in everyday structures was important to Förderer. It is a core topic in his book *Kirchenbau von heute für morgen?* (Zürich: NZN-Buchverlag, 1964). He would have undoubtedly preferred to have incorporated the entire building programme, including the school, within his single composition. gta Archives of ETH Zurich
21. 'The profusion of recesses, facets, and various cut-outs does not resolve the impression of heaviness foreign to this country's tradition of simplicity. / We would have wished for a more elegant expression, more elevated, supple, and harmonious.' ('La profusion de décrochements, facettes et découpages divers, n'élimine pas une certaine impression de lourdeur étrangère à la tradition de simplicité de ce pays. / Nous souhaiterions une expression plus élégante, plus élevée, plus souple et plus harmonieuse.' Jury sitting protocol, 9 February 1963, gta Archives Zurich ETH, Nachlass Hermann Baur).
22. Jury sitting protocol, 6 July 1963 (gta Archives Zurich ETH, Nachlass Hermann Baur).
23. On the topic of the relief in Förderer's work, see further Martin Tschanz, 'The Relief between Art and Architecture', in Roger Boltshauser, *Otto Müller, Trudi Demut, Hans Josephson*. Carousel, Confessions, Confusion, set 2, zine 1 (London: Koenig Books, 2020), 57–63.
24. Bächer, *Walter M. Föderer* (see note 9), 29.
25. The spaces in the archive I was given access to were cramped, meaning that it cannot be ruled out that the large model is either stored in another room or that it has been disposed of.
26. Förderer wrote that with its extremely different viewing points from above or below, for him the church 'has become the haute école of vision in perspective' (Bächer, *Walter M. Föderer*, see note 9, 38).
27. 'anhand dessen sich die Arbeiter orientieren konnten' (Zara Reckermann, *'Gebilde von hoher Zwecklosigkeit': Walter Maria Förderers Gratwanderung zwischen Architektur und Skulptur am Beispiel St-Nicolas in Hérémence*, Weimar: VDG, 2009, 33).
28. Conversation with Willy Jeiziner and Xavier Furrer, 14 November 2018.
29. 'As for me, I imagined that a rock had fallen down into the space. And into the rock, I sculpted a church, giving it the jagged and irregular shapes that the terrain imposed and that are found elsewhere in the village and surrounding landscape' ('Pour ma part, j'ai imaginé un rocher tombé en cet emplacement. Et dans ce rocher, j'ai sculpté une église en lui donnant les formes découpées et irrégulières qu'impose le terrain et qui se trouvent d'ailleurs dans l'aménagement du village et le paysage environnant.' Marius Charbonnet and Oswald Ruppen, *L'Église d'Hérémence en Valais. Témoignage de notre siècle*, Sion: Imprimerie Valprint SA, 1980, 29).
30. See Betonsuisse (ed.), *Merkblatt für Sichtbetonbauten / cemsuisse Merkblatt – MB 02* (Bern: Betonsuisse Marketing, 2012). This fact sheet has been updated and was re-issued in 2020.
31. 'Da sie das Volumen der Neubauten aufgebläht und das Kloster seiner Rolle als Dominante beraubt hätten.' 'In grossen hintereinander liegenden Flächen leicht volumentötend wirkt, besonders in unserem nebelgrauen Klima.' 'Eine warme, erdfarbene Tönung.' (Rudolf Guyer, Materialversuche für die Erweiterungsbauten des Seminars Kreuzlingen, *Schweizerische Bauzeitung* 84, no. 13, 1966, 243–4, here 243).
32. '"Uhrmachergeist"' (ibid., 244).
33. Guyer mentions the possibility of additionally dyeing the cement, and recommended a procedure that was about 30 per cent more expensive than exposed concrete as an alternative to the quarry stone cladding of the sustaining walls (ibid., 243–4).
34. 'Wenn auch das Konstruktionsprinzip der Altbauten "Last – Stütze" aus verschiedensten Gründen nicht einfach von den Neubauten übernommen werden kann, so sollen die Bauten unserer Zeit die Möglichkeit des "Spannungsbaues" nicht grosssprecherisch demonstrieren. Die bei den Altbauten so stark zur ruhigen, getragenen Wirkung beitragende

[34 cont.] "optische Statik" soll bei den Neubauten gesinnungsgemäss berücksichtigt sein. Aggressive Vorstösse dagegen führen hier zu einer Disharmonie.' ('Wettbewerb Neubau des Lehrerseminars Kreuzungen', *Schweizerische Bauzeitung* 84, no. 13, 1966, 233–42, here 242).

[35] Hannes Ineichen (ed.), *Rudolf + Esther Guyer: Bauten und Projekte 1953–2001* (Blauen: Schweizer Baudokumentation, 2002), 291.

[36] Adrian Forty, 'Ohne Zeit', *Werk, Bauen + Wohnen* 95, no 1/2 (2005), 16–9.

[37] 'Die oft anzutreffende Vorstellung vom Mehrzweck-Betonelement für verschiedene Funktionen [...] unrealistisch.' ('Gewerbeschule für Verkaufspersonal in Zürich', *Detail*, no. 2, March–April 1975, 177–88, here 180).

[38] 'Vor allem aber auch hinsichtlich der Qualität und der Möglichkeit reichhaltigerer architektonischer Gestaltung' (ibid., 180 and 183).

[39] 'What then should be the Aesthetic of Concrete? / Is it Stone? Yes and No. / Is it Plaster? Yes and No. / Is it Brick or Tile? Yes and No. / Is it Cast Iron? Yes and No. / Poor Concrete! Still looking for its own at the hands of Man.' (Frank Lloyd Wright, 'In the Cause of Architecture, VII: The Meaning of Materials – Concrete', *The Architectural Record* 64, no. 2, 1928, 98–104, here 102).

[40] Hubert Theler, *Die Felsenkirche St. Michael von Raron* (Visp: Mengis Druck und Verlag, 2001).

[41] See Erhard Wagner and Christoph Schubert-Weller, *Erd- und Höhlenhäuser von Peter Vetsch / Earth and Cave Architecture* (Sulgen: Verlag Niggli, 1994).

[42] The author is deeply greatful for the support by the community of Hérémence, namely Kilian Dayer, Willy Jeiziner and Xavier Furrer, Rudolf and Esther Guyer and – last but not least – the gta Archives of ETH Zurich and Daniel Weiss who advised me of the documents in the Hermann Baur bequest.

'In our country, it is practically impossible not to build in concrete'[1]

Brief Notes on Exposed Reinforced Concrete in the Architecture of Ticino

Nicola Navone

In the 1980s, the architecture of Ticino enjoyed its greatest moment of critical attention and was subsumed into a 'School', the existence of which, however, was denied by its principal protagonists.[2] Reinforced concrete, in particular the various types of exposed concrete, was elected as the qualifying material of this 'School', to the point that the editors of the magazine *archithese* dedicated an issue to it, opening with a round table involving Aurelio Galfetti, Luigi Snozzi, and Livio Vacchini.[3]

This circumstance would suggest specific characteristics inherent to reinforced concrete construction in the canton of Ticino, the history of which remains to be written, but this, however, is not the subject of these pages. Our intention is rather to investigate why so many of the protagonists of that fortunate period chose to privilege this material and how they interpreted it in their works, beginning, as a necessary premise, with a pivotal figure of the time, Rino Tami.

From the Cantonal Library to the Chiasso–Saint Gotthard Motorway

The first important public building in exposed reinforced concrete in Ticino was the Cantonal Library, built in Lugano between 1936 and 1941 to a project by the brothers Carlo and Rino Tami (fig. 1). This outstanding work was among the few in those early years to be published outside of Ticino (famously earning the praise of Giuseppe Pagano in the influential architecture journal *Costruzioni-Casabella*; and moreover, it was also the only building in Ticino selected by George Everard Kidder Smith for his book *Switzerland Builds*).[4] Assisted by the engineer Agostino Casanova,[5] the Tami brothers first proposed facades with plastered surfaces, as stated in the cost estimate dating from 1938, before finally opting to leave the reinforced concrete exposed. The construction of the library was entrusted to Lonati e Cavadini, a building firm in Lugano, on 24 July 1939. Careful attention was paid to the selection of the inert materials (sand and gravel

1. Rino Tami with Carlo Tami, Cantonal Library, Lugano, 1936–41. View of the north elevation of the book depository, photograph Vincenzo Vicari.

from the Ticino River, extracted from the Castione quarries), to the execution of the formwork in planed boards, and to the facade finishes, bush-hammered with the exception (probably for cost reasons) of the south and west facades of the book depository.

According to Riccardo Bergossi, the choice of reinforced concrete would have been motivated by the example of the Institute buildings at the University of Bern (1929–31) by Otto Brechbühl and Otto Rudolf Salvisberg (an important figure for Tami and the design of the Cantonal Library[6]), though for Kenneth Frampton the bush-hammering of the Cantonal Library indicates an influence of Auguste Perret's works.[7] On the one hand, Tami's choice of material seems consistent with the thoughts he expressed a few years earlier, in a combative article entitled 'I sepolcri imbiancati dell'architettura', in which he put forth a proposal to 'prohibit for an adequate number of years the use of plaster on facades',[8] so as to restore the correct use of materials and ensure their perfect execution. Even so, references to demands for 'architectural honesty' advanced by Tami in his few writings[9] and during his brief tenure at the Federal Institute of Technology in Zurich[10] do not seem to provide a definitive answer to the question. The project for the Church of the Sacred Heart in Bellinzona was begun in October 1936, while the Tami brothers were still occupied with their competition submission for the Cantonal Library, and was completed in 1939.[11] On the advice of the engineer Agostino Casanova (who was also involved, as we have seen, in the project for the Cantonal Library), Rino Tami concealed few structural elements in reinforced concrete within the walls of the church (on the interior in terracotta brick and on the exterior in granite ashlars extracted from various quarries, squared, sized, and laid in such a way as to break the continuity of the horizontal courses).[12] Later, having been commissioned to design the facades of the Lucendro electric power plant, together with his brother Carlo, Tami again decided on granite ashlar masonry,[13] which he justified *a posteriori* as a desire to harmonise with the alpine landscape.[14] Thus, the choice of bush-hammered concrete for an important public building like the Cantonal Library should not be attributed to a generic 'modernist' aspiration, but rather to a series of specific considerations regarding the functional purpose and character of the building (also supported by the similar finishes of the facades of the book depository tower at the Swiss National Library, in Bern, inaugurated in 1931), and in fact he made the decision at a very advanced project stage, when the opening of the construction site was imminent.

In the post-war period, Rino Tami's experimentation with reinforced concrete would continue in the form of structural frames combined with brick infill, at first in silica-calcareous clay, and later with sanded facing terracotta brick. One of the first times he articulated this theme was with the Fischer Marcionelli apartment house, also known as Casa Solatia, built in Lugano between 1949 and 1951.[15] Here, the concrete structural frame is limited to the south elevation, where it manifests itself in the diaphanous volume of the loggias. It was in some of the industrial buildings designed by the Tami brothers, just prior or contemporary to the above projects, that the reinforced concrete structure became a characteristic element of the elevations. With the La Fleur pharmaceutical plant in Lugano (1946–50, with Carlo Tami), their initial idea of columns tapered at the sides and top, and projecting out from the facade plane, was abandoned (though the Tami brothers would later use them for the expansion of the Frieden Factory in Balerna, 1951–53, albeit with less lateral tapering).[16] Instead, Rino Tami created a coplanar framework of columns and floors that mark the rhythms of the main elevations.[17] With the Usego warehouse in Bironico (1950–52, with Carlo Tami, tragically demolished in 2004[18]) (fig. 2), the framework is articulated on the facades, with configurations that differentiate between the warehouse, the garage, and the administration volumes. While the structure of the latter building is close to that of the La Fleur plant, in the warehouse, structural reinforcement at the nodes allude to the mushroom pillars of the interior structure. The surfaces of the infill walls, again in silica-calcareous brick, are interrupted before they reach the beams to leave space for a ribbon window. This solution permitted natural lighting and ventilation of the warehouse, while ensuring the necessary surface area for shelving and eliminating the need to cut the infill bricks to fit the contours of the structural frame.

Tami's reflections and experiences regarding this series of buildings were to lead to an ulterior evolution, this time in the complex formed by the Cinema Corso and the 'La Piccionaia' and 'Il Cardo' buildings, in Lugano (1952–57, with Carlo Tami and Peppo Brivio) (fig. 3). Here, the silica-calcareous brick was replaced by terracotta facing brick, which Tami considered more suited to the Lombard character of the canton of Ticino[19] and which at that time, according to Tita Carloni, had 'disappeared from the construction sites of Ticino and was literally destined to come back and invade them in one way or another'.[20]

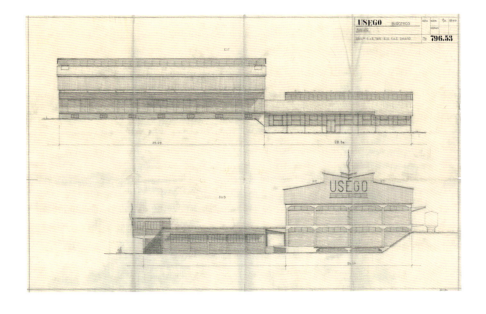

2. Rino Tami with Carlo Tami, Usego warehouse, Bironico, 1950–52. East and south elevation drawings, 23 August 1951.

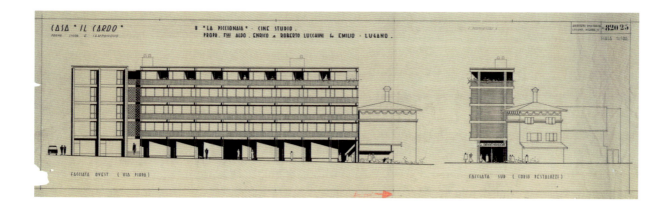

3. Rino Tami with Carlo Tami and Peppo Brivio, Cinema Corso, Casa 'La Piccionaia' and Casa 'Il Cardo', 1952–57. West and south elevation drawings, December 1954.

Brivio (who was then collaborating with Tami, even though he had his own studio),[21] must have made a significant contribution to the project. A reconstruction of its genesis demonstrates, in the mixed-use building 'Piccionaia', the transition from facades not unlike those of the Frieden factory, to a clear predominance of horizontal lines delineated by the edges of the floor slabs, completed by the downstands concealing the roller shutters, and punctuated by corbels that reveal the position of the pillars set back from the surface of the facade. The entire composition is enlivened by the play of shadows that appears particularly at noon, when the sun's rays are tangent to the facade.[22] The configuration of the structure emerges only in the side facade, which directly faces the fifteenth-century building to the south. The surfaces of the exposed reinforced concrete were bush-hammered, with the exception of the edges, which were finished with the characteristically smooth 'bindello'[23] (as Perret used to do). In the adjacent building, 'Il Cardo', after having expanded the facade of the 'Piccionaia' and inserted a connecting bay that hosts the entrance, Tami chose, in contrast, to emphasise the vertical lines in the residential part of the building. He did this by means of projecting pilasters and brick infill from floor to floor on the main facade, along with full-height windows, while the lateral facade, along Via Frasca, features wooden parapets below the windows. The differentiated treatments of the facades distinguishes the offices from the apartments, and we can suppose that in the latter area, the use of French windows was a further tribute to Perret.[24] While those who have investigated these works have had the opportunity to highlight their formal sources,[25] on these few pages, instead of expanding the 'intertextual network' of references, I will simply observe that Tami was not aiming for an ostentatious representation of structure, but instead articulated his overt demand for 'architectural honesty' in a more subtle way, consistent with the usual mix of 'sprezzatura' and elegance that characterised his personality: by showing and concealing at the same time, and by devoting special attention to the balance of the composition and to the construction details.

Tami would continue to develop the combination of a reinforced concrete frame with infill in terracotta facing brick (with sanded surfaces) in other urban buildings,[26] contributing to the diffusion of this language not only amongst the architects of his own generation – in particular Alberto Camenzind and above all Augusto Jäggli, who would later collaborate with Tami on the design for the headquarters of Radio della Svizzera italiana (Public Radio for Italian-speaking Switzerland) in Lugano-Besso (1951–62)[27] – but also of the younger generation, such as, for instance, Tita Carloni who, more than the others, would use it for numerous urban buildings,[28] and to a lesser degree Peppo Brivio.[29] We could furthermore add a long list of lesser known professionals,[30] ranging from excellent architects to competent professionals, who made the system their own by articulating it in various ways and with varying results throughout the 1970s.[31]

Tami, in the meantime, was able to further test the technical and formal potential of reinforced concrete with Casa Torre, a tower in Cassarate (1953–58) that he designed again in collaboration with Peppo Brivio. The concrete structure and brick infill that characterised the first versions of the project made way for massive facade walls in exposed reinforced concrete on the lateral elevations, oriented to overlook the lake.[32] But it was above all in the construction of the Chiasso–Saint Gotthard motorway (at that time the N2 national highway) that reinforced concrete would play a crucial role, becoming, in fact, thanks also to Tami's efforts of persuasion, the material that gave a unified character to the entire motorway. Tami had participated in the project from the very beginning; he served on the competition juries for the major works along the stretch between Chiasso and Lugano and in October 1963 he was named 'aesthetics consultant for the motorway', permitting him to impose his artistic vision onto the design of every one of its elements over the course of twenty years.

On the construction of this infrastructure and on Tami's fundamental contribution, see the essay dedicated specifically to him in this book.[33] It is worth remembering here that Tami was assisted by Aurelio Galfetti[34] (fig. 4) and, later on, by Flora Ruchat-Roncati, who, thanks to his help, was commissioned in the early 1970s for the design of two service areas, one in Chiasso–Brogeda (not built) and one in Coldrerio (built to a different project)[35]. Their experience with the N2 motorway project would, in fact, play a crucial role in their careers. Without this background, it is difficult to imagine Flora Ruchat-Roncati's work for the N16 Transjurane motorway (for which she designed, together with Renato Salvi, a series of major structures, following their victory in the competition launched in 1989, on which jury Tami served), or – as a member of the Beratungsgruppe für Gestaltung Alptransit – her work for the Saint Gotthard high-speed railway line.[36] Galfetti, the author of remarkable proposals for road, railway, and hydroelectric infrastructure, also devoted considerable efforts in the initial planning phase of the new railway route.[37]

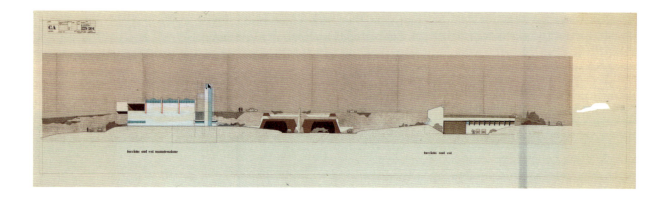

4. Rino Tami with Aurelio Galfetti, control centre at the Gotthard motorway Tunnel, Airolo, inaugurated 1980. South-east elevation drawing of the ventilation centre, the tunnel portal, and the vehicle and salt depot (intermediate version), 26 October 1972, with modifications up to 30 May 1973.

The *Tendenzen* Generation

Questioned by the editors of *archithese* on why he decided to give the reinforced concrete of Casa Rotalinti an untreated, 'brut de décoffrage' finish, Galfetti cited, on the one hand, the authoritativeness of Le Corbusier's work and, on the other, a desire to distance himself from the organicist approaches that had been so successful in Ticino from the second half of the 1950s. The effects of this wish could be seen at a glance on the hill overlooking Bellinzona, in the contrast between Galfetti's first work, Casa Rotalinti, before this was swallowed up by vegetation, and the nearby Casa Verda – built at almost the same time, between 1961 and 1962, by Rino Tami. The stone walls and carefully articulated roof pitches of Tami's house were meant to help integrate it into the landscape.[38] Galfetti even confessed (with his usual intellectual honesty and understatement) that at that moment in time, he had not really reflected on certain choices, and that it was only over the course of years that they became loaded with more complex and layered meanings. (Among other things, Galfetti also disclosed that, not unlike Rino Tami with his Cantonal Library, he had hesitated at length about whether to plaster the facades of Casa Rotalinti.)[39] Thus, towards the mid-1980s, by which time his partnership with Flora Ruchat-Roncati and Ivo Trümpy had dissolved more than a decade earlier, and having begun his arduous and passionate search for a new language, Galfetti would tend to think of Casa Rotalinti as a sort of 'fourth Castle' overlooking Bellinzona, and the rugged surfaces of his reinforced concrete facades as a revisitation of, and in 'analogical' harmony with, the granite of Bellinzona's fortifications, on which he was working at that time as part of the project for the restoration of Castelgrande (1981–2000).[40] This analogy between stone and concrete was also one of the motifs in the project for the Bagno di Bellinzona (a public swimming pool complex, 1967–70), designed by Galfetti together with Flora Ruchat-Roncati and Ivo Trümpy.[41] The reinforced concrete surfaces of the swimming pools were left exposed (they would be painted, for maintenance reasons, a few years after the complex was inaugurated), permitting them to re-propose the unity of material that Galfetti and his friends loved about a popular nearby landmark: the Lavertezzo bridge. Built of stone over the granite swimming holes in the Verzasca River, it condenses some of the fundamental themes that reappear in the Bagno. The architects themselves made references to the bridge in the first board of the winning competition project. The exposed concrete of the pools would cause the water to take on a colour much like the rivers and streams of the Sopraceneri valleys, thus avoiding the frivolous cliché of the blue-painted swimming pool while making an allusive reference to a geometrised, artificially natural context. Though much has been written about the elevated walkway and the relationship it establishes between the city and the river, and between those walking or standing on it and the surrounding landscape, another fundamental element of the project worth noting is how the configurations of the swimming pools and entire complex leave their imprint in the alluvial plain of the Ticino River (which the reclamation works had transformed into a sort of artefact in itself). Clearly the architects paid particular attention to this aspect, as demonstrated by the long genesis of the magnificent children's pool. This attests to the capacity of reinforced concrete to bring forms and elements together into a unitary whole (the pool and the slide, in the specific case), but it also reminds us of the necessary complexity of the design and construction process behind the creation of such forms. The plans drawn by the architects, complete with the conformation of contour lines to create an artificial topography (fig. 5), and those by the engineers (in this case, Guido Steiner for the pools and Enzo Vanetta as co-designer of the elevated walkway) (fig. 6), as well as the photographs of the building site, in particular the construction of the formwork for the slide (fig. 7), also illustrate this necessary level of complexity.[42]

The project for the Bagno di Bellinzona demonstrated once again the polysemous nature of reinforced concrete, which Aurelio Galfetti continued to deal with on numerous occasions, articulating it in various ways, but always with his open and anti-dogmatic approach to architecture. Consider, for example, his combination of pigmented reinforced concrete and thin stone inserts in three apartment buildings in the Via Vela residential quarter of Bellizona ('Al Portone', 1984–85, and 'Bianco' and 'Nero', 1984–86),[43] or his precast concrete panels, traversed by vertical slits, in another apartment building in the same neighbourhood (Casa Ghidossi, 1994–95), or his corrugated concrete wall for the Bellinzona tennis club, situated to the north of the Bagno (inaugurated in 1986).

Luigi Snozzi had different reasons for his predilection for exposed reinforced concrete, at least from the moment that he parted ways with Livio Vacchini, with whom he had also experimented with steel frameworks, plastered masonry walls, and timber-framed curtain walls. In my opinion, at the heart of his decision to use reinforced concrete was its ability to fuse, in a single gesture, the act of shaping the ground (for example, by means of retaining walls) and of staging the landscape through a calibrated sequence of views along a pathway. The paradigm of this approach is, of course, Casa Kalman, in Brione sopra Minusio (1974–76) (fig. 8), which accepted the challenge of an 'impossible' plot of land – one that was steep and curved – to delineate a route that offers the experience of both domestic space and landscape. The path to the house (which in the original project unfolded in parallel to the contours of the land and reached the entrance by means of a small bridge over the river) culminates on the opposite side with a

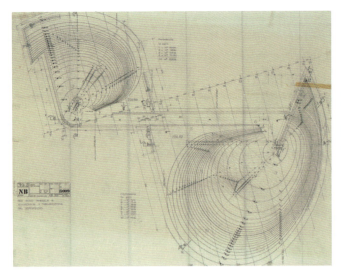

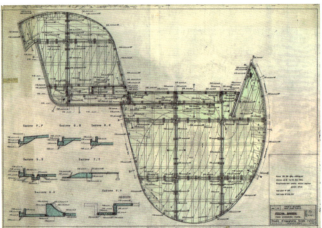

5. Aurelio Galfetti, Flora Ruchat-Roncati, and Ivo Trümpy, Bagno di Bellinzona, 1967–70. Plan drawing of the children's pool, 7 October 1968.

6. Aurelio Galfetti, Flora Ruchat-Roncati, and Ivo Trümpy, Bagno di Bellinzona, 1967–70. Plan drawing of the reinforcing for the children's pool by engineer Guido Steiner, 29 October 1968.

7. Aurelio Galfetti, Flora Ruchat-Roncati, and Ivo Trümpy, Bagno di Bellinzona, 1967–70. Construction of the formwork for the slide into the children's pool, November 1968.

pergola framing a distant view of Lake Verbano. Both in reality and in the drawings that represent it, including the site plan, the house, terrace, and pergola all combine into a single figure that acquires, despite the small size of the home's interior, a distinct presence in the landscape. A similar argument could be made for Casa Bianchetti in Locarno-Monti (1975–77) or Casa Heschl in Agarone (1983–84). In Casa Cavalli in Verscio (1976–78) (fig. 9), the reinforced concrete walls establish a close dialogue with the existing granite enclosures and retaining walls, reiterating the leitmotif of the round table between Galfetti, Snozzi, and Vacchini with which we started our discussion, that is, the analogy between stone and concrete.

For Luigi Snozzi, reinforced concrete (as articulated by him, always re-proposing the same finish and avoiding experimentation with surfaces textures or colours) was one of the tools that served to implement that process of formal reduction that characterises his architecture (and its design genesis) and to 'give meaning to the relationships between things, rather than to the things in themselves'.[44] The authoritativeness of his work, combined with his role as a full professor of design at the Swiss Federal Institute of Technology in Lausanne, greatly contributed to the diffusion of this material amongst both the architects closely associated with him and the next and more recent generations.

Numerous other Ticinese architects of the generation born in the 1930s used exposed reinforced concrete with impressive results, for instance Mario Campi and Franco Pessina (the two partnered with Niki Piazzoli from 1969), Giancarlo Durisch, and Dolf Schnebli (Ticinese by adoption), as well as other, lesser-known figures (at least in terms of attention by the critics), including Alberto Finzi, Sergio Pagnamenta, and Vittorio Pedrocchi.[45] Together their works testify to the variety of orientations and experiments that coexisted during a historic period of great cultural fermentation, the narration of which was certainly flattened and oversimplified by the controversial definition of a 'Ticinese School'.[46] If we do not linger on the work of these architects, it is to devote our attention to the person who, more than anyone else, contributed to reflections on the structural use of reinforced concrete in Ticino – Livio Vacchini.

Vacchini's first work, Casa Beheim (1961–62), is a small building in exposed concrete (unfortunately painted a few decades ago in a colour partway between cream and apricot) clinging to the hillside overlooking Solduno. However, the decision to adopt reinforced concrete as his material of choice only came about in the 1980s, by this time well-prepared by the tectonic discipline he had acquired over his long experience with steel[47] and anticipated (with a preponderance of a tectonic approach, in the form of an extensive use of prefabricated concrete elements) by his gymnasium for the Saleggi primary school in Locarno (1976–79).[48] His new predilection for concrete found its first full manifestation in the Collina d'Oro primary school (1977–84)[49] (fig. 10) and an ulterior, decisive, maturation in the house he would build for himself at Costa di Tenero (1986–92) (fig. 11), in his gymnasium in Losone (1990–97), and in his remarkable submission for the competition for the new town hall in Nice, France (1999–2000, with Silvia Gmür, and with the fundamental contribution of the engineer Aurelio Muttoni).

8. Luigi Snozzi with Walter von Euw, Casa Kalman, Brione sopra Minusio, 1974–76. View of the pergola towards the house, photograph Jan Derwig.

9. Luigi Snozzi with Walter von Euw, Casa Cavalli, Verscio, 1976–78. South view.

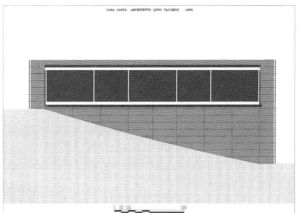

10. Livio Vacchini, Collina d'Oro primary school, Montagnola, 1977–84. View of the courtyard, photograph Alberto Flammer.

11. Livio Vacchini, house in Costa di Tenero, 1986–92. Side elevation, drawing for publication, 1992.

Much has been written on the role of the structure as a generator of form in the architecture of Livio Vacchini. The critical interpretations that have prevailed thus far, endorsed by the architect himself,[50] emphasise the logic and (presumed) insight of his works. Vacchini himself wrote in one of his notebooks that one must 'reflect on the art and make the object intelligible. Observers must bring their own intelligence to the game. However, they must understand how the building (or the game) works'.[51] And yet, if we investigate the nature of his architecture, beginning with archival documents (applying the tool of genetic criticism) and proceeding unfettered by the prevailing interpretation, a complexity and richness emerges, determined by a coexistence of possible readings that make his work appear far less apodictic and even more interesting.[52] (After all, it was Vacchini himself who noted, in November 2002, that 'a work "holds up" over time when it is capable of eliciting new interpretations. A new gaze creates a new work').[53]

The possibilities offered by reinforced concrete associated with prestressing have long been at the heart of Vacchini's design investigations, but his interest in this material was also fuelled by a search for 'unity', because 'the architect searches for unity. This reasoning incites him to choose a material that is suited to the construction of foundations as well as walls and floor slabs: a universal material'.[54]

A Digression in the Form of a Conclusion: Mario Botta and the Success of BKS in Ticino

The reader will have noticed that no mention has been made thus far of Mario Botta. The fact is that exposed reinforced concrete holds a secondary role in his architecture, and it was limited to certain buildings, such as his early Casa Della Casa in Stabio (1965–67) and, using lightweight concrete with expanded clay aggregate, his famous Morbio Inferiore middle school (1972–77), and his municipal gymnasium in Balerna (1976–78). In the first phase of his career, Botta preferred using concrete block in the version imprinted with the acronym BKS. The blocks were manufactured in Ticino by Agglomerati di Cemento, a private company at the time, founded in 1934 by Arnoldo Bariffi.[55] They were originally made 'with air chambers in a concrete, tuff, and terracotta conglomerate', and later, at the peak of their diffusion, with a mix of 'sand, gravel, "Larges" expanded clay, Portland cement, iron oxides, and water'.[56]

Nonetheless, Mario Botta was not the first to explore the constructive and aesthetic potential of BKS concrete face block. His first teacher and mentor, Tita Carloni, had already used concrete block for his Casa-atelier for the artist Edmondo Dobrzanski in Gentilino (1965–66) and, in the same years, for a single-family home in Rovio, a temporary building at the Beata Vergine hospital in Mendrisio (with Luigi Snozzi and Livio Vacchini), and the Pinacoteca Giovanni Züst in Rancate (1965–67).[57] It should also be pointed out that Carloni had a certain aversion for unfinished reinforced concrete and for the precariousness (if not total inadequacy) of certain structural solutions explored by his younger colleagues.[58] Instead (like Tami and Brivio), he put considerable emphasis on the importance of attention to details and perfect execution. The discipline imposed by the modularity of masonry was seen by Carloni as a resource (unlike Luigi Snozzi, who saw it as a useless bother),[59] while the rough, wrinkled surface of the BKS block evoked a 'threshold' condition between natural and artificial (a sort of rusticity imbued with urbanity that Carlo Cattaneo had recognised, in the 1800s, as a characteristic of Ticino).[60]

Mario Botta's decision to use BKS concrete blocks (also to avoid the construction problems attributed to exposed reinforced concrete) in his early works (fig. 12) was decisive for the success of this material in Ticino. It was supported by an effective business and media operation[61] that was so widespread 'that it almost became a symbol of the region'.[62] However, this sudden success was followed by an equally rapid decline, perhaps also due to the formal connotations often associated with the material.[63] This has not been the case of exposed reinforced concrete, which attests to how the polysemous nature of this endlessly adaptable material continues to fuel the design thinking and practice of the younger generations of Ticinese architects.

12. Cover and double internal page, dedicated to the house in Ligornetto by Mario Botta (1975–76), from *BKS Architettura in Ticino / Architektur im Tessin / Architecture au Tessin*, published in 1986.

Notes

[1] This essay is based on research carried out as part of a project funded by the Swiss National Science Foundation, 'Architecture in Canton Ticino, 1945–1980', promoted by the Archivio del Moderno of the Università della Svizzera italiana–Academy of Architecture, and directed by the author.
'Dans notre pays, il est à peu près impossible de ne pas construire en béton.' The affirmation, by Livio Vacchini, is from 'Beton/Béton. Gespräch über Beton als Bau- und als Ausdrucksmaterial mit Aurelio Galfetti, Luigi Snozzi und Livio Vacchini', *archithese* 16 (1986), no. 2, 4–14, 32, here 12 (note that the German version is a little different: 'unter unseren Bedingungen ist es nicht möglich, nicht mit Beton zu bauen', ibid., 6).

[2] Nicola Navone, '"Exercer son propre métier jusqu'au bout". Architecture récente dans le canton du Tessin/"Practicing craft to its fullest". Recent Architecture in the Canton of Ticino', *Faces*, no. 74 (Autumn 2018), 6–18.

[3] 'Beton/Béton' (see note 1).

[4] *Costruzioni-Casabella* 15, no. 173 (1942), 24–31. George Everard Kidder Smith, *Switzerland Builds: Its Native and Modern Architecture* (New York: Bonnier, 1950), 212–3. For the bibliography (updated in 2006) of writings devoted to the Cantonal Library by the Tami brothers, see the relative entry by Riccardo Bergossi in Kenneth Frampton and Riccardo Bergossi, *Rino Tami. Opera completa* (Mendrisio: Mendrisio Academy Press, 2008), 200–15. Riccardo Bergossi's monograph, *La Biblioteca cantonale di Lugano di Carlo e Rino Tami*, Mendrisio Academy Press, is in the course of publication. I would like to thank Riccardo Bergossi for his generosity in sharing his profound knowledge of Tami's work.

[5] Having graduated in civil engineering at the Swiss Federal Institute of Technology in Zurich (information from *Schweizerische Bauzeitung* 99, no. 3, 1932, 36), and being the same age as Rino Tami, Agostino Casanova (1908–94) opened a studio in Lugano in association with the engineer Spartaco Prada (who, like him, was a native of Mendrisiotto). He continued to work with Rino Tami on numerous occasions, forming a solid professional partnership with him; see Frampton and Bergossi, *Rino Tami* (see note 4).

[6] Another example of the use of this material on the part of Salvisberg is the district heating plant at the Swiss Federal Institute of Technology in Zurich, completed in 1935. It is also worth remembering that Tami attended Salvisberg's design studio at the Swiss Federal Institute of Technology in Zurich the year before, in 1934.

[7] On what the design of the Cantonal Library owes to Salvisberg's architecture, see, in particular, the essays by Kenneth Frampton, 'L'architettura di Rino Tami' and Riccardo Bergossi, 'Rino Tami e l'architettura in Ticino negli anni Trenta', in Frampton and Bergossi, *Rino Tami* (see note 4), 10–37 (the reference to Perret is on p. 13) and 38–83 (the reference to the Institutes of the University of Bern is on p. 67).

[8] 'Proibire per un adeguato numero di anni l'uso dell'intonaco sulle facciate' (Rino Tami, 'I sepolcri imbiancati dell'architettura', in *Il 900 e il 900 da noi. Numero unico Gauno d'architettura*, Lugano: Mazzuconi, 1936, 28–31).

[9] See, for example, Rino Tami, 'Della verità in architettura', in Tita Carloni (ed.), *Rino Tami. 50 anni di architettura* (Lugano: Fondazione Arturo e Margherita Lang, 1984), 167–174 (text of the inaugural lecture held at the Swiss Federal Institute of Technology in Zurich). But see also Rino Tami, 'Problemi estetici dell'autostrada', *Rivista tecnica della Svizzera Italiana* 60, no. 24 (1969), 1607–20; (German transl.: 'Die Beteiligung des Architekten bei Ingenieurbauten. Ästhetische Probleme beim Bau von Autobahnen', *Deutsche Bauzeitung* 104, no. 9, 1970, 715–20); later republished in *Brücken-, Tunnel- und Strassenbau im Gebirge/Construction de ponts, tunnels et routes dans les massifs montagneux*, proceedings of the day of study (Lugano, 24–25 September 1982) (Zürich: 1982), 23–9 and idem, 'L'autostrada come opera d'arte', in Carloni (ed.), *Rino Tami*, ibid., 122–5.

[10] In 1957, Rino Tami was appointed full professor of architectural design at the Department of Architecture of the Swiss Federal Institute of Technology in Zurich, a position he gave up in 1961 to devote himself entirely to his profession.

[11] On the Church of the Sacred Heart of Jesus and the adjacent residence of the Capuchin Fathers, see Riccardo Bergossi, 'Rino Tami con Carlo Tami, Chiesa del Sacro Cuore a Bellinzona', in Nicola Navone (ed.), *Guida storico-critica all'architettura del XX secolo nel*

Cantone Ticino, vol. I (Balerna: Archivio del Moderno, 2020) (with previous bibl.), I.CF.1.01–06. The work is available in Open Access at the webpage https://www.ticino4580.ch/, together with the version in English: Nicola Navone (ed.), *A Historical-Critical Guide to 20th-Century Architecture in Canton Ticino*, vol. I (Balerna: Archivio del Moderno, 2021).

[12] Agostino Casanova appears, together with his associate Spartaco Prada, as the person responsible for the 'calcoli statici cem[ento] arm[ato]' (static calculations for the reinforced concrete) in the table summarising the architects, consultants, builders, and suppliers on the construction site in 'Nuova Chiesa del Sacro Cuore', published 16 November 1939 by the *Gazzetta ticinese*.

[13] The masonry was meant to be modelled after that of the Church of the Sacred Heart, with squared ashlars of various sizes, in white Osogna granite, Nero di Lodrino granite, and white and grey Castione granite, but in the end it was simplified at the request of the project management company, Motor-Columbus, based in Baden. See Riccardo Bergossi, 'Facciate per la Centrale elettrica del Lucendro', in Frampton and Bergossi, *Rino Tami* (see note 4), 234–7.

[14] Rino Tami, 'L'architettura delle centrali idroelettriche', *Wasserwirtschaft – Naturschutz, Sonderheft der Schweizerischen Monatszeitschrift Wasser- und Energiewirtschaft* 15, no. 8/9/10 (1959), 259–63.

[15] Riccardo Bergossi, 'Casa d'appartamenti Fischer Marcionelli (Casa Solatia)', in Frampton and Bergossi, *Rino Tami* (see note 4), 270–3.

[16] See Riccardo Bergossi, 'Rino Tami con Carlo Tami, Fabbrica Frieden', in Navone (ed.), *Guida storico-critica all'architettura*, vol. I (see note 11), I.IND.1.01–04.

[17] With the exception of the volume that hosts the storage area on the second floor, the infill panels of which are finished with wooden slats in place of the silica-calcareous bricks used for the rest of the building.

[18] See Riccardo Bergossi, 'Stabilimento Usego', in Frampton and Bergossi, *Rino Tami* (see note 4), 276–81.

[19] According to testimony by Tita Carloni recorded in the documentary *Il club degli architetti*, by Wladimir Tchertkoff and Michele Fazioli, originally aired on 15 November 1983, episode on 'Orsa Maggiore', https://www.rsi.ch/play/tv/dossier-alla-scoperta-dellarchitettura-in-ticino/video/il-club-degli-architetti?id=12854728, last accessed 20 April 2020.

[20] 'Scomparso dai cantieri ticinesi e destinato poi ad invaderli per dritto e per traverso, nel senso letterale della parola' (Tita Carloni, 'Tra conservazione e innovazione. Appunti sull'Architettura nel Canton Ticino dal 1930 al 1980', in P. Disch, ed., *50 anni di architettura in Ticino. Quaderno della Rivista tecnica della Svizzera italiana*, Bellinzona–Lugano: 1983, 4–11, also published in *Ingénieurs et architectes suisses* 109, no. 10, 1983, 161–7, here 165).

[21] On Peppo Brivio, see Annalisa Viati Navone, *Verso un'architettura concreta. Peppo Brivio, le prime opere* (Bellinzona–Gentilino: Edizioni Sottoscala–Fondazione Archivi Architetti Ticinesi, 2021).

[22] On the origin of the building, see Riccardo Bergossi, 'Rino Tami con Carlo Tami e Peppo Brivio, Cinema Corso, Case "La Piccionaia" e "il Cardo"', in Navone (ed.), *Guida storico-critica all'architettura*, vol. I (see note 11), I.DM.1.01–06.

[23] Related to the dialect term 'bindell', the 'bindello' is the 'narrow strip that concrete finishers, plasterers, and painters would respect in the proximity of edges, in order not to alter them' ('stretta striscia che i cementisti, i modellisti e i pittori erano soliti rispettare in vicinanza degli spigoli, per non alterarli.' Tita Carloni, 'Trasformare gli edifici moderni: una pratica complessa', in *Progetto Biblioteca. Spazio, storia e funzioni della Biblioteca cantonale di Lugano*, Lugano–Losone: Biblioteca cantonale di Lugano–Edizioni Le Ricerche, 2005, 81–5).

[24] I am referring to the Perret–Le Corbusier polemic, masterfully investigated by Bruno Reichlin, 'L'"intérieur" tradizionale insidiato dalla finestra a nastro. La Petite Maison a Corseaux, 1923–1924', in idem, *Dalla 'soluzione elegante' all'"edificio aperto'. Scritti attorno and alcune opere di Le Corbusier*, edited by Annalisa Viati Navone, (Mendrisio–Cinisello Balsamo: Mendrisio Academy Press–Silvana Editoriale, 2013), 87–132 (with previous bibl.).

[25] See Bergossi, 'Cinema Corso, Case "La Piccionaia" e "il Cardo"' (see note 22).

[26] See, in addition to the headquarters of the Radio della Svizzera italiana, discussed below, in particular the Palazzo delle Dogane (Federal Customs Administration building)

(1958–62) and the Casa Boni e Regazzoni (1959–62) in Lugano (for which see Riccardo Bergossi, 'Rino Tami con Francesco van Kuyk, Palazzo delle Dogane e Casa Boni e Regazzoni', in Navone (ed.), *Guida storico-critica all'architettura*, vol. I (see note 11), I.DM.2.01–04; Case Skory in Sorengo (1960–66), Casa Dufour Anstalt in Lugano (1961–63) and Casa Beretta in Locarno (1962–65), for which see Frampton and Bergossi, *Rino Tami* (see note 4), 388–93, 394–7 and 402–4.

27 Nicola Navone, 'Alberto Camenzind, Augusto Jäggli, Rino Tami, Studio della Radio della Svizzera italiana', in Navone (ed.), *Guida storico-critica all'architettura*, vol. I (see note 11), I.CU.1.01–06. For Alberto Camenzind, as well as Werner Oechslin and Flora Ruchat-Roncati (eds.), 'Alberto Camenzind. Architekt, Chefarchitekt Expo 64, Lehrer' (Zürich: gta, 1998), see, for example, Alberto Franchini, 'Alberto Camenzind e Bruno Brocchi, Edificio Partimco', in Nicola Navone (ed.), *Guida storico-critica all'architettura del XX secolo nel Cantone Ticino*, vol. II (Balerna: Archivio del Moderno, 2021, forthcoming publication); for Augusto Jäggli, among other works, see the expansion of the Nord primary schools in Bellinzona (1959) and the Bianchi and Monti apartment buildings on Via Ciseri in Lugano (1959) in Paolo Fumagalli (ed.), *Augusto Jäggli architetto 1911–1999* ([Gentilino]: Fondazione Archivi Architetti Ticinesi, 2003).

28 From one of his very first works, the Arizona Hotel in Lugano (1955–57, for which see Franz Graf and Britta Buzzi-Huppert (eds.), *Tita Carloni. Albergo Arizona, 1955–1957* (Mendrisio: Mendrisio Academy Press, 2016), to other works, for which refer to Alberto Franchini, 'Tita Carloni, Edificio a destinazione mista in via Franchini', 'Tita Carloni, Immobili d'abitazione in via Beltramina', in Navone (ed.), *Guida storico-critica all'architettura*, vol. I (see note 11), I.DM.3.01–06, I.AB.8.01–06 and 'Complesso a destinazione mista Albergo Milano', in Navone (ed.), *Guida storico-critica all'architettura*, vol. II (see note 27)).

29 I am thinking in particular about the departure station of the Orselina–Cardada cable car (1951–52, unfortunately demolished) and the Casa Rosolaccio in Chiasso (1958–60).

30 Among whom we could mention, for example, Oscar Hofmann, Alex Huber, and Luigi Nessi.

31 In this regard, please refer to the results of the research conducted by Alberto Franchini as part of the SNSF research project 'Architecture in Canton Ticino, 1945–1980', promoted by the Archivio del Moderno and directed by the author of this essay.

32 See Riccardo Bergossi, 'Rino Tami con Peppo Brivio, Casa Torre', in Navone (ed.), *Guida storico-critica all'architettura*, vol. I (see note 11), I.AB.3.01–06. The structure was calculated by the engineer Walter Krüsi, Appenzeller by origin but Ticinese by adoption, and one of the pioneers of reinforced concrete in the subalpine canton.

33 Ilaria Giannetti, 'The N2 Chiasso–Saint Gotthard Motorway: Design and Construction of One Hundred and Forty-Three Kilometres of Reinforced Concrete', 63–76.

34 See Serena Maffioletti, 'L'"orgogliosa modestia" della N2', in Frampton and Bergossi, *Rino Tami* (see note 4), 137–75 and Nicola Navone, 'Rino Tami, architecte-conseil de l'autoroute Chiasso–Saint-Gothard', *fabricA* 11 (2017), 12–43.

35 See Serena Maffioletti, 'Composizioni infrastrutturali: i sogni ad occhi aperti di Flora Ruchat-Roncati', in Serena Maffioletti, Nicola Navone, and Carlo Toson (eds.), *Un dialogo ininterrotto. Studi su Flora Ruchat-Roncati* (Padova: Il Polifilo), 2018, 159–84.

36 For this and other infrastructure projects, see ibid.

37 See Laurent Stalder, 'La topografia di Aurelio Galfetti / Aurelio Galfetti's Topography', in Franz Graf (ed.), *Aurelio Galfetti. Costruire lo spazio / The Construction on Space* (Mendrisio–Cinisello Balsamo: Mendrisio Academy Press–Silvana Editoriale, 2021), 121–34.

38 An amusing anecdote about Galfetti in 'Beton/Béton' (see note 1), 4.

39 Ibid.

40 On Casa Rotalinti as the 'fourth Castle' of Bellinzona, see ibid., 6 and 'Una conversazione con Aurelio Galfetti', P.-A. Croset (ed.), *Casabella* 49, no. 518 (1985), 56–7.

41 On Bagno di Bellinzona, see Nicola Navone and Bruno Reichlin (eds.), *Il Bagno di Bellinzona di Aurelio Galfetti, Flora Ruchat-Roncati, Ivo Trümpy* (Mendrisio: Mendrisio Academy Press, 2010, 3ed. 2021) and N. Navone, 'Dagli esordi al Bagno di Bellinzona. Congetture sull'architettura di Flora Ruchat-Roncati', in Maffioletti, Navone, and Toson (eds.), *Un dialogo ininterrotto* (see note 35), 31–90.

42 For these documents, see, respectively, Fondo Aurelio Galfetti, Fondo Guido Steiner, Enzo

Vanetta – Bagno di Bellinzona, and Fondo Flora Ruchat-Roncati of the Archivio del Moderno.

[43] In particular for the 'Bianco' and 'Nero' apartment buildings, see Nicola Navone, 'Il Mediterraneo tra le Alpi. Un progetto e un'opera di Lio Galfetti / The Mediterranean amid the Alps. A Project and a Work by Lio Galfetti', in Graf (ed.), *Aurelio Galfetti* (see note 37), 78–105.

[44] 'Beton / Béton' (see note 1), 6. I have translated here from the German version '…der Beziehung zwischen den Dingen Bedeutung zu geben, und weniger der Dingen selber', which differs, once again, from the French version ('Je vise ainsi à favoriser les relations entre les éléments, les volumes, plutôt que les éléments proprement dits'). Just a bit further down (ibid., 11), Snozzi describes reinforced concrete as an 'elementary' material: 'A concrete wall forms a whole; it is not made up of stones piled upon each another, it is, in and of itself, *one* stone; it is a monolith' ('Un mur en béton forme un tout; il n'est pas constitué de pierres empilées les unes sur les autres, il est à lui seul *une* pierre; il est un monolithe') (the italics are in the original).

[45] For Alberto Finzi see, for example, Francesco Tadini, 'Alberto Finzi e Paolo Zürcher, Fercasa', in Navone (ed.), *Guida storico-critica all'architettura*, vol. I (see note 11), I.AB.7.01–06 and Leone Carlo Ghoddousi, 'Alberto Finzi, Centro scolastico Nosedo a Massagno', in Navone (ed.), *Guida storico-critica all'architettura*, vol. II (see note 27). For Sergio Pagnamenta, see, for example, the Casa al Lago in Lavena (1958, mentioned also by Carloni, 'Tra conservazione e innovazione', see note 20, 165) or his primary schools in Viganello (1974–78); for Vittorio Pedrocchi, see, for example, the Muralto primary school (1963–69) and the Gordola middle school (1978–81).

[46] To contradict those who use the term in the singular, *Tendenza* ticinese, forgetting that not by chance (as we have been recently reminded again by Luca Ortelli, 'Architettura nel Cantone Ticino. Da Tendenzen alla condizione contemporanea', *Archi*, no. 6, 2017, 25–9), the 1975 exhibition and book were titled *Tendenzen*, in the plural.

[47] Consider, for example, the Fabrizia administrative building in Bellinzona (with Luigi Snozzi, 1962–66), the Macconi commercial and office building in Lugano (with Alberto Tibiletti, 1969–75), and the Losone secondary school (with Aurelio Galfetti, 1972–74), for which, regarding the steel construction, see Franz Graf, 'De la vulnérabilité à la solidité', *matières*, no. 16 (2020), 199–209.

[48] See Roberta Grignolo, 'Livio Vacchini. Scuola elementare ai Saleggi di Locarno', in Navone (ed.), *Guida storico-critica all'architettura*, vol. I (see note 11), G I.SC.4.01–06.

[49] See Martino Romani, 'Livio Vacchini. Scuola elementare della Collina d'Oro', in Navone (ed.), *Guida storico-critica all'architettura*, vol. I (see note 11), I.SC.7.01–06.

[50] In particular, I have in mind the interpretation of Vacchini's work offered on multiple occasions by Roberto Masiero, who enjoyed the esteem and friendship of the Ticino architect, and for whom see idem, *Livio Vacchini. Opere e progetti*, (Milano: Electa, 1999) (English ed. Barcelona: Gustavo Gili, 1999).

[51] 'Bisogna riflettere sull'arte e rendere l'oggetto intelleggibile [sic]. Lo spettatore deve partecipare con la sua intelligenza al gioco. Si deve però capire come l'opera è fatta (o il gioco)', from a notebook presently conserved in the architect's studio in Locarno, undated, noted on the title page 'Livio Vacchini / via Bramantino 22 / CH 6600 Locarno'.

[52] In this regard, see the research project promoted by the Archivio del Moderno on the work of Livio Vacchini, directed by Paolo Amaldi and by the author of this essay, the first results of which are contained in Paolo Amaldi, 'Livio Vacchini, les multiples chemins de la forme', *matières*, no. 16 (2020), 183–197 and idem, *Logotecnica. I paradossi della forma nell'opera di Livio Vacchini*, Mendrisio Academy Press (forthcoming publication, February 2022). On the various possible interpretations of a work by Vacchini, see also Martino Pedrozzi, *Il Lido di Ascona di Livio Vacchini. Una teoria del giunto* (Bellinzona: Casagrande, 2017).

[53] 'L'opera "tiene" nel tempo quando è capace di suscitare una nuova interpretazione. Un nuovo sguardo fa un'opera nuova', from a notebook presently conserved at the architect's studio in Locarno (on the title page: 'Livio Vacchini / Annotazioni / 1968–'). The citation is dated November 2002.

[54] 'L'architecte recherche l'unité. Son raisonnement le pousse à choisir un matériau qui se prête aussi bien à la réalisation des fondations, qu'à celle des murs et des dalles, un matériau universel' ('Beton / Béton', see note 1, 12).

[55] The information on the foundation of the 'Agglomerati di Cemento' company is in *Foglio*

ufficiale svizzero di commercio, no. 9 (2 January 1934), 99. Besides Bariffi, the original board of directors included Aldo Veladini, the engineer Ugo Früh, Fritz Wullschleger, and Carlo Vicari.

[56] The two quotations are from, respectively, an advertisement that appeared in the pages of the *Gazzetta ticinese*, dated 29 September 1934, and *BKS Architettura e tecnica / Architektur und Technik / Architecture et Technique* (Bellinzona: Salvioni, 1992), 14.

[57] The OTAF Building in Sorengo (1968–71) and Casa Jelmorini in Pregassona soon followed (1968–69).

[58] Carloni makes his criticism clear in 'Tra conservazione e innovazione' (see note 20), 165.

[59] 'You have all gone crazy with these concrete blocks, it never ends! I don't want to see them anymore! Reinforced concrete! I'm not the least bit interested in knowing that there are thirty-seven and three-fourths modules! There's a window here: that's it. It's this big. End of story! And now I have freedom of composition.' ('Voi siete matti con questi mattoni, non si finisce più! Non voglio più vederli! Cemento armato! A me non interessa sapere se qui ci sono trentasette moduli e tre quarti, no! Qui c'è una finestra: è così. Ha questa misura. Fine! E ho libertà di composizione.' 'Tita Carloni, una voce critica dell'architettura ticinese', interview by S. Martinoli and F. Mena, *Archivio Storico Ticinese* 48, no. 149, 2011, 33–62, here 51).

[60] That is, 'a unique mixture of rustic customs and worldly experience' ('una singolar mistura di costumi rusticali e d'esperienza mondana.' C. Cattaneo, *Notizie naturali e civili sulla Lombardia*, printed by G. Bernardoni, Milan: 1844, paragraph XLV, cited from the Rizzoli edition, Milano: 1990, 301).

[61] The manufacturing company sponsored the publication of two books, in Italian, French, and German, dedicated to a collection of works built with BKS concrete blocks. See *BKS Architettura in Ticino / Architektur im Tessin / Architecture au Tessin* (Bellinzona: Salvioni, 1986) and *BKS Architettura e tecnica* (1992) (see note 56). Numerous articles in the local press have been dedicated to the material and its use by the principal Ticinese architects.

[62] Paolo Fumagalli, 'Il significato di un materiale / Die Bedeutung eines Materials / La signification d'un matériau,' in *BKS Architettura in Ticino* (see note 61), 6. It should also be noted that BKS blocks were also used outside of Ticino, for example, in the work by Vincent Mangeat, who not by chance was a friend of Aurelio Galfetti and Mario Botta.

[63] A few years later Fabio Reinhart would controversially insert, in the north elevation of one of the entrance volumes of his Bellinzona Motorway Hotel, an elaborate composition in BKS blocks and prefabricated concrete elements, depicting (after long and careful observation) the faint image of a skull, to signify the death of (Ticinese) architecture.

Concrete in the Early Works of Herzog and de Meuron

Roberto Gargiani

The romantische Haus der Zukunft

Joseph Beuys studied the transformation processes – up to deterioration – of organic substances such as wax, grease, and vegetables, as well as materials such as oil painting itself. The phenomenon of programmed deterioration suffered by the concrete surfaces of some works by Herzog and de Meuron is the experimentation, in architecture, of the processes of continuous material transformation assumed in Beuys's artistic creation.

'He showed us – Herzog and de Meuron remember of their meeting with Beuys in 1977–78 – things we had never seen before: e.g., the way he operated with materials, he didn't use them only in a mono-functional way like architects tend to do – he had a much more sensual approach and he attributed symbolic meaning to materials. This symbolic side however never became part of our own work'.[1] The rough concrete cast in situ is, in the works of Herzog and de Meuron of the 1980s, the material for the construction of plinths and stairs. When it becomes part of the visible body of a building it assumes the form of blocks, plates, or skeletons so thin and fragmented that they appear as graphic lines, expressions of a concept, rather than real load-bearing structures. Outside of their work on industrial buildings, Herzog and de Meuron look for various ways to engender an artistic treatment of concrete, which has been increasingly pushed over the years to decorative excesses, searching for new artistic potential beyond the usual constructive or technical logic, according to Beuys' lesson. In their first works, certain characteristics – comparable to those of the materials in the works of Beuys and Arte Povera – are impressed on the concrete, to the point that it is possible to trace that 'quelque chose d'archaïque' felt by Herzog in the works of Beuys.[2] It is, however, significant that Herzog, specifically in regard to concrete, also refers to the architecture of Rossi, of whom he was a student during his time at the Swiss Federal Institute of Technology: 'In his earliest buildings made of poorly processed concrete, we discovered an affinity, something that swung to rest between Pasolini and Arte Povera'.[3]

The Blue House in Oberwil, in the countryside near Basel, built between 1979 and 1980, can be considered one of Herzog and de Meuron's first explorations on the nature of banal and poor materials in architecture. The image of the traditional house, seen through Rossi's lesson, becomes the first element – the ideal type – to undergo a transformation akin to those made by Beuys to felt or grease.

1. Herzog & de Meuron, the Blue House in Oberwil, 1979–80. Photograph by author.

2. Herzog & de Meuron, the Blue House in Oberwil, 1979–80, detail of the corner. Photograph by author.

A Gordon Matta Clark-like cut seems to have pulled out one of the walls of the house, the one facing the garden, in place of which a closure, inspired by the modernist genre of the thirties, is set. Another wall, the one along the road, is folded to accommodate other fragments of modernism (recalling the curved wall ramp in the gallery of the hôtel particulier La Roche, by Le Corbusier and Pierre Jeanneret). It is already clear, from the monstrous configuration derived from the manipulations to the ideal type, that the house can no longer be traditional. Similar operations are carried out on the construction materials themselves. The concrete is proposed in two of its basic states, poured on site and prefabricated (figs. 1–2).

In the house in Oberwil, the value attributed to in-situ concrete as a building material in direct contact with the earth is already evident. The concrete barely emerges from the ground, creating a visible plinth on which the walls of the house rest. The concrete cast on site, including that of the access steps (and that of the flat canopy, set on four steel beams and used as a terrace), is left exposed without painting, as if it were a natural geological substructure protecting the house from the infiltrations of water. A sewer pipe, also in unpainted concrete, is embedded in the plinth like an *objet trouvé*, bringing light to the underground room and evoking the main function of the plinth as a water collector.

The three traditional walls of the house are built not of brick or stone, but of ordinary concrete blocks. With this type of concrete, Herzog and de Meuron raise the question of visibility, which takes on different connotations and moves away from the truth conferred to the concrete of the plinth. The blocks are not plastered, revealing the extent to which that truth is at the centre of reflection on the material, nor are they left exposed because a thin layer of ultramarine blue paint is spread on the walls, 'with a very watered-down pigment',[4] which transforms the perception of the construction and the material – 'we used pure ultramarine blue (Yves Klein blue) pigment to destabilize the building brick walls,' says Herzog.[5] That colour makes it possible to unify the precast concrete of the blocks with the cast in situ pieces, creating openings of the most singular shapes – asymmetrical eyes, inspired by the house in Jacques Tati's film, *Mon oncle*, and the irregular horizontal slot cut out at the height of a bed.

The choice of ultramarine blue makes the concrete block masonry special. 'Destabilising', as Herzog states, means creating a feeling of ambiguity in the perception of the masonry, projecting it into a fairy tale dimension, similar to Adam's house in paradise, which detaches it from the brutalist declinations still present in Botta's early villas built with those same blocks. It is not surprising that the fairy tale house is covered with a steeply sloping gable roof, made with exposed and protruding wooden joists on which a roof covering – derived from Eternit concrete – is laid.

The image of the ordinary house has been violated by the blue colour, by the asymmetries, by the cut and by the folding walls, which have transformed it into a surprisingly 'ugly' work. The calculated use of the various forms of concrete – from cast on site, to the block, and to Eternit – is essential for the transfiguration of the traditional house into a work of Arte Povera. Up until the early decades of the 2000s, this 'betrayed' house is destined to become a recurring presence at various moments in the work of Herzog and de Meuron – an oft-repeated question awaiting an answer on what the 'romantische Haus der Zukunft'[6] is.

Everything changes concerning the form of Herzog and de Meuron's concrete in the house for E. K. Meid, in Tavole, in the mountains of Liguria, designed and built between 1982 and 1988, as well as in the 1984 competition project for the theatre in Visp, at the bottom of the Valais mountain landscape. In both works, the material is forced to become the supporting structure of a masonry made of local stones, which is not intended to be reduced to the worn expression of the infill or the covering. For this reason, the reinforced concrete does not take on the visible form of a regular spanned skeleton.

In the house in Tavole, the reinforced concrete simultaneously forms the two walls intersecting in a cross (which in the rectangular plan delineates four rooms without corridors), the four pillars in the corners, the slabs including that of the roof, and the trellis of the pergola. All these elements are visible except for the four pillars in the corners, which are hidden by the dry stone envelope. Thanks to their suppression, the cross walls become the iconic figure of the house, as in Fujii's Todoroki House. The geometry of the pergola also follows the same game of the suppression of elements, as demonstrated by the enigmatic arrangement

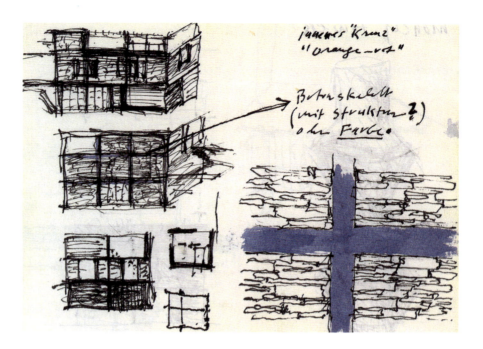

3. Herzog & de Meuron, Stone House, house for E. K. Meid in Tavole, 1982–88, sketch.

of the pillars (what static reason causes the median beam to rest on an intermediate pillar, which does not exist along the other two beams of the same length?) The fact that in the studies the concrete strips emerging from the dry stone walls are intended to be painted blue is an indication of the desire to make another artistic transfiguration of the material, as in the case of the concrete blocks of the Oberwil house. In the sketch, the opposition between two words, *struktur* and *farbe*, is indicative of the different role given to the bands of the *betonskelet*.[7] Even the hypothesis of colouring the *inneres 'kreuz'* orange confirms the role still given to colour in the aesthetic transfiguration of concrete.[8] (fig. 3)

'The house in Tavole – declares Herzog – is built on a grid structure of cast in-situ concrete beams; part of this grid structure is filled in with natural stones collected together by local masons. This architecture can of course be interpreted in different ways; but in fact we are here applying this serial principle for the first time, this "significance-free" structure, and we attain the "significance", the specific aptitude for the site through the limitation of this structure and through its cladding, or, in this case, its filling'.[9]

If the play of suppression makes the skeleton ambiguous, no less surprising are the effects, on the infill concept, of the intuition of resorting to dry stone masonry, widespread in local construction for terracing and small agricultural buildings. The absence of visible mortar corresponds to the invisible pillars in the house's corners, and therefore, even in the case of masonry, one is forced to wonder how those layers of stones remain standing and what their relationship is with the enigmatic skeleton. The work that at first glance seemed trivial turns out to be full of potential difficulties.

The paradox of the construction in the house in Tavole lies precisely in the combination of fragments of reinforced concrete skeleton and fragments of stones, without the two materials combining into a unity that had previously been seen. The stones themselves look as if they are dry mounted; in reality they are held together by a miracle, not without generating technical defects that have emerged over time, starting with the mortar applied to the base so as not to be visible.

It is evident that both the concrete and the stones are not treated according to a logical technique but according to the artists' impulse to want to test their nature. 'We push the material, we use to an extreme to show it dismantled from any other function than "being"', is the crucial statement of Herzog and de Meuron regarding the house in Tavole.[10]

It is worth emphasising that the skewed theorem of the house in Tavole rejected the use of colour envisaged in the initial phases of the project and appearing in its most perfect formulation. Only in the works of the following decades will ornamentation intervene to help the enunciation of the largest possible number of corollaries. For the theatre in Visp, once the pentagonal shape of the plan has been determined, Herzog and de Meuron study the geometry of internal beams and walls in order to avoid, as in the house in Tavole, the literal coincidence between the edges of the pentagon and the arrangement of the structure, from which one would have derived a logic of reinforced concrete bands visible along the facades, traceable to that of the frame and infill. The pattern of walls and beams more expressive of the disjunction between the perimeter envelope and the internal structure sought by Herzog and de Meuron produces a spiral-shaped dynamic figure. It so happens that the German name for Valais, Wallis, is also the name of the English mathematician John Wallis, who popularised a spiral assembly system of wooden beams later taken up by Christopher Wren in a project for the coverage of the Sheldonian Theatre in Oxford. The geometric scheme of Wallis and Wren coincides with that studied by Herzog and de Meuron for the structures in the Visp theatre, taking the place of the cross in the Tavole house. From the irregularly squared granite blocks, set up to create the thick walls of the theatre, as in Tavole, the frameworks emerge, still arranged according to an irregular geometry, where the pillars never coincide with the edges of the pentagon – 'a controlling geometric concrete-frame structure'[11] (fig. 4).

The value given by Herzog and de Meuron to exposed reinforced concrete, used in the basement of a house, becomes even more eloquent with the house of art collectors H. and M. Vögtlin-König, in Lerchenreinstrasse 5, in Therwil near Basel, built between 1985 and 1986. It is in this house that the materials' articulation, typical of traditional Swiss constructions with a masonry base and an upper wooden structure, is transposed into a reinforced concrete base on which the wooden structure of the house rests. The two parts give rise to two different compositions: the base responds to the question posed by the authors themselves, 'Abstraktion in der Architektur?',[12] thanks to the essential shapes of the walls which welcome the public with the courtyard leading into the artwork gallery; whereas the long rectangular house is the representation of the traditional Swiss house, yet another ideal type as in the Oberwil house. As seen in the Oberwil and Therwil houses, concrete plays a fundamental role in the aesthetic transfiguration of the type, but it can no longer be used in the form of blocks because Herzog and de Meuron are guided by a real passion for experimentation with materials (figs. 5–6).

4. Herzog & de Meuron, competition for the theater in Visp, 1984, sketch.

5. Herzog & de Meuron, house for art collectors Vögtlin-König in Therwil, 1985–86. Photograph by author.

6. Herzog & de Meuron, house for art collectors Vögtlin-König in Therwil, 1985–86. Photograph by author.

The artwork gallery is the most unpolished and most ancestral place in the house, built with concrete cast in place and concrete blocks, without any coating or paint. The atmospheric effect is due to the light hitting the back wall, pouring down as it does from the long skylight designed to be invisible. Rectangular concrete plates are used for the house, designed as if they were wooden boards and fixed to fir poles. These same plates are also laid to create the path adjacent to the house on the garden side. The covering of the pitched roof is also made with concrete tiles. The gesture of entering the gallery by walking over the gravel in the courtyard – the same used in the concrete compound cast on site – is not merely a simple technical detail, but rather the confirmation that Herzog and de Meuron have built a coherent theory dedicated to the different possible natures of concrete.

By now the 'romantische Haus der Zukunft' has taken on the appearance of an unusual concrete shed, which brings the traditional ideal type – after the tests in Oberwil or Tavole – to the extreme. It is precisely the grey colour of the concrete that unifies the two worlds represented in the house in Therwil, the 'Abstraktion in der Architektur' of the base and the 'romantische Haus der Zukunft' resting on it. Here the concrete is applied in its two fundamental technical forms – cast on site and prefabricated – in order to avoid falling into the superimposition of different materials typical of the Swiss building tradition.

'In the case of the Therwil House – explains Herzog – we at first considered building a prefabricated building on top. We then noticed that this alien body, as a kind of *objet trouvé*, a kind of stage set, would run counter to what we were trying to achieve. A path leads from the courtyard into the house, not only in reality but in terms of materials as well. We represented various versions of concrete as a masonry material, not because we are especially interested in concrete, but because it gave us the opportunity to define the coherent construction of this place. The image of the shed increasingly became a form of wooden boards and prefabricated concrete panels, which are structurally just as related to the wooden boards as they are to the architecture of the courtyard and the plinth. The longer we dealt with this theme of concrete, the more the image of the shed was relinquished to a structural idea. In the end, the shed actually became unimportant to us and we were able to move more freely *vis-à-vis* this image.'[13]

The filiations between the works of Herzog and de Meuron, which began to multiply at the end of the 1980s, may seem to have been lost in different streams due to the variety of expressions; yet a path, sometimes even linear, crosses them all. The representation of the 'romantischen Hauses der Zukunft' in Therwil, which proceeds by inversions and discontinuities from the works of Oberwil and Tavole, is projected onto the envelope construction – made of the same material and chromatic substance of cement and wood – that wraps the simple steel structure of the Ricola storage building built in Baselstrasse, Laufen, in 1986–87 (fig. 7). This time the concrete does not even need on-site work or special prefabrication forms. Herzog and de Meuron take a typical product of twentieth-century Swiss construction culture, Eternit, in the form of thin grey plates, which become the iconic element of the warehouse. It is even logical, from an artistic point of view owed to Duchamp, that in order to identify the intrinsic quality of a room intended to store finished products, one makes use of products available on the market, chosen from the warehouse's stocks of Eternit products. The very nature of the cement selected by Herzog and de Meuron to build the envelope of the warehouse in Laufen is therefore intrinsically iconic. The way of mounting the plates only adds further degrees of expressiveness, after the crucial choice of employing Eternit, which still contains the consequences of the design process. Even the slender structure made of thin wooden rods is designed according to the assembly of the Eternit plates. The use of industrial products demonstrates that the Ricola warehouse is Herzog and de Meuron's work with the greatest affinities to the sculptures of Arte Povera. It is worth remembering that in 1986, Herzog created a sculpture, exhibited at the Galerie Stampa in Basel, made with wooden panels mounted to create stacked conduits, in the manner of the works of Andre or Boetti.[14] The same idea of stacking guides the assembly of the Eternit plates for the Ricola warehouse. However, if Herzog and de Meuron can indicate, as a reference for their project, the stacks of wooden planks commonly found in the Laufen valley or the geological stratification visible in the abandoned quarry next to which their warehouse stands, it is only because in contemporary art the theme of the stack had long since become fundamental in everyday, sparse, and serial sculpture. The importance of the radical change in the poetics of Herzog and de Meuron inherent in the transition from the elevation study (in which the stratification was planned to be executed with plates of the same dimensions) to the definitive version (in which the plates are instead in groups of three different widths, causing a variation in height in the layers of the envelope) cannot be overemphasised. In this transition, the subversive potential of Arte Povera present in the first study is diluted in a design composed of rhythmic sequences, a prelude to the other and more sophisticated

7. Herzog & de Meuron, Ricola storage building in Laufen, 1986–87. Photograph by author.

modulations that will distinguish Herzog and de Meuron's subsequent works. The whole design, from the simple stratification of an everyday industrial product, inevitably ends up evoking geological stratification with an antique constructive character, such as the one that qualifies the equipment of the mighty stones of Palazzo Medici in Florence, which pass from rustic to polished in a succession of three main levels, ending with a projecting cornice, just like the Eternit plates of the Ricola warehouse.

Epilogue: 'Material's Atomic Structure' or Surface Ornaments of Concrete?

In the works of Herzog and de Meuron in Oberwil, Tavole, Therwil, or Laufen one feels a slight reluctance to surpass certain limits in the use of materials or go beyond certain principles in the working and implementation of the elements. From the courage to move with and against these limits came a tension, which infused these early works with a radical strength, making them exemplary of a way of proceeding in search of an architecture made of simple, conventional, everyday materials, implemented in surprising ways. Yet in the early 1990s this way of proceeding changes its course, and the desire to discover what lies beyond those limits begins to prevail, perhaps without realising that beyond that there can only be ornament, or, more likely, that encroachment occurs consciously under the pressure of an attraction, which could already be perceived in details such as the sophisticated modularity introduced in the stratification of the Eternit plates of the Ricola warehouse.

What happens in two works under construction around 1992 is destined to change not only the orientation of Herzog and de Meuron's work but, more generally, that of contemporary architecture: the Ricola Europe warehouse in Mulhouse, built in 1992–93, and the Pfaffenholz Sports Centre, in St. Louis, designed in 1989–90 and built in 1992–93. In both works, the overwhelming reappearance of the ornament that pervades the surfaces of polycarbonate or glass panels is at stake and ends up investing the concrete parts with the aim of recreating the unity achieved at the Therwil house thanks to the use of grey concrete, applied in different ways and with different textures. It is as if technical research on the nature of the material was supplanted by technical research on ways of impressing the ornament onto those materials.

Looking at the different external coverings of each from a distance, the buildings in Mulhouse and St. Louis are two similar creations. Both have canopies that project extraordinarily far, not only to provide shelter, but to appear like a piece of clothing placed around the head and in the same fabric as the dress, in order to show off the ornament in all its splendour. The working of concrete is the most surprising aspect of the rediscovery of ornament.

To understand what happens to the concrete of Ricola Europe, it is first necessary to evaluate the building design in the phase where the envelope is decorated with a repeated Achillea plant motif, in the manner of a Warhol serigraph, designed by Karl Blossfeldt to symbolise the herbal composition of the

Ricola candies. In that project, the ornament also pervades the blind sides to be made in concrete, and its presence is linked to the research undertaken to decorate the concrete of the St. Louis sports centre. The decision to remove the leaf ornament from the concrete surfaces is made due to a lack of time available for experimentation with the impression technique. It is at this point in the project that Herzog and de Meuron discover the ingredient that will make the hard and impenetrable concrete wall just as ethereal, reflective, and shimmering in the light as the ornate polycarbonate walls: rainwater. In the rain, the concrete is sporadically washed by the water collected on the roof and by the water sliding down the two walls due to the lack of eaves; in those moments, the surface of the wall becomes shiny and iridescent like that of the polycarbonate panels. It is this kind of momentary dematerialisation of concrete – thanks to the veil of water – that Herzog and de Meuron seek by employing the solution of the washout of the two walls – 'it raises questions about solidity and transparency'.[15] Thus the layer of water, which makes the concrete reflect, turns out to have the same value as the ultramarine blue paint applied on the blocks of the Oberwil house.

However, that layer of water has other consequences on the concrete surface, which, once the transparency and shine effect has ceased, appears soiled by gouges and over time also by moss. 'When it dries, it gets muddy, but it is still beautiful. And the water layer is a natural protection on the concrete surface', affirms Herzog.[16] The gouges are interpreted by Herzog himself as natural artistic phenomena – 'The "pencil of nature" would also become the pencil of architecture!'[17] – in harmony with the manifestations of contemporary art in which even mould becomes a material, whilst in the historical perspective of the variegated evolution of concrete during the twentieth century, they appear to be even new and sought-after *malfaçons* of the *béton brut* second era. Over time, a sort of natural wall plant decoration is born, a precursor to other solutions by Herzog and de Meuron to decorate the walls – 'The water running down the walls will form a fine film of plant life; a natural drawing will ensue'.[18] In Herzog and de Meuron's view, the climbing vegetation transforms the concrete wall into a stone wall.[19] A strip of pebbles at the foot of the two walls creates the system for collecting water in the ground. The run-off device for the Mulhouse warehouse is taken up with other intentions in some subsequent works, with details modified according to the desired effects. The first variant is the studio for Rémy Zaugg, also in Mulhouse, built in 1995–96. The device looks identical; but this time Herzog and de Meuron are not interested in the effects of transparency but in the accelerated decomposition of the concrete surface, which in the Ricola warehouse had been recorded as an almost accidental consequence. Thus, specifically to accentuate the stains on the concrete, they implement an automatic painting process using rainwater; the roof is designed as a tank for collecting water and preventing excessive heating of the premises in summer, but when the water overflows, it carries with it particles of iron dioxide from the concrete-sand mix, which scar the walls with dense streaks of rust, like colour slipping onto a canvas.[20] Brilliance and climbing vegetation at the Ricola Europe warehouse and rusty streaks in Zaugg's studio are different ways of treating the concrete surface, both of which match the different character of the two buildings. The intentions expressed during the studies for the Ricola Europe warehouse of an extended decoration also on concrete, are implemented in the construction of the Pfaffenholz Sports Centre in St. Louis. It is in this building that the concrete changes radically, in form and substance, compared to projects by Herzog and de Meuron prior to this time. It is no coincidence that this is the work in which the concrete is transformed from a wall or block to a cladding panel, just as Herzog and de Meuron enter the universe of the ornament applied to the material. It is significant in this regard that the tests to impress the ornament also take place with cast-in-place concrete walls. Although the work determines the appearance of the ornament on concrete, the meaning of that ornament with respect to the concrete construction process is not easy to define.

The introduction of the panel, among the technical forms of concrete by Herzog and de Meuron, is a consequence of their choice to experiment with a sophisticated kind of ornamental modelling of the material. The large panels are prefabricated in the workshop where they are treated with a photographic technique, spreading a film with the image imprinted and treated with retarding products on the bottom of the mould, so that the different drying times produce fragments of polished and rough surfaces, depending on the motif imprinted on the mould.[21] Thus the layer of paint spread on the concrete block walls of the house in Oberwil only now reveals its secret meaning of alteration to the material not accomplished in the primeval and symbolic significance of Beuys. The panels are applied to the lower body of the building with the entrance, both along the wall and against the ceiling of the projecting canopy; the same panels are also laid on the ground to form a wide pavement in front of the building. The concrete poured in place, which forms the body of the building partly dressed by the panels, is not left exposed so as not to create colour conflicts with the panels but is painted green to make the building lose itself in the landscape. A similar chromatic tone is possessed by the glass, which provides the backing to the large rear building in which the three gyms and services are housed. Upon entering the building, one is enveloped by the atmosphere of greys generated by the poured concrete of inclined pillars, beams, and walls, exposed and without surface work after dismantling, and by the acoustic panels applied to the ceilings (figs. 8–10). The manufacturing of the concrete panels for the Pfaffenholz Sports Centre marks the beginning of an experimentation on ornament that will pervade in various forms – not only on the surfaces of the prefabricated panels, but also in the configuration of Herzog and de Meuron's structures themselves. The fact that the ornamental motif imprinted on the concrete panels does not propose any clearly recognisable figure, but produces the effect of an approximate and unsuccessful processing of the concrete, is important for understanding its impact in the evolution of Herzog and de Meuron's work. The specifically graphic nature of the ornament and, above all, its generation through a retarding agent, an ingredient intrinsic to the manufacturing process of concrete, introduces a significant ambiguity to the question of the ornament as proposed with the leaves of the Ricola Europe warehouse,

8. Herzog & de Meuron, Pfaffenholz Sports Centre in St. Louis, 1989–93. Photograph by author.

9. Herzog & de Meuron, Pfaffenholz Sports Centre in St. Louis, 1989–93, detail of panels. Photograph by author.

10. Herzog & de Meuron, Pfaffenholz Sports Centre in St. Louis, 1989–93, detail of a panel. Photograph by author.

to the point of being able to include even the panels of the Pfaffenholz Sports Centre among the kinds of *malfaçon* of the *béton brut* second era, even if by now the *malfaçon* has become more sophisticated than natural ones, which stain the concrete walls of both buildings in Mulhouse. However, confirmation that the ornamentation operations carried out in the building in St. Louis arose from a continued desire to retain the nature of the material could come from the fact that to decorate the glass panels of the same building, Herzog and de Meuron transform the photograph of the panels into a printed figure, which is then applied onto the outside of the walls for thermal insulation and which is visible behind the same glass panels.

The trajectory that Herzog and de Meuron are tracing through the sequence of their works, from the house in Oberwil to the sports centre in St. Louis, is becoming more and more precise, and it is pushing concrete towards the loss of its own presumed identity, derived from experiences and discussions on truth, *béton brut*, and brutalism; and the more the trajectory advances and becomes clear, the more the first works lose that aura of simple architecture and their ambiguities vanish. In this perspective, the Pfaffenholz Sports Centre is the work that marks an epochal turning point. And it is no coincidence that the irregular stains on the panels mark the beginning of a reflection on what will become the ornament imprinted in concrete, even though they are not yet completely independent from the logical manufacturing process of the concrete. The fact that those spots are obtained not with a sculptural modelling of the formwork but with a thin film spread on the panel means that the formal result revives questions of the relationship between *Kernform* and *Kunstform* that Bötticher wants to coincide (what can be seen on the surface, the *Kunstform*, must correspond to the structure, or *Kernform*), and that instead Semper wants to keep distinct, even if it is only a thin layer of paint that differentiates them. If we push further the reasoning on the Pfaffenholz Sports Centre panel, we discover that the effects produced by the irregular density of the retarding agent make the particle size of the conglomerate appear, namely the *Kernform*, and act like a *décollage* of the cement film, which is deposited directly against the formwork, namely the *Kunstform*. If what looks like simple ornaments are seen through the process of their manufacture, then the effects of the retarding agent cannot fail to be regarded as the interrupted unveiling of the truth of the matter, the partial development of a photographic image, an unfinished element, whose true image can only be guessed at, emerging beyond the polished surface. Is the panel by Herzog and de Meuron not more coherent with the principle of truth professed at the time of brutalism, since the concrete surface is not touched after having extracted the element from the mould and does not undergo any working after the disarming, as happens, for example, with the pebble stone technique, in which one wants to reveal the nature of the compound, hidden under the cement film formed during the setting as a coating layer inherent in the process itself?

It is now clear that with Ricola Europe and the Pfaffenholz Sports Centre, Herzog and de Meuron have voluntarily questioned the very meaning of the two main materials, the transparent polycarbonate panels with the imprinted ornament and the opaque concrete panels again with an imprinted ornament, as if they wanted to create, with those two works, a sort of reasoning on the dematerialisation of concrete through the processing of its surface. The fact that the concrete is not limited to the side walls, as in Ricola Europe, where its dematerialisation was obtained by the washing away, but that in the Pfaffenholz Sports Centre it occupies the facade, explains the profound reasons for the ornamental pattern imprinted on the concrete panels. Precisely through the surface treatments and the impression of ornaments, Herzog and de Meuron now seek the sublimation of the material according to theoretical and artistic processes comparable to those of Otto Wagner in the subway station in Karlsplatz in Vienna.

'The longitudinal facades and square in front of it – explain Herzog and de Meuron – are covered in prefabricated concrete slabs whose surfaces have been roughened with a specially-developed printing technique that makes them appear to be like photographic surfaces. The concrete surfaces mediating between outer and inner space at this entry point seem softer, almost textile-like. The printing of the glass plates and the concrete slabs permits the assimilation of two materials highly differing in appearance'.[22]

In light of the ornate prefabricated panel of the Pfaffenholz Sports Centre, Herzog's statements on the 'material's atomic structure' made in 1988, just one year before the start of the St. Louis project, take on a fundamental value. Does the technical process for impressing an image on the surface of the matter contradict or negate the aspiration to understand the molecular structure of concrete from which is derived a different 'truth' to that which the masters of the twentieth century believed, as Herzog rightly proclaims? Are Herzog's statements on the need to understand the molecular structure itself not similar to those made in the 1960s and 1970s by Morris or Smithson, no longer to be verified depending on the fluid or solid state of concrete, but on that complex limit which is its surface, where two worlds act: the resistance of the formwork panel and the pressures of the compound against that panel, and all the phenomena related to the presence of water and its evaporation which occur on that surface? What is certain is that the prefabricated panels at St. Louis reflect the desire of Herzog and de Meuron to discover the very structure of concrete and therefore to give it an artistic form, in a way never attempted before, not even by Kahn.

'First of all – explains Herzog in 1988 – the material experiences a further division: our attempt to reach, as it were, the material's atomic structure. We have little faith in the material's external appearance because we are unable to derive any self-evident quality from it. After all, we are dealing with solid bodies, which therefore have a crystalline structure, understood in the chemical sense. These crystalline structures, which represent a kind of spatial imprint of the forces that exist between the individual atoms, are invisible to the naked eye. Yet they are a reality; they permit access to an understanding of the materials' qualities, which are more interesting and complex than the usual applications of the construction industry or the understanding that the creators of Modernism had of the concept of honesty towards materials. We will see to what extent we will be able to incorporate such considerations in our architectural work. There are beginnings in the Therwil House, where the various forms that reinforced concrete takes have experienced a kind of decomposition, or in the Schwarz Park project, where the forms of the configuration can be understood as a geometric expression of the place's natural morphology'.[23]

Notes

1. Jeffrey Kipnis, 'A Conversation with Jacques Herzog', *El Croquis. Herzog & de Meuron 1993–1997*, no. 84 (1997), 7–21, here 15.
2. 'Herzog & de Meuron et Philip Ursprung', in Philip Ursprung (ed.), *Herzog & de Meuron. Histoire naturelle* (Baden: Lars Müller Publishers, 2002), 84–88, here 85.
3. Herzog & de Meuron, 'Pritzer Prize Speech', in Gerhard Mack, *Herzog & de Meuron 1997–2001. The Complete Works* vol. 4 (Basel: Birkhäuser Verlag, 2009), 227–31, here 228.
4. Mack, *Herzog & de Meuron 1997–2001. The Complete Works* vol. 4 (see note 3), 15.
5. Alejandro Zaera, 'Continuities: Interview with Herzog & de Meuron', *El Croquis. Herzog & de Meuron 1983–1993*, no. 60 (1994), 6–23, here 22.
6. See the note on the drawing, Gerhard Mack, *Herzog & de Meuron 1978–1988. The Complete Works* vol. 1 (Basel: Birkhäuser Verlag, 1997), 133, sketch F.
7. Ibid., 61, sketch C.
8. Ibid.
9. 'Conversation between Jacques Herzog and Bernard Bürgi, Basel, 8th November 1990', in Gerhard Mack, *Herzog & de Meuron 1989–1991. The Complete Works* vol. 2 (Basel: Birkhäuser Verlag, 1996), 183–88, here 184.
10. Zaera, 'Continuities. Interview with Herzog & de Meuron' (see note 5), 23.
11. 'Conversation between Jacques Herzog and Theodora Vischer, May 1988', in Mack, *Herzog & de Meuron 1978–1988. The Complete Works* vol. 1 (see note 6), 212–7, here 215.
12. Mack, *Herzog & de Meuron 1978–1988. The Complete Works* vol. 1 (see note 6), 132, sketch A.
13. 'Conversation between Jacques Herzog and Theodora Vischer, May 1988' (see note 11), 214.
14. Mack, *Herzog & de Meuron 1978–1988. The Complete Works* vol. 1 (see note 6), 158, drawing C.
15. Kipnis, 'A Conversation with Jacques Herzog' (see note 1), 11.
16. Ibid.
17. Ibid., 15.
18. *El Croquis. Herzog & de Meuron 1993–1997*, no. 84 (1997), 94.
19. Kipnis, 'A Conversation with Jacques Herzog' (see note 1), 15.
20. *El Croquis. Herzog & de Meuron, 1993–1997* (see note 18), 128.
21. Gerhard Mack, *Herzog & de Meuron 1989–1991. The Complete Works* vol. 2 (Basel: Birkhäuser Verlag, 1996), 61.
22. *El Croquis. Herzog & de Meuron, 1993–1997* (see note 18), 81. The interest in concrete ornaments is not surprising. 'I was particularly interested in his ornamental friezes in concrete', affirms Herzog in relation to the works of Wright seen in Chicago (William J. R. Curtis, 'The Nature of Artifice. A Conversation with Jacques Herzog', *El Croquis. Herzog & de Meuron 1998–2002*, no. 109/110, 2002, 16–31, here 26).
23. 'Conversation between Jacques Herzog and Theodora Vischer, May 1988' (see note 11), 216.

Southern Fragments of Swiss Asbestos-Cement, 1940 to 2040

Hannah le Roux

A Fragmented History

As storms in the tropical belt make the news with their increasing ferocity and frequency, a photographic trope recurs: the piled debris of rolled cars, uprooted trees, wires, pooled runoff, and smashed buildings they leave behind. Amongst the twisted metal, broken timber, and displaced fittings, there are fragments of building materials. If the images are taken in the older, working class areas of the global South – Latin America, South East Asia or Africa – there are likely to be asbestos-cement fragments in the mix, and specifically, remnants of sheets produced by a machine made in Kriens, Switzerland.[1] In the swirl of vectors and extreme events where globalised materials meet climate change, the patented technology behind these fragments links them back to a common origin.

The Bell asbestos-cement machines were used from the mid 1940s by subsidiaries of the interlinked Swiss asbestos and cement companies under the Schmidheiny family,[2] who were controllers of Holderbank Financière Glarus in the post-Second World War period. Financed by the Holderbank group, Ernst Schmidheiny II (1902–1985), often in collaboration with the Belgian Emsens family and sometimes the French Cuvelier family, created many country level subsidiaries in this period, notably in South America and South Africa, under Eternit or similar names, that held the license to use the Hatschek process for manufacturing asbestos-cement products. Following their initial collaboration with national governments, from the 1960s the growth in asbestos-cement industries coincided with transnational and United Nations extension of programmes for social housing projects. As a consequence of their interactions with technical advisors, Swiss asbestos-cement was used to roof and carry water to millions of houses, schools, and clinics in the global South.

There is significant public interest in the location and impact of asbestos-cement products,[3] which present a residual risk to health in their potential to fragment and release fibres into the environment at large. Along with the impact of storms and fires, the degradation over time of the cement matrix that holds the asbestos fibres in pipes and roof sheeting can also release fibres into soil and watercourses, and potentially into the air where they can be inhaled and damage human health over the long term. Due to its link with slow acting fatal diseases, asbestos has been banned in some materials used in buildings since the 1970s, with a near global ban by 2004,[4] and many countries have made it mandatory to label and sometimes remove its existing sources.

The dominance of the Holderbank subsidiaries in asbestos-cement industries would make them a useful ally in public programmes of identification, removal, and safe disposal of the material in the global South. But neither Everite, the South African company set up by Eternit, whose assets and liabilities are currently being sold to undisclosed parties,[5] nor Becon AG, the Swiss asset management company that inherited the liabilities of Eternit SA,[6] have been willing or able to allow access to the company archives of the preceding ventures, citing either their loss or corporate restructuring as the reason.[7] However, because the design of buildings materialises ephemeral relations, the activities of the company remain in time and place as a concrete – if episodic – record within architecture. Buildings, along with the drawings, specifications, and product catalogues that produce them are a substitute history of Swiss asbestos-cement. By reading between the buildings, as it were, architectural history can reproduce the missing lineages of financial transfers, product development, intellectual property, locational decisions, legal judgements, and material consequences over Eternit's half-century of operation in the global South.

This form of historical work is redolent of fragments. In its method, it brings together the remaining elements of company history with the fragmented material of asbestos-cement itself, particularly in the tropical countries of the global South where already dangerous climatic and public health events are likely to increase substantially over the next decades. In doing so it contrasts the North, and Switzerland in particular, with its financial liquidity and command of technology, with the precarious regimes of governmental care and climatic risks in the countries where they amassed significant profits. Like the drawing stencil Everite designed for architecture students in the 1980s (fig. 1), fragments can be read through negative and positive form: they can appear as missing pieces in a template or as its trace. Placed back together, these pieces reconstruct a troubling history of Swiss asbestos-cement.

Piece 1: Dislocations (1941–1947)

The first fragment is a detail of the roof of a model house (fig. 2), proposed as an exemplar of material substitution during the Second World War. These standardised elements of curved mappings and sheets are the consequence of co-operative interaction between the international asbestos-cement cartel and the South African state's industrial development complex. The South African market for asbestos-cement had been expanded by the war as metals and timber were tightly controlled for use in armaments and military structures. By 1944, the Central Housing Board of South Africa was detailing roofs, doors, shelves, and rainwater goods from the material and testing their potential in low-cost housing.[8] The Turner & Newall (also known as Turnall) group produced a corrugated asbestos roof sheeting product called 'Bigsix' that was used in the United Kingdom for buildings associated with flammable products, and later in garden sheds and colonial buildings,[9] and this profile was used in South Africa used as a substitute for corrugated iron.

1. Everite, tracing stencil for architects, ca. 1989. Photograph by author.

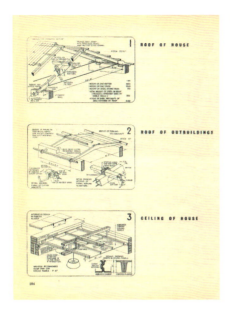
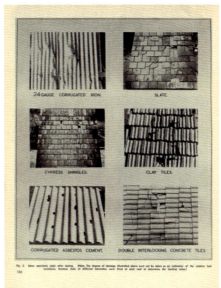

2. Roof of a model house, 1943.

3. Some specimen roofs after testing for hail impact, 1952.

The Holderbank group, through Amiantus AG, first competed with and then took over the production of South African asbestos-cement from the British company Turner & Newall, who focused on their operations in Rhodesia. The Swiss company had made their first investments in building materials outside of Europe in Egypt in 1927.[10] In 1937 Ernst Schmidheiny II secured quarries near Cape Town for a new South African cement company, the National Portland Cement company. By the outbreak of the Second World War, they had established two asbestos fibre mining companies in the Northern Cape province, Kuruman Cape Blue Asbestos and Danielskuil Cape Blue Asbestos.[11] This investment gave the Holderbank group access to rare blue asbestos fibres from a site outside of the war arena, and bypassed the quotas controlled by the two major British firms that owned most South African and Rhodesian mines, Turner & Newall and Cape. The Holderbank investments were consolidated by the financing of a new asbestos-cement enterprise, Everite Limited, in April 1941.[12] The South African state encouraged the new Everite enterprise through the Director General of War Supplies, Hendrik van der Bijl,[13] who had earlier founded the state-owned company, Iron and Steel Corporation (ISCOR).

Everite's factory was located on farmland at Kliprivier, midway between the industrial town of Vereeniging and the gold mining belt of the Witwatersrand, and a rail siding was constructed alongside it to link the production facility both with fibre sources and potential markets. A second plant was constructed at Brackenfell near Cape Town. Both factories operated as self-contained settlements for black workers who were accommodated in hostels constructed in the first few years of operation.[14] Kliprivier had bungalow houses for European workers in a suburban layout just beyond the factory fence, and within a decade the settlement had a sports club and fields and a medical facility.

The construction of this medical facility alongside the factory in 1950 suggests that Everite's practices aligned with those of the other international

Southern Fragments of Swiss Asbestos-Cement, 1940 to 2040

asbestos-cement producers who regularly examined their workers.[15] These rooms applied apartheid segregation to the layout.[16] The design allocated separate waiting areas and inspection rooms to 'Europeans' and 'Natives', with the doctor and nurse having access to each set of bodies without them ever overlapping. The unequal facilities shown in the plans – two examining rooms and an enclosed lobby for whites, versus one room off an open waiting area for blacks – inscribed the different values assigned to racialised bodies within measures and practices of occupational health.

This racial differentiation of workers at the scale of their bodies was in line with the policies applied by the National Party that came to power in South African in 1948 with the vote of the marginalised white Afrikaner population, for whom they built up the modernising but deeply unequal policy of (racially) separate development or *apartheid*. This policy was manifest at an urban scale through the construction of segregated new townships for black workers who were housed in minimal dwellings with their own reductive standards for building sizes and materials specifications. The Everite company was to supply roofs for around half[17] of these low-cost housing projects for Africans, so benefiting from the state's new policies.

Piece 2: Specifications (1949–1970)

On the afternoon of 17 November 1949, a severe and disastrous hailstorm struck Pretoria, the administrative capital city of South Africa and the seat of the National Building Research Institute. Chas Rigby and Keep Steyn, the engineer-researchers on a research project on hail damage, gathered samples of the hailstones and calculated their terminal velocity. They used this data to reproduce the event in a monitored and comparative experiment that involved shooting ice blocks from a grenade thrower mounted on a twenty-foot-high tower onto thirty-nine different roofing materials. Noting that there had been eighteen other hailstorms with stones of three to four inches in diameter over the country in recorded history, they suggested that these conditions were a matter of public interest, especially in relation to the new types of building materials coming on to the market.[18] Rigby and Steyn's experiment produced holes in the three brands of locally made corrugated asbestos cement sheets, but not in an imported sample of American asbestos cement with a narrower pitch and thicker material (fig. 3). The corrugated iron sheets did not fail at all at the maximum velocities tested of 10,000 ft-pdls (420 Joules), far outperforming the local asbestos-cement samples that broke at 700–900 ft-pdls (38 Joules).

By 1951, the South African state had developed a standard set of plans and specifications for low-cost housing for blacks, the Minimum Standards of Accommodation[19] through a long period of committee deliberations.[20] Although these research groups were all associated with the National Building Research Institute, there is no record of the consequences of the tests on the two choices for roof sheeting that were embedded in this document, corrugated iron or asbestos-cement, which remained an acceptable alternative. The standards had been applied in three pilot projects for townships on the Witwatersrand, which remain lived in today,[21] where the two materials were used alternately in the prototype units. In line with the minimum standards specifications, roofs were supplied without ceilings or gutters, and many remain in that condition after decades.[22]

The state's adoption of asbestos-cement as a standard material also ignored international studies such as that of G. Anthony Atkinson who wrote in a report for the United Nations on *Design and Construction in the Tropics* that 'materials and equipment may behave differently. Climatic effects such as high temperature and humidity, strong sunlight, etc., may make some materials weaker or less durable. Earthquakes and hurricanes may create special problems.'[23] In another well-circulated report, *Overseas Building Notes*, the cover showed a storm damaged asbestos-cement roof in Uganda that had been patched with bitumen.[24]

Up until the mid 1970s, the South African apartheid state was the supplier and manager of almost all houses occupied by blacks. These tenants paid rent related to their income levels in formal jobs, the criterion for the allocation of a house. As apartheid policies developed, blacks would come to be considered temporary residents in a white majority state, holding citizenship only in rural ethnic homelands such as the Transkei, Ciskei, KwaZulu, and Bophuthatswana. Those living in mixed race parts of towns were moved to newly built, ethnically segregated townships.

In 1959 the private company, Everite (Pty) Ltd, listed shares on the South African stock exchange and became a public company, although over 50 per cent of its capital remained private. The chairman of the board was Ernst Schmidheiny, and both his brother Max (1908–1991) from Holderbank and André Emsens (1900–1992) of the Belgian Eternit family were on the board.[25] The growth of Everite's valuation was very strong, from the initial investment of R700 000 in 1941 to over R11 million in 1968, with annual dividends of 12 per cent to 19 per cent of the share capital paid out to its investors through the mid 1960s.[26]

Alongside the production of three kinds of roof sheeting and underground piping for black townships, the company produced a wide range of products for a market that included white homeowners. The 1968 annual report includes a list of thirty-nine asbestos-cement products[27] including the range of planters and seating designed by Willy Guhl that another publication shows being marketed at the company's pavilions at the popular Rand Easter Show along with the more prosaic pipes and water tanks.[28] Everite's marketing to architects was also robust, engaging them through detailed technical catalogues in binders, the distribution of copies of *AC: The International Asbestos Cement Review*, which regularly featured an Everite advertisement on its back cover, and a design competition for a model black township in 1956.[29] Yet despite the vigorous marketing and growth of the market for asbestos-cement, the presence of an on-site technical department, and an international network of expertise, it appears that the inherent brittleness of the roof sheets tested in 1949 was not successfully addressed. In the 1973 catalogue for their Longspan Profile B sheeting, Everite noted under a section on physical characteristics that 'the possibility of damage during storms of an unusually severe nature does exist.'[30] Asbestos cement was, for all this apparent corporate strength, still fragile.

Piece 3: Channels (1962–1972)

In 1964, the experimental station of the French Centre Scientifique et Technique du Bâtiment (CSTB) conducted 'flexion' or breaking point tests to guarantee the safety of a new type of asbestos-cement roofing channel in areas where storms might occur[31] (fig. 4). The sample channels were sent to Champs-sur-Marne by Asbestos de Mexico at their own expense through the instructions of their designer, the Harvard trained architect and United National technical assistance consultant Alvaro Ortega.[32] The experiment concluded that the sheets were only suitable for use in areas without cyclones, providing there were sufficient fixings. Despite this failure, Eternit marketed many variations of this profile from the 1960s to the 1980s in Latin America, Africa, and South East Asia.

In Latin America and Asia, the asbestos-cement companies that the Holderbank invested in from the late 1930s onwards faced a political context that was more dynamic than the South African apartheid regime. Many of the subsidiaries were run though Max Graf, a close family acquaintance appointed by Ernst Schmidheiny in 1944 who reported directly to the Eternit base in Niederduren. Graf 'supervised existing asbestos-cement plants in Brazil, Colombia, and Venezuela, and from 1958 to 1965… directed the takeover or establishment of companies in Ecuador, El Salvador, Guatemala, Costa Rica, Honduras and Nicaragua',[33] eventually managed by the Amindus AG organisation in Switzerland. The company was also reportedly present in Mexico, Panama, Argentina (1937–), Bolivia, Chile, Uruguay (1945–) and Peru (1940–).[34]

The 'Canal', 'Canaleta', or 'Canalit' product that Eternit introduced to this market in the early 1960s was an innovative profile that Ortega first trialled in 1959 in Guatemala, when he transformed uncured asbestos-cement pipes into self-spanning roof troughs.[35] In 1960, working for the United Nations as a technical advisor, Ortega prototyped a more sophisticated open-source version for the UN that was also used by Eternit in some countries. This work was publicised internationally in architectural media.[36] The Canaleta profile had two specific qualities that linked it to development agendas. Firstly, the profile width and lengths, unlike earlier Imperial profiles, fitted into metric grids and so could work with a ten-centimetre modular building system more common to Latin countries. Further, the product was self-spanning for six metres, allowing it to be used to roof buildings without the need for timber or concrete substructures.

These asbestos-cement channel roofing products were brought onto the market at a moment when the demand for housing for urbanising communities had become a global political concern. However, with the rapid increase in urbanisation, housing agencies were unable to provide for complete dwellings for the urban poor. The challenge that the Swiss subsidiaries faced was to partially, rather than fully replace the self-built approaches that architects like John Turner had observed in Peru,[37] where existing working-class housing was often competently built by artisans. Surveys of such practices showed many local techniques for roofing and walls were in use, including ceramic tiles, thatch, and

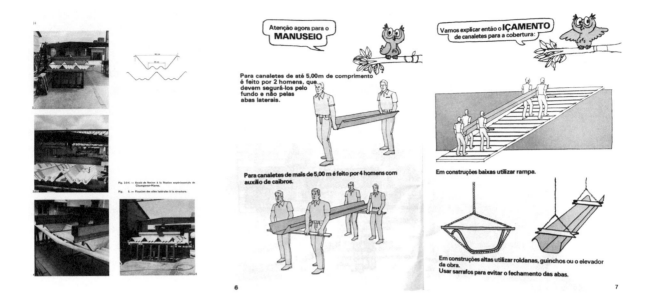

4. Flexion tests at the experimental station of Champs-sur-Marne, 1964.

5. Instructions for carrying asbestos-cement canaletas, 1983.

concrete slabs.[38] One such study conducted by Ortega with the Pratt Institute in 1964 surveyed United Nations representatives from the tropics and Middle East on the forms of vernacular and self-built architects in their countries.[39] The survey requested their feedback on typical urban and rural technologies used for specific parts of buildings like floors, walls, and roofs. Without proposing any design approach, the survey findings aimed to create a 'framework, a structure of order' for housing that could be mass produced. By design, however, by asking representatives to describe the roof in relation to forms that could be constructed with the canal profiles – support span, flat roof, pitched roof, double roof, and overhang – the survey was collecting data to justify the substitution of local materials and approaches with mass produced self-spanning roofing.

Piece 4: Self-help (1967–2002)

Their growing alignment with developmental discourse brought materials manufacturers into engagement with agencies like the United Nations in which activist voices from the global South and trade unions increasingly took on multinational capital and public health issues.[40] Asbestos-cement was vulnerable to criticism both because of the foreign exchange costs of the materials involved for countries without their own fibre mines[41] and because of growing public health advocacy. The transnational transmission of research around the link between asbestos and mesothelioma had increased after the 'Biological Effects of Asbestos' conference at the New York Academy of Sciences in October 1964 and became a cause for organised labour and litigation.[42] As the evidence of builders getting cancers from occupational exposure accrued ahead of a series of litigious actions in the United States, asbestos-containing building materials became seen as sources of lethal fibres that could be released when used without extreme care.[43]

Southern Fragments of Swiss Asbestos-Cement, 1940 to 2040

The United Nations conference on the Human Environment in Stockholm from 5–16 June 1972 was a seminal moment in relinking ecological agendas to those of the human-made environment.[44] The role of observing the impacts of development shifted away from nation states alone to global entities in the form of Non-Governmental Organisations, Earthwatch, and UNEP, the United Nation Environmental Programme. The official conference statement on environmental risks was, however, broad and intentionally ambivalent, supporting the technological advances of industrialised nations while acknowledging the ambitions of people in the global South to reach developmental goals: 'In our time, man's capacity to transform his surroundings, if used wisely, can bring to all peoples the benefits of development and the opportunity to enhance the quality of life. Wrongly or heedlessly applied, the same power can do incalculable harm to human beings and the human environment.'[45]

An instructive sales pamphlet issued by Eternit Brazil in 1983 for Canaleta 49 (fig. 5), a lighter and simpler version of the channel profile, showed asbestos-cement being 'wrongly or heedlessly' handled. Without cranes, scaffolding, trucks, or protective workwear, a small team of men are shown lifting Canaletas up ramps or with winches, as might be anticipated in self-building on a site in a hillside favela. By ensuring that materials could be handled by the human body, asbestos-cement products could be distributed into the spaces of the marginalised poor where monitoring by the state or multilateral agencies would be near impossible.

Such forms of monitoring were emerging, but not from the global South. In 1972 Denmark issued the first ban on the use of asbestos as insulation.[46] In 1974, the International Labour Organisation held an occupational cancer convention, issuing recommendations for the substitution of carcinogenic substances and agents that impact workers.[47] In the same year the United States National Research Council convened a committee for research on new technologies for roofing in 'Developing Countries', which included representation from the American asbestos-cement company Johns Manville on the special advisory committee along with Eric Carlson and Alberto Gonzalez-Gandolfi from the United Nations.[48] Then in late December a tropical cyclone hit Darwin in northern Australia, destroying 80% of its houses and prompting further North American research[49] that called for additional work on 'brittle materials' like asbestos-cement, and updated building codes.

Following up on the Stockholm conference, the Conference on Human Settlements and Sustainable Urban Development (Habitat I) held in Vancouver in 1976 shifted the emphasis of national agencies towards housing and human settlements, with particular emphasis on conditions of poverty in rapidly growing cities. Although both Switzerland and South Africa were on the margins during this event due to their respective self-elected and enforced suspension from United Nations debates, the delivery mode for asbestos-cement products changed quickly in its wake. In place of using the state or multilateral agencies as specifiers, the subsidiaries in South America and South Africa developed strategies for delivering their asbestos-cement materials directly to the poor. Their approach claimed to draw on the work in the 1950s by three United Nations advisors, Otto Koenisberger, Vladimir Bodiansky, and Charles Abrams[50] who had promoted the 'roof loan' scheme as a way to emancipate home builders on the Gold Coast (now Ghana) from their long wait to save enough funds to put roofs on their incrementally built homes. However, Eternit's roof loan schemes inverted the African practice of building from the ground up. They proposed that finance should be given by development banks for 'core' or 'shell' housing that provided sanitary elements of bathrooms and kitchen sinks along with an over-spanning roof, typically of channel asbestos-cement sheets, that the indebted owners would need to complete themselves over time.[51]

In 1972 Max Schmidheiny's son, Stephan (1947–) completed his thesis on investment guarantees for developing countries.[52] He then spent time in South Africa where he worked in the marketing department of Everite in 1973, and then in Niederurnen, before he took full control of the Holderbank asbestos-cement businesses from 1984 to 1989 when it reverted to Holcim's control under his brother Thomas (1945–).[53] The transnational fluidity of finance in relation to the static products of housing was reflected in several company strategies. In the late 1970s, following the liberalisation of black housing rights to include ownership in South African townships, Everite's marketing manager researched housing finance mechanisms.[54] More significant in its global impact was Stephan Schmidheiny's relationship since the 1980s with Hernando de Soto.[55] De Soto's influential proposition is that the world's urban poor with claims on land in informal settlements should be given title to their land claims to use as an asset in securing loans for, amongst other things, building materials.

Funded by newly minted loans for the poor, asbestos-cement products then could be distributed within the space of self-help housing. In the late 1970s, Everite began to focus on opportunities offered by the Southern African homelands system that the apartheid government was developing with increasing urgency. The company devised a marketing scheme for self-built core housing for the nominally independent territories of the Ciskei, Transkei, and Bophuthatswana that began with a core and Canalit roofs.[56] The National Building Research Institute assisted with some of the research into the building process and produced a demonstration project in the Winterveld,[57] a sprawling resettlement camp for blacks who had been evicted from Pretoria as 'surplus people'.[58]

By this stage asbestos bans were being effected in richer countries – though not South Africa and Brazil – but access to finance allowed Stephan Schmidheiny to invest in forests and a sawmill in Chile in 1982.[59] This shift in resource investment[60] coincided with Eternit developing 'NuTec' or 'New Technology' fibre cement products that aimed to replace asbestos fibres with cellulose ones derived from timber.

Aftermath

> 'Often I wonder where all the Everite material produced by us goes to. I give you one figure: our yearly production is equal to a band of Asbestos-Cement going from Johannesburg to Cape Town and from there to Port Elizabeth, East London to Durban of 1/4' width and 12' wide.'
>
> H. R. Benecke, Managing Director, Everite, 1966[61]

In a study conducted in 2000, researchers found that 52 per cent of a sample of 1,488 six-month-old infants lived in asbestos-roofed houses in the South Africa township of Soweto.[62] Over 60 per cent of these dwellings did not have ceilings, and a similar proportion of the roofs were in some way degraded (fig. 6). Of the few occupational health reports that have sampled such houses for asbestos fibres, a 1992 report that found dangerous levels appears to have been removed from public circulation.[63] The conditions within these houses are therefore 'uncertain', to use the term coined by Michelle Murphy in her history of 'sick building syndrome',[64] as the presence of asbestos fibres is likely, but their measurability is ambivalent. Measuring their impact on bodies is even more difficult, given the proximity of township houses to many other forms of industrial emissions including coal-fired power stations and stoves and dust from mine tailings, along with underlying health conditions of many residents.[65] As in Latin America, activists have for this reason focussed on documenting asbestos-related diseases in areas with close proximity to fibre mines or factories, as well as amongst former factory workers.[66] Reciprocally, in 2006 the former asbestos mining companies in South Africa, through asset management companies, established trusts to compensate people who would contract debilitating and terminal asbestos-related diseases through working on mines or living near them,[67] while excluding claims related only to exposure to asbestos-cement building materials.

Yet as time goes on since the banning of asbestos-cement in the early 2000s in Southern countries, the material becomes increasingly, rather than less risky. The studies of the 1940s and '70s that highlighted the brittle nature of asbestos-cement and its lack of suitability for countries prone to cyclones and hail damage were effectively ignored, and most roofs sold by Eternit linked companies to such places in that period have not been removed. Yet the projections for extreme weather events increase with climate change, while the material itself is prone to degradation with time.[68] Set against this slow and inevitable fragmentation of the matrix of cement, releasing asbestos fibrils, is the accelerating fragmentation and mobility of capital, including the significant profits accrued by the Holderbank in the global South. The difficulties in accessing company archives reflects the steps taken by the Holderbank companies – Amiantus, Eternit, Anova, Becon, Everite, and others – to separate these two types of fragments, the dangerous fibres, and the residues of their profits. Yet it is likely that these fragments may still co-exist in some places – Panama, or the Bahamas, perhaps – suggesting that there is still much work to be done in bringing the material legacy and business history of Swiss asbestos-cement together if we hope to repair them.

6. Asbestos-cement on roofs and in rubble in public open space, KwaThema, South Africa. Photograph by author, 2019.

Notes

[1] Bell Engineering Works Ltd. (ed.), 'Asbestos Cement Machines' (Kriens-Luzern: Escher Wyss Gruppe, 1978).

[2] Biographies of the Schmidheiny family include Paul Eisenring, Alfred Hummler, and Willi Rohner, *Spectrum 2000: Festschrift zum 60. Geburtstag von Max Schmidheiny*, Heerbrugg, 3 April 1968 (Heerbrugg: Rheintaler Druckerei und Verlag, 1968); Werner Catrina, *Der Eternit Report: Stephan Schmidheinys schweres Erbe* (Zürich, Schwäbisch Hall: Orell Füssli, 1985); Hans O. Staub, *Von Schmidheiny zu Schmidheiny*. Schweizer Pioniere der Wirtschaft und Technik, 61 (Meilen: Verein für Wirtschaftshistorische Studien, 1994); The Schmidheiny Story: The Sustainable Truth https://espacioschmidheiny.net/en/biografia/bio/, accessed 26 January 2021.

[3] David Cogley et al., *Life Cycle of Asbestos in Commercial and Industrial Use Including Estimates of Releases to Air Water and Land: Final Inhouse Report* (Washington: Environmental Protection Agency, 1982); Barry I. Castleman and Stephen L. Berger, *Asbestos: Medical and Legal Aspects* (Englewood Cliffs, NJ: Aspen Law & Business, 1996); Jock McCulloch, *Asbestos Blues: Labour, Capital, Physicians & the State in South Africa* (Oxford: James Currey and Bloomington: Indiana University Press, 2002); Guadalupe Aguilar-Madrid et al., 'Globalization and the Transfer of Hazardous Industry: Asbestos in Mexico, 1979–2000', *International Journal of Occupational and Environmental Health* 9, no. 3 (2003), 272–279; Lundy Braun et al., 'Scientific Controversy and Asbestos: Making Disease Invisible', *International Journal of Occupational and Environmental Health* 9, no. 3 (2003) 194–205; R. F. Ruers and N. Schouten, *The Tragedy of Asbestos: Eternit and the Consequences of a Hundred Years of Asbestos Cement* (Netherlands: Socialistische Partij, 2006) https://international.sp.nl/sites/international.sp.nl/files/tragedyofasbestos_0.pdf, accessed 25 January 2021; Jock McCulloch and Geoffrey Tweedale, *Defending the Indefensible: The Global Asbestos Industry and its Fight for Survival* (Oxford: Oxford University Press, 2008).

[4] Laurie Kazan-Allen, 'Chronology of Asbestos Bans and Restrictions' http://www.ibasecretariat.org/chron_ban_list.php, accessed 20 April 2019.

[5] Peter van der Steen and Dave Lake, 'Business Rescue Plan' http://www.g5.co.za/pdfs/business-rescue/group-five-construction-pty-ltd-business-rescue-plan.pdf, accessed 26 January 2021.

[6] AG means 'Aktiengesellschaft' or limited company. In 2018, Becon AG, based in Switzerland, reduced its capitalisation from 30 million to 300 000 Swiss francs. See '4343485 – Calls to Creditors/Reduction of the Share or Participation Capital and Call to Creditors', in *Swiss Official Gazette of Commerce SOGC*, 6 July 2018 https://www.sogc.ch, accessed 26 January 2021.

[7] Personal communication with Brian Gibson, Everite, and Martina Neumüller-Kast, Eternit Schweiz, 2018.

[8] Central Housing Board, Drawing 299. Details of corrugated iron and corrugated asbestos roofs in lieu of concrete roofs for Types 292 and 248, blueprint by A. Dykstra (Clelland Archive, University of Pretoria).

[9] 'Turners Asbestos Cement Company' (Manchester: Turners Asbestos Cement Company, 1935).

[10] Dominique Barjot, 'Holcim: From the Family Business to Global Leadership (1993–2007)', *Revue française d'histoire économique*, no. 1 (September 2014), 56–85; Staub, *Von Schmidheiny zu Schmidheiny* (see note 2).

[11] P. A. Van Zyl, *A History of Asbestos Mining in South Africa* (Johannesburg: Asbestos Relief Trust, 2017).

[12] Staub, *Von Schmidheiny zu Schmidheiny* (see note 2).

[13] *25th Anniversary – Everite Limited* (Johannesburg: Everite, 1966).

[14] Kirchhofer archive, University of the Witwatersrand.

[15] In her study of the Johns Manville owned mines in Canada, Jessica van Horssen found that the company examined workers but did not share their findings with them, but with a company laboratory in New York. See J. Van Horssen, *A Town Called Asbestos: Environmental Contamination, Health and Resilience in a Resource Community* (Vancouver: University of British Columbia Press, 2016).

[16] Max Kirchhofer, 'Proposed New Doctor's Residence and Consulting Rooms on Stand No. 1 Garthdale Agricultural Holdings Farm Waterval 47, Kliprivier, District Vereeneniging for Everite (Pty) Ltd. Johannesburg', 1950

[17] S. Bannister, 'Use of Asbestos Cement in Low-Cost Housing' (Department of Housing, Republic of South Africa, 2001).

[18] C. A. Rigby and K. Steyn, 'The Hail Resistance of S.A. Roofing Materials', *South African Architectural Record* 37, no. 4 (1952), 101–7.

[19] National Planning and Housing Commission, *Minimum Standards of Housing Accommodation for Non-Europeans* (Pretoria: National Housing and Planning Commission, 1951).

[20] Derek Japha, 'The Social Programme of the South African Modern Movement', in Hilton Judin and Ivan Vladislavic (eds.), *Blank_ Architecture, Apartheid and After* (Rotterdam: NAi Publishers, 1998), 423–37.

[21] Hannah le Roux, 'Designing KwaThema: Cultural Inscriptions in the Model Township', *Journal of Southern African Studies* 45, no. 2 (2019), 1–29.

[22] Bannister, 'Use of Asbestos Cement in Low Cost Housing' (see note 17).

[23] G. A. Atkinson, 'Design and Construction in the Tropics', *Housing and Town and Country Planning*, no. 6 (1956), 9.

[24] Department of Scientific and Industrial Research, 'Asbestos-cement Roofing and Other Products', *Overseas Building Notes* (Garston: Tropical Building Section, Building Research Station, 1962).

[25] List of Directors, *Everite Annual Reports 1965–1985*.

[26] Everite Limited, *Annual Report 1968* (Johannesburg: Everite Limited, 1968).

[27] Ibid, inside cover.

[28] *25th Anniversary – Everite Limited* (see note 13).

[29] Douglas M. Calderwood, Max Kirchhofer, and M. D. Ringrose, 'Architectural Competition. The Grouping of Non-European Houses and the Use of Asbestos-Cement Products', *South African Architectural Record*, no. 2 (1956).

[30] Everite Limited, *Longspan Profile B' Sheets/ Plate* (Johannesburg: Everite, 1973), 5.

[31] Correspondence between Ortega and CSTB, 2 June 1964 (Alvaro Ortega archive, McGill University, Montreal).

[32] See Alvaro Ortega, 'Las Canaletas. Una aplicación reciente para cubiertas economicas', *AC: The International Asbestos-cement Review*, no. 22 (February 1961), 47–9.

[33] Staub, *Von Schmidheiny zu Schmidheiny*, 108 (see note 2).

[34] Catrina, *Der Eternit Report* (see note 2).

[35] 'Pleated Asbestos Roof for Low-Cost Housing', *Architectural Record* 129, no. 2 (February 1961), 175.

[36] 'Sophisticated Roof Component Widely Used for Self-help Housing', *Architectural Record* 141, no. 12 (December 1967), 156.

[37] John Turner and Robert Fichter, *Freedom to Build: Dweller Control of the Housing Process* (New York: The MacMillan Company, 1972).

[38] Marvin Sevely, Yury Sokolov, and Alvaro Ortega, 'Low Cost Housing Program in the Tropics', (New York: United Nations Committee on Housing, Building and Planning and Pratt Institute, Center for Middle Eastern and Tropical Architecture, 1965).

[39] Ibid.

[40] United Nations Department of Economic and Social Affairs, United Nations Secretary-General, and United Nations Group of Eminent Persons to Study the Impact of Multinational Corporations on Development and on International Relations, *The Impact of Multinational Corporations on Development and on International Relations* (New York: United Nations, 1974).

[41] See, for instance, Nkrumah's criticism of Turner & Newall in Kwame Nkrumah, *Neo-Colonialism: The Last Stage of Imperialism* (London: Thomas Nelson, 1965).

[42] Irving J. Selikoff, 'Opening Remarks', *Annals of the New York Academy of Sciences* 132, no. 1 (1965).

[43] See the chronology and description of the tort cases in Castleman and Berger, *Asbestos: Medical and Legal Aspects* (see note 3).

[44] See Felicity D. E. Scott, *Outlaw Territories: Environments of Insecurity/Architectures of Counterinsurgency* (New York: Zone Books, 2016).

[45] United Nations, *Report of the United Nations Conference on the Human Environment, Stockholm, 5–16 June 1972* (New York: United Nations, 1973), 3.

[46] For a chronology of asbestos bans, see Kazan-Allen, 'Chronology of Asbestos Bans and Restrictions' (see note 4).

[47] International Labour Organization, *Occupational Cancer Convention and Recommendation C139* (Geneva: International Labour Organization, 1974).

[48] Special Advisory Committee on Roofing in Developing Countries, *Roofing in Developing Countries. Research for New Technologies* (Washington: National Research Council, 1974).

[49] Richard D. Marshall, *Engineering Aspects of Cyclone Tracy. Darwin, Australia, 1974*, NBS Building Science Series 86 (Washington: National Bureau of Standards, 1976).

[50] See Charles Abrams, Vladimir Bodiansky, and Otto Koenigsberger, *Report on Housing in the Gold Coast* (New York: United Nations, 1956).

[51] See Llewellyn B. Lewis, 'Power and Influence Relations between a Firm and Its Environment and the Development of a Political Strategy for a Firm in the Black Market', Masters in Business Law, University of South Africa, 1977.

[52] Stephan Schmidheiny, 'Die Investitionsrisikogarantie', Hochschulschrift, Universität Zürich, 1972.

[53] Staub, *Von Schmidheiny zu Schmidheiny* (see note 2).

[54] Llewellyn B. Lewis, unpublished report on low cost housing finance, 1980.

[55] Schmidheiny 'supported' the Institute of Liberty and Democracy (ILD) in Peru where de Soto was based. See Hernando de Soto, *The Mystery of Capital: Why Capitalism Triumphs in the West and Fails Everywhere Else* (London: Black Swan, 2000).

[56] Lewis, 'Power and Influence Relations between a Firm and Its Environment and the Development of a Political Strategy for a Firm in the Black Market' (see note 51); Everite Limited, 'Everite: Self-help and Low Cost Housing (including plans)' (Johannesburg: Everite, 1978).

[57] See 'NBRI and Government on Core Housing Project', *Housing in Southern Africa* 8 (March/April 1980), 2–4.

[58] For perspectives on displacements under the Homelands policy, see Surplus People Project, *Forced Removals in South Africa* (Cape Town: Surplus People Project, 1983).

[59] Stephan Schmidheiny, 'Forests and Globalization: A Business Perspective', in James Gustave Speth (ed.), *Worlds Apart: Globalization and the Environment* (Washington: Island Press, 2003).

[60] In 1980 Everite still owned asbestos mines in South Africa through a 43.6 per cent stake in Asbestos Investments Pty Ltd (Asbesco) which operated mines and mills in South Africa and Zimbabwe. Jonathan Myers, *Asbestos and Asbestos-Related Disease in South Africa*, Saldru Working Papers no. 28 (Cape Town: Southern African Labour and Development Research Unit, 1980), 8.

[61] *25th Anniversary – Everite Limited* (see note 13).

[62] Angela Mathee et al., 'Potential Risk Factors for Asbestos Exposure Amongst Six-month-old Infants Living in the Township of Soweto, South Africa', *International Journal of Environmental Health Research* 10, no. 2, (2000), 135–9.

[63] An unpublished survey carried out by the National Centre for Occupational Health (NCOH), South Africa, of asbestos levels in Soweto houses by Enoch Mogomotsi, D. Rama, and R. Du Toit (1992) was cited in the 2001 report on asbestos use in low cost housing by Bannister, which notes it found that 'in certain samples, fibre levels nearly 10 times higher than the recommended 0.1 f/millilitre safety level were recorded' (Bannister, 'Use of Asbestos Cement in Low Cost Housing', 13, see note 17). The report was withdrawn by the NCOH 'due to weaknesses identified in the methodology' (Bannister, 'Use of Asbestos Cement in Low Cost Housing', 13, see note 17) and a new survey of three houses was conducted in the neighbourhood of Mofolo South in 1999. Various papers published by the National Institute for Occupational Health using the 1999 data that found levels of airborne fibres in the house to be within minimal detectable concentrations, but dangerous accumulations of fibres in the soil below the roof run off lines. See James I. Phillips and David Rees, 'The Legacy of in situ Asbestos Cement Roofs in South Africa', *Occupational and Environmental Medicine* 74, suppl. 1 (2017), A76–7.

[64] Michelle Murphy, *Sick Building Syndrome and the Problem of Uncertainty: Environmental Politics, Technoscience, and Women Workers* (Durham N.C.: Duke University Press, 2006).

[65] Eric D. Bateman and Anamika Jithoo, 'Lung Diseases in South Africa: An Overview', in Derek J. Chadwick and Jamie Goode (eds.), *Innate Immunity to Pulmonary Infection*. Novartis Foundation Symposium 279 (Chichester: John Wiley & Sons, 2006), 4–11; discussion 11–16, 216–9.

[66] Aguilar-Madrid et al., 'Globalization and the Transfer of Hazardous Industry' (see note 3); Lundy Braun and Sophia Kisting, 'Asbestos-Related Disease in South Africa: The Social Production of an Invisible Epidemic', *American Journal of Public Health* 96, no. 8 (2006), 1386–96; Fernanda Giannasi, 'Eternit

in Brazil', in Laurie Kazan-Allen and David Allen (eds.), *Eternit and the Great Asbestos Trial* (London: IBAS, 2012), 65–71.

[67] Kgalagadi Relief Trust, 'History of the Trust' (2018), https://asbestostrust.co.za/krt/history/, accessed 26 January 2021. The trust was funded by Becon.

[68] Cleber M. R. Dias et al., 'Long-term Aging of Fibre-cement Corrugated Sheets – The Effect of Carbonation, Leaching and Acid Rain', *Cement Concrete Composites* 30, no. 4 (2008), 255–65.

CONCRETE STORIES

Sarah Nichols

Introduction

What do we talk about when we talk about concrete? Buildings out of concrete? Concrete as material in the abstract? The wet slurry? What about as a commodity – an industrialised product? Or is concrete not a material but instead an assemblage? Or is it all of them? As a recipe, concrete at its most basic is a composite of cheap and readily available substances: cement, water, sand, and aggregate. These are mixed, cast into a form, and left to hydrate to form a solid. More often than not, it is embedded with steel to add tensile strength at which point it is referred to as reinforced concrete. It is a messy process that uses inexpensive ingredients and yet structures out of it can be incredibly refined. Yet to succinctly describe the material process is only part of the picture and although concrete is messy and contradictory on site, as a cultural object it is just as complicated.

Modern concrete is a material with many origin points, some of which have been recorded and heroised while other developments occurred anonymously and have been forgotten. Though the use of concrete extends back millennia and can be found in many places and in many variations, what we commonly refer to as concrete today has relatively recent origins that are closely tied to the industrial revolution. In the second half of the nineteenth century, Portland cement became a normalised product. Meanwhile, patented reinforced-concrete building systems like Monier and Hennebique were introduced and provided not just a new type of construction but new ways of managing the construction process. In Switzerland, domestic cement production took off rather late in the 1870s, but reinforced concrete construction soon rapidly gained popularity.

Over the first half of the twentieth century, concrete came to prominence as a material for daring works of civil engineering, modernist architecture, and as the often-hidden structure of ubiquitous, quotidian construction both above and below ground. In Switzerland, even as concrete became more and more common for everyday construction, its use in buildings tended – with a few notable exceptions – to be pragmatic rather than polemic. Civil engineering works in concrete elicited attention for their daring and began to be associated with a particular 'Swissness'. From Maillart's bridges to the hairpin turns of Alpine passes, these projects began to broadcast expertise in concrete that was sellable abroad, as Swiss contractors and engineers competed in the global construction business. Over these decades, industrial organisations, technical education systems, and the building trades all developed sophisticated ways of managing concrete as a product, as a scientific test subject, and as a substance for both technics and craft. As the economy in Switzerland boomed after the Second World War, this knowledge and organisation sprang into action pouring a nearly unending stream of concrete. By the late 1950s, Switzerland used more cement per capita than any other nation on earth – a marker that was reached multiple times before the 1973 oil crisis. At the same time, a generation of Swiss architects completed ambitious projects in concrete that became well known within the country yet still receive less attention abroad than more recent works. As the construction industry crashed in the wake of the oil crisis, concrete also fell out of favour, becoming a scapegoat in the popular imagination for the ills of postwar development. Even as structures continued to use reinforced concrete, exposed concrete facades fell largely out of favour. Yet by the 1990s exposed concrete – this time still heavy and massive but also smooth and refined – returned in a new generation of minimalist projects that vaulted the 'Swiss box' to international attention.

Today, concrete is not only a dominant construction material in Switzerland but also the most widely used building material on earth. Concrete can be found in buildings but also in infrastructure: as small elements like concrete masonry units and as large monolithic structures. It is used for high-tech and low-tech applications, by engineers and architects as well as hobbyists and self-builders. It is something that can be almost anything, almost anywhere. In terms of public opinion, it is polarising. While many architects appreciate and even fetishise concrete as a surface material, the feeling of the general public ranges from apathy to distaste or even disgust for its roughness, coldness, and greyness. The link between exposed concrete and the large projects of postwar welfare states that often left promises unfulfilled and maintenance deferred strengthened this distaste for the perceived hubris of a material associated with a modernity gone awry. Dislike of the aesthetics and ideologies of concrete now compound with ethical objections due to concrete's significant impact on climate primarily through the CO_2 released by cement production. Yet environmental concerns go beyond the specifics of greenhouse gases because concrete has been used pervasively to intervene on the environment: from changing the course of rivers in ways that impact habitat, to covering surfaces that no longer absorb rainfall, or to imperfectly sealing away radioactive waste.

The statements and images that follow reproduce the organising structure of the exhibition. The nine statements represent different ways concrete has been conceptualised while eschewing definitive categorisation or periodisation. Each theme shows how ideas persist or recur through time, even as the expression of these notions has changed. Material is not neutral matter. Rather, it is a construct – designed in ways that are important but also often overlooked. Thus to consider concrete as a whole, any one codified approach – concrete as engineering material, concrete as craft material, concrete as modern material – is insufficient to understand it. Through different modes of being, concrete appears and acts in different ways. The exhibition is thus structured around a series of statements that take the form of a declarative 'concrete is…'. Each statement posits a way in which concrete can be understood, from 'concrete is rock' to 'concrete is fluid.'

Each statement represents a powerful imaginary about what concrete is or should be. Yet the statements, like the material, do not add up to an easy whole. Rather, the intention is that the different statements allow enough points of entry to understand concrete as the complex and sometimes contradictory material that it is, sketching a discursive field rather than following a single argument.

The exhibition is the result of the first research collaboration between the S AM Swiss Architecture Museum and the Archives de la construction moderne (Acm) at EPF Lausanne, the Archivio del Moderno dell'Accademia di architettura at the Università della Svizzera italiana, and the gta (Institut für Geschichte und Theorie der Architektur) Archiv at ETH Zurich. The three archives are the main sources for the material presented here. Reflecting the archival holdings, most of the material shown is from the twentieth century, mainly from the 1910s through the 1970s but with earlier and later material as it was available. This has the effect of excluding some of the most well-known projects from recent years while also making it possible to highlight the wealth of exceptional but sometimes lesser-known projects from earlier eras. As needed, material from additional archives has been brought in to better demonstrate the full range of construction in concrete – from retaining wall, to anti-tank barrier, to building, to gravity dam. Following from the curatorial decision to take on concrete as a complex field rather than a narrow argument, it was crucial to bring in this supplementary material not just to show the variety of construction in concrete but also to be able to display the vital links through engineers, material suppliers, and contractors between architecture and other forms of construction.

It is a poignant time to look back at the history of concrete because the framework with which we approach materials is fundamentally shifting – a shift which is not yet complete but one that seems foundational. Performance, aesthetics, ethics, supply chains, lifecycle, toxicity – important lenses of analysis are being fleshed out even as basic approaches – sometimes as fundamental as qualitative or quantitative, carrots or sticks – continue to be debated. Many of these dilemmas are predicated on the fact that we are always designing buildings for an uncertain future. With the dust that these debates have sent up not fully settled, there is sometimes a whipsaw effect looking back at the projects enclosed within: nostalgia for an era of societal projects combines with distaste for the hubris or even sometimes wilful naiveté of some gestures.

As just one front in which criteria are changing, it is clear that questions of environment are of utmost urgency today. This exhibition looks back at a generation of projects where the idea of architecture having a cumulative climatic effect was not fully formed. Yet as awareness of the impact of CO_2 has become widespread, the scale of the problem has only increased. In 2018, the six remaining cement factories in Switzerland were responsible for 9 per cent of the country's carbon dioxide output. Today, if worldwide cement production were a country, it would be the third largest emitter of atmospheric carbon dioxide after China and the United States. The significant and borderless climate impact of concrete use is now a fundamental challenge to our continued concrete dependency. At the same time, even just the maintenance of existing concrete structures will keep cement production at a considerable level.

Will concrete, which seemed to explode onto the scene in a wave of urban expansions at the end of the nineteenth century, now fade just as quickly away? Concrete's basic promise of solidity and economy has had remarkable staying power. Yet if these values have followed us into the twenty-first century, they are not absolute. Would concrete still be considered cheap if material prices accounted for the true environmental cost of the material throughout its lifespan? What are the limits to the framework in which cheapness is even desirable? A number of very fundamental arguments about concrete are no longer being taken for granted. At the same time, material scientists are seeking ways of fundamentally changing concrete that would shift the calculus of the cost of the material. Yet as is so often the case with concrete, the question of its future is not only about the material itself. As pervasive and adaptable as concrete is, its future will not be determined in isolation but rather by a new politics of material. With political will, the playing field could shift in such a way that assessments of economy, durability, and environmental impact force a revaluation of the whole culture of construction. If this feels impossible because concrete has become so naturalised, it is a good moment to reflect on the history, myths, and contradictions of concrete to understand how constructed and how tenuous our relationship to this material is.

CONCRETE is ROCK

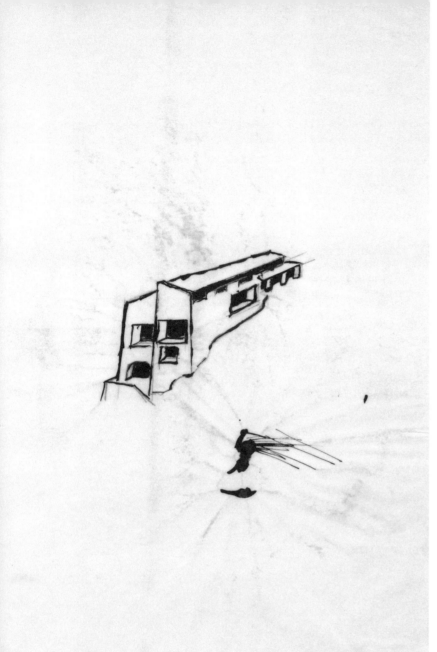

Concrete, geologically speaking, is a rock. This has been a strong, recurring notion from its modern introduction in the nineteenth century through to today. Even in one of the first articles on modern concrete from 1839, an engineer Johann Telesphor Zetter from Solothurn tried to position concrete as a natural material by claiming it was a mere reproduction of naturally occurring conglomerates like *Nagelfluh* (*breccia helvetica*).[1]

Rudolf Olgiati, Casa Las Caglias, Flims, 1959–60. Sketch, n.d., ink on tracing paper. Building in cast-in-place concrete with plaster facade.

Blasting in a cement factory quarry, from E. G. Portland (ed.), *Die schweizerische Zement-Industrie*, 1958.

Removal of lime and clay marl for cement production, from E. G. Portland (ed.), *Die schweizerische Zement-Industrie*, 1958.

[1] 'In dieser Art hat ihn die Baukunst nicht eben erfunden sondern bloss der Natur nachgeahmt, die mit selbem grossartige Gebäude ausgeführt hat, nämlich die Gebilde der Nagelfluh (breccia helvetica).' (Johann Telesphor Zetter, 'Über die Bereitung und Anwendung des Betons', *Zeitschrift über das gesamte Bauwesen* 3, no. 2, 1839, 56). *Nagelfluh*, a composite stone with visible pebbles bound together in a larger piece of sandstone, had long been used as a building material in southern and western Switzerland, though what is referred to here is not buildings of *Nagelfluh* – whose Latin name, *breccia helvetica*, refers to its Swiss provenance – but its natural formations as cliffs or erratics in the Alps.

195

Removal of lime and clay marl for cement production, from E. G. Portland (ed.), *Die schweizerische Zement-Industrie*, 1958.

Swiss Federal Strength Testing Institute Zurich in collaboration with Prof. Dr A. Jaccard & Prof. Dr A. Heim, overview map of the locations of raw materials for lime, cement, and gypsum production in Switzerland, 1894.

Yet if concrete is a rock, it is also one that is man-made. Producing cement – the binder in concrete – from rock (limestone) requires an energy-intense industrial process of extraction and high-heat sintering that not only uses tremendous amounts of fuel but also releases tremendous amounts of carbon dioxide into the atmosphere. This process is, in turn, dependent on research and testing that precisely determine the proportion of ingredients and properties of the concrete mix, resulting in a material that is far more homogenous and predictable than a natural stone.

Claims that concrete is a rock are often meant to obscure these crucial scientific and industrial steps that happen between the quarry and the finished building. In Switzerland, particular emphasis was put on associations between Alpine cliffs and the concrete in buildings – creating a powerful cultural imaginary of buildings supposedly produced from and visually linked to the Alps.[2]

[2] Despite the rhetorical importance of such claims, the cement industry has mostly proliferated along the riverbeds of the lowlands rather than in the Alps.

Karl Moser and Robert Curjel, Basel Badischer Bahnhof, 1909–13. Perspective drawing, March 1908, plan copy with handwritten notes. Coffered barrel vault built in concrete.

197

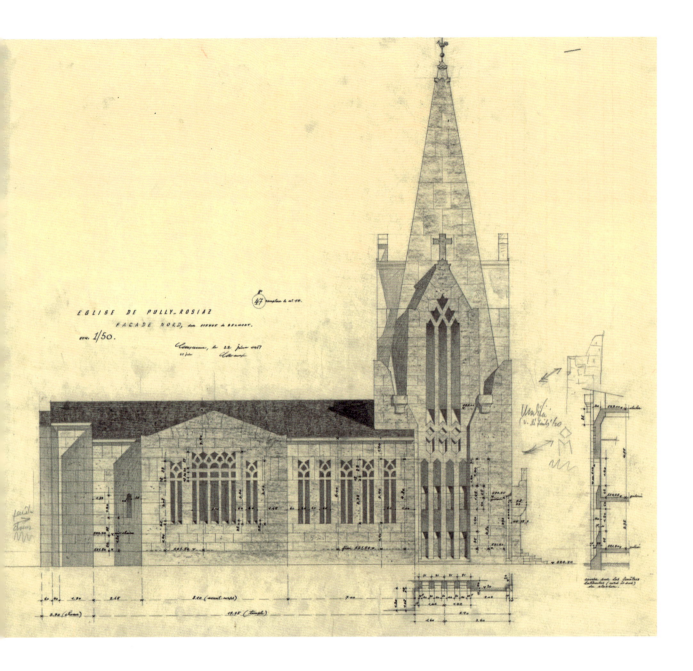

Paul Lavenex, Pully-La Rosiaz Church, 1951–53. North facade, front elevation, June 1951, ink and pencil on tracing paper. Concrete blocks moulded on site.

Paul Lavenex, Pully-La Rosiaz Church, 1951–53. Main entrance, postcard, n.d.

For architects and material producers, the story of concrete as stone was particularly important for protagonists who viewed industrialised construction with ambivalence or scepticism. In the early decades of the twentieth century, concrete was used as masonry blocks (*Kunststein*) visually indistinguishable from stone but stronger and less expensive, following a long history of artificial stones made from mortar.³

³ Artificial stones, including ceramics, have a longer history. Mortar-based artificial stones were used in regions of Italy since at least the seventeenth century for the corners of houses and for river embankments, while Pulhamite stone of Portland cement, sand, and rubble was used for the fashionable rockeries and grottos of nineteenth-century England.

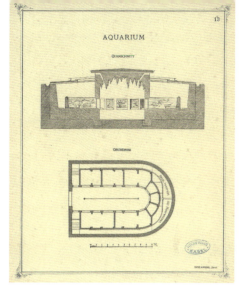

The first 'exposed concrete' facades thus appeared well before Brutalism – they are simply a visual expression so in line with natural stone that they often do not seem to be anything else. In Switzerland, a famous example of this is Gustav Gull's extension and renovation of the Swiss Federal Institute of Technology Semperbau, during which the original Ostermundingen sandstone was replaced with stone-like concrete blocks.

Della Torre & Greppi with Borgari, Aquarium, Swiss National Exhibition Zurich 1883. Entrance, photograph Romedo Guler, 1883. Aquarium structure and artificial stones made of concrete.

Della Torre & Greppi with Borgari, Aquarium, Swiss National Exhibition Zurich 1883. Plan and section drawings, from Alfred Pfister (ed.), *Bauten der Schweizerischen Landesausstellung Zürich 1883*, 1883. Aquarium structure made from mass concrete.

Jakob Haller and Carl Schindler, Du Pont office building, Zurich, 1913–14. Sculptural elements at entrance and integrated fountain by sculptor Adolf Meyer, from *Zeitschrift für Beton- und Eisenbetonbau*, 1914. Facade at building base including sculptural elements made from artificial stone with black pigmented cement and glass fragments.

199

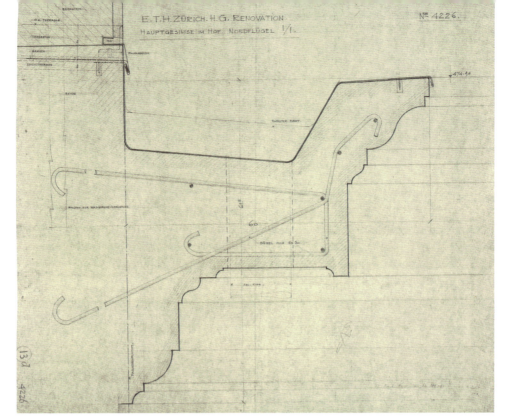

Gustav Gull, Swiss Federal Institute of Technology main building renovation, Zurich, 1914–25. Section drawing of reinforced artificial stone cornice, October 1923, plan copy.

Advertisement for Beton-Werke AG in Schmerikon, from Gustav Gull, *Orientierungs-Schrift über die an den Erweiterungs-Bauten beteiligten Unternehmer und Lieferanten*, 1924. As depicted, Beton-Werke AG was one of the producers of artificial stone elements for Gull's renovation and extension work at ETH.

Gustav Gull, Swiss Federal Institute of Technology main building renovation, 1914–25. A man installing an artificial stone block on the facade of the south wing, anonymous photograph, November 1921.

Gull, while drawing on Polytechnic knowledge of the Swiss Federal Institute of Technology in the project through the development of the *Kunststein* blocks, as well as the reinforced concrete frame of his extension, nevertheless refused to reveal this reliance, hiding his concrete in plain sight.

 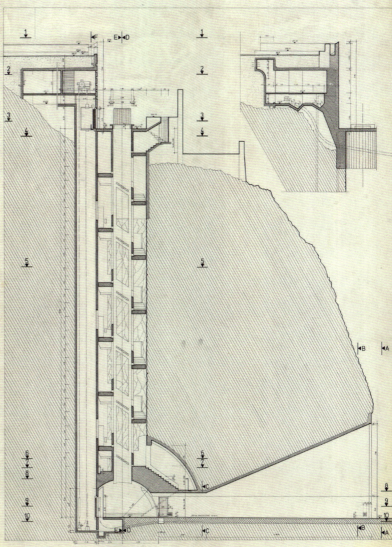

In the 1960s and 1970s the rock-like nature of concrete was again emphasised. This time however, instead of using masonry, whole concrete structures were treated as rock-like, either set against stone surfaces like cliffs, above and following page, or appearing as the solitary figures of glacial erratics, as in the work of Rudolf Olgiati, another protagonist who preferred to view building culture as a continuation of tradition.

Aurelio Galfetti, entrance to Castelgrande Bellinzona. 1991. Anonymous photograph, n.d.

Aurelio Galfetti, restoration of Castelgrande, Bellinzona. 1981–2000. Longitudinal section drawing of the lifts and stairs with access from Piazza del Sole. January 1983–June 1985, ink on polyester film.

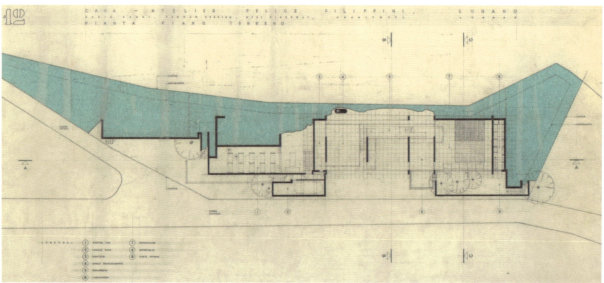

Mario Campi, Franco Pessina, and Niki Piazzoli, Casa Filippini, Muzzano, 1967–69. The courtyard towards the quarry, anonymous photograph, n.d.

Robert Maillart, rockfall protection roof near Tiefencastel, 1904. Anonymous photograph, n.d.

Mario Campi, Franco Pessina, and Niki Piazzoli, Casa Filippini, Muzzano, 1967–69. The interior looking towards the courtyard and the quarry, anonymous photograph, n.d.

Mario Campi, Franco Pessina, and Niki Piazzoli, Casa Filippini, Muzzano, 1967–69. Plan drawing of the ground floor, n.d., pencil and coloured screentone on tracing paper.

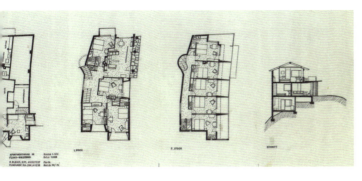
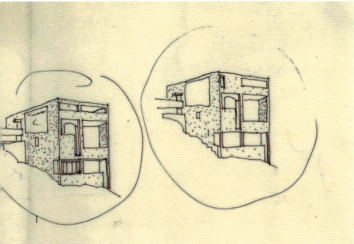
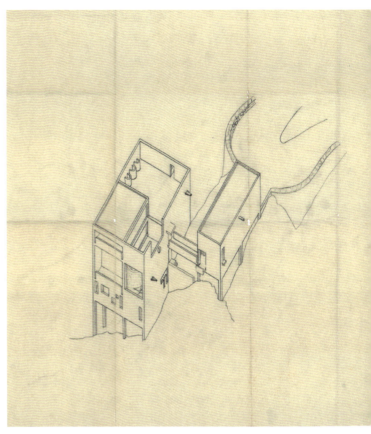

Rudolf Olgiati, Casa Las Caglias, Flims, 1959–60. Plan and section drawings, February 1965, ink on tracing paper.

Aurelio Galfetti, Casa Rotalinti, Bellinzona, 1960–61. Concept sketches of the main facade and perspective studies, n.d., ink and coloured pencil on tracing paper.

Aurelio Galfetti, Casa Rotalinti, Bellinzona, 1960–61. Axonometric view, n.d., pencil on tracing paper.

Rudolf Olgiati, Casa Las Caglias, Flims, 1959–60. Anonymous photograph, n.d.

Mario Campi and Franco Pessina, Casa Vanini, Muzzano, 1962–64. Ground floor, anonymous photograph, n.d.

CONCRETE is UNDERGROUND

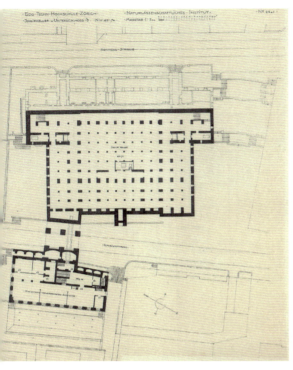
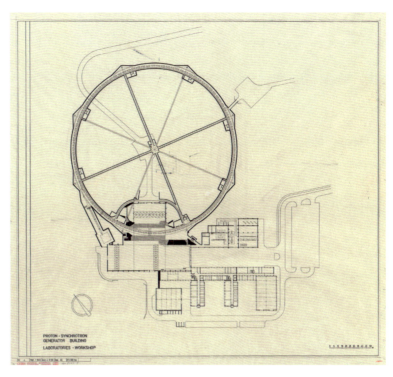

Some of concrete's most widespread uses often go unseen because they are below ground level or underwater. In the nineteenth century, concrete was viewed as a foundation material – appropriate for use below ground due to its economy, strength, and water-resistance. Early applications of concrete included foundations (shown in the Swiss Federal Institute of Technology student notebooks) and water supply projects (seen in the canalisation plan of Winterthur). Only slowly, in Switzerland and elsewhere, did concrete emerge from the ground. But even as it did, the close connection between concrete and the underground was never broken. Still today, concrete lines a subterranean network of spaces that support life above ground. They are part of a powerful imaginary of a nation that is both connected and insular.

Gustav Gull, the Institute of Natural Sciences of the Swiss Federal Institute of Technology, Zurich, 1912–16. Plan drawing, n.d., ink on tracing paper. Basement level in mass concrete.

Rudolf Steiger and Peter Steiger, Fietz & Hauri engineers. CERN proton-synchrotron generator building, Geneva, 1954–60. Plan drawing, September 1959–July 1960, ink on tracing paper. Synchrotron ring in reinforced concrete.

Henri-Robert von der Mühll, student notebook, 1919. Pencil and ink on paper.

Alfred Roth, Heinrich Pestalozzi School, Skopje, 1966–69. Seismic base isolation, photograph C. Hubacher, n.d. Raw reinforced concrete base structure before addition of rubber cushions and building.

207

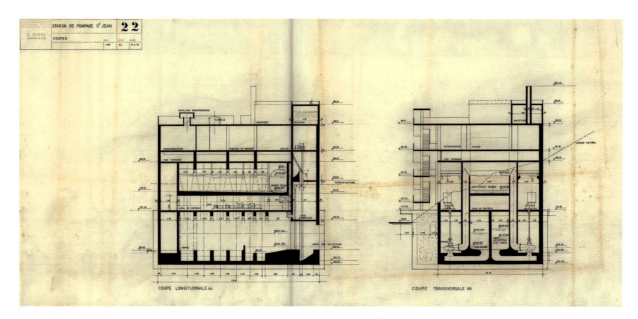

Georges Brera, Saint-Jean pumping station, Geneva, 1963–67. Section drawings, February 1964, ink on tracing paper. Structure in reinforced concrete.

Sewerage network for the city of Winterthur, 1890. Map from *Schweizerische Bauzeitung*, 1890. Conduits and access shafts in mass concrete.

Conrad Zschokke SA, reservoir, Bernex, 1963–64. Anonymous photograph, n.d.

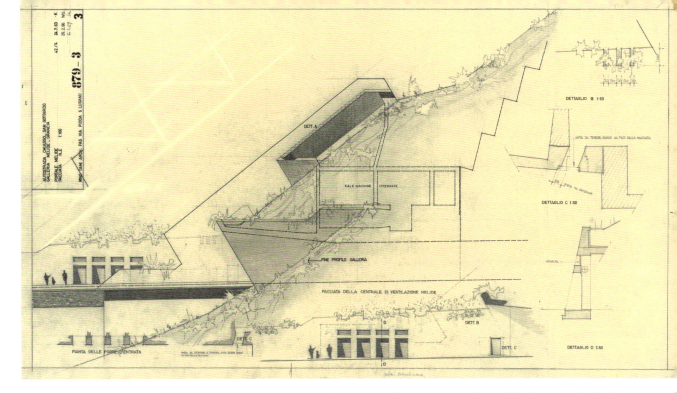

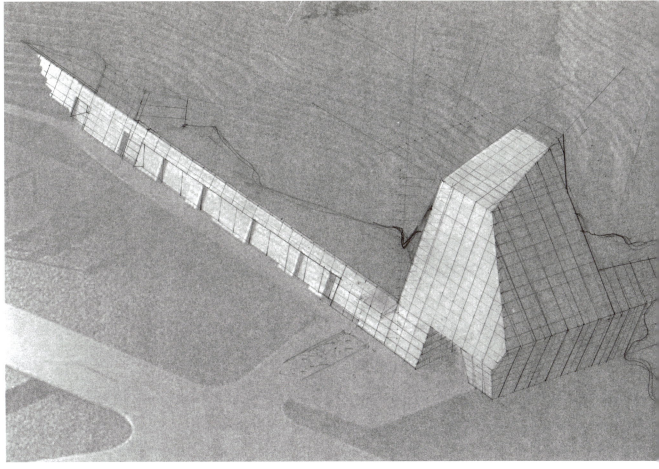

Rino Tami, Chiasso–Gotthard motorway, Melide portal of the Melide-Grancia tunnel, 1963–70. Side elevation drawing, July 1963–November 1969, ink and pencil on tracing paper.

Beratungsgruppe für Gestaltung Alptransit, multifunction station, Faido, 2012–14. Concept sketch Flora Ruchat-Roncati, n.d., pencil on sketch paper applied to xerographic photocopy.

Flora Ruchat-Roncati and Renato Salvi, N16 Transjurane motorway, Terri Nord ventilation station, 1989–98. View from south-east, photograph Heinrich Helfenstein, n.d.

Entreprises Électriques Fribourgeoises, J.-F. Bruttin and Henri Gicot, hydroelectric development, Rossens, 1943–48. Water supply and water discharge tunnels, anonymous photograph, n.d.

T. R. Schneider, New Rail Link through the Alps (NRLA), Gotthard Base Tunnel, 1998–2016. Geological horizontal section, December 1987, plan copy.

Tunnels cut through the Alps, easing transit across the country for goods and people by road or rail in a way that exemplifies the infrastructural necessities of the global economy, posing a view of the underground that reinforces Switzerland as an interconnected global economic hub. While tunnels predate industrial concrete, in the nineteenth century, new cements and additives were increasingly relied upon for waterproofing and securing a new generation of tunnels built as critical parts of the modern national transit network. As tunnelling operations moved into the twentieth century, concrete was cast as tunnel walls, for air supply, egress, and as sculptural tunnel entrances.

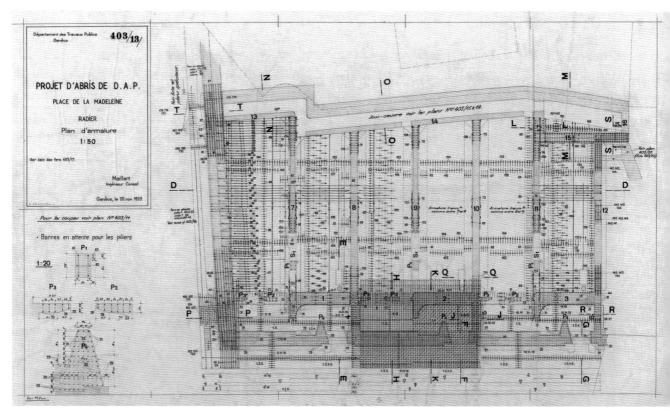

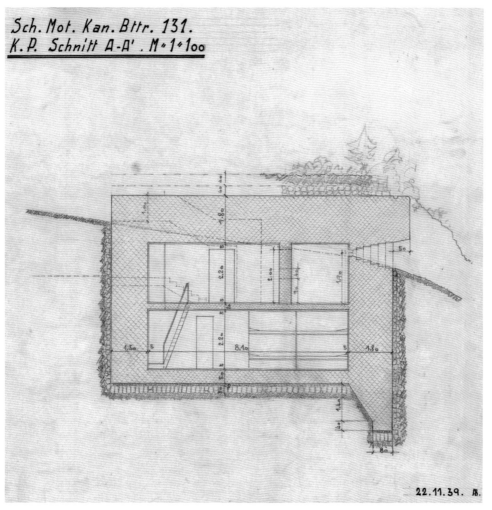

Robert Maillart, bomb shelter at the Place de la Madeleine, Geneva, 1939. Plan drawing, November 1939, ink and pencil on tracing paper.

Arnold Itten, military bunker, 1939. Section drawing, November 1939, pencil on tracing paper.

Bunker entrance camouflaged as rock, Andermatt. Photograph Leo Fabrizio, 2002.

Innumerable bunkers fortify Switzerland against the outside world as part of the country's famed national defence strategies. In the popular imagination, bunker networks in the Alps are so vast that the mountain range is practically hollow, displacing rock with concrete caverns. In some instances, tunnels act as bunkers, such as at the A2 Sonnenberg tunnel in Lucerne constructed both as part of a north-south connection across the country and as civil defence shelter for 20,000 of Lucerne's inhabitants. Yet, as is known within the country, defence begins at home with the pervasive network of domestic civil defence bunkers of thick reinforced concrete in the basement of most urban buildings. By 1961, reinforced concrete was specifically called for in civil defence requirements as a means of protection against all types of weapons feared during the Cold War: atomic, biological, and chemical. Yet if concrete was deployed as a means of protection from a *possible* threat, the concrete spaces built for such protection had the *real* effect of militarising the intimate sphere of the country.

Unbeknownst to many, Robert Maillart's office designed several bunkers, producing beautiful drawings of the unseen reinforcement for spaces that were themselves unremarkable, as with the reinforcement plan for the bunker at Place de la Madeleine in Geneva. Arnold Itten designed bunkers during conscripted service in the early 1940s; his drawings reveal a perverse proportion of material to space.

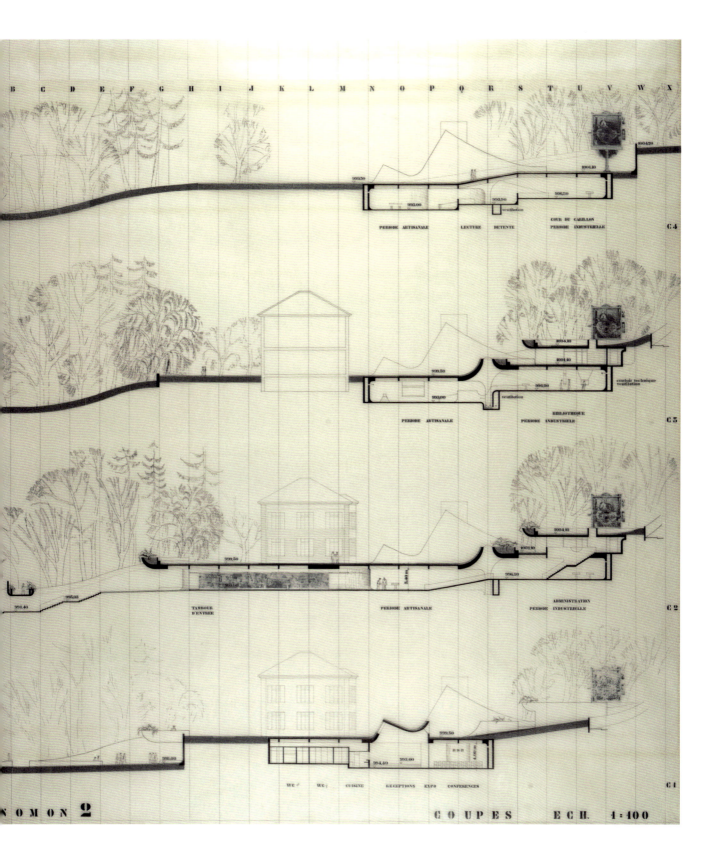

Georges-Jacques Haefeli and Pierre Zoelly, competition for a watchmaking museum, La Chaux-de-Fonds, 1968. Section drawings, n.d., ink on tracing paper. Structure in reinforced concrete.

Glaus Allemann + Partner, competition for spa planning and thermal baths, Baden-Baden, 1974–76. Section drawings, n.d., plan copy. Proposed structure in reinforced concrete.

Designing the underground has in fact been a key site of work for architects and engineers, both as practical and speculative proposals. By the 1960s, the concrete underground had become a space for visionary proposals. Pierre Zoelly documented 'found' sites of design in the underground and, alongside them, proposed expanded notions of the underground as another ground plane that allowed transit networks to be buried underneath a second layer of the city – notions that he brought to fruition on a more limited scale in projects such as the Watch Museum in La Chaux-de-Fonds.

CONCRETE *is* ENERGY

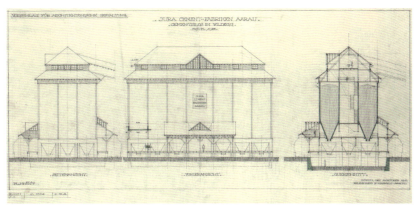
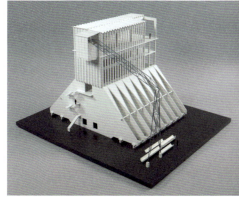
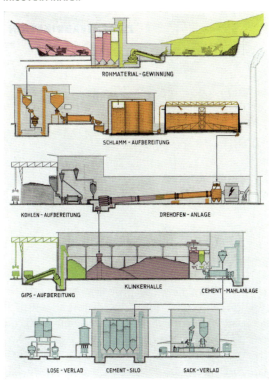

Concrete is in a reflexive relationship with energy. Over the course of the twentieth century, a growing cement industry needed more and more energy to produce the key ingredient for concrete. At the same time concrete was increasingly put to use to produce energy. Concrete use was thus both a precipitator and a provider of energy demand, helping drive the spiral of increasing energy intensity at both ends.

Otto Pfeghard and Max Haefeli, cement silos for the Jura Cement-Fabriken Aarau, Wildegg, 1918. Elevation and section drawings, October 1918, pencil on tracing paper.

Heinz Hossdorf, gravel and concrete plant, Günzgen, 1960–62. Model, 1998, wood. Photograph gta Archiv, ETH Zürich, 2021.

Diagram of the 'wet process' in cement manufacturing, from E. G. Portland (ed.), *Die schweizerische Zement-Industrie*, 1958.

Worker examining a cement kiln, from E. G. Portland (ed.), *Die schweizerische Zement-Industrie*, 1958.

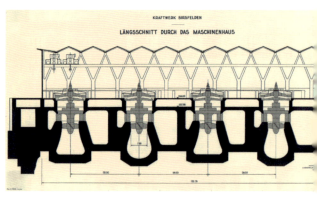

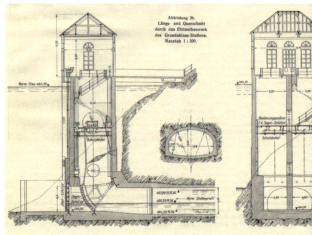

Wooden formwork for the turbines at the Niederried Electric Plant, from Losinger + Co AG (ed.), *Losinger*, vol. 'Kraftwerkbau', 1967.

Hans Hofmann, Birsfelden Hydroelectric Power Plant, Birsfelden, 1953–54. Section drawing of building and turbines, December 1956, plan copy.

Gabriel Narutowicz, hydroelectric power plant, Mühleberg, 1917–20. Section drawing, from *Schweizerische Bauzeitung*, 1926.

To produce cement clinker, limestone is sintered in a high-temperature kiln in a process that requires large amounts of fuel and releases tremendous amounts of carbon dioxide into the atmosphere.[1] Cement kilns operate continuously regardless of demand, consuming a steady stream of fuel. The vast majority of energy came from fossil fuels, initially, coal. In 1929, the production of a specified amount of cement required a staggering half its weight in coal.[2] From the 1960s onwards, production switched to oil. Incremental efficiency gains were offset by increased cement production:[3] in 1977, the cement industry was responsible for 2 per cent of the country's total energy consumption.[4]

Despite the fact that concrete is considered a local material because it is usually produced close to where it will eventually be poured, fuel – which concrete is just as heavily predicated upon – has almost always been imported, complicating this narrative. The cement industry has had to be adept at ensuring a constant supply of fuel even at times of extreme scarcity, and the growth of the cement industry over the course of the twentieth century was contingent upon its access to carbon energy.[5]

[1] Most of the CO_2 released during cement production is due to calcination of the heated limestone.
[2] Eduard Weckerle, *Industrien der Steine und Erden: Zement, Kalk, Gips, Ziegelsteine, Glas, Keramik*, Die schweizerische Industrie und ihre Arbeiter 1 (Olten: Hauenstein-Verlag, 1944), 12.
[3] Energy per tonne of cement from 1.3 mil kCal in 1959, 1.02 in 1975, to .9 kCal in 1976. Hans Eichenberger, *Die Zementindustrie im Überblick*, Wirtschaftspolitische Mitteilungen (Zürich: Wirtschaftsförderung, 1977), 16.
[4] Eichenberger, *Die Zementindustrie im Überblick* (see note 3), 15.
[5] Cement kilns also serve as waste dumps of sorts, burning an assortment of leftovers as a secondary fuel supply, from trash to animal cadavers.

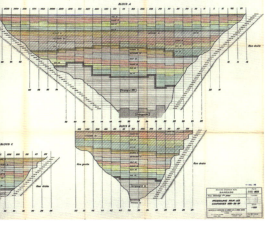
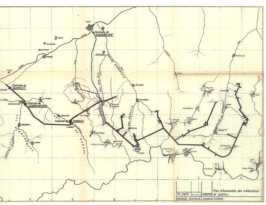

While concrete relies on energy, it is also an essential material in the production of energy. In Switzerland, where fossil fuels are largely imported, dams took on a political dimension as a means of achieving energy autarchy. Hydropower produces the majority of electricity in the country, typically using concrete to redirect and hold water. While imposing Alpine dams are the most prominent image of hydropower, there are also a number of river dams built in concrete in the flat areas of the country. In section, the light structure of Hans Hoffmann's Kraftwerk Birsfelden is revealed as a thin crown on top of the heavy concrete base through which water flows into the turbines. Building hydropower structures is a matter of technics and craft. The fluid shapes for the formwork of river dams were so complex that boatbuilders were sometimes brought in to fabricate them. In gravity dams such as the Grande Dixence, the mass of concrete holds back water that can then be sent down concrete-lined chutes to turbines below. Further incisions into the mountain range bring water from across the region to the dam.

Alfred Stucky, Grande Dixence Dam, 1950–61, Phasing plan for concrete pours, February 1954, plan copy.

Alfred Stucky, Grande Dixence Dam, 1950–61, Overview of water conduits and spillways, 1951, plan copy.

Alfred Stucky, Grande Dixence Dam, 1953–61, Photograph Walter Binder, October 1969.

Otto Rudolf Salvisberg, District Heating Power Plant and Machine Laboratory of the Swiss Federal Institute of Technology, Zurich, 1930–35. Photograph Heinrich Wolf-Bender, 1932.

Pierre Zoelly, Aubrugg Combined Heat and Power Plant, Wallisellen, 1975–78. Cutaway bird's-eye drawing, n.d., ink on paper.

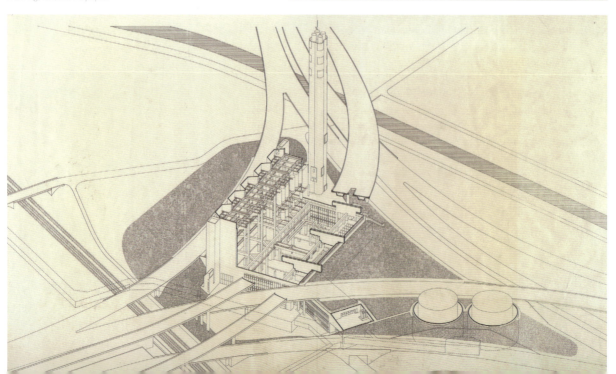

Otto Rudolf Salvisberg, District Heating Power Plant and Machine Laboratory of the Swiss Federal Institute of Technology, Zurich, 1930–35. Concrete reinforcement, photograph Heinrich Wolf-Bender, October 1931.

Gebruder Rank, Coal Warehouse II at the Zurich Municipal Gasworks, 1904–08. Warehouse exterior, from *Schweizerische Bauzeitung*, 1909. Silos and structure in reinforced concrete.

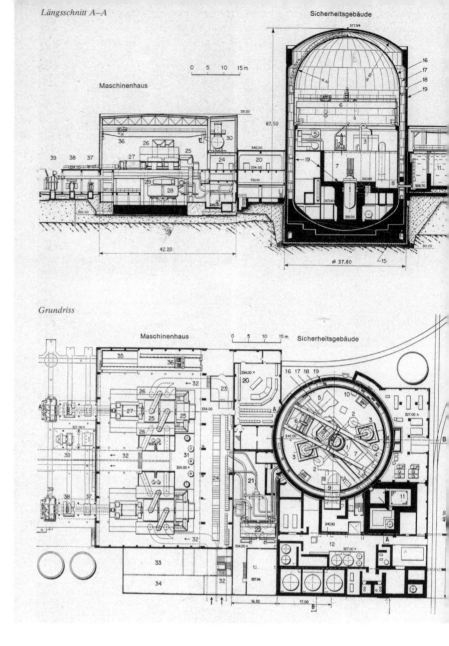

Westinghouse International Atomic Power Co. Ltd. and AG Brown, Boveri & Cie, Beznau Nuclear Power Plant, Döttingen, 1965–71. Section and plan drawings, from *Das Werk*, 1976.

While concrete has a particularly close association with hydropower, concrete has also been integral to the construction of other types of power plants. A special type of heavy concrete (Schwerbeton) with iron filings added to the mix is used in nuclear power plants for protection against radiation. The much-emphasised fire-resistant properties of concrete have been put to use for coal- and gas-fired power plants and for waste incinerators. For coal, concrete was deployed along the supply chain for storage as coal silos as well as for the structure of power plants themselves, with both uses relying upon the idea of a heat- and fire-resistant material. Salvisberg's Machinenlabor and Fernheizkraftwerk for the Swiss Federal Institute of Technology in Zurich presents an institutional facade as the famous concrete piece of Zurich's 'Stadtkrone'. Yet the facade wraps a building that is less uniform and less object-like than its exterior suggests. As shown in section, the building contains a vertical shaft that connects the building's foundation to a rail tunnel far below – a connection needed to deliver coal to the building's silos.

CONCRETE *is* SECOND NATURE

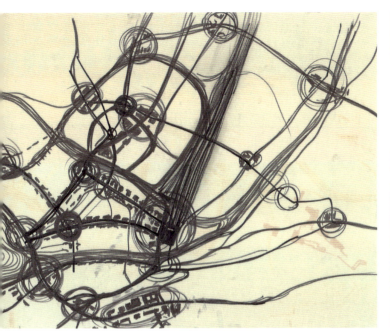

The use of concrete has systemic effects that go well beyond individual structures. Concrete is not only very common, but it is also used for projects that change both landscape and nature. In the words of Giedion in 1928, the ultimate effect of concrete buildings and public works is an 'Umgestaltung der Erdoberfläche' (redesign of the earth's surface).[1]

[1] Sigfried Giedion, *Bauen in Frankreich, Bauen in Eisen, Bauen in Eisenbeton* (Leipzig/Berlin: Klinkhardt & Biermann, 1928), 8.

Otto Glaus and Ruedi Lienhard, Sihlraumplanung, Zürich, 1964–68 (unrealised). Drawing of traffic flows in Zurich, n.d., marker on tracing paper.

Max Vogt, SBB signal-box tower, Buchs, 1980. Photograph Heinrich Helfenstein, 2006.

The 'Säubodenkehre', a hairpin corner paved in concrete in the Klausen Pass (Uri), 1934. Photograph Erwin Thomann, n.d.

Jean-Claude Piguet, Roland Hofer, and Maurice Tappy, Chillon viaduct, 1966–69. Photograph Walter Binder, June 1970.

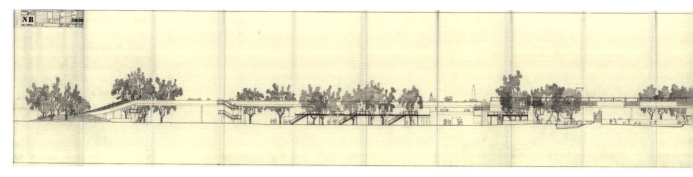

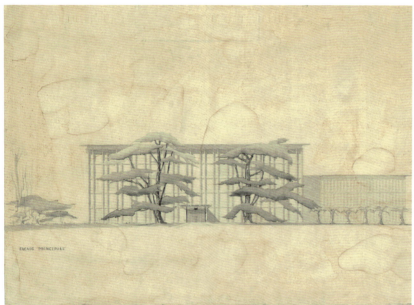

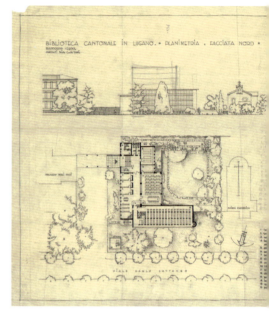

Aurelio Galfetti, Flora Ruchat-Roncati, and Ivo Trümpy, Bagno di Bellinzona, 1967–70. North elevation of the final design, March 1969, ink and pencil on tracing paper.

Jean Tschumi, Mutuelle Vaudoise Accidents headquarters, Lausanne, 1953–56. Elevation drawing, north facade, preliminary sketch, n.d., wash and pencil on paperboard.

Rino Tami with Carlo Tami, Cantonal Library, Lugano, 1936–41. Plan and north elevation drawings, [March 1938], ink and pencil on tracing paper. Built as exposed concrete. At this phase in the project, the blank north facade of the east wing as shown in elevation was planned to be finished with stucco.

Hermann Siegrist, Leimenegg Housing Estate, Winterthur, 1930–32. Anonymous photograph, 1932.

Concrete is used to structure and manage the landscape. The profusion of even small objects like the 'Toblerone' for tank defence or avalanche protection barriers become motifs that repeat across the country, tying disparate regions together and giving a sense of measure and narrative. These repetitive elements in even remote places are markers of specific readings of territory as, for example, something that is unpredictable but sought to be brought under control, or peaceful but always anticipating defence.

Concrete is also used to create lines that smooth the passage of people and goods across the countryside. Roads with concrete hairpin turns and railways with concrete avalanche galleries snake up mountainsides while bridges and tunnels allow straighter paths at a lower elevation. The repetition of accessory infrastructures along these lines also reinforces continuity across regions, such as the exposed concrete train stations and control towers completed as a family of forms for the SBB by Max Vogt, each entrance from train into town coded with the same material language, emphasising connectivity rather than difference.

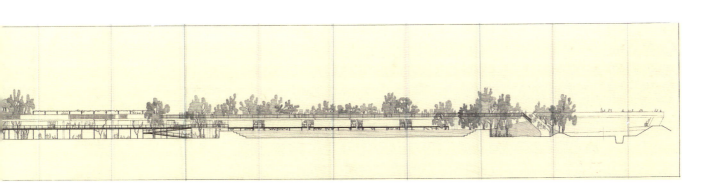

Otto Glaus, Lugano-Agno Airport Hotel, Agno, 1956–58. Perspective drawing, n.d., ink on tracing paper.

Otto Glaus and Ruedi Lienhard, Jakobsgut Housing Estate, Zurich, 1966–69. Sketch of facade with integrated vegetation, n.d., plan copy. Building in exposed concrete cast in place.

Mario Campi and Franco Pessina, Casa Vanini, Muzzano, 1962–64. Perspective cross-section drawing of the swimming pool, July 1964, ink and pencil on parchment paper.

At another scale, the relationship between concrete buildings and their immediate surroundings has shifted over time, becoming increasingly entangled. A first modest step in this line of thinking was a tendency from the 1920s onwards to depict concrete buildings in relation with their natural surroundings. In drawings and photographs, concrete facades are shown as the backdrop to trees and other types of plants rather than as isolated objects – a modest but notable shift in representation. The depiction of these foregrounded plants became more specific – avoiding the trope of the architect's geometrisation of trees – as well as denser and more varied. From a singular tree framed by the building emerged instead clusters or groves of plants that seemed to extend beyond the frame, varied between tree canopy, mid growth, and ground cover. As these shifts happened, plants were also integrated into the buildings themselves, not just crawling up a wall like ivy or placed in a window box like the pervasive geranium but sometimes seemingly taking over – vibrantly erupting from generous planters that form the facade of the building rather than being attached onto it.

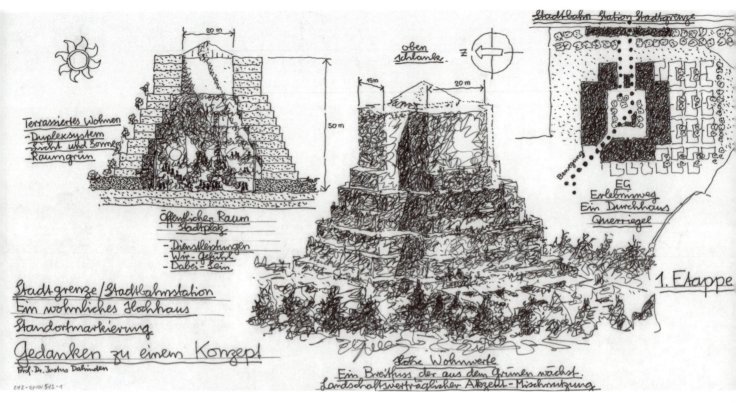

Justus Dahinden, Stadthügel Europolis, Baar, 2003–09 (unrealised). Conceptual sketches with section, perspective, and site plan, n.d., ink on tracing paper.

Hans Ulrich Scherer, Mühlehalde Terraced Housing, Umiken, 1963–66. Photograph Walter Binder, October 1969.

Jakob Zweifel, Heinrich Strickler, and Bernhard Schorderet, Im Moos Primary School, Rüschlikon, 1969–71. The school yard with concrete topography, photograph Fritz Maurer, n.d.

While repeated marking of the territory can produce systemic effects, other projects have sought to challenge more directly the long-held dichotomy between land and building and nature and artifice. Landform buildings that gained popularity in the 1960s and 1970s used concrete to create artificial, inhabitable topographies. The most common type of concrete landform is the Terassenhäuser (terraced housing) found across Switzerland, typically in hilly areas of suburban sprawl. These multifamily buildings discard traditional relations to the ground to produce buildings that carve an existing slope into a series of flat planes partially embedded in the hillside. Other proposals suggested using concrete as a way of creating artificial mountains that, independently of existing topography, would be ringed with terraced units on all sides, forming autonomous urban units. Inverting this idea, Walter Jonas instead imagined funnel-shaped structures that would also create an artificial topography but one that was obviously detached from the ground plane, with a narrow base and widening top that also created a ring of terraced units.

Walter Jonas, Intrapolis, 1962 (unrealised). Perspective drawing of funnel-shaped housing estates, n.d., mixed media on paper. The material for the buildings remained unspecified, but the structural qualities of the constructions imply reinforced concrete.

231

Otto Glaus and Ruedi Lienhard, Jakobsgut Housing Estate, Zurich, 1966–69. Perspective drawing, n.d., print copy on tracing paper.

Otto Glaus and Ruedi Lienhard, Sihlraumplanung, Zurich, 1964–68 (unrealised). Perspective drawing of elevated highway above the Sihl, 1967, plan copy with newspaper clipping.

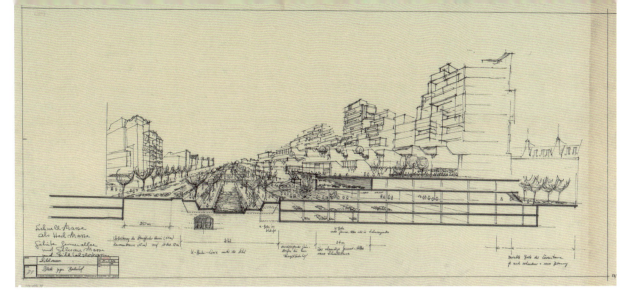

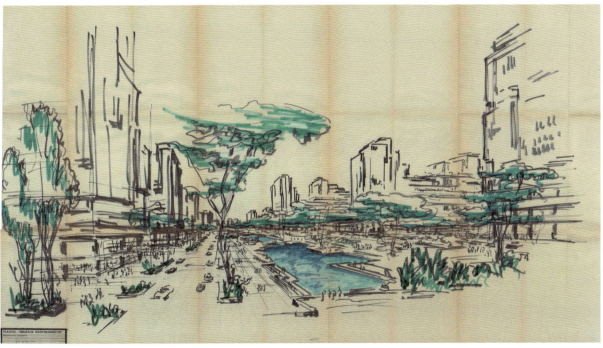

While concrete was used to explore new relations to the ground plane, it was also used to explore new relations to nature. For some architects in the postwar period, among them Walter Maria Förderer, Otto Glaus, and Eduard Neuenschwander, the boundary between natural and artificial had been eroded by centuries of anthropogenic transformations, something they felt was accelerating as highways, hydropower projects, and new housing spread across the landscape at a rapid pace. As a response, they sought new relations not just between the building and the ground but also between the building, the city, and nature. Proposals to bury infrastructure below ground were paired with new visions for an artificial ground plane that could be used to bring nature back into the city – no matter how artificial a form such nature took. Going farther than the idea of the integrated planter, the scale and intention of such proposals change so that buildings or whole cities were viewed as backdrops for a lush and possibly even wild artificial ecology.

Otto Glaus and Ruedi Lienhard, Sihlraumplanung, Zurich, 1964–68 (unrealised). Section through the Sihl with adjoining housing estates, view towards Zurich Main Station, n.d., plan copy.

Otto Glaus and Ruedi Lienhard, Sihlraumplanung, Zurich, 1964–68 (unrealised). Perspective drawing of Sihl and adjoining housing estates, June 1964, plan copy.

CONCRETE is MONOLITHIC

Concrete holds the possibility of making a building out of a single piece of material – or can appear as such. The allure and horror of such a proposition clearly distinguishes concrete from other materials. The idea of the building as a solid whole, as opposed to most methods of construction that join discrete parts together, is one way of understanding concrete as monolithic. Yet for such a solid term, monolithic has been understood in multiple ways.

Otto Ingold, Volkshaus Bern, 1911–14. Main facade, from *Das Werk*, 1915. Building, including exposed facade, in reinforced concrete.

237

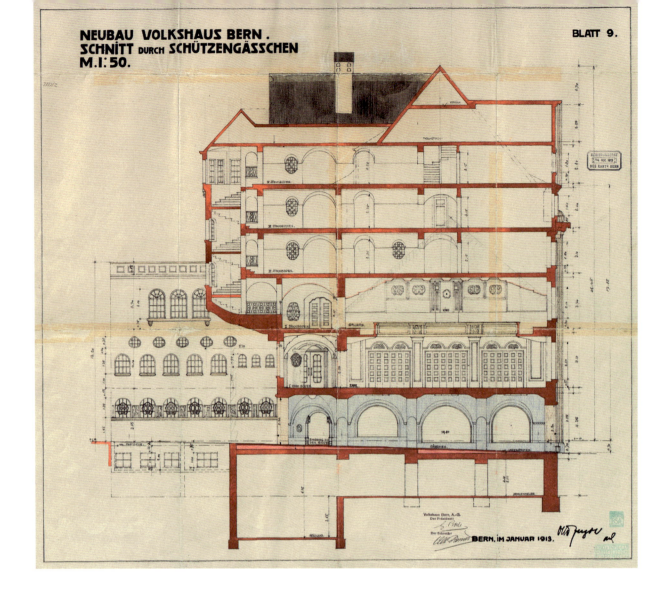

Otto Ingold, Volkshaus Bern, 1911–14. Section drawing, January 1913, print copy with watercolour, colour ink, ink, and pencil.

Otto Rudolf Salvisberg and Otto Brechbühl, Lory Hospital, Bern, 1927–29. Anonymous photograph, n.d.

Karl Indermühle and Werner Luder, competition for Lorraine Bridge, Bern, 1911. Perspective drawing of pier, from *Schweizerische Bauzeitung*, 1911. Bridge designed as reinforced concrete with fluting to express hidden reinforcement.

Rino Tami with Carlo Tami, Cantonal Library, Lugano, 1936–41. Main entrance, photograph Enrico Cano, 2006.

When concrete is cast in place, it can be understood as one block of material from foundation to roof. The promise of a building as a single, solid piece has been a powerful ideal for concrete structures even though it is far from the reality of most completed buildings. Using concrete not just as a structural frame but for a whole facade radically departs from classical tectonics that articulates parts and their structural role. As reinforced concrete began to be used for buildings, how to express a poured building with hidden reinforcement inside was a matter of concern in an era that sought truth to materials. While some architects exposed concrete but tried to relate it to classic orders, others suggested expressing the hidden reinforcement. The 'pure' forms of unfinished buildings fresh out of their formwork also became a trope of their own, showing the possibility of the single material.

LORRAINEBRVECKE IN BERN

MOTTO: "EINFACH"

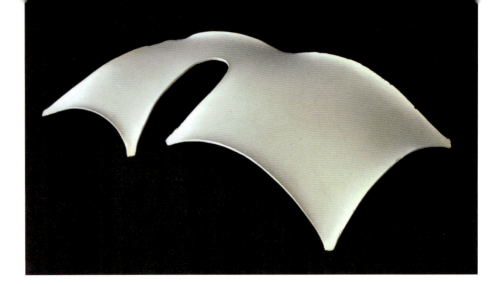

Heinz Isler and Constantin Hilberer, Sicli Fire Extinguisher Factory, Geneva, 1966–70. Model of shell for reinforced concrete structure, n.d., polystyrene foam board, anonymous photograph, n.d.

Marcel Taverney, Maurice Schobinger, and Robert Gétaz, Alexandre Sarrasin, engineer, Galeries du Rivage, Vevey, 1934–35. Market hall, photograph de Jongh, n.d.

Robert Maillart, Federal Granary, Altdorf, 1912–13. Interior with mushroom ceiling construction, photograph Heinrich Wolf-Bender, n.d.

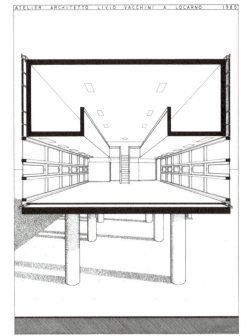
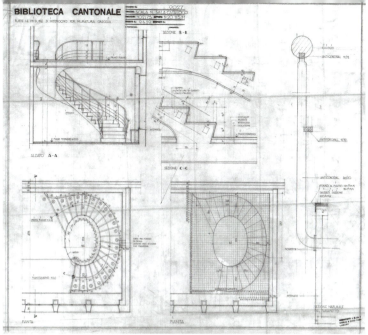
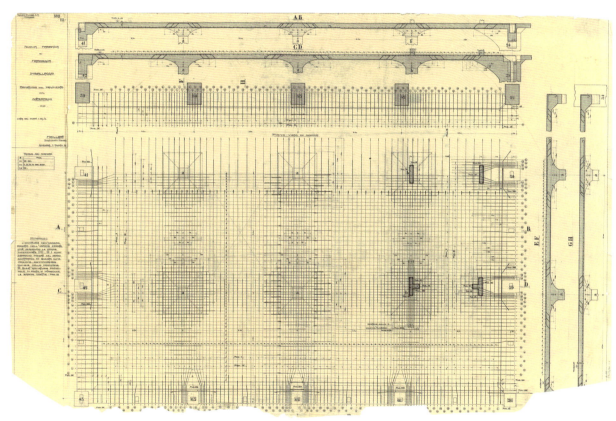

Monolithic is also understood as the structural performance that can be achieved in reinforced concrete. Using the tight bond between concrete as a compressive material and the tensile strength of embedded reinforcement, reinforced concrete structures are understood to transfer stresses throughout a structure, allowing the whole to be more than the sum of its parts. While the idea of a single pour often resulted in buildings that expressed their solidity, a performance-based understanding of the monolithic suggested the opposite: lightness. By optimising performance, monolithic structures could use less material, producing light structures and impressive spans.

Livio Vacchini, Studio Vacchini in Locarno, 1984–85. Perspective section drawing, 1985, ink on polyester film.

Rino Tami with Carlo Tami, Cantonal Library, Lugano, 1936–41. Plans, elevation, section, and detail drawings of the stairway in the Catalogue Room, June 1939, pencil and ink on tracing paper.

Robert Maillart, tanning agent factory for Tannini Ticinesi SA, Maroggia, 1929–30. Reinforcement plan, August 1929, ink and pencil on tracing paper.

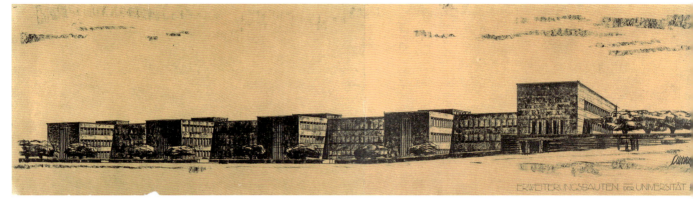

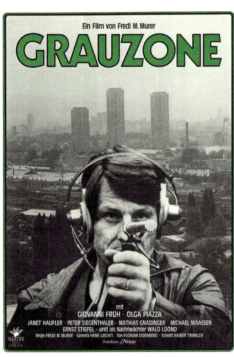

Otto Rudolf Salvisberg and Otto Brechbühl, Extension Building for the University of Bern and the Cantonal Chemical Laboratory, Bern, 1929–31. Perspective drawing of south facade, n.d., print copy.

Film poster for Fredi M. Murer (dir.), *Grauzone*, 1979. This dystopian science-fiction film implicates the concrete cityscape of Zurich as a possible cause for a mysterious epidemic.

Claude Paillard, Fred Cramer, Werner Jaray, and Peter Leemann, Grüzefeld Housing Estate, Winterthur, 1965–68. The estate from surrounding fields, anonymous photograph, n.d.

While the idea of monolithic performance or a monolithic pour are related to the individual structure, the notion of the monolith also carried over to the relation between concrete buildings and their surroundings. The notion of the monolith was also understood as a solitary figure: a block standing alone and apart. Despite concrete's prevalence, this idea of concrete being able to express a project's formal apartness or autonomy has been powerfully deployed. For projects as varied as Salvisberg's University of Bern or Isler's bubbles or Dahinden's triangles, concrete has been used to create structures that are intentionally detached from their surroundings both in form and through their materiality. This could create 'islands' within the city or the countryside. While architects used this effect with intention, the notion that concrete buildings did not blend in also became a target of critique, a marker of development and modernity that became shorthand for larger societal critiques.

CONCRETE is COMPOSITE

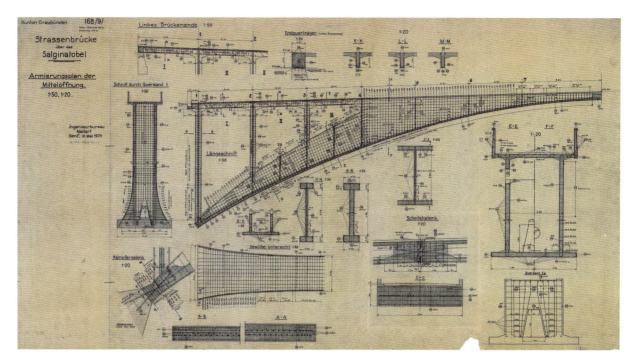

Much has been made of the idea that concrete can be used to build so many different things: it can form a column or wall, floor or roof, flowerpot or cornice, tunnel or dam. Yet while concrete does find a wide variety of applications, none of these uses are fulfilled using concrete alone. Concrete relies on other materials to make buildings: it needs formwork so that it can take shape, reinforcement for strength, and insulation for thermal performance. Materials are interdependent; just as concrete needs other materials, buildings that appear to be out of other materials also sometimes rely on concrete as well, for example, as a foundation or a structural frame.

A first simple example of the relation between concrete and other materials is reinforced concrete. Steel is embedded within concrete to form a composite material capable of acting in both tension and compression. This reinforcement is not visible on the outside of a completed structure but in order to build, reinforcement plans are drawn by engineers to indicate the type of rebar and ties used and how they should be placed. Rebar is not the only thing below the surface in even the most reduced monolithic concrete buildings. Sometimes, cables are used for post-tensioning to stiffen structures and allow longer spans. Insulation is also usually needed for buildings, either as a hidden layer or sometimes as expanded clay aggregate in the concrete mix itself.

Robert Maillart, Salginatobel Bridge near Schiers, 1929–30. Reinforcement plan, May 1929, ink and graphite on tracing paper.

Francis Isoz, Banque Cantonale Vaudoise, Lausanne, 1897–1903. Bétons armés système Hennebique, first basement floor, stirrup distribution, May 1899, blueprint.

Jean Tschumi, Nestlé headquarters, Vevey, 1956–60. Reinforcement of the floor over the gantry, photograph de Jongh, n.d.

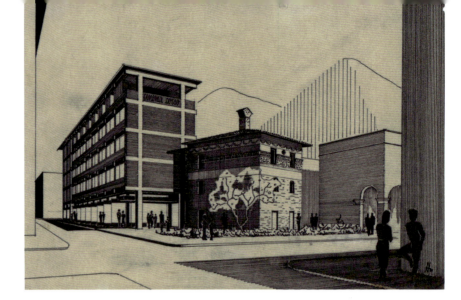

Rino Tami with Carlo Tami and Peppo Brivio, Cinema Corso, Casa 'La Piccionaia' and Casa 'Il Cardo', 1952–57. Perspective drawing Oscar Hofmann, November 1956, ink on tracing paper.

Lux Guyer, Pre-Fra office building, 1948. Perspective drawing, 1948, pencil on tracing paper. The 'Pre-Fra' concept combines a prefabricated skeleton of prestressed, prefabricated concrete elements with infill.

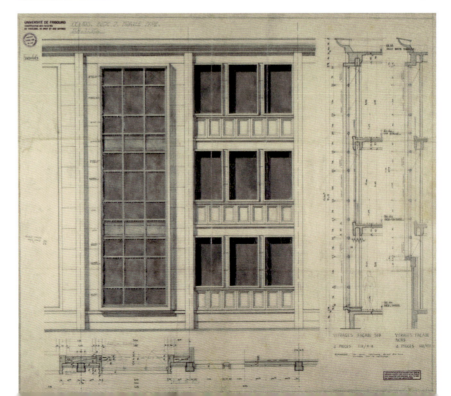

Fernand Dumas and Denis Honegger, Université Miséricorde, Fribourg, 1937–41. Plan, elevation, and section drawings of a bay, December 1938, ink, pencil, and wash on tracing paper.

For many buildings, reinforced concrete forms a structural frame that is filled in with lighter elements. The concrete frame defines only a skeleton while the infill can be anything or, should the intention be to completely disguise its appearance, can be entirely clad, the frame concealed behind other materials. In the examples shown here, the frame is articulated as an ordering device that displays the difference between structure and enclosure, revealing beams and columns with infills of glass, brick, or even prefabricated concrete wall panels.

Max Ernst Haefeli, Werner Max Moser, and Rudolf Steiger, University Hospital Zurich, 1941–53. Interior showing concrete skeleton and infill elements, anonymous photograph, n.d.

247

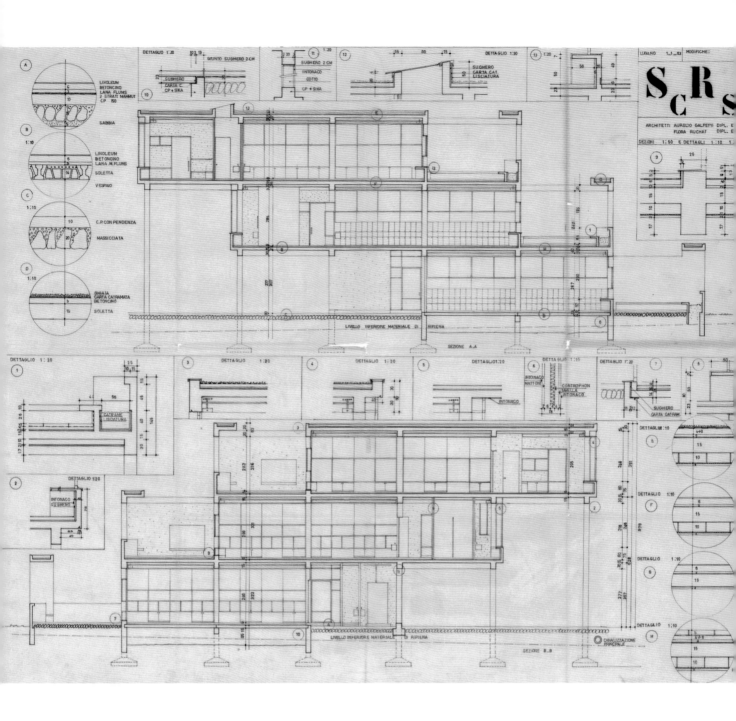

Aurelio Galfetti, Flora Ruchat-Roncati, and Ivo Trümpy, primary school in Riva San Vitale, first phase 1961–64, second phase 1970–73. Section drawings with details, January 1963, ink on tracing paper.

248

Buildings with exposed concrete facades are the most visible types of concrete buildings but what about buildings when concrete is used but its presence is hidden? Despite the dominant role exposed concrete plays in discussions about materiality, concrete is frequently used in mixed construction in everything from a minor supporting role to a major structural role. This is significant because concrete is often perceived as antagonistic towards other materials that are understood as more traditional or familiar. Such a sentiment is often expressed in assessments of the urban environment, where concrete buildings

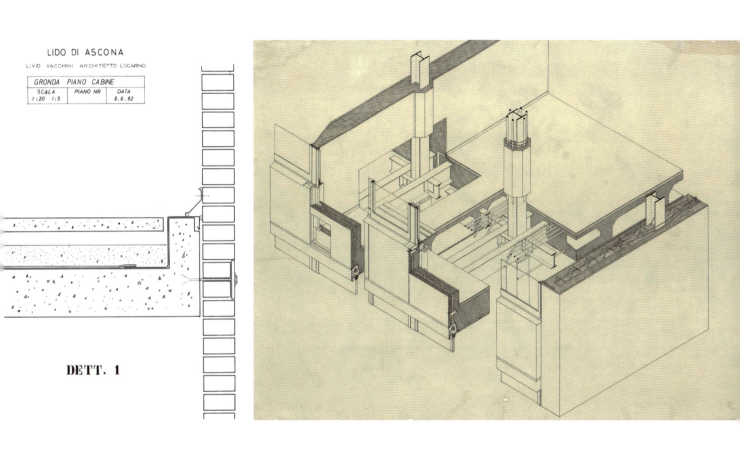

are often seen as a-contextual and at odds with the rest of the city. Yet, the aesthetic contrast presented by exposed concrete buildings against wood or masonry belies how entangled concrete is in making the city. Concrete buildings do not necessarily reveal their materiality: a reinforced concrete frame can disappear altogether or be only slyly revealed. Such buildings – a far more common way of building in concrete than the monolithic – receive far less attention yet are much more common.

Livio Vacchini, Lido Ascona municipal beach, Ascona, 1980–86. Details of the gutter at the level of the changing cabins, partial plan and section drawings, June 1982, ink and pencil on polyester film.

Rudolf Steiger, Flora Steiger-Crawford, Carl Hubacher, and Robert Winkler, Zett-Haus, Zurich, 1929–32. Cut-away perspective drawing showing mixed construction system with concrete used to encase steel columns, n.d., ink on tracing paper.

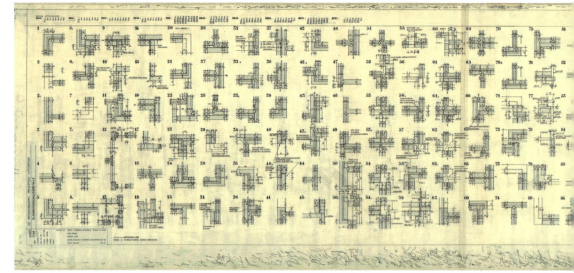

Claude Paillard, Fred Cramer, Werner Jaray, and Peter Leemann, Grüzefeld Housing Estate, Winterthur, 1965–68. Drawing showing various joint details used throughout estate, September 1964, ink on tracing paper.

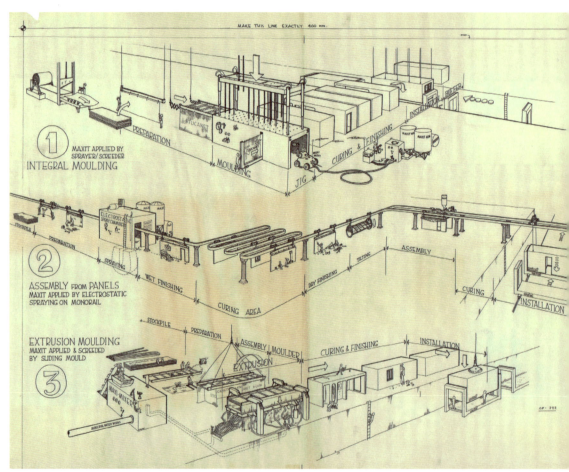

Fritz Stucky, production line diagram for Variel System, n.d., ink on transparent paper. Stucky's Variel line of prefabricated concrete elements was a popular and affordable choice for new construction during the building boom of the decades following the Second World War.

Prefabrication allows concrete to be cast off-site prior to construction. Parts are then brought into place and assembled. While prefabrication is considered distinct from cast-in-place construction, there are a number of different scales and methods that can be used to prefabricate. Prefabrication can be as simple as producing masonry blocks to panelise construction to prefinished units that are transported in a near-complete

Ernst Göhner AG, Housing Estate in Greifensee, 1967–75. Workers moving a prefabricated concrete element into place, from Werner Sigmund, *Ernst Göhner (1900–1971): Bauen in Norm*, 1990.

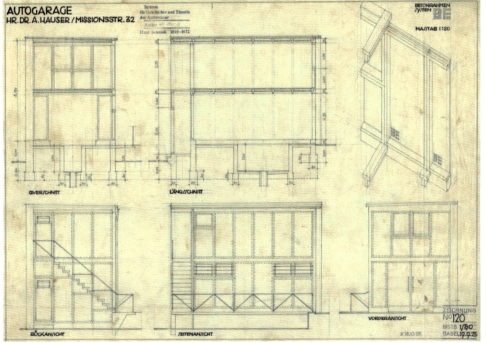

Hans Schmidt, automobile garage for Dr A. Hauser, Basel, 1925–26. Elevation and section drawings, September 1925, pencil on tracing paper. The garage was built using prefabricated elements assembled on site.

state with integrated systems and finishes, which only need to be fixed in place. Prefabrication often goes hand in hand with a desire to standardise through the use of fixed modules with the aim of achieving an economy of scale. But the idea of bringing construction into the factory is also appealing as it allows a more controlled environment and the possibility of compensating for seasonal swings in on-site construction.

CONCRETE *is* IMMATERIAL

Graffiti 'Beton Grau wie die Zukunft' (Concrete gray like the future), Zurich. Photograph Gertrud Vogler, 1981.

The 'Concrete Procession', Zurich, October 1986. Photograph Gertrud Vogler, October 1986. As part of a demonstration against urban redevelopment, activists marched through the streets of Zurich with a massive concrete block.

Graffiti 'Wo der Beton wächst stirb das Leben' (Where concrete grows, life dies), Zurich. Photograph Gertrud Vogler, December 1982.

Graffiti 'I long for betong', Zurich. Photograph Gertrud Vogler, February 1981.

ABC: Beiträge zum Bauen, no. 3/4, 1925, page 1.

Martin Moser, Poster for the Citizens' Initiative 'Stopp dem Beton – für eine Begrenzung des Strassenbaus' (Stop the Concrete – for a Limit on Road Construction), 1990. The initiative was not adopted, with 71.5 per cent of eligible voters voting against it.

Diverse forms of knowledge, public and professional discourse, and organisational structures all shape how concrete is used and understood. From patents to university lectures to protests, the perception of concrete is shaped by ever-shifting notions about what concrete is and how such ideas are transmitted.

While in the 1920s architects such as the editors of the avant-garde journal *ABC* saw concrete as a modern material that brought hope not just of new aesthetics but also of newer, more industrialised and rationalised construction processes, protests in the 1980s were more pessimistic about the future promised by concrete, declaring the concrete was 'grey like the future' and 'where concrete grows, life dies'. As Adrian Forty has observed, reactions to concrete can act as a mirror to larger attitudes about modernity and development.

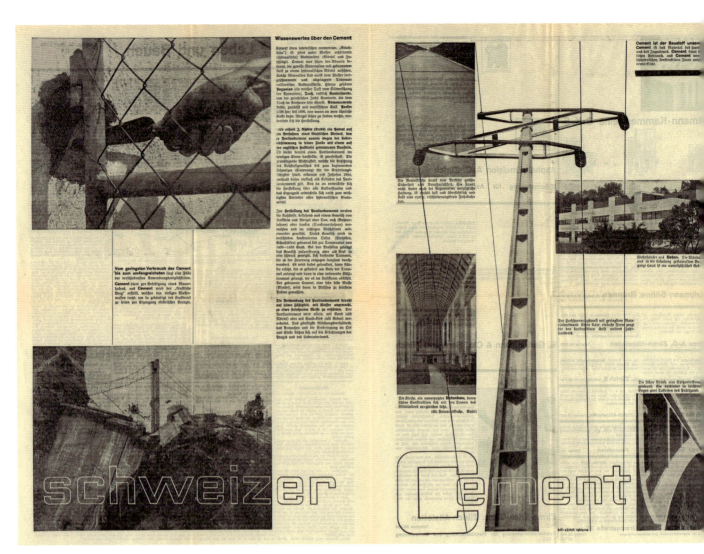

Neue Zürcher Zeitung, advertisement for Swiss cement within a special section of the paper, guest-edited by Sigfried Giedion, June 1934.

'Göhnerswil' Wohnungsbau im Kapitalismus, 1972, cover.

Architekturpreis Beton 97, 1997, cover. This copy, belonging to the journalist and architectural historian Adolf Max Vogt, features the following handwritten commentary: 'Das unschuldige Material / Das Böse / Der Fortschreitschritt' (the innocent material / the evil (material) / a step forward and away).

Of course, one powerful agent in shaping the understanding of concrete was the material industry itself. The cement industry in particular was an influential, centralised voice that was well coordinated and successful in advocating for concrete and related materials both to public building authorities and to the general public. Through lobbying, advertising, sponsoring of competitions and awards, it is no surprise that the cement industry helped position concrete as a material of progress and technological achievement.

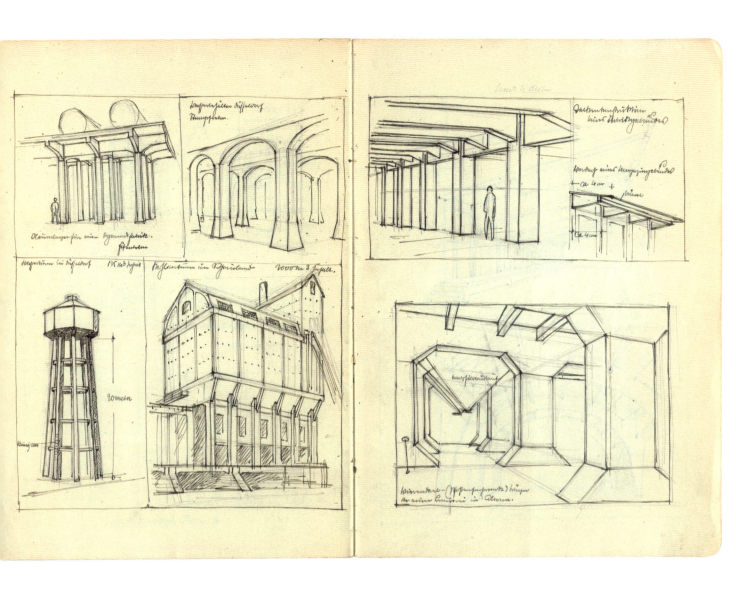

Other immaterial aspects of concrete are more disciplinary or exist even as legally protected knowledge. Understanding of concrete and the knowledge of how to build in concrete is passed on in education, whether in lectures and exercises in technical and trade schools or on site through apprenticeships. From rules of thumb to theoretical coefficients, different types of knowledge and know-how are held by many actors involved in construction – from engineers to architects to contractors and masons. Whether the knowledge of how to build in concrete should be prescribed in norms making it accessible to non-specialists or constrained to those with experience was the subject of repeated debate over the course of the twentieth century, with a tendency to keep knowledge to the few but allow specialists as much freedom as possible.

Hans Schmidt, student notebook, winter 1917–18.

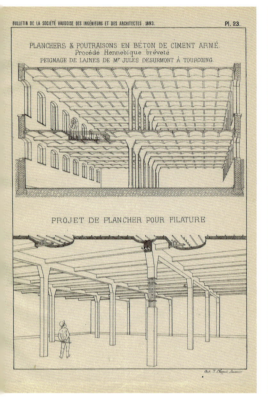 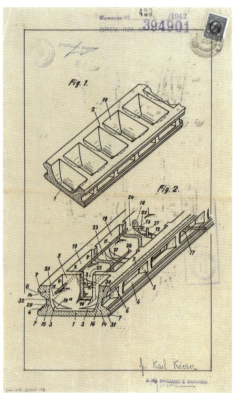 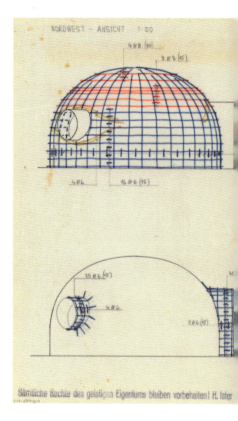

Filature de Tourcoing (France), spinning mill with Hennebique-system reinforced concrete frame, from *Bulletin de la Société vaudoise des ingénieurs et des architectes*, 1893.

Karl Kieser, patent for Kieser Construction System, Italy, May 1942. Drawing of patented prefabricated concrete plank system, ink on tracing paper.

Heinz Isler, office building for S. Kisling & Cie, Langenthal, 1978. Northwest elevation drawings, n.d., marker on tracing paper. Building constructed according to Isler's Bubble System.

The introduction of patented reinforced concrete construction systems – of which Monier and Hennebique were some of the most prominent in Switzerland – changed the organisation of the construction industry across Europe, shifting, as Giedion suggested, architects into the role of designers whose buildings would be transformed into construction documents by another party: the new expert concrete engineer. As specialised ways of constructing in concrete began to be developed, they were frequently patented as products and systems – a marked difference from the tacit shared knowledge of the construction site.

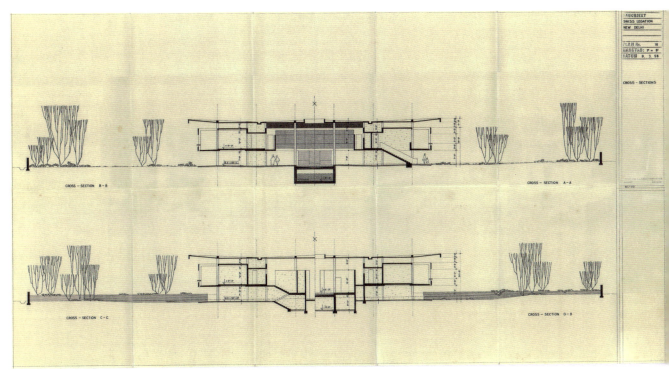

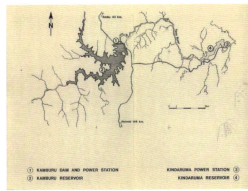

The precision and quality with which concrete is used in Switzerland developed into a form of advertising that gives Swiss architects, engineers, and contractors a strong reputation internationally. Swiss engineers and architects are prolific internationally, exporting expertise about concrete construction since the early twentieth century. Landmark projects in concrete were thought to also have an advertising function, displaying Swiss quality and leading to commissions for Swiss companies and professionals outside of the country. Many infrastructure development projects abroad that have left a complicated legacy were financed, designed, and built by Swiss companies. Yet typically, the 'export' of concrete related to such projects was

Hans Hofmann and Walter Rüegg, Swiss Embassy in New Delhi, India, 1957–63. Section drawings, March 1958, ink on paper. Pretensioned concrete structure.

Entreprises de grands travaux hydrauliques and Omnium d'entreprises, dam in El Kansera on the Oued Beth, Morocco, 1927–35. View of the test plant, anonymous photograph, May 1931.

Justus Dahinden and Heinz Isler, Bubble System for Housing, Moghan (Iran), 1976–81. Perspective drawing, May 1975, marker on tracing paper.

Engineering Power Development Consultants, dam in Kamburu, Kenya, 1971–74. Site plan, n.d., plan copy.

259

Entreprises Campenon Bernard, Dragages TP, and Conrad Zschokke SA, Dhahran International Airport, Dhahran (Saudi Arabia), 1980–81. Construction workers pouring concrete, anonymous photograph, n.d.

Robert Maillart, cement factory in Tourah, Cairo (Egypt), 1928–29. Cement silos, photographic print, n.d.

Maillart & Cie, industrial buildings in concrete, from Julius Vischer and Ludwig Hilberseimer, *Beton als Gestalter*, 1928.

immaterial, the concrete itself would usually be sourced locally, though some imaginative hybrid models were notable exceptions. As the Swiss cement industry expanded around the word from the 1920s onwards it also exported management and financing, and, sometimes, machinery, establishing local subsidiary cement plants. In this way, the Swiss cement industry has played a key role in propagating concrete as a global building material. Often, the operations of Swiss cement companies abroad differ markedly from operations at home. Their subsidiaries have been criticised for labour violations, the support of oppressive regimes, and using inefficient cement kilns while touting the efficiency and thereby lower climate impact of their domestic plants.

CONCRETE *is* PRAXIS

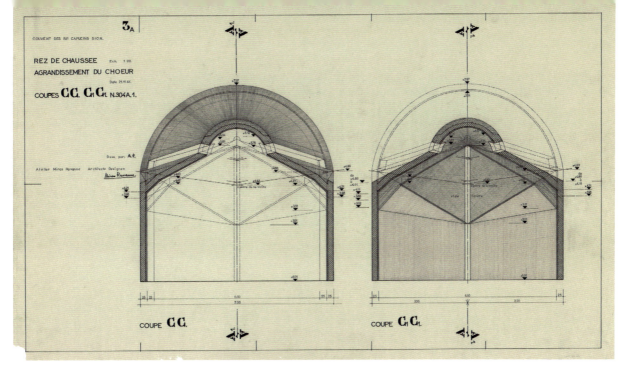

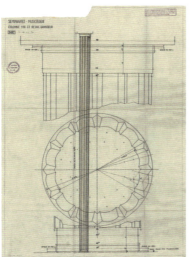

Concrete is a matter of practice and process. It is a material whose quality is determined not just by its composition but also by how it has been handled on site. Controlled, concrete can be as smooth and precise as it appears in Vaccini's presentation drawing on the following page or it can be made intentionally rough. Yet this control can also be hard to achieve as it entails so many discrete steps and so many different actors. The concrete mix not only needs to be properly defined but it also needs to be cast before it has hydrated too much. Wet concrete must fill all the nooks and crevices in the formwork without anyone on site being able to see whether it has actually done so. Gaps or warping in the formwork result in permanent bends in the surface. Each successive pour must match the previous one and be precisely calibrated and timed so that the individual pours are not visible in the whole. In short, as has been much observed, concrete is difficult to control.

Mirco Ravanne, Capuchin monastery, Sion, 1964–68. Choir enlargement, section view, November 1964, ink and graphite on tracing paper.

Fernand Dumas and Denis Honegger, Université Miséricorde, Fribourg, 1937–41. Column, elevation and 1:1 detail drawings, May 1939, ink, pencil, and pastel on tracing paper.

Fernand Dumas and Denis Honegger, Christ-Roi Church, Fribourg, 1951–53. Constructing a capital, anonymous photograph, May 1952.

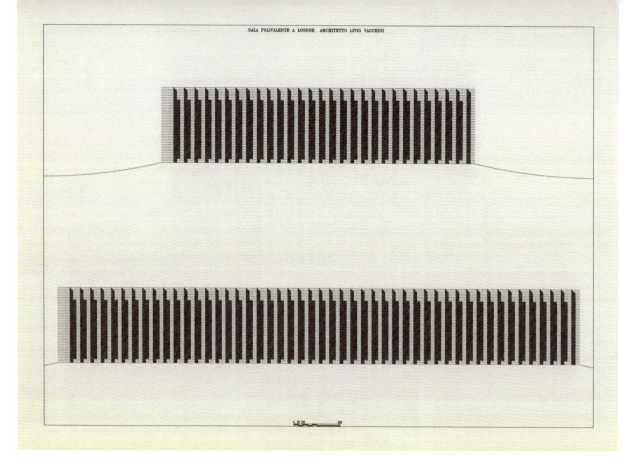

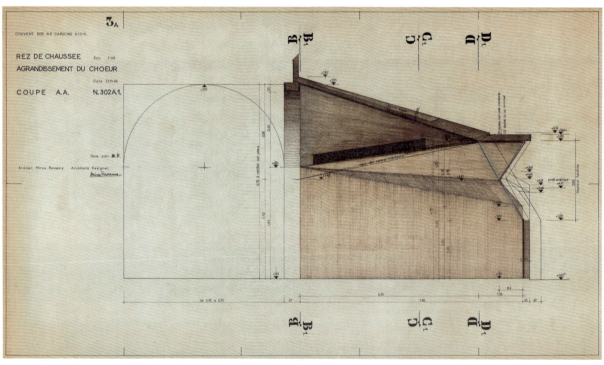

Livio Vacchini, gymnasium, Losone, 1990–97. Elevation drawings, n.d., digital print on tracing paper.

Mirco Ravanne, Capuchin monastery, Sion, 1964–68. Choir enlargement, section drawing, November 1964, plan copy on transparent film.

Jean Tschumi, Mutuelle Vaudoise Accidents headquarters, Lausanne, 1953–56. West facade, photograph de Jongh, n.d.

Jean Tschumi, Mutuelle Vaudoise Accidents headquarters, Lausanne, 1953–56. Installing prefabricated reinforced concrete panels into the frame of the western facade, anonymous photograph, April 1955.

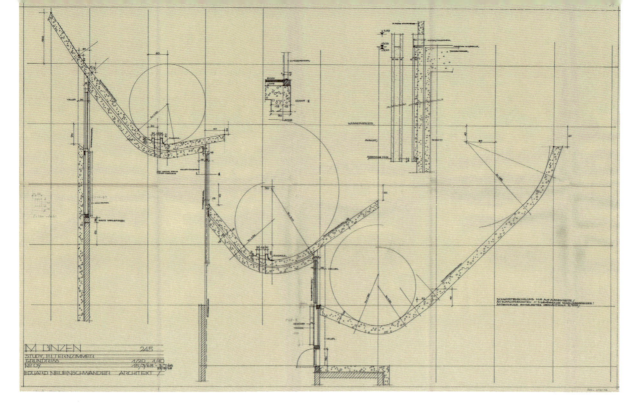

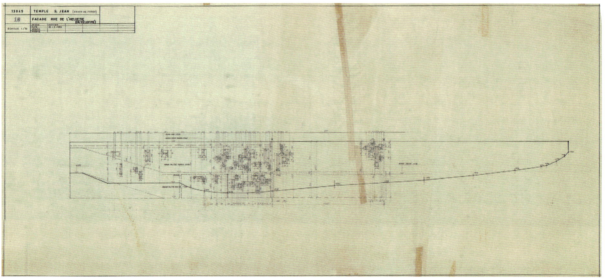

Eduard Neuenschwander, Single-Family House Im Binzen, Gockhausen, 1968–69. Partial plan of the study/parents' room with sections showing wall detailing, March–August 1968, ink on tracing paper.

André Gaillard, Francis Gaillard, and Daniel Grataloup, Saint-Jean protestant church, La Chaux-de-Fonds, 1963–72. Elevation drawing of facade on Rue de l'Helvétie (completed), March 1963, ink and pencil on tracing paper.

Controlling this difficult-to-control material is seen as particularly Swiss, especially when the result is a concrete structure built to a high degree of precision. Close connections along the chain from drawing to building are crucial. Drawings that describe geometry with precision are constructed with complementary precision of timing, construction, and material selection in the field. Larger factors such as the apprenticeship system for ensuring skilled labour on the construction site, high construction budgets that prioritise durable construction, and a more diffuse cultural sense that quality is something to be strived for all help make precision both possible and desirable.

Roland Vigier, concrete bridge at the Swiss National Exhibition, Zurich, 1883. Testing the bridge's load-bearing capacity, 1883. Photograph Romedo Guler, 1883. The bridge was erected for demonstration purposes by Vigier, who owned a Portland cement factory in Luterbach near Solothurn.

Roland Vigier, concrete bridge at the Swiss National Exhibition, Zurich, 1883. Photograph Romedo Guler, 1883. The aftermath of the bridge's collapse after having carried a weight of 35.75 tonnes over two days.

Robert Maillart, full-scale test model for mushroom floor-slab construction, 1910. Photographic print, n.d. The unusual name refers to the mushroom-shaped transition from column to slab.

Hans Leuzinger and Robert Maillart, Cement Hall at the Swiss National Exhibition, Zurich, 1939. The hall after load and explosives testing, anonymous photograph, 1940.

Max Ernst Haefeli, Werner Max Moser, Rudolf Steiger, and André Studer, High-Rise Building Zur Palme, Zurich, 1959–64. Load-bearing test for the entry ramp of the parking garage using construction workers, anonymous photograph, June 1962.

Heinz Isler, prototype for a dome-shaped house, Lyssach, 1976. Workers applying the concrete surface, anonymous photograph, 1976. He built this prototype for an experimental concrete house in his own backyard.

Heinz Isler, prototype for a dome-shaped house, Lyssach, 1976. The prototype after its collapse, anonymous photograph, 1976.

Rudolf Linder, Hotel Zum Bären, Basel, 1901–02. Damage after the building's collapse, which occurred during construction, anonymous photograph, 1901. The structure had been built in reinforced concrete using the Hennebique system. The collapse spurred the first provisional norms for reinforced concrete.

Early-age cracks in concrete due to premature drying-out of material, from *Cementbulletin*, 1973.

Collapsed concrete bridge. Photograph Erwin Thomann, n.d.

Fernand Dumas and Denis Honegger, Université Miséricorde, Fribourg, 1937–41. Defective pillars in need of repair, photograph Civelli, n.d.

Practices for managing concrete are developed through experience and testing. At every scale, concrete structures are tested and studied both in the laboratory and in the field. When reinforced concrete was a new material, such tests were important not just for knowledge of material performance but also to prove to a sceptical public that reinforced concrete was safe. In structural engineering, Switzerland is known for having placed particular emphasis on full-scale load testing of reinforced concrete to verify that theories of structural performance aligned with the reality of how structures actually performed.

Accidents often became lessons from which new knowledge could be drawn. Uneven surfaces or exposed rebar were documented and used to improve rules of thumb for concrete mixes, coverage depth, and pouring processes. Buildings and bridges that collapsed – often before the concrete had fully hardened – were studied to determine the cause of failure. These reports – which Swiss authorities were particularly diligent in producing – then became importance evidence for improving the understanding and handling of concrete.

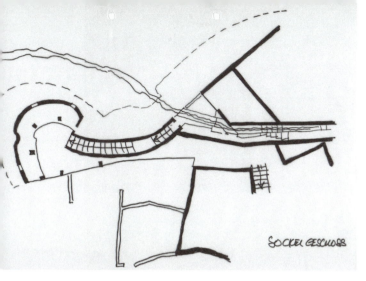
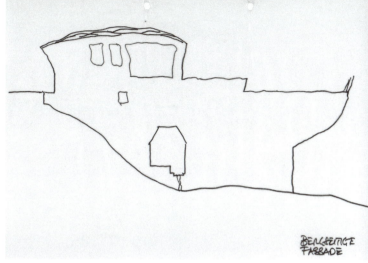

Self-built house known as 'Beton Meier', n.d. Plan sketch of the ground floor, Pierre Zoelly, n.d., ink on tracing paper. Zoelly was fascinated by this self-built house that he called 'Beton Meier', which he documented through drawings and photographs.

Self-built house known as 'Beton Meier', n.d. Elevation sketch, Pierre Zoelly, n.d., ink on tracing paper.

Self-built house known as 'Beton Meier', n.d. Detail of facade, photograph Pierre Zoelly, n.d.

Self-built house known as 'Beton Meier', n.d. Photograph Pierre Zoelly, n.d.

Abb. 2. Nordansicht des von Dr. Rudolf Steiner projektierten Versammlungshauses der Anthroposophen (sog. Goetheanum) auf dem Schlachtfeld ob Dornach. Die architektonisch dilettantische Lösung des in kolossalen Ausmassen gehaltenen, grundhässlichen Steiner-Baues rufen zum energischen Protest gegen dessen Ausführung. — Fig. 2. Le projet du Dr. Rudolf Steiner, d'un bâtiment destiné aux réunions des anthroposophes sur le champ de bataille de Dornach (Goetheanum). Face nord. Des protestations énergiques doivent empêcher l'exécution de cet édifice monstrueux, œuvre d'un dilettante.

SO WIRD DAS HAUS AUCH AM ENDE NOCH AUSSEHEN

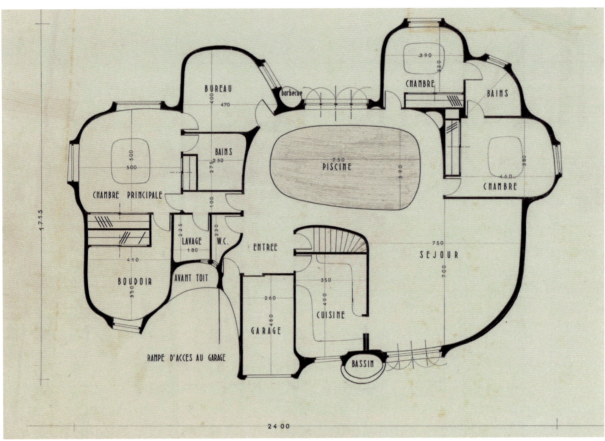

Rudolf Steiner, Goetheanum, Dornach, 1925–28. Drawing of Goetheanum with critical caption, from *Heimatschutz*, December 1924. The caption translates as follows: 'View from the north of the meeting house of the anthroposophists (the so-called Goetheanum) planned by Dr Rudolf Steiner on the battlefield above Dornach. The architecturally dilettantish design of the colossal, hideous building by Steiner calls for an energetic protest against its construction.'

Heidi and Peter Wenger, Grenzsanität, a centre for mandatory immigrant health screening, Brig, 1955–57. Under construction, photograph Peter Wenger, n.d.

Daniel Grataloup and André Gaillard, Villa Binggeli, Le Grand-Saconnex, 1969–74. Plan drawing, December 1969, ink and graphite on tracing paper.

If concrete can be mastered with precision, it was also looked upon with both promise and trepidation for its potential for more aesthetic and formal freedom paired with relatively low cost and ease of handling. The democratisation of concrete in Switzerland was actively opposed by engineers who successfully sought to keep it largely a specialised domain. Yet at times, the sense that concrete could form anything provoked backlash from conservative critics that still saw too much potential for dilettantism, both in the form of self-construction by laypeople and in excesses of formal freedom. As the second Goetheanum was under construction in Dornach, near-universal horror at its organic form created a rare moment of unity across an architectural culture deeply fractured between modernist and historicist camps. While self-built houses in concrete are common in many parts of the world, in Switzerland these were exceptions within a highly regulated construction climate. Despite this, architects like Pierre Zoelly and Heidi and Peter Wenger found inspiration in autodidactic and incremental building processes. Yet many more purportedly dilettantish constructions were in fact highly controlled, with forms that were precisely described or surfaces with an intentional roughness.

CONCRETE *is* FLUID

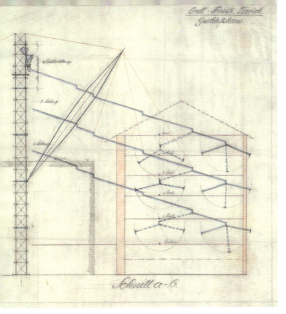

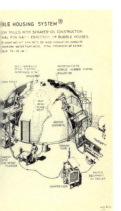

Concrete is constantly in flux. It is poured into a formwork where it then hardens in a process called hydration, shifting from soft and creamy to solid. Today this process often takes place on site within a matter of days. Afterwards, the formwork is removed and the structure reaches most of its strength. Yet around the turn of the twentieth century, concrete took much longer to harden and needed to be left in the formwork far longer – sometimes for months at a time – instilling a sense of the process of transformation that was invisibly occurring within the mould. The flow of wet concrete on site is carefully calibrated, with the exact mix changing according to the means of delivery and even the weather conditions. In different eras and for different applications, concrete has been rammed, poured, pumped, or sprayed into a formwork with each method using a different relative fluidity. Debates about how fluid concrete should be concerned not just the material properties but the labour process, with the idea that a more liquid mix would allow greater mechanisation, thereby reducing reliance on skilled labour.

Hermann Weideli, Orell Füssli Building (Dietzingerstrasse 3–15), Zurich, 1921–24. Schematic section drawing showing chutes for pouring concrete, n.d., pencil on tracing paper.

Schrah Dam, Wägital, 1922–24. Cable crane for pouring concrete, anonymous photograph, n.d.

Hans Leuzinger and Robert Maillart, Cement Hall at the Swiss National Exhibition, Zurich, 1939. Workers spraying concrete onto reinforcement, anonymous photograph, November 1938.

Justus Dahinden and Heinz Isler, Bubble System for Housing, Moghan (Iran), 1976–81 (partially realised). Perspective drawing showing spray-on construction process, n.d., plan copy.

Otto Rudolf Salvisberg and Otto Brechbuhl, Lory Hospital, Bern, 1927–29. Raw structure after concrete has been poured, anonymous photograph, n.d.

Heinz Isler, prototype for a dome-shaped house, Lyssach, 1976. Spray application of concrete onto reinforcement structure, anonymous photograph, 1976.

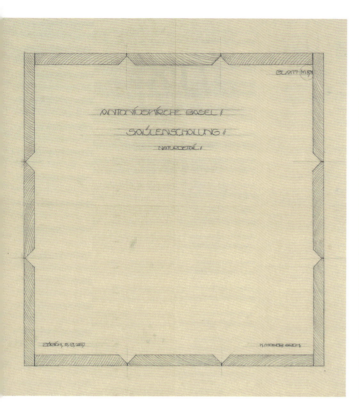

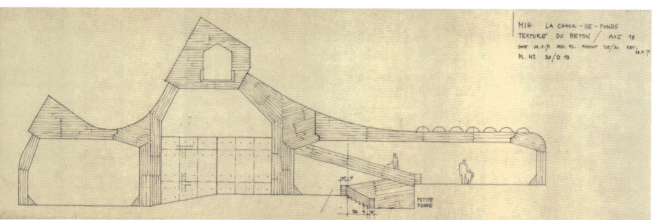

Karl Moser, St. Anthony's Church, Basel, 1925–27. Formwork for columns, plan drawing. September 1925, pencil on paper. The original drawing was realised at the scale 1:1.

Karl Moser, St. Anthony's Church, Basel, 1925–27. Perspective drawing of interior, n.d., charcoal on tracing paper.

Georges-Jacques Haefeli and Pierre Zoelly, Musée international d'horlogerie, La Chaux-de Fonds, 1972–74. Section drawing, February–April 1971, plan copy on transparent film.

When removed from the formwork, the vestiges of this fluid state remain as formwork marks – intentional or unintentional – reproduced in the negative on the surface of the concrete. In Switzerland, Karl Moser was one of the first to make use of this at St. Anthony's Church in Basel where he carefully drew the formwork to ensure that the board marks would turn out as he had envisioned. Later, the art of leaving traces became so widespread that it turned into an industry unto itself. As architects favoured leaving concrete raw in the 1960s and 1970s, products like formwork inserts were developed to produce a range of patterns. The *Technische Forschungs- and Beratungsstelle* of the Swiss cement industry also pivoted to address questions related to exposed concrete, from the appropriate mix to detailing and to the expected weathering of a material that was previously more often used as a substrate.

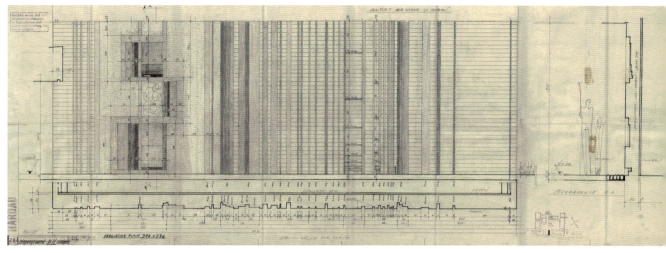

Otto Glaus and Ruedi Lienhard, Hardau Vocational School, Zurich, 1963–64. Elevation and section drawings of interior wall patterning, August 1962, ink and pencil on tracing paper.

Otto Glaus, Lugano-Agno Airport Hotel, Agno, 1956–58. Patterning of facade, anonymous photograph, n.d.

Hans Leuzinger and Robert Maillart, Cement Hall at the Swiss National Exhibition, Zurich, 1939. The hall under construction, anonymous photograph, December 1938.

Rudolf Olgiati, house for Dr G. Olgiati, Flims/Waldhaus, 1964–65. Detail of window, anonymous photograph, n.d.

Otto Glaus and Ruedi Lienhard, Hardau Vocational School, Zurich, 1963–64. Interior wall patterning, anonymous photograph, n.d.

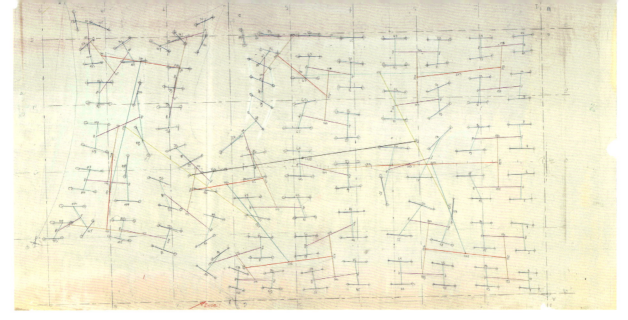

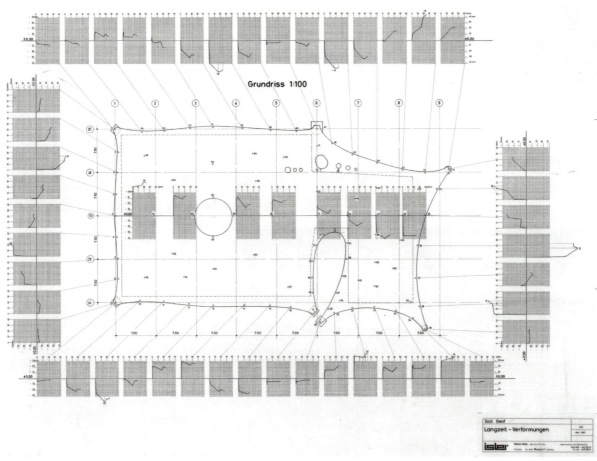

Heinz Isler and Constantin Hilberer, Sicli Fire Extinguisher Factory, Geneva, 1966–70. The drawing shows the movement of various measurement points on the concrete shell due to deformation over time, n.d., colour pencil on paper. The building is constructed as a thin concrete shell, executed in a single pour.

Heinz Isler and Constantin Hilberer, Sicli Fire Extinguisher Factory, Geneva, 1966–70. The plan shows the movement of various measurement points on the concrete shell due to deformation over time, November 1997, ink on tracing paper.

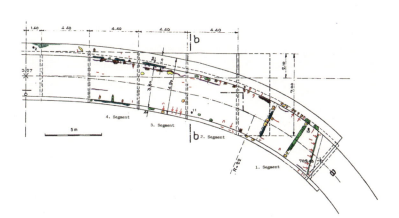

Yet the transformation of concrete does not stop when it is taken out of the formwork. Concrete continues to harden for decades, gaining strength long after construction has been completed. At the same time, concrete also reacts with environmental agents, cracking and crumbling. Concrete is thus both simultaneously hardening and decaying while moving in opposite directions: stronger and more vulnerable. The stains or cracks on exposed concrete facades are often evidence of these changes. Many people who object to concrete as a material base their objections on these changes: that when concrete is visible, it does not stay the same. Yet, somewhat astoundingly, claims that concrete would stay the same – that it would be not just durable but immutable and devoid of maintenance – were put forward in recurring waves by the building material industry from the turn of the twentieth century onwards. Even as each generation saw concrete weathering, those in the concrete business would claim that such problems had been solved and that while the last generation's concrete crumbled, a new generation was immutable.

Robert Maillart, Schwandbach Bridge near Hinterfultigen, Rüeggisberg, 1933. The plan shows cracks and other problems with the concrete almost 60 years after completion, November 1990, plan copy.

Mirko Roš, *Versuche und Erfahrungen an ausgeführten Eisenbeton-Bauwerken in der Schweiz*, Title page, 1937. This report by the Swiss Federal Laboratories for Materials Science and Technology (EMPA) contains the results of tests on reinforced concrete bridges and provided evidence that elastic theory corresponded with actual performance over time.

Image Credits

ESSAYS
The numbers refer to the figures.

Laurent Stalder
Archivio del Moderno, Balerna, Fondo Jachen Könz: **9** / Max Bill, *Moderne Schweizer Architektur = Architecture moderne suisse = Modern Swiss Architecture: 1925–1945* (Basel: Verlag Karl Werner, 1949): **3, 4** / Justus Dahinden, *Stadtstrukturen für morgen : Analysen – Thesen – Modelle* (Stuttgart: Verlag Gerd Hatje, 1971): **7** / ETH-Bibliothek Zürich, Bildarchiv: **5** (WIH_FLs21-034/CC BY-SA 4.0), **6** (Com_FC30-0001-241/CC BY-SA 4.0) / gta Archiv, ETH Zürich, Nachlass Pierre Zoelly: **8** / Rolf Keller, *Bauen als Umweltzerstörung : Alarmbilder einer Un-Architektur der Gegenwart* (Zürich: Verlag für Architektur Artemis, 1973): **2** / Made-in, Geneva: **10** / Bruno Taut, *Alpine Architektur* (Hagen i.W: Folkwang, 1919): **1**

Marcel Bächtiger
An heiligen Wassern, dir. Alfred Weidenmann (Switzerland/West Germany, 1960): **2** / *Cascade*, dir. Lumière brothers (Switzerland, 1896): **1** / *Dene wos guet geit*, dir. Cyril Schäublin (Switzerland, 2017): **8** / *Grande-Dixence*, dir. Claude Goretta (Switzerland, 1960): **3** (© RTS Radio Télévision Suisse; émission d'archives 'Le barrage de la Grande Dixence', 12 May 2021) / *Messidor*, dir. Alain Tanner (France/Switzerland, 1979: **4** / *Reisender Krieger*, Christian Schocher (Switzerland, 1981): **5, 6, 7**

Salvatore Aprea
Archives de la construction moderne, EPFL, Lausanne, fonds Morsier et Weibel: **4** / *Le béton armé, organe des concessionnaires et agents du système Hennebique*: **3** (1, no. 2, 1898), **6** (1, no. 1, 1898), **9** (10, no. 105, 1907) / Éditions Art. Perrochet-Matile, private collection: **8** / Mobimo Lausanne: **1** / Musée Historique, Lausanne: **2, 5, 7** / Swiss Confederation, Federal Intellectual Property Agency: **10**

Aurelio Muttoni
ETH-Bibliothek Zürich, Bildarchiv: **3a** (Hs_1085-1905-6-1-160/Public Domain Mark), **3b** (Hs_1085-1912-8-530/Public Domain Mark), **3c** (Hs_1085-1935-36-1-24/Public Domain Mark) / Musée Historique, Lausanne: **1** / Aurelio Muttoni: **5** / Aurelio Muttoni, *Introduction à la norme SIA 262*, Documentation SIA D0182 (Zürich: SIA, 2003): **2** / Aurelio Muttoni, Franco Lurati and Miguel Fernández Ruiz, 'Concrete Shells – Towards Efficient Structures: Construction of an Ellipsoidal Concrete Shell in Switzerland', in *Structural Concrete* 14, no. 1 (2013): **4**

Ilaria Giannetti
Archivio del Moderno, Balerna, Fondi: Renato Colombi: **5** (top); Rino Tami: **2, 7** (bottom) / Archivio Storico Ufficio federale delle strade (USTRA), Bellinzona: **3, 4, 5** (bottom), **6, 7** (top) / Ilaria Giannetti: **1**

Silvia Berger Ziauddin
Bernhard Chiquet: **6, 7** / Eidgenössisches Justiz- und Polizeidepartement, Bundesamt für Zivilschutz, *TWP 1966: Technische Weisungen für den privaten Schutzraumbau* (Bern: Eidgenössische Drucksachen- und Materialzentrale, 1966, appendix): **1** / Federal Office for Civil Protection: **4, 5** / *Schweizerische Bauzeitung* 93, no. 36 (1975): **2, 3**

Lorenzo Stieger

Archive of the architectural collective Atelier 5, Bern: **5, 9** / gta Archiv, ETH Zürich, Nachlass Claude Paillard: **3** / gta Archiv, ETH Zürich, Sammlung Prof. Alexander Henz: **7** ('Häuser am Hang', *Schöner Wohnen*, no. 10, 1966) / Stephan Kunz (ed.), *Ziegelrain '67–'75* (Aarau: Aargauer Kunsthaus, 2006): **8** / Erwin Mühlestein, 'Variables Terrassenhaus-Bausystem', *Bauen + Wohnen* 26, no. 12 (1972): **6** / Hans Ulrich Scherer, 'In ein paar Jahrzehnten', *Brugger Neujahrsblätter* 69 (1959): **4** / Stadtarchiv Zug: **1** (E.13-1.6736; E.13-1.6736; E.13-1.6297), **2** (E.13-1.624)

Silvia Groaz

Reyner Banham, *Brutalismus in der Architektur* (Stuttgart: Krämer Verlag, 1966): **4** / *Bauen + Wohnen* 18, no. 11 (1964): **2** / Walter Häberli, *Beton, Konstruktion und Form* (Dietikon-Zürich: Verlag Stocker-Schmid, 1966): **5** / Museum für Gestaltung Zürich/Plakatsammlung/Zürcher Hochschule der Künste: **1** / *Das Werk* 53, no. 9 (1966): **3**

Giulia Marino

Archives architectures Genève, Fonds Zschokke Constructions, Série 2: **7** / Archives de la construction moderne, EPFL, fonds IGECO: **3** / *Bauen + Wohnen*: **1** (1966), **2** (1969) / ETH-Bibliothek Zürich, Bildarchiv: **4** (Com_C15-171-002/CC BY-SA 4.0, Com_C15-171-001/CC BY-SA 4.0, Com_C15-171-001/CC BY-SA 4.0), **5** (Com_FC24-8604-0002/CC BY-SA 4.0), **6** (Stiftung Luftbild Schweiz: LBS_L1-841043/CC BY-SA 4.0) / Claudio Merlini: **8, 9, 10**

Martin Tschanz

Archive Xavier Furrer: **2** / Commune d'Hérémence: **3, 4, 5** / Hannes Ineichen (ed.), *Rudolf + Esther Guyer: Bauten und Projekte 1953–2001* (Blauen: Schweizer Baudokumentation, 2002): **8** (bottom), **10** / *Schweizerische Bauzeitung* 84, no. 13 (1966): **8** (top) / Martin Tschanz: **1, 6, 7, 9, 11**

Nicola Navone

Archivio del Moderno, Balerna, Fondi: Aurelio Galfetti: **5**; Flora Ruchat-Roncati: **7**; Luigi Snozzi: **8, 9**; Guido Steiner e Enzo Vanetta – Bagno di Bellinzona: **6**; Rino Tami: **1, 2, 3, 4**; Livio Vacchini: **10, 11** / *BKS Architettura in Ticino/Architektur im Tessin/Architecture au Tessin* (Bellinzona: Salvioni, 1986), private collection: **12**

Roberto Gargiani

Roberto Gargiani: **1, 2, 5, 6, 7, 8, 9, 10** / Gerhard Mack, *Herzog & de Meuron 1978–1988. The Complete Works* vol. 1 (Basel: Birkhäuser Verlag, 1997): **3, 4**

Hannah le Roux

Building Control Investigation Section, 'The Experimental House', *South African Architectural Record* 28, no. 11 (1943): **2** / Centre Scientifique et Technique du Bâtiment (ed.), *Bâtiment tropical*, no. 4 (1964): **4** / Eternit Brasil, 'Canalete 49, Manual do montador', pamphlet, 1983: **5** / C. A. Rigby and K. Steyn, 'The Hail Resistance of S.A. Roofing Materials', *South African Architectural Record* 37, no. 4 (1952): **3** / Hannah le Roux: **1** (private collection), **6, 7**

CONCRETE STORIES
The numbers refer to the pages, the letters to the position on the page.

ABC: Beiträge zum Bauen, no. 3/4 (1925): **255e** / *Architekturpreis Beton 97* (Zürich: 1997): **256c** / Archives architectures Genève, Fonds Zschokke Constructions: **208c** (Série 1463), **210b** (Série 0193), **219a** et **219b** (Série 0338), **259b** (Série 0026), **259d** (Série 2780), **260a** (Série 4784) / Archives de la construction moderne, EPFL, Lausanne, Fonds: Emilio Antognini: **263c**; Georges Brera & Paul Waltenspühl: **208a**; Charles Brugger: **245b**; Fernand Dumas et Denis Honegger: **246c, 263b, 268d**; André Gaillard: **266b, 270c**; Georges-Jacques Haefeli: **213, 274c**; Paul Lavenex: **198a, 198b**; Mirco Ravanne: **263a, 264b**; Philippe Sarrasin: **240b**; Jean Tschumi: **226b, 245c, 265a, 265b**; Heidi et Peter Wenger: **270b** / Archivio del Moderno, Balerna, Fondi: Aurelio Galfetti: **201b, 203b, 203c, 226a, 248**; Mario Campi: **202a, 202c, 202d, 203e, 229**; Flora Ruchat-Roncati: **209b, 210a**; Rino Tami: **209a, 226c, 239c, 241b, 246a**; Livio Vacchini: **241a, 249a, 264a** / Autorenkollektiv an der Architekturabteilung der ETH Zürich, *'Göhnerswil' Wohnungsbau im Kapitalismus* (Zürich: Verlagsgenossenschaft, 1972): **256b** / *Bulletin de la Société vaudoise des ingénieurs et des architectes* 19, no. 6/7 (1893): **258a** / *Cementbulletin* 41, no. 11 (1973): **268b** / ETH-Bibliothek Zürich: **196c** / ETH-Bibliothek Zürich, Bildarchiv: **199a** (Ans_05425-01-039-FL/Public Domain Mark), **267a** (Ans_05425-02-012-FL/Public Domain Mark), **267b** (Ans_05425-02-013-FL/Public Domain Mark) / Leo Fabrizio: **212** / gta Archiv, ETH Zürich, Nachlässe: Walter Binder: **219c, 225d, 230b**; Justus Dahinden: **230a, 259c, 273d**; Otto Glaus: **214, 225a, 228a, 228b, 232a, 232b, 233a, 233b, 275a, 275b, 275e**; Gustav Gull: **200a, 207a**; Lux Guyer: **246b**; Haefeli Moser Steiger: **207b, 247, 249b, 267e**; Heinrich Helfenstein: **225b**; Hans Hofmann: **218b**; Heinz Isler: **240a, 258c, 267f, 267g, 273f, 276a, 276b**; Arnold Itten: **211b**; Walter Jonas: **231**; Hans Leuzinger: **273c**; Fritz Maurer: **230c**; Karl Moser: **197, 274a, 274b**; Eduard Neuenschwander: **266a**; Rudolf Olgiati: **195a, 203a, 203d, 275d**; Claude Paillard: **242c, 250a**; Pfleghard & Haefeli: **217a**; Alfred Roth: **207d, 273b**; Walter Rüegg: **258b, 259a**; Otto Rudolf Salvisberg: **220a, 221a, 239a, 242a, 273e**; Hans Schmidt: **251b, 257**; Gottfried Semper: **200c**; Hermann Siegrist: **227**; Fritz Stucky: **250b**; Henri-Robert Von der Mühll: **207c**; Pierre Zoelly: **201a, 220b, 269a, 269b, 269c, 269d** / gta Archiv, ETH Zürich, Sammlungen: Modellsammlung: **217b**; NEAT: **210c**; Schweizerischer Werkbund: **240c**; Prof. Erwin Thomann: **225c, 268c** / Gustav Gull, *Orientierungs Schrift über die an den Erweiterungs-Bauten beteiligten Unternehmer und Lieferanten* (Zürich: 1924): **200b** / *Heimatschutz* 19, no. 8 (December 1924): **270a** / Hochschularchiv ETH Zürich: **211a, 241c, 244a, 260b, 267c, 267d, 275c, 277a** / Losinger + Co AG (ed.), *Losinger*, vol. 'Kraftwerkbau' (Bern, 1967): **218a** / Museum für Gestaltung Zürich/Plakatsammlung/Zürcher Hochschule der Künste: **255f** / *Neue Zürcher Zeitung NZZ*, no. 1135 (1934): **256a** / Alfred Pfister (ed.), *Bauten der Schweizerischen Landesausstellung Zürich 1883* (Zürich: Hofer & Burger, 1883): **199b** / E.G. Portland (ed.), *Die schweizerische Zement-Industrie* (Zürich: 1958): **195b, 195c, 196a, 196b, 217c, 217d** / Mirko Roš, *Versuche und Erfahrungen an ausgeführten Eisenbeton-Bauwerken in der Schweiz* (Zürich: Eidgenössische Materialprüfungs- und Versuchsanstalt für Industrie, Bauwesen und Gewerbe, 1937): **277b** / *Schweizerische Bauzeitung*: **208b** (15, no. 9, 1890), **218c** (87, no. 24, 1926), **221b** (54, no. 11, 1908), **239b** (58, no. 3, 1911) / Schweizerisches Sozialarchiv: **255a** (F_5107-Na-10-107-032), **255b** (F_5107-Na-14-080-008), **255c** (F_5107-Na-14-121-021), **255d** (F_5107-Na-10-104-003) / Werner Sigmund, *Ernst Göhner (1900-1971): Bauen in Norm* (Meilen: Schweizer Pioniere der Wirtschaft und Technik 49, 1990): **251a** / Staatsarchiv Basel Stadt: **268a** (Gerichtsarchiv VV 5) / Stadtarchiv Bern: **238** (SAB 1038 5 6879) / Stadtarchiv Zürich: **273a** (VII.308.C.a) / Swiss Architecture Museum S AM: **242b** / Julius Vischer, Ludwig Hilberseimer, *Beton als Gestalter. Bauten in Eisenbeton und ihre architektonische Gestaltung: ausgeführte Eisenbetonbauten* (Stuttgart: Hoffmann, 1928): **260c** / *Das Werk*: **237** (2, no. 3, 1915), **222** (3, no. 4 1976) / *Zeitschrift für Beton- und Eisenbetonbau: Mitteilungen über Zement-, Beton- und Eisenbetonbau* 5, no. 9 (1914): **199c, 199d**

Author biographies

Salvatore Aprea is an architect and architectural historian. He is currently the director of the Archives de la construction moderne at the Swiss Federal Institute of Technology in Lausanne, where he also lectures. He has published several essays on the history of concrete and the book *German Concrete: The Science of Cement from Trass to Portland, 1819–1877*, in addition to articles on the history of modern architecture in Switzerland and the book *Habiter la modernité*. He has also curated several architecture exhibitions, including most recently *La macchina delle meraviglie*, Rome, 2019, and *Habiter la modernité*, Lausanne, 2018.

Marcel Bächtiger studied architecture at the Swiss Federal Institute of Technology in Zurich (EPFZ). Since graduating he has been working as a filmmaker, lecturer, researcher, and editor at the renowned magazine *Hochparterre*. In his doctoral thesis *Augen, die anders sehen*, he analyses the cinematographic foundations of Le Corbusier's œuvre and the numerous crossfades between film theory and architectural theory in the twentieth century. At the EPFZ Department of Architecture he teaches 'Spatial Concepts in Film and Architecture' as an elective course and focus work.

Silvia Berger Ziauddin is a professor of Swiss and contemporary history at the University of Bern. Her research and teaching interests include the history of Switzerland in the global Cold War, cultural histories of the atomic age, underground spaces, vertical technologies and resources, the history of bunkerisation, gender and emotions in the 1980s, and the history of epidemics. She is a member of the 'Silicon Mountains' research group at the Walter Benjamin Kolleg and is on the advisory board for the Interdisciplinary Centre for Gender Studies at the University of Bern, as well as the international advisory board for the Lund Centre for the History of Knowledge in Sweden.

Roberto Gargiani has taught the history of architecture in Florence, Rouen, Paris, Venice, and Rome. He is currently a professor of the history of architecture at the Swiss Federal Institute of Technology in Lausanne. He is the author of *Karsten Födinger: Toward a Radical Sculpture* (with A. Rosellini, 2020), *Le Corbusier: Béton Brut and Ineffable Space, 1940–1965* (with A. Rosellini, 2011), *A New Era of American Architectural Concrete: from Wright to SOM* (2020), *The Rhetoric of Pier Luigi Nervi: Concrete and Ferrocement Forms* (with A. Bologna, 2016), *Louis I. Kahn, Exposed Concrete and Hollow Stones, 1949–1959* (2014) and *Concrete, from Archeology to Invention, 1700–1769* (2013).

Ilaria Giannetti is an architect and associate professor at the Università degli Studi di Roma 'Tor Vergata' – Department of Civil Engineering and Computer Science. She specialises in contemporary construction and engineering history.

Her main research interests lie in the history of building techniques and structural engineering of the nineteenth and twentieth centuries, focusing on the history of building industrialisation and on interrelations between architecture and engineering.

Silvia Groaz, PhD, is a postdoc at the Laboratory of History and Theory and a curator for the exhibition gallery Archizoom, at the Swiss Federal Institute of Technology in Lausanne (EPFL). Her research focuses on postwar historiography, the architectural discourse, and the relations between art and architecture. During her doctoral studies, she was a visiting scholar at Columbia University, New York. She obtained an MA in architecture history at the Bartlett School of Architecture (UCL), an MSc in architecture at the EPFL, and a BSc at the Accademia di Architettura, Mendrisio. She has received grants from the Swiss National Science Foundation and the Getty Research Institute and has disseminated her research in international conferences and reviews.

Hannah le Roux is an architect and associate professor at the University of the Witwatersrand in Johannesburg. Her work moves between modalities of design research, architectural history, urbanism, and curation to engage with the impacts of modern architecture and its transnational networks on Africa, and vice versa. She researched the toxic legacy of asbestos-cement as a fellow on the Mellon/Canadian Centre for Architecture within the project 'Architecture and/for the Environment', from 2017 to 2019, and continues that work through the Aggregate collective project, 'Toxics'.

Giulia Marino has a master's degree in architecture from the University of Florence and a PhD from the Swiss Federal Institute of Technology in Lausanne (EPFL). She is a professor at the Université catholique de Louvain in Brussels and associate researcher at the Laboratory of Techniques and Preservation of Modern Architecture at the EPFL. Her scientific interests are centred on the conservation of modern and contemporary heritage, and in the history of twentieth-century construction techniques and building services. She is a member of ICOMOS Schweiz, co-chair of Docomomo Switzerland, and a member of the International Specialist Committee on Technology at Docomomo International.

Aurelio Muttoni is a professor of structural engineering at the Swiss Federal Institute of Technology in Lausanne. He received his diploma and PhD in civil engineering from the Swiss Federal Institute of Technology in Zurich. He is the author of several publications, amongst them the book *The Art of Structures* dedicated to both engineers and architects. Aurelio Muttoni is also cofounder of and partner at the Muttoni & Fernández consulting office. This office is active in the conceptual design, analysis, and dimensioning of load-bearing structures in architecture and civil engineering constructions, as well as in consulting activities in the field of structural engineering.

Nicola Navone, architect and PhD, is the deputy director of the Archivio del Moderno, a lecturer at the Accademia di architettura di Mendrisio, Università della Svizzera italiana, and a member of the Collegio di Dottorato 'Architecture. Innovation and Heritage', Università degli Studi di Roma Tre. Among his research interests, ranging from the sixteenth to the twentieth centuries, he pays particular attention to the emergence of an internationally recognised architecture in Ticino, a subject to which he has dedicated numerous publications as well as the research project 'Architecture in Canton Ticino, 1945–1980', which was funded by the Swiss National Science Foundation.

Sarah Nichols is an assistant professor of architecture at Rice University in Houston, Texas. Her scholarly work focuses on building materials, particularly concrete, looking at how materials are designed and the relation between conceptions of materials and their use in architecture. She is guest curator for the exhibition *Beton* at the S AM Swiss Architecture Museum (11.2021–04.2022) and is currently working on a book manuscript based on her dissertation *Opération Béton: Constructing Concrete in Switzerland* (2020), for which she was awarded the silver medal of the Swiss Federal Institute of Technology in Zurich.

Laurent Stalder is a full professor at the Swiss Federal Institute of Technology in Zurich as of 2018. The main focus of his research and publications is the history and theory of architecture from the nineteenth to the twenty-first centuries where it intersects with the history of technology. His main publications include *Hermann Muthesius 1861–1927: Das Landhaus als kulturgeschichtlicher Entwurf* (2008), *Der Schwellenatlas* (2009), *Fritz Haller: Architekt und Forscher* (2015), *Architecture/Machine* (2017), and *Architectural Ethnography* (2018).

Lorenzo Stieger is an architect with a research focus on urban design, and architectural theory and history. He earned both his 2009 architecture degree and his 2018 doctorate from the Swiss Federal Institute of Technology in Zurich (ETHZ). For several years, he practised in various offices in Los Angeles and Zurich before becoming a researcher and co-lecturer at the Department of Architecture and Urban Design in Singapore and at the ETHZ. He is currently conducting post-doctoral research at the Academy of Architecture at the Università della Svizzera italiana in Mendrisio, Switzerland.